JSP™: A Beginner's Guide

Gary Bollinger
Bharathi Natarajan

Osborne/**McGraw-Hill**

New York Chicago San Francisco
Lisbon London Madrid Mexico City Milan
New Delhi San Juan Seoul Singapore Sydney Toronto

Osborne/**McGraw-Hill**
2600 Tenth Street
Berkeley, California 94710
U.S.A.

To arrange bulk purchase discounts for sales promotions, premiums, or fund-raisers, please contact Osborne/**McGraw-Hill** at the above address. For information on translations or book distributors outside the U.S.A., please see the International Contact Information page immediately following the index of this book.

JSP™: A Beginner's Guide

1234567890 FGR FGR 01987654321

ISBN 0-07-213319-8

Publisher Brandon A. Nordin
Vice President & Associate Publisher Scott Rogers
Acquisitions Editor Ann Sellers
Senior Project Editor Carolyn Welch
Acquisitions Coordinator Paulina Pobocha
Technical Editor Phil Hanna
Copy Editor Bob Campbell
Proofreader Susie Elkind
Indexer Valerie Perry
Computer Designers John Patrus, Roberta Steele
Illustrators Michael Mueller, Lyssa Wald
Series Design Gary Corrigan
Cover Illustration Kevin Curry

This book was composed with Corel VENTURA™ Publisher.

About the Authors

Gary Bollinger is Chief Product Architect and co-founder of Artesia Technologies. He is the author of several articles appearing in *JavaPro* and *JavaReport* magazines. He has several undergraduate and graduate degrees in literature, computer science, theology, and a Ph.D. in philosophy. He also has 15 years' professional experience programming RPC, CORBA, and J2EE architectures. He loves his dogs.

Bharathi Natarajan is a Lead Engineer at Artesia Technologies and has co-authored articles appearing in *JavaPro* and *JavaReport* magazines. He has an undergraduate degree and a graduate degree in computer science. He has 8 years' professional experience programming in C/C++, distributed programming, and J2EE architectures. He also loves his dogs.

To my father, Leonard Bollinger, whom I admire more than I tell him, and in memory of my late mother-in-law, Nancy Royston Jones Winters, who encouraged me and loved me.
---Gary Bollinger

To my father, Udayampalayam Subbian Natarajan, who has been my inspiration since childhood. My road to success started with his guidance and encouragement.
---Bharathi Natarajan

Contents

PART III

Appendices

Acknowledgments

Writing a book is the sort of thing one might never start if from the beginning one understood the challenges. There is nothing quite like putting in a 10-hour day (or more) at one's "real job," only to begin again, each night, the second job (*the Book*) shortly after dinner. That said, it has been enormously rewarding, thanks in part to the efforts of our family, friends, and editors.

Our wives, Mary Bollinger and Sandra Natarajan, have been extremely patient with our distraction over the last 10 months. Sandy and Mary encouraged us and pitched in to help edit and proofread the book at crucial points. Their encouragement and help were invaluable. We could not have finished the book without their support. We know that there could be no one more proud of our achievement that the two of them.

We offer special thanks to Phil Osip, a friend and colleague, who wrote the applet we used in our discussion of the `<jsp:plugin>` tag in Module 5. We also thank David Smith, another friend and colleague, who read and helped edit Modules 4 and 5.

Our technical editor, Phil Hanna, provided invaluable technical criticism on the finer points of servlet and JSP technology. He knows the material well, and we gratefully accepted his insights. Any remaining errors are all ours, of course!

The Osborne editors—we had several—were always professional and helped us work through the challenges to deliver the book on time.

Not to forget, our dogs Caramel, Chachu, Emily, and Socrates were always with us, providing valuable company during those long hours when everyone else was long asleep.

Acknowledgments

Introduction

Are you a student trying to understand the fundamentals of modern Web development? Do you wonder how JavaServer Pages (JSP) work together with HTML, Java servlets, and databases to build scalable Web architectures? Have you been looking for a clear, structured introduction to JavaServer Pages?

Do you develop Web sites and wish you could improve the performance of your CGI scripts? Have you ever wanted to use program loops or variables directly in your Web pages? Do you grow weary of writing obscure Perl programs that exert much of their effort printing out static HTML?

Do you develop Java servlets to generate Web pages? Do you yearn for a more natural way to write dynamic pages? Do you seek a clean way to separate programming language constructs from HTML elements?

Do you develop Active Server Pages (ASP) and hope to create Web sites on non-Microsoft platforms? Do you think there is a market for your skills on UNIX?

Are you interested in design patterns and wonder how you should apply them to Web architectures?

If you answered *yes* to any of these questions, this book is for you! The JavaServer Pages technology was developed by Sun Microsystems, Inc. Most obviously, the technology provides a better way to write dynamic Web pages. Web page development must often include both static HTML and dynamic content in its pages. Suppose, for example, you want to target the content of a page specifically for the person accessing the page. Most of the page provides the same look-and-feel for every person who accesses it. But some part of the page pulls content from a database tailored by user demographics or a pre-established login identity. Amazon.com, for example, provides a welcome message with a user's name and targeted advertisements. How might we imitate Amazon.com?

Traditional CGI development uses a programming language, probably Perl or C/C++, to create a program that prints out large amounts of static HTML interleaved with responses from database queries. Even Java servlets (a companion Java technology) follow this basic paradigm; the only difference is that servlets live in a process thread, while Perl scripts execute as standalone processes. JavaServer Pages invert this approach, starting with static HTML and interleaving "tagged" Java code into the static HTML. The fact that the Java code is "tagged" is important—it means there is a clear separation between HTML and code. Consider the following JSP fragment (don't worry about the details right now):

```
<%
   for(int i = 0; i < 3; i++) {
%>
  <TR>
     <TD> "Cell 1" </TD>
     <TD> "Cell 2" </TD>
  </TR>
<% } %>
```


This JSP fragment consists of two Java code sections and an HTML section. The point to notice is that we insert both HTML and Java using tags. Of course, what goes between the Java tags is more complicated than what goes between the HTML tags, but we will show later on in Modules 5 and 6 how even Java scripting can be simplified using JSP.

Now look at this servlet code fragment doing the same job performed by the JSP fragment:


```
PrintWriter out = response.getWriter();
for (int i = 0; i < 3; i++) {
   out.println("<TR>\n<TD> Cell 1</TD>\n<TD> Cell 2 </TD>\n</TR>");
```

This servlet fragment buries static HTML in a Java *println* function call. The little piece of HTML shown here is comprehensible, but it is easy to see how confusing such statements can become. The problem lies with the inability of servlets to separate Java code from static HTML. It is the same problem when using Perl or C/C++ CGI scripts. JavaServer Pages solve this problem.

Prerequisites

We target this book at students and beginning Web and Java developers who seek a clear introduction to fundamental JSP concepts and techniques. While some of the material is difficult, we fill the book with examples, tips, and explanations that make it accessible to Web developers and programmers with modest experience. We address Java servlet programming in the context of JSP application architectures and in general provide what we believe is the necessary background information to use JavaServer Pages effectively. Still, we assume and require some familiarity and experience with programming languages, preferably Java. We also assume some familiarity with the Internet.

Structure of the Book

We divide the book into three parts:

Part I lays the technical foundations for building JavaServer Pages, focusing on syntax elements and their appropriate use. We divide Part I into six modules addressing the foundations of Internet technologies and each of the specific elements of JavaServer Pages.

Part II introduces fundamental aspects of practical JSP development and focuses on the issues and techniques necessary to build "real-world" JSP applications. We divide Part II into four modules addressing common software patterns in Web architectures, Web security, application workflow, and integration of databases. By using such patterns, Web developers can create Web applications more quickly with fewer errors.

Part III provides four appendices supplying ancillary information supporting our basic discussion.

Part I—JSP Foundations

Module 1 presents the broader world of Web technologies. It first describes the core architectural elements of Web application development, the Hypertext Transport Protocol (HTTP) and basic client-server issues. Then it provides an overview of the client and server technologies that extend the functionality of Web browsers and Web servers to support "real-world" applications. At the end of Module 1, you will understand the general universe of Web technologies.

Module 2 narrows the focus to two JSP syntax elements, comments and directives, and their appropriate use in Web applications. Module 2 also describes the basics of a JSP page and lays the foundations for good programming style. At the end of Module 2, you will have built and displayed your first simple JSP page.

Module 3 describes JSP scripting elements. We showed a few examples earlier in this Introduction. In Module 3 we describe scripting elements in detail and begin to build more complex JSP application elements. At the end of Module 3 you will be able to build complete JSP applications that exploit Java to script dynamic content.

Module 4 describes implicit objects in JavaServer Pages. These objects provide a framework for passing and using information between the parts of a JSP application. At the end of Module 4 you will have built a JSP page that interactively responds to an HTML form.

Module 5 describes standard JSP actions. JSP actions function as callouts (external references) to Java functionality. Among other things, standard actions provide a simple mechanism for incorporating helper JavaBeans in one's application. At the end of Module 5 you will be able to incorporate JavaBeans into your JSP application, thereby improving its style and professionalism.

Module 6 presents custom JSP actions. Such actions provide one of the most powerful features of the JSP architecture. When writing custom JSP actions one is really extending the JSP engine itself. At the end of Module 6 you will have built your first such extension to the JSP engine.

Part II—Building Real-World Applications

Module 7 begins our discussion of some major aspects of "real-world" application development using JavaServer Pages. It introduces software patterns and their application to JSP architectures. We pay special attention to these patterns:

- Model-View-Controller (MVC)
- Mediator
- Command
- Strategy
- Bridge

We also mention other patterns, but spend less time on them. These include factory, interceptor/filter, and callback.

Module 8 addresses security issues. We describe some of the common security techniques used in Web architectures, including those required by the Servlet 2.2 specification.

Module 9 describes issues surrounding application workflow—the control and movement from page to page in a JSP application.

Module 10 addresses the role of databases in JSP architectures. We describe the JDBC data access API. Then we describe various techniques required to integrate a database into a JSP application.

Part III—Appendices

The appendices provide ancillary information supporting the rest of the book. Appendix A provides answers to special **Mastery Check** questions posed at the end of each module.

Appendix B explains how to create and deploy a Web server and JSP environment. We concentrate on the Tomcat implementation of the Servlet and JSP containers and on the Apache Web Server.

Appendix C describes how to set up and configure a MySQL database. This database engine is free and provides a fine platform for personal development projects.

Finally, Appendix D describes the changes that occur between the current JSP specification (JSP 1.1) and the proposed final draft of the JavaServer Pages 1.2 specification.

Special Features

Each module includes ***Hints***, ***Tips***, ***Cautions***, and ***Notes*** to provide additional reference information wherever needed. Detailed ***code listings*** are included in gray boxes, many times with certain tags or features highlighted with further explanation.

Most modules contain ***Ask the Expert*** question-and-answer sections to address potentially confusing issues. Each module contains step-by-step ***Projects*** to give you a chance to practice the concepts taught thus far. You can download the content for the projects from Osborne's Web site (`www.osborne.com`).

Mastery Checks are included at the end of all modules to give you another chance to review the concepts taught in the module. The answers to the **Mastery Checks** are in Appendix A.

Notational Conventions

At several points, we present formats derived from formal specifications. When we do so, we use the following conventions:

- We display all literals in courier font: `literal`.
- When we treat collections of elements as a single unit, we display them in parentheses: (element1 element2).
- We indicate zero or more instances of an element using an asterisk: (element1 element2)*.
- We indicate an optional term between brackets: [element].
- We indicate a carriage return character followed by a line feed character using the hyphenated sequence: `CR-LF`.
- We indicate symbolic elements such as variables or placeholder names using italics: *element*.
- We indicate environment variables in courier font, capitalized with '`%`' signs around the variable (Windows notation): `%TOMCAT_HOME%`.
- We indicate directory names, relative paths, and file names in courier font using the backward-slash character for a file separator (Windows syntax): `%TOMCAT_HOME%\webapps\Book`.
- We indicate Java Class names, interface names, and method names using italics: *HelperBean.getProperty*.

Throughout the development of this book, our objective has always been to provide you with a cohesive, easy-to-understand guide for coding JavaServer Pages that helps you get up and running in no time. We applaud your decision to learn JavaServer Pages and encourage you to use the Internet to its fullest potential, both during the learning process and in your ensuing Web application development. Have fun and good luck!

Other Readings

1. Alexander, C., S. Ishikawa, and M. Silverstein. *A Pattern Language*. Oxford University Press, 1977.

2. Alexander, C. *The Timeless Way of Building*. Oxford University Press, 1979.

3. Alur, Deepak, John Crupi, and Dan Malks. *Core J2EE Patterns: Best Practices and Design Strategies*. Sun Microsystems Press, Prentice Hall, 2001.

4. Berners-Lee, Tim, with Mark Fischetti. *Weaving the Web: The Original Design and Ultimate Destiny of the World Wide Web by Its Inventor*. Harper San Francisco, 1999.

5. [DBTags] http://jakarta.apache.org/taglibs/doc/dbtags-doc/intro.html

6. Gamma, Erich, Richard Helm, Ralph Johnson, and John Vlissides. *Design Patterns: Elements of Reusable Object-Oriented Software*. Addison-Wesley Publishing Company, 1995.

7. Geary, David. "JSP Templates." *Java World*, September, 2000. http://www.javaworld.com/javaworld/jw-09-2000/jw-0915-jspweb_p.html

8. Lea, Doug. "Christopher Alexander: An Introduction for Object-Oriented Designers." SUNY Oswego/NY CASE Center, December, 1993. http://g.oswego.edu/dl/ca/ca/ca.html

9. [MySQL] http://www.mysql.com

10. [Struts] http://jakarta.apache.org/struts/index.html

11. [Taglibs] http://jakarta.apache.org/taglibs/index.html

12. [Tomcat] http://jakarta.apache.org/tomcat/index.html

Part I

JSP Foundations

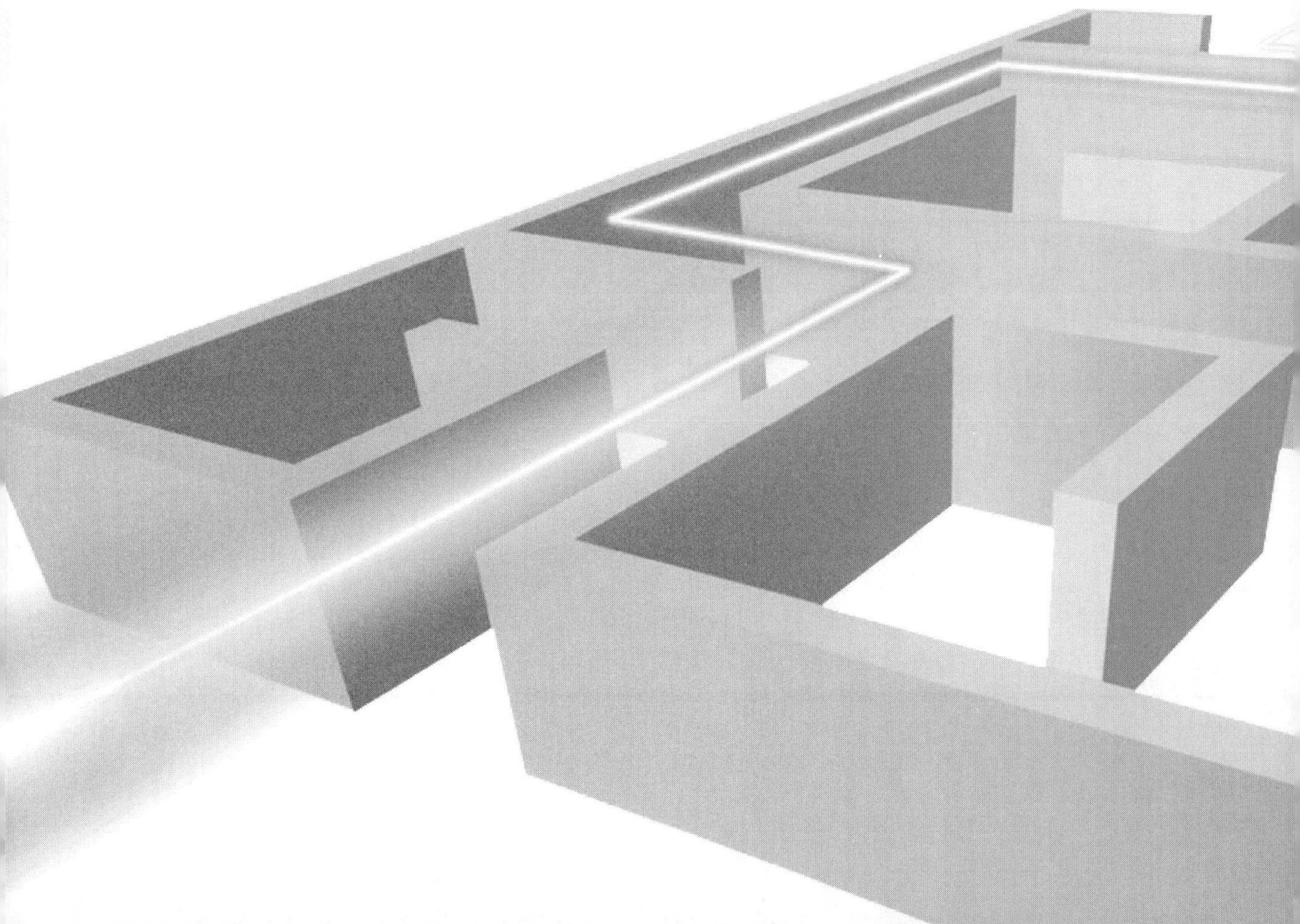

Module 1

Introduction to Internet Technologies

The Goals of This Module

- Learn features of client-server architectures and the HTTP protocol
- Become familiar with client-side Internet development technologies
- Understand fundamental server-side Internet development technologies

Understanding JavaServer Pages (JSP) begins with understanding the Hypertext Transfer Protocol (HTTP). A *protocol* is a set of rules for encoding and transmitting requests for data over a computer network. You can think of protocols as languages spoken by computer networks. The Internet speaks HTTP as its mother tongue. HTTP lets one computer pass a document to another computer anywhere in the world. Put another way, HTTP provides the wire over which Web clients talk to Web servers.

Of course, other protocols like the File Transfer Protocol (FTP) also send documents across networks, but HTTP does it best. HTTP beats other protocols, not because it is faster or more powerful, but because it is simple. HTTP, with help from the Hypertext Markup Language (HTML), implements the idea that a word or concept in one document, a *source*, points directly at a word or concept in another document, the *destination*. HTTP lets readers of a document follow "links" from source to destination without the reader logging in to the remote server or performing any of the other cumbersome network handshakes required by protocols like FTP. The concept of hypermedia linking and a simple network transfer protocol provide the foundations of what we know today as the World Wide Web.

The World Wide Web Consortium (W3C) eventually standardized HTTP as specification HTTP/1.0. A newer specification, HTTP/1.1, provides for several optimizations and scaling advantages over HTTP/1.0 and will eventually supercede HTTP/1.0. Our discussion in this module assumes HTTP/1.1.

Note

Tim Berners-Lee invented HTTP and HTML in 1990 and founded the W3C, the most influential specifications group for Internet protocols. (See Tim Berners-Lee with Mark Fischetti, *Weaving the Web: The Original Design and Ultimate Destiny of the World Wide Web by Its Inventor* [San Francisco: HarperSanFrancisco, 1999], pp. 28–29.)

The Internet as a Client-Server Architecture

Based on HTTP, the Internet provides the world's greatest client-server application architecture. Client-server architectures organize computing services into centralized processes that provide resources such as storage space, database management, and file transfer. Clients then request the resources they need from these centralized processes. Figure 1-1 shows a diagram of the client-server architecture.

Client-server architectures seek to combine and coordinate resources to achieve efficiencies of scale. By centralizing and sharing resources, client-server architectures can provide more services at a cheaper cost to more clients. At the same time, client-server architectures try to hide the existence of the network from clients. When they do their job effectively, clients seem to own the server resources they use. Such *network transparency* is an admirable goal. In fact, however, network servers can never fully hide the existence of the network. Let's look at some of the reasons for this.

Tip

Network printers provide what is perhaps the most familiar example of client-server resources. Consider how often printer problems occur to realize the difficulty of network transparency.

Network Transparency Issues

Three traits of all networks make network transparency a difficult goal:

- **Latency** The time requests take to travel to servers and return responses
- **Reliability** The likelihood of answers to client requests
- **Concurrency** The execution order of client requests by the server

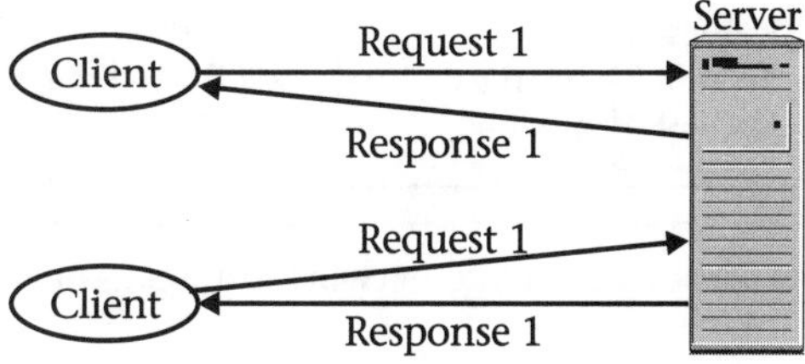

Figure 1-1 Clients request resources from centralized servers.

Clients cannot predict the impact of any of these network traits. If a server must handle more requests than it can respond to in a timely way, clients will wait or time out. If the network path to a server crashes, possibly because someone temporarily removed an intermediate machine from the network, client requests go unanswered.

Tip

To picture the effect of latency and reliability, consider all the times you have accessed an Internet site that did not respond.

If a client sends multiple, simultaneous requests to a server, it must not make any assumptions about the order in which the server responds to these requests. If the client does make assumptions, these assumptions can cause data inconsistencies between the client and server. Remove the network, and all these factors are predictable; add the network layer back in, and these factors become unpredictable once more. Figure 1-2 shows the challenges to network transparency.

While it is impossible to ignore network traits in client-server architectures, server traits magnify the impact of network problems. Server *state* impacts network problems the most.

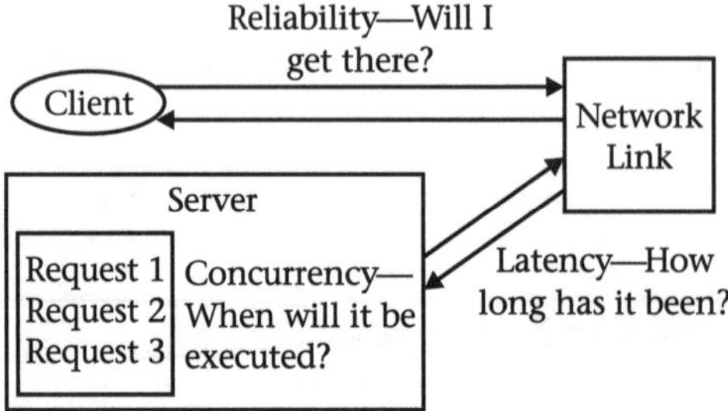

Figure 1-2 Three network traits make network transparency difficult.

Stateful Servers

In a client-server architecture, a server's *state* refers to the information it manages during and between client requests. All servers must manage some state to do their job. File transfer servers, for instance, maintain a marker or bookmark indicating the state of a client's file transfer request.

Stateful servers, however, do more than maintain state *during* a client request. They also preserve client information *between* client requests. For example, a stateful server might manage client *session* information that persists across multiple client requests to the server. Session information helps servers tailor responses to specific client characteristics like access rights or preferences.

Session management also helps servers direct clients through specific states in a workflow. For example, a server might manage a client's passage through an online catalog purchase.

Transactions are another type of state that servers use to help clients make sequences of requests that build on each other. In effect, transactions let clients bundle multiple actual service requests into a single logical request. Database servers best illustrate the importance of transactions. A single user activity such as accessing a bank account, withdrawing money, and reflecting the change to the user account must happen *all at once* or not at all. This means multiple requests to a database server must maintain temporary state as the server executes each request. After all requests have completed, the server either commits or discards the effects of the entire set of requests.

Stateful servers find it more difficult to establish network transparency because they must keep client and server information *synchronized*. Synchronization refers to the act of maintaining consistency between a server's picture of the client and the actual state of the client. The most obvious challenge to such consistency occurs when a client disconnects from a server without notifying the server. Suppose, for instance, that a user turns off the client machine in the middle of a session with a server. Handling this very typical occurrence introduces great complexity into stateful servers. The server must somehow determine the real state of the client (the client is gone) and modify its picture of the client accordingly (remove its client information). The logic and code to do such synchronization is complex. Current HTTP servers remain simple by not managing client state. HTTP servers are stateless servers.

HTTP Servers Are Stateless

The stated goal of HTTP servers since 1990 has been to serve up information to Web browsers as fast as possible. In the early days, this meant serving up HTML documents and images. Today's Web servers deliver video, audio, animated images, and many other rich format types to browsers. Throughout this evolution, HTTP servers remained lightweight and stateless, reflecting the protocol's basic request-response paradigm. Assuming no problems, a typical round trip from Web browser to Web server and back traces these steps:

1. The browser establishes a connection with the Web server.
2. The browser sends an HTTP request to the Web server.
3. The Web server sends an HTTP response to the browser over the established connection.
4. The Web server closes the connection. Any premature closure of the connection, whatever the cause, terminates the current request.

A basic understanding of the details of the HTTP protocol is imperative for developers writing JavaServer Pages or Java servlets, so let's look more closely at the HTTP message format. (This discussion derives from the HTTP/1.1 protocol specification. See RFC 2616, at `http://www.ietf.org/rfc/rfc2616.txt`.)

1-Minute Drill

- What are client-server architectures?
- What is network transparency?
- What is a stateless server?

- Client-server architectures organize computing services into centralized processes that provide resources such as storage space, database management, and file transfer.
- Network transparency occurs when a client-server architecture hides the existence of the network from clients.
- A stateless server is one that retains no client state information *between* client requests.

HTTP Requests

HTTP requests follow some variant of this general format:

```
Request line
*(Message header CR-LF)
CR-LF
[Message body]
```

For example, here is an actual HTTP request sent by Microsoft Internet Explorer 5.5:

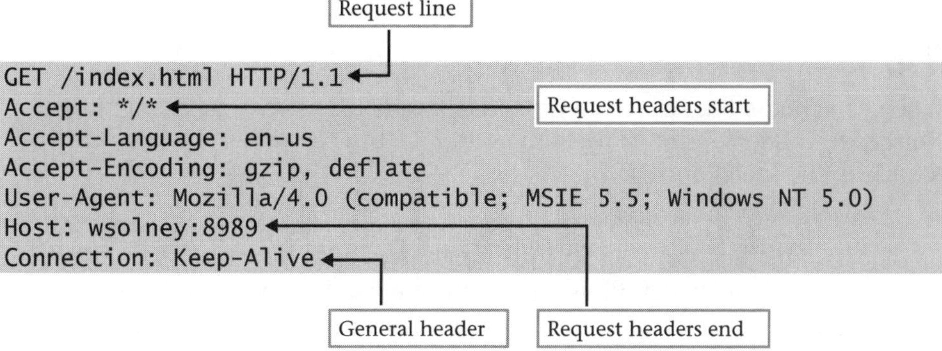

Request line
GET /index.html HTTP/1.1
Accept: */*
Request headers start
Accept-Language: en-us
Accept-Encoding: gzip, deflate
User-Agent: Mozilla/4.0 (compatible; MSIE 5.5; Windows NT 5.0)
Host: wsolney:8989
Connection: Keep-Alive
General header
Request headers end

Let's try to understand this request format better by breaking it down into its separate elements.

The Request Line

The *request line* requires the following three fields separated from each other by a SPACE character:

- Request method
- Request URI
- HTTP version

The request line ends with a CR-LF character sequence.

Request Methods

The method field determines the basic variations of the request message. The two most important method types for JSP development are GET and POST.

GET The GET method retrieves a specified Web resource from a remote server. Most HTTP requests use the GET method. In fact, every time you surf to a particular main Web site, you implicitly issue a GET request. In that respect, the GET request acts as the workhorse of the Web. To help limit the number of browser network requests, the GET method typically caches information it retrieves, and for a period thereafter returns this cached information rather than a new response from a Web server.

Tip

When you choose the Refresh command in Internet Explorer (or Reload in Netscape), you force your browser to go to a Web server rather than its cache to pick up the site information.

The GET method can also *send* information to a Web server. To do this, browsers encode information using a Multipurpose Internet Mail Extension (MIME) standard called *application/x-www-form-urlencoded.* They concatenate the encoded information to the request URI (Uniform Resource Identifier) using a question mark (?) character. The format encodes data as name-value pairs. In each name-value pair, an equal sign (=) character separates the name from the value. An ampersand (&) character separates different name-value pairs. Spaces are encoded as the plus sign (+) character. The format replaces non-alphanumeric characters with *%HH*, where *HH* stands for hexadecimal values representing the ASCII value of the character.

The GET method suffers from real-world limitations on the size of the URI that Web servers accept. Additionally, Web servers typically log requests, so sensitive data encoded in the URI can end up in server logs. Here is an example of a GET request line:

Content is urlencoded

```
GET /cgi-bin/Scripts/foo.perl?
   FormField1=value1&FormField2=value2 HTTP/1.1 CR-LF
```

POST The POST method, like the GET method, both retrieves information from Web servers and sends data to Web servers. Unlike the GET method, though, the POST method attaches its client data to the end of the request as a special content message. This content message *can* use the application/x-www-form-urlencoded MIME standard that the GET method uses. Unlike the GET method, it can also use a different encoding standard called *multipart/form-data*. This alternative encoding standard packages client information as a series of parts, where each part can have a different content type.

The POST method can send more information to Web servers than the GET method because it does not rely on the request URI to package the data. Further, sensitive data never ends up in a server log. Here is an example of a POST request (which leaves out several headers you would normally see):

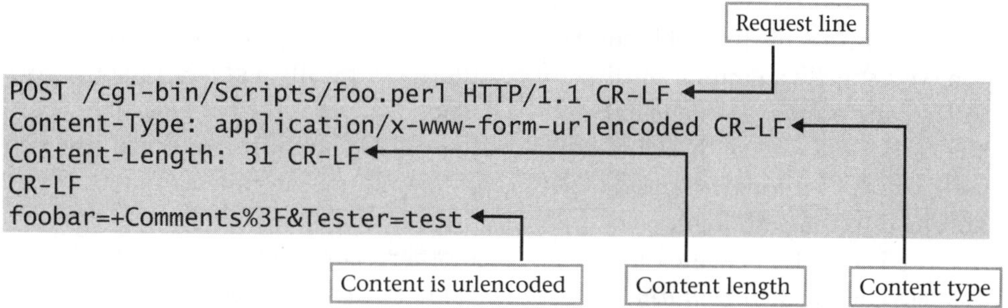
Request line
POST /cgi-bin/Scripts/foo.perl HTTP/1.1 CR-LF
Content-Type: application/x-www-form-urlencoded CR-LF
Content-Length: 31 CR-LF
CR-LF
foobar=+Comments%3F&Tester=test
Content is urlencoded
Content length
Content type

The second field in an HTTP request is the request URI, which is related to the links you traverse in Web pages or type into the address field of your browser. Let's look more closely at URIs.

Request URIs

HTTP requests must specify a Web resource as the object of the request. They do this using Uniform Resource Identifiers (URIs). The URI specification provides a way to uniquely identify Internet resources. (See RFC 2396, at `http://www.ietf.org/rfc/rfc2396.txt`.) URIs are characterized by three definitions:

- **Uniform** URIs support multiple resource types but follow a common syntactic form
- **Resource** URIs identify resources that can be documents, images, resource collections, or, indeed, any entity with an identity
- **Identifier** URIs include syntactically restricted references to resources

To clarify these definitions, consider Table 1-1, which shows some examples of common types of Internet URIs:

As the examples illustrate, URIs follow this general format:

scheme scheme-specific-notation

The scheme part identifies a formal specification or grammar for the URI. Every such naming scheme requires a scheme-specific syntax or notation. Some hierarchically organized URIs share a more specific four-part format:

```
scheme // authority[ path [ ? query ] ]
```

Network protocols like FTP and HTTP fall into this category. Such URIs require that you specify a naming or directory authority, typically a server on a network host. Some protocols, like HTTP and FTP, support a resource path starting from the authority's root path. Some schemes, like HTTP, support a query string as well, which functions as a mechanism for passing runtime arguments to the object specified in the path field.

The HTTP/1.1 specification provides another, more familiar name for HTTP request URIs, called *Uniform Resource Locators* (URLs). The general form of an HTTP URI (URL) follows this format:

```
http: // origin-server [ :port ] [absolute_path [ ? query] ]
```

The optional *port* qualifier in the HTTP URI format specifies the network port serviced by the HTTP authority. When you don't specify this port, HTTP assumes port 80.

URI	**Definition**
`http://www.w3c.org/`	HTTP messages
`ftp://ftp.NCSA.uiuc.edu/`	FTP messages
`telnet://grex.cyberspace.org/`	Telnet protocol messages
`news:comp.lang.java`	Usenet news group messages
`mailto:aboll@bell.net`	Electronic mail messages

Table 1-1 Common Internet URIs

Note

Tim Berners-Lee (inventor of the Web) describes the politics behind the naming of URIs and URLs (in *Weaving the Web*, p. 62). While he argued for "Universal" rather than "Uniform" and "Identifier" rather than "Locator," the majority of participants in the Internet Engineering Task Force (IETF) URI working group argued for "Uniform" and "Locator." Eventually, "Uniform" was adopted and "URI" came to stand for URLs as well as broader categories of identifiers.

The HTTP/1.1 specification also describes two types of request URIs relevant to `GET` and `POST` methods:

- Absolute URI
- Absolute path

The *absolute URI* form provides a complete URI as described earlier. This is an example of a request line specifying a complete URI:

```
GET http://www.w3c.org/index.html HTTP/1.1
```

The HTTP/1.1 specification suggests that a future specification might require that every `GET` and `POST` request use absolute URIs. Today, however, most HTTP requests send the *absolute path* form for request URIs. This form strips the `http://` preface and the origin server out of request URIs and passes the origin server as part of a request header using a `Host:` field. For example, the browser renders this absolute URI request line

```
GET http://www.w3c.org/index.html HTTP/1.1
```

as

```
GET /index.html HTTP/1.1
```

and adds the line

```
Host: www.w3c.org
```

to a request header following the request line. After stripping out the origin server from the request URI, the browser uses it to establish a connection.

HTTP Protocol Version

The HTTP protocol version is the third part of the HTTP request line. Currently, this usually has the value `HTTP/1.1` but could have the value `HTTP/1.0`.

Note

HTTP/1.1 offers a significant performance advantage over HTTP/1.0 by supporting persistent connections. Web browsers and servers specify whether to keep a connection open using the `Connection:` field in the general header. For example, a client sends the following header string to keep its connection alive: `Connection: Keep-Alive`.

Message Headers

HTTP supports three kinds of message headers in request messages:

- **General headers** Provide information about the message including such information as the date. For example, a general header will include a `Connection:` field.
- **Request headers** Provide information about the request and the client making the request. For example, a request header will include a `Host:` field.
- **Entity headers** Provide information about data being sent to the server by a `POST` method. For example, an entity header includes `Content-Type:` and `Content-Length:` fields.

Each message header ends with a `CR-LF` character sequence. Another `CR-LF` follows the complete sequence of all message headers.

Message Body

The `POST` method uses its message body to send data to the Web server. Browsers send this data as an encoded byte stream (an entity body) that the server must then decode using information supplied in a corresponding entity header. Browsers specify the end of an entity body using the `Content-Length:` field in an entity header.

HTTP Responses

After receiving and interpreting a request message, Web servers return a response message. HTTP responses follow some variant of this general format:

```
Status line
*(Message header CR-LF)
CR-LF
[Message body]
```

For example, here is an actual HTTP response returned by the Apache 1.3 Web server:

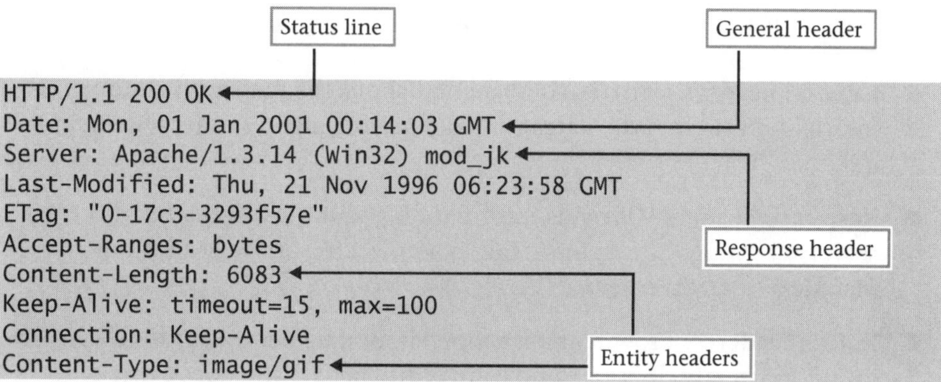

We can understand this response format better by breaking it down into its separate elements.

The Status Line

The status line requires three fields separated from each other by a `SPACE` character:

- HTTP version
- Status code
- Reason phrase

The status line ends with a `CR-LF` character string.

The HTTP Protocol Version

The HTTP version field is the same as that discussed for requests. Currently, both requests and responses usually send either version `HTTP/1.1` or `HTTP/1.0`.

Status Codes and Reason Phrases

The status codes indicate the completion status of a request while the reason phrases give a short description of the codes. Table 1-2 lists a few common status codes, their associated reason phrases, and short explanations of the codes.

Message Headers

HTTP supports three kinds of message headers in response messages:

- **General headers** Provide information about the message including information such as the date. For example, a general header will include a `Date:` field.
- **Response headers** Provide information about the response and the server returning the response. For example, a response header can include a `Server:` field.
- **Entity headers** Provide information about data being sent to the server by a POST method. For example, an entity header includes `Content-Type:` and `Content-Length:` fields.

Status Code	Reason Phrase	Explanation
200	OK	The request succeeded.
301	Moved Permanently	The requested Web resource has permanently moved to a new URL.
400	Bad Request	The request had a malformed syntax.
404	Not Found	The server could not find the requested URL.
503	Service Unavailable	The server has an overload of requests or some other temporary problem and cannot service a specific request.

Table 1-2 Table of Common HTTP Response Codes and Reason Phrases

General headers and entity headers work the same way in response messages as they do in request messages. Response headers replace request headers in response messages. Each separate message header ends with a CR-LF character sequence. Another CR-LF follows the complete sequence of all message headers

Message Body

The message body section works the same way in responses as in requests. A message body is optional in the sense that not all responses return entity bodies. Servers return a message body to GET and POST requests, depending on the status code. When responses return an entity body, it may have a zero length (if this makes sense for the resource requested). New pages, images, videos, or any other new content come from GET and POST requests that return both an entity header and an entity body.

- What is a URI?
- How do GET and POST HTTP methods differ in the way they send content to a Web server?

The Rest of the Story

While the HTTP protocol and client-server paradigm provide the wire over which the Internet passes requests and responses, Web browsers and Web servers supply the rest of the architecture. We address these parts of the architecture next, starting with the browser. Part of the story concerns the technologies that browsers and Web servers support to provide richer network architectures.

- A URI is a Uniform Resource Identifier that uniquely identifies a network resource.
- A GET method sends content to the Web server as part of the request URI using the application/x-www-form-urlencoded format. A POST method sends content to the Web server using a message body encoded in either the application/x-www-form-urlencoded format or the multipart/form-data format.

HTTPEcho.java

Project 1-1: Echoing the HTTP Protocol

The HTTP protocol can confuse even experienced programmers. In the spirit that "a picture is worth a thousand words," here's a simple Java program that lets you see some of the protocol as it passes from Web browser to Web server and back.

Step-by-Step

1. Download and install the Java 2 SDK Standard Edition (J2SE) from the JavaSoft Web site: `http://java.sun.com/j2se`.
2. Create a *JAVA_HOME* environment variable pointing at the installation directory for J2SE. Configure your *PATH* environment variable to include `%JAVA_HOME%\bin`.
3. Download the *HTTPEcho.java* program file from the Osborne Web site (`www.osborne.com`) into a temporary directory on your desktop:

```
import java.net.Socket;
import java.net.ServerSocket;
import java.io.IOException;
import java.io.InputStream;
import java.io.OutputStream;
import java.io.BufferedInputStream;

public class HTTPEcho {
   private static final int BUF_SIZE = 1024;
   private Socket browserSocket = null;
   private Socket webServerSocket = null;
   private ServerSocket browserListenerSocket = null;
   private OutputStream toWebServer = null;
   private BufferedInputStream fromWebServer = null;
   private OutputStream toBrowser = null;
   private BufferedInputStream fromBrowser = null;

   private ServerSocket createListenerSocket(int portNum)  {
      ServerSocket socket = null;
      try  {
         socket = new ServerSocket(portNum);
      }
      catch (IOException ioe)  {
         System.out.println(ioe.getMessage());
         System.exit(-1);
      }
      return socket;
   }
```

```
private Socket createClientSocket(String host, int portNum)  {
   Socket socket = null;
   try  {
      socket = new Socket(host, portNum);
      toWebServer = socket.getOutputStream();
      fromWebServer =
         new BufferedInputStream(socket.getInputStream());
   }
   catch (IOException ioe)  {
      System.out.println(ioe.getMessage());
      System.exit(-1);
   }
   return socket;
}

private Socket accept ()  {
   Socket socket = null;
   try {
      socket = browserListenerSocket.accept();
      toBrowser = socket.getOutputStream();
      fromBrowser =
         new BufferedInputStream(socket.getInputStream());
   }
   catch (IOException e) {
      System.out.println("Accept failed: " +  e.getMessage());
      System.exit(-1);
   }
   return socket;
}

private void setBrowserListenerSocket(ServerSocket socket)  {
   browserListenerSocket = socket;
}

private void setWebServerSocket(Socket socket)  {
   webServerSocket = socket;
}

private void setBrowserSocket(Socket socket)  {
   browserSocket = socket;
}

private int readLine(InputStream in,
                     byte[] b,
                     int off, int len)
      throws IOException {
   if (len <= 0) {
      return 0;
```

```
    }
    int count = 0, c;
    while ((c = in.read()) != -1 && count < len) {
       b[off++] = (byte)c;
       count++;
       if (c == '\n') {
          break;
       }
    }
    return count > 0 ? count : -1;
 }

 /*
    read from in socket,
    echo to console,
    write to out socket
 */
 private void echoBuffer(BufferedInputStream in,
                         OutputStream out)  {
    byte[] readBuf = new byte[BUF_SIZE];
    try  {
       int rlen = -1;
       int bodyLen = 0;
       String line = null;

       do  {
          line = null;
          rlen = readLine(in, readBuf, 0, BUF_SIZE);
          if (rlen > 0)  {
             line = new String(readBuf, 0, rlen);
             System.out.print(line);
             if (line.startsWith("Content-Length: ")) {
                String size =
                   line.substring("Content-Length: ".length(),
                                  line.length());
                bodyLen = Integer.parseInt(size.trim());
             }
             out.write(readBuf, 0, rlen);
          }
       } while ((rlen > 0) && !(line.equals("\r\n")));

       if (bodyLen > 0) {
          System.out.println("<Entity-Body>");
          int count = 0;
          do  {
             rlen = in.read(readBuf, 0, BUF_SIZE);
             if (rlen > 0)  {
                out.write(readBuf, 0, rlen);
                count += rlen;
```

```
            }else break;
         } while (count < bodyLen);
      }
      out.flush();
   }
   catch (IOException ioe)  {
      System.out.println(ioe.getMessage());
   }
   finally  {
      readBuf = null;
   }
}

/*
   read and echo request read and echo reply
*/
private void echo()  {
   System.out.println("\nHTTP REQUEST:");
   echoBuffer(fromBrowser, toWebServer);

   System.out.println("\nHTTP REPLY:");
   echoBuffer(fromWebServer, toBrowser);
}

/*
   close all client sockets and open file descriptors
*/
private void closeClientDescriptors()  {
   try  {
      fromWebServer.close();
      toWebServer.close();
      webServerSocket.close();
      fromBrowser.close();
      toBrowser.close();
      browserSocket.close();
   }
   catch (IOException ioe)  {
      System.out.println(ioe.getMessage());
   }
}

/*
   All request/response pairs are
   serialized - so there is no thread
   contention for instance variables.
*/
public static void main(String [] args) {
   HTTPEcho echo = new HTTPEcho();
```

```
        if (args.length > 1)  {
            /* echo command-line args */
            System.out.println("Starting HTTPEcho on port: " +
                               args[0] + ". ");
            System.out.println("Web server host: " +
                               args[1] + ".");
            System.out.println("Web server is on port: " +
                               args[2] + ".");

        /* parse command-line args */
        int interceptorPort = Integer.parseInt(args[0]);
        String webServerHost = args[1];
        int webServerPort = Integer.parseInt(args[2]);

        /*
            Create listener socket and begin
            echoing Web browser requests and
            Web server responses
        */
        echo.setBrowserListenerSocket(
            echo.createListenerSocket(interceptorPort));
            while (true)  {
                echo.setBrowserSocket(echo.accept());
                echo.setWebServerSocket(
                echo.createClientSocket(webServerHost,
                                        webServerPort));
                echo.echo();
                echo.closeClientDescriptors();
            }
        }
        else {
            System.out.println("Usage: java HTTPEcho " +
                               "interceptorPort " +
                               "webServerHost webServerPort");
        }
    }
}
```

4. Execute the following command in the temporary directory:

```
%>javac HTTPEcho.java
```

This compiles the Java file and creates a file called *HTTPEcho.class* in the same temporary directory.

5. *HTTPEcho* takes a few simple command-line arguments:

```
%>java HTTPEcho <interceptor-port> <web-server-host> <web-server-port>
```

Invoke HTTPEcho like this:

```
%> java HTTPEcho 8989 www.yahoo.com 80
```

6. Now open a Web browser on your desktop and type the URL **http://localhost:8989** and press the RETURN key. You should see a stream of HTTP scroll across your console window as your browser is slowly loaded with information from the Yahoo! Web site.

The *HTTPEcho* program doesn't provide a perfect echoing of the HTTP protocol. Entity bodies may contain binary information like images that would be meaningless if echoed to the console. Further, some of the more complex requests and responses send their requests in parts using the same connection for each part. *HTTPEcho* cannot handle such a complex use of the protocol. On the other hand, *HTTPEcho* can help you get a better sense of the HTTP protocol.

How does *HTTPEcho* work? It intercepts your browser's HTTP requests and forwards them to the location (Web server host and the port) specified on the command line when you started the *HTTPEcho* program. We started *HTTPEcho* using `www.yahoo.com` as an argument, so *HTTPEcho* intercepts HTTP requests, dumps them to the console, and then forwards them to the Yahoo! Web server. The Yahoo! Web server then responds to *HTTPEcho*, which dumps the response to the console before forwarding it to your Web browser.

Client-Side Web Programming

Web browsers have become the preferred user interface for most applications. This trend away from traditional GUI applications is somewhat surprising. Traditional GUI applications respond to user events such as menu selections or button pushes in *asynchronous* threads of activity. The windows in which users perform work are asynchronous in the sense that an activity in one window does not stop the activity in another window. Consequently, multiple, simultaneous activities can occur in the same application at the same time.

You cannot program such behavior into typical browser applications. Imagine clicking on a button in your standard Windows application and having the whole window replaced. We would find this behavior unacceptable in a Windows application, but, for the most part, we tolerate it from our browsers. Furthermore, browsers provide only a few application controls, which solicit user input or provide information to users. (For example, an application might display a user prompt with a text entry field next to it. This combination of prompt and text entry field is a text box control.)

The HTML 4.0 specification lists the following controls:

Buttons	**Check boxes**
Radio buttons	Menus
Text input	File selection
Objects	Hidden fields

Compare this HTML list to the list of controls shipped "out-of-the-box" with Visual Basic:

Check boxes	**Combo boxes**	**Command buttons**
Data	Directory list boxes	Drive list boxes
File list boxes	Frames	Horizontal scroll bars
Images	Labels	Lines
List boxes	Menus	OLE containers
Option buttons	Picture boxes	Shapes
Text boxes	Vertical scroll bars	Timers

In addition to these basic controls, third-party vendors offer virtually hundreds of additional controls written for Visual Basic. Visual Basic provides a much richer toolkit for building sophisticated user interfaces than does HTML and the browser.

Given the deficiencies of the Web browser as an application user interface, why is it so popular? In our opinion, the popularity of browser applications comes primarily from their ability to provide a single, simple means to access distributed resources, especially Internet resources. We accept much to get those resources in a simple way.

Following are some of the specific advantages of browser applications:

Simple Access to Server Resources Browser applications make it easy to implement client-server user interfaces while providing a general platform to do it. Before browser applications, clients and servers were *hard-coded* to each other, each speaking a private language (protocol). Some of the common applications were Telnet, FTP, Gopher, and electronic mail. Browsers package these separate applications into a single application launched with a couple of mouse clicks.

Common Platform HTML provides a simple way to program applications within the browser page itself, thereby transforming it from a single application into an application platform.

Ease of Application Installation, Deployment, and Training Web applications require no installation beyond installation of the browser. (And these days, the browser is often bundled with the operating system.) The popularity of the Web browser has also achieved a kind of critical mass—so many applications use a browser that people understand and feel comfortable with the browser as their platform. People rarely need much training in the mechanics of using a Web browser.

The popularity of browser applications does not mean that users are completely happy with their limitations. Most recent developments in the browser and the Web server aim to overcome the limits of the basic Web technology. Although this book describes JavaServer Pages, a server technology, let us briefly address browser technologies.

Extending the Web Browser

In recent years, various vendors have spent great effort extending the capabilities of the browser as an application interface. This usually happened under the auspices of making browser pages "more dynamic." The most important of these client-side extensions have been these:

- Helper applications
- Browser plug-ins
- JavaScript
- VBScript
- Dynamic HTML
- Java applets

Helper Applications

Browsers do not know how to handle most format types they encounter on the Web. This is partly because so many format types exist and partly because new format types keep appearing. Browsers compensate by launching other applications based on media format. For example, a browser may not handle RealVideo files but can be configured to launch the RealPlayer application to handle a RealVideo download.

Tip

The MIME standard that provides the basic scheme for HTTP request formatting also provides the basis for launching helper applications. The idea is that the browser passes MIME format types that it cannot handle to helper applications.

Recently, helper application functionality has tended to migrate into browser plug-ins. We discuss plug-ins next.

Browser Plug-Ins

Browser plug-ins seamlessly extend browser functionality so that they appear to be part of the browser itself. For example, Adobe Software provides a plug-in for viewing Adobe's Portable Document Format (PDF). Other plug-ins support audio and video formats. RealNetworks, for example, has plug-ins to play RealAudio and RealVideo files directly in the browser. Dozens of such plug-in programs now exist for both Netscape and Internet Explorer. Such plug-ins are loaded into the browser's own address space for execution. Vendors deploy plug-ins in browsers as shared libraries.

Note

Shared libraries are specially packaged units of code (usually written in C or C++) that can be loaded and executed in an application at runtime. On Microsoft Windows platforms, shared libraries use Microsoft's Dynamic Link Library (DLL) format that has a .dll file extension. On UNIX platforms, shared libraries use the Dynamic Shared Object (DSO) format that has a .so file extension.

Both helper applications and plug-ins suffer from the limitation that they are not general purpose programming languages. They provide one proprietary function and only that function. JavaScript, on the other hand, provides a truly flexible programming language for browsers.

JavaScript

JavaScript was the first general purpose, "dynamic" client-side scripting language for browsers. Netscape first delivered JavaScript in 1995 but called it LiveScript. (See Steenson's article, "JavaScript: Past, Present, and Future," at `http://home.netscape.com/computing/webbuilding/studio/feature19981111-1.html`.)

Netscape quickly renamed LiveScript to JavaScript, thereby confusing many people who had just started to hear about Java. The confusion was somewhat lessened by Sun, the developer of Java, when it issued a joint press release with Netscape that same year. The press release proclaimed Java and JavaScript to be complementary but very different technologies. (See `http://home.netscape.com/newsref/pr/newsrelease67.html`.)

JavaScript provides a scripting language for creating user interface controls. In effect, JavaScript inserts code logic into the browser. It supports such effects as validation of user input and image swapping as the mouse cursor rolls over a spot on a Web page.

Microsoft almost immediately wrote its own version of JavaScript and called it JScript. Both Microsoft and Netscape supported a scripting language standard encompassing the core features of JavaScript and JScript and controlled by the European Computer Manufacturers Association (ECMA) standards organization. ECMA named this scripting language ECMAScript. (See `http://www.ecma.ch/`.) Despite the respective commitments by Microsoft and Netscape to the ECMAScript standard, they continue their separate, proprietary and divergent enhancements to JavaScript. This means heavy dependence on JavaScript often requires separate code bases for different browsers.

VBScript

Alongside JavaScript, Microsoft also developed VBScript as an interpreted subset of its Visual Basic programming language. Microsoft developed VBScript specifically for use in Microsoft's Internet Explorer to support ActiveX controls. ActiveX is a proprietary Microsoft object-oriented software component model. Like JavaScript, VBScript requires interpreter support in the Web browser. Microsoft positions VBScript as an alternative to JavaScript for those programmers who already know

Visual Basic. Only Microsoft's browser, Internet Explorer, and Microsoft's Web server, the Internet Information Service (IIS), support VBScript.

Dynamic HTML

Dynamic HTML (DHTML) supports multiple technologies such as JavaScript and Java, but it is most strongly identified with *Cascading Style Sheets* (CSS), a W3C specification. (See `http://www.w3.org/TR/REC-CSS1`.) Cascading Style Sheets help page developers separate presentation elements from content elements. For example, exact pixel layout, similar to page layout for books or magazines, requires Cascading Style Sheets. Cascading Style Sheets also support such page element traits as colors, font specifications, display layers, and page margins.

Dynamic HTML also provides access to a browser page's Document Object Model (DOM). DOM is the internal representation of the elements of a page, along with their attributes. Dynamic HTML supports runtime access to some of these elements and in some cases, enables runtime modifications. For example, suppose we have this page element:

```
<h1 id=myPageElement>Dynamic HTML Features</h1>
```

Both JavaScript and VBScript can dynamically set the color of this element. Here is the JavaScript:

```
<script language="JavaScript1.2">
   myPageElement.style.color="#FF012F"
</script>
```

DHTML has a low level of standardization. Microsoft added support for its proprietary technologies, ActiveX and VBScript, which Netscape does not support. Both Netscape and Internet Explorer support CSS, but to different degrees for different features. Both the event model and DOM for Internet Explorer and Netscape differ, making cross-platform use of DHTML quirky. (See `http://www.dhtmlzone.com/`.)

Java Applets

Java was announced by Sun Microsystems in February of 1995, the same year that Netscape announced JavaScript. (See Richard Morin's article "Oak and WebRunner" in *Sun Expert Magazine,* 1995, Vol. 6, No. 2. Also see `http://java.sun.com/pr/1995/02/pr950201-01.html`.)

Its original name was Oak. Sun described Oak as a simplified derivative of C++ and described its features as including the following:

- Dynamic linking of program functionality into a running application using a network download
- Independence from any CPU platform
- Guaranteed security from viruses

Oak was renamed Java by April of 1995. (See Chris Rose's article, "It's the World Wide Web, But Not as We Know It," in *PowerPC News*: Apt Data News Ltd, 1995, Issue Number 534, UG534-17. Also see `http://java.sun.com/pr/1995/04/pr950417-01.html`.)

From that quiet beginning as Oak, Java has captured unprecedented mind-share among programmers. Initially, this popularity focused on the client side, especially Java applets.

The idea behind applets was to provide full-featured programming capabilities to browser applications without sacrificing security. Both Netscape and Microsoft licensed Java and integrated it into their respective browsers. Today, Sun provides a Java plug-in for both browser platforms. Special HTML tags invoke the plug-in to load applets into a Java virtual machine (JVM). This plug-in bridges the browser and an external JVM. The Sun Java plug-in removes developer dependence on the "out-of-the-box" versions of the Java Virtual Machine supported by browser vendors. This allows developers to remain current with the Java releases. For example, at this time you must use the Sun plug-in to run Java 2 applets in a browser.

1-Minute Drill

- What is the difference between browser plug-ins and JavaScript?
- What is Dynamic HTML?

- Browser plug-ins extend the browser and get loaded into the browser at runtime. You deploy them as shared libraries. They typically handle a single proprietary media format type. JavaScript, on the other hand, is a general-purpose programming language interpreted by the browser.
- Dynamic HTLM refers to a loose collection of browser enhancements but is most closely identified with a W3C specification called Cascading Style Sheets (CSS) and with technologies that expose the Document Object Model (DOM).

The Role and Limits of Browser Technologies

All of the client-side technologies add functionality to Web browsers and help make Web applications more intuitive, easier to use, and more interesting. Despite their clear value, however, none of these technologies deliver services. Their role is limited to improving how users see and request such services.

Java applets are arguably the most general and powerful of the client-side technologies. With sophisticated caching, streaming techniques, or clever programming, applets may seem almost like standard desktop applications. A slow network connection, however, or interrupted Internet service quickly dispel this illusion. Network transparency is a goal that client-server applications never completely achieve.

The power that client-side extensions add to browsers can even be counter-productive. The trend in recent years has been to move functionality from the client to the server. People describe this as a movement away from a *thick client* to a *thin client*. A thin client separates the presentation of an application user interface from the control logic of the presentation. This movement away from fat clients provides several advantages. We list some of the most important:

- **Centralized application deployment** Developers can deploy applications and application upgrades to a centralized application server rather than to the myriad client machines accessing the applications.
- **Enforcement of information consistency** Every user shares the same view of the information rather than the view deployed on his or her client machine.
- **Centralized security management** Administrators can control access to information at the server rather than on each client machine.

Most of us have grumbled at one time or another at Web sites that take too many long minutes to display because we must first install an application plug-in or download a Java applet. The more Web sites rely on such technologies, the fatter Web clients become and the more the Internet clogs down distributing these fat clients. Java applets have lost their luster as a preferred development strategy largely because they tend towards a fat client paradigm. JavaScript still enjoys a loyal following in part because it attempts far less than a typical Java applet. The paradigm shift in modern computing puts clients on a diet and fattens up the server.

1-Minute Drill

- What role do Web browser extensions play among Internet technologies?
- What is the primary limitation of such browser extensions?

Server-Side Web Programming

Given the advantages provided when you move application functionality to the server, how is it done? Initially, the only answer was to use the Common Gateway Interface (CGI).

Note

In his early proposals to CERN, the European Center for High-Energy Physics in Geneva, Switzerland, Tim Berners-Lee already anticipated the requirement that Web servers present "legacy" information stored in databases as HTML views. (See Tim Berners-Lee's "Information Management: A Proposal" at `http://www.w3.org/History/1989/proposal.html`. [1989, p. 12].) This requirement eventually led to the CGI standard.

The CGI standard specifies the approved mechanisms for integration of *external gateway programs*—programs that provide gateways between non-HTML information sources and the Web server. Figure 1-3 shows the CGI architecture accessing a relational database.

A Web server and a CGI program talk at the operating system process level. In an operating system, a process is the most fundamental executable unit for programs. Processes can launch other processes and hand off information while doing so. The Web server launches a CGI process and therefore can hand off request information. For example, the Web server packages the data passed in `GET` requests as an environment variable named *`QUERY_STRING`*. Suppose we send this URL to a Web server using a `GET` request:

```
http://myserver/cgi-bin/Scripts/foo.perl?name=emily
```

- Browser extensions add functionality to Web browsers and help make Web applications more intuitive, easier to use, and more interesting.
- Browser extensions do not supply services and their use encourages fatter clients.

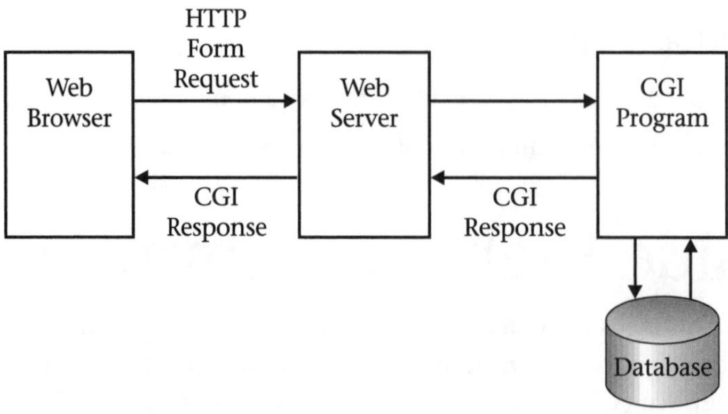

Figure 1-3 The Common Gateway Interface

A CGI program can access its *QUERY_STRING* environment variable to retrieve the fact that `name` has the value `emily`.

Alternately, if we send the URL using a `POST` request, a CGI can read the value of `name` out of its standard input file descriptor. The `POST` request sets two environment variables that support retrieving this content: *CONTENT_LENGTH* and *CONTENT_*TYPE.

CGI is a powerful tool and literally "rules" the Web—but its days are numbered. Launching programs to handle client requests wastes server resources (including the CPU) and complicates generation of response pages. In a worst-case scenario, every client request could require launching one or more additional processes. When Perl or some other scripting language implements a CGI program (the typical case on the modern Internet), the inefficiencies get much worse because scripting languages typically launch additional processes to handle operating-system queries. This proliferation of CGI processes limits the scalability of Web applications.

Further, because CGI programs do not persist across client requests, they must store state information related to clients (e.g., session information) in a database or file system. In general, we want a more tightly coupled relationship between our server extensions and the Web server so we can improve response times and scalability and support efficient management of client state. Fortunately, better techniques than CGI exist today.

Question: I don't understand. What do you mean by a tightly coupled relationship between server extensions and the Web server?

Answer: Software modules are more or less tightly coupled. Loosely coupled software modules make few assumptions about each other and pass information generically. CGI scripts, for example, live in a separate address space from Web servers. They make no assumptions about the features of Web servers. They exchange information with Web servers using standard operating-system features like environment variables and standard file operations. All these traits mean CGI programs couple very loosely with Web servers. Tightly coupled software modules, on the other hand, exploit each other's implementation details to optimize cooperation. For example, they typically share the same memory address space, pass specific data structures back and forth, and share proprietary features of common code libraries.

Question: Isn't it risky to create a tight coupling between the Web server and custom extensions?

Answer: Yes, it is. By creating a tight coupling between server extensions and the Web server, you make it possible for extension code to destabilize or even crash the Web server.

Question: Then why do you say tight coupling is desirable?

Answer: Loose coupling between software modules is generally better because it reduces software complexity and isolates software problems. When performance and responsiveness are requirements, however, tight coupling can sometimes optimize these features. The performance degradation caused by launching CGI programs is often unacceptable in modern Web architectures. A tightly coupled Web server extension can overcome this performance problem with CGI scripts.

Question: Which techniques help reduce the risk posed by tightly coupled server extensions?

Answer: You can reduce the risk by limiting server extensions to small, discrete functions. The less code that you add to the Web server, the less risk that it will degrade the reliability of the server. One useful approach is to build bridging code in the server that handshakes with more loosely coupled software, perhaps over a network socket.

Extending the Web Server

Modern server-side programming architectures include the following technologies:

- **Server-side JavaScript** A JavaScript programmer's toolkit for Web servers
- **Server plug-ins** Functions the server calls when processing a request
- **Active Server Pages (ASP)** A proprietary Microsoft technology for scripting Web server extensions
- **Servlets** A Sun Microsystems technology that handles client HTTP requests using Java
- **JavaServer Pages (JSP)** A Sun Microsystems Java technology for scripting Web server extensions
- **Java 2 Enterprise Edition (J2EE) Application Server** A Java process that, among other technologies, supports a Web server, servlets, and JSPs

Let's look at each of these technologies to understand their basic features.

Server-Side JavaScript

Server-side JavaScript adds APIs to access databases, file systems, and electronic mail. The primary problem with server-side JavaScript is that IIS supports JScript, a different implementation of JavaScript than that supported by iPlanet. In other words, when you use server-side JavaScript you must commit yourself to a specific Web server. This is a reasonable requirement for companies that have standardized on technology vendors, but completely unreasonable for product companies who must be all things to as many customers as possible.

Note

One of the interesting stories of the modern Internet has been the ongoing tension between proprietary technologies and open standards. HTML is probably the most obvious example of the struggle between proprietary enhancements and the attempt to create an open standard. JavaScript, DHTML, Java, browser plug-in architectures—indeed, practically every Internet technology—have their own tale to tell.

Server Plug-Ins

Web servers add plug-in capabilities by loading runtime libraries. The mechanisms for doing this differ between Microsoft's IIS and Sun Microsystems iPlanet. The former uses the Internet Service Application Programming Interface (ISAPI), the latter the Netscape Application Programming Interface (NSAPI). Another popular Web server, Apache, uses a similar architecture. Figure 1-4 shows the plug-in architecture.

ISAPI IIS requires that developers implement ISAPI functionality as a Windows DLL. When a request for this functionality arrives at the server, the server loads it into local memory and executes it. This means that bad programming can crash IIS. Alternately, you can configure ISAPI functions to run in a separate address space (i.e., a separate process) from IIS. Finally, you can configure ISAPI applications to load and unload for every request. ISAPI functionality runs fastest when it runs in the address space of IIS. When you run an ISAPI application in a separate process or dynamically load and unload it, you degrade its performance.

NSAPI Sun's iPlanet requires developers to implement NSAPI functionality as a DSO that it loads into its own address space. There the NSAPI application runs as a service thread.

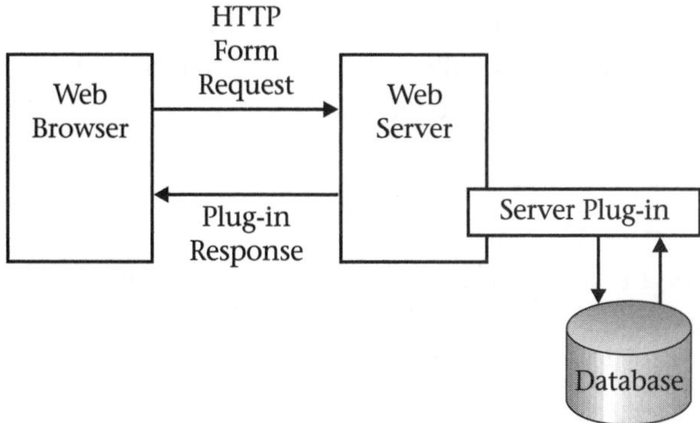

Figure 1-4 Web server plug-in architecture

Apache API Apache supports the idea of handlers associated with request format types. To extend Apache, you must compile a handler into Apache at the source code level. Apache source code is freely downloadable from their Web site. (See `http://httpd.apache.org/docs/install.html`.)

ASP

ASP provides a powerful basis for combining static HTML, Extensible Markup Language (XML), Web scripts like JavaScript and VBScript, and Microsoft's Component Object Model (COM) components into a single Web page. ASP's syntax is much like that of JavaServer Pages. Its advantages over JavaServer Pages are its support for several different scripting languages and the large catalogue of Microsoft COM components you can embed in ASPs. ASPs have big disadvantages, however, because they confine developers to Microsoft platforms and a fixed set of ASP tags. (In Module 6, we describe how you extend JSP tags.)

Java Servlets

Java servlet technology provides an extensible, platform-neutral, Web server extension methodology. Pure Java Web servers or application servers might implement the servlet container as a thread inside the main process. The more popular Web servers like Apache, iPlanet, or Microsoft's IIS require a different architecture based on their proprietary interfaces. This architecture includes a plug-in to the Web server that redirects servlet requests to a separate Java process implementing the servlet container. This use of a Web server plug-in provides a compromise between tight coupling and loose coupling. The Web server plug-in provides a tightly coupled bridge to pass information between Web server and a loosely coupled servlet engine. The servlet container listens on a configurable network port dedicated to such redirections. Figure 1-5 shows this architecture.

JSP

JSP complements the Java servlet architecture by providing a JSP container that manages parsing and compilation of JavaServer Pages into servlets. Figure 1-6 shows the general JSP architecture.

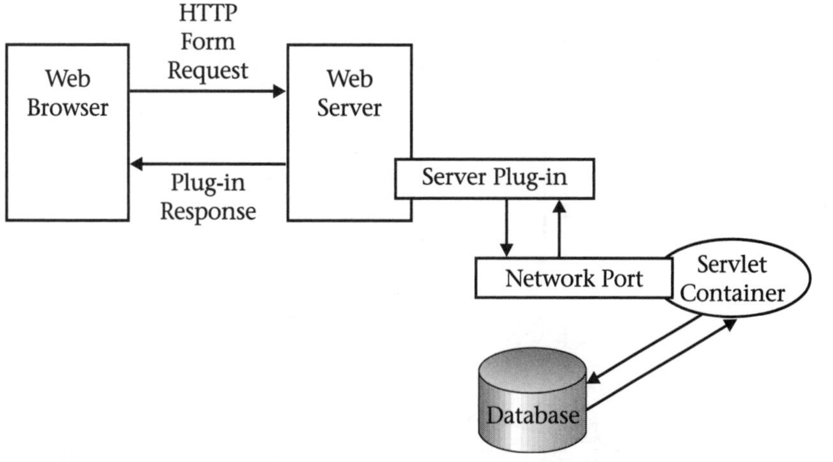

Figure 1-5 Servlet architecture for IIS, iPlanet, and Apache

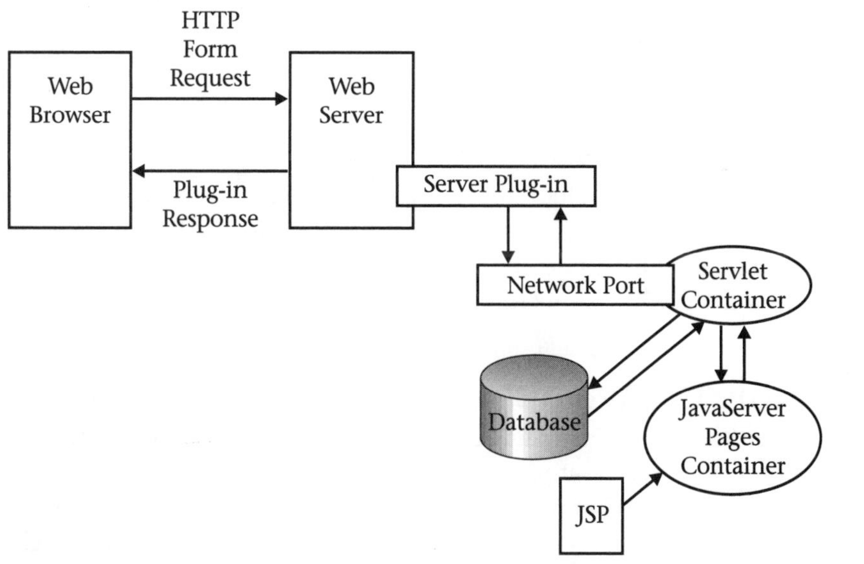

Figure 1-6 JavaServer Page architecture

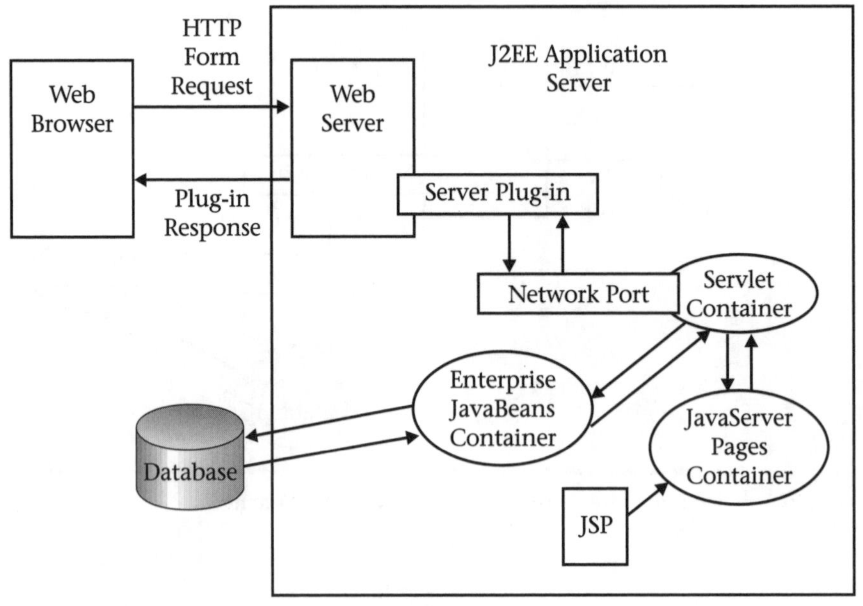

Figure 1-7 Java 2 Enterprise Edition application server architecture

J2EE Application Servers

The J2EE specification includes both Java servlets and JavaServer Pages. J2EE application servers typically provide a Java platform for Web services as well as other services like Enterprise JavaBeans and the Java Messaging Service that we do not discuss here. We show the J2EE platform architecture in Figure 1-7.

The Role of Java Servlets and JavaServer Pages

Vanilla Web servers deliver static content efficiently and effectively. Modern Web applications, however, require more than static content. Client-side extensions to browsers help meet this need but do not really address the special purpose of the client-server paradigm—to provide remote services. Server-side JavaScript is popular but proprietary. Web server plug-ins provide useful but proprietary extensions. Further, as you will see in Part 2 of this book, enterprise applications require all the features of servers that Web servers avoid. They require sophisticated security services and session management. They must track client state. They must manage database access including connection pooling. The list is long and inescapable.

Imagine programming such enterprise server features using CGI scripts or server plug-ins. W3C never intended that CGI scripts provide general-purpose server platforms. They intended to provide gateways to legacy data. Similarly, server plug-ins provide efficient gateways to external applications but do not provide a complete server-side development platform.

Active Server Pages provide a platform for server-side Web application development, but the platform works only with Microsoft technologies. Servlets and JavaServer Pages, on the other hand, provide a server-side platform for non-proprietary, cross-platform, scalable, and extensible Internet applications.

1-Minute Drill

- What is a server plug-in?
- Why are the days of CGI dominance numbered?
- What is the role of Java servlets and JavaServer Pages?

Project 1-2: Running Your First JSP Program

This exercise requires you to set up a working Web server on your development machine. Appendix B explains installation and configuration of Apache and Tomcat. If you read and followed the instructions in Appendix B, skip to Step 4. If you have not already installed and configured Apache and Tomcat, follow Steps 1 through 3 first.

Step-by-Step

1. Follow the instructions in Appendix B to install the Tomcat servlet container. You can install Apache as well, but this project only requires Tomcat.

- Server plug-ins extend Web servers using proprietary Web server programming interfaces. The three most common APIs are
  - **ISAPI** APIs for Microsoft's IIS
  - **NSAPI** APIs for the iPlanet
  - **The Apache Web Server API** APIs for the Apache Web Server
- CGI scripts waste server resources and complicate generation of response pages. Recent technologies like Active Server Pages, Java servlets, and JavaServer Pages provide more efficient and simpler ways to develop complicated Web applications.
- These Java technologies provide a general platform for server-side Web application development that is non-proprietary, cross-platform, scalable, and extensible.

2. Go to the `bin` directory under *%TOMCAT_HOME%*. (You created this variable in Step 1.)
3. At the command prompt, type

```
%> startup
```

   This should start the Tomcat servlet container. To shut down the Tomcat servlet container, type

```
%> shutdown
```

4. Start a browser (Internet Explorer or Netscape Navigator) and because Tomcat runs on port 8080 by default, type this URL into the appropriate field of your browser window:

```
http://localhost:8080
```

   You should see the Tomcat welcome page.
5. Find the hyperlink titled *JSP Examples* and click on it. This takes you to a Web page that shows a list of JSP examples that you can execute.
6. Select the *Execute* hyperlink for any of the examples. The JSP example should execute correctly. For example, if you select *Numberguess* to run, you should see a page that requests you to enter a number between 1–100. If you see this, you installed and configured your Tomcat servlet container correctly.
7. Select the *Source* hyperlink for any of the examples. You should see the actual code used to create the JSP page.
8. Congratulations! You have taken an important first step into the world of JavaServer pages! You must get the JSP configuration working so you can build and execute the projects we describe in this book. By exercising the example JavaServer pages, you assure that the basic Tomcat installation works and you get a good look at how a JSP page maps to an HTML response page.

Mastery Check

1. HTTP stands for ____.

2. List three computer network traits that make network transparency difficult to achieve.

____

____

3. List two types of HTTP requests.

____

____

4. Explain why standard Web browser–Web server architectures fail to provide an adequate basis for many modern Web applications.

____

____

5. List three types of Web browser extensions.

____

____

6. List three kinds of Web server extensions.

____

____

Module 2

JSP Elements: Comments and Directives

The Goals of This Module

- Understand the JavaServer Pages (JSP) container
- Understand how to use comments when coding JavaServer Pages
- Know the basic JSP directives

A JSP page looks like a Hypertext Transfer Protocol (HTML) page with special syntactic elements. These elements help provide the dynamic behavior that today's Web pages require. In this module and the following four, we explain JSP elements.

The JSP life cycle differs from that of a static HTML document. In a simple handshake between a Web server and a Web browser, the Web server fetches a file requested by the Web browser and streams it back to the browser. Then the browser renders this stream in its view panel. If the requested file happens to be static HTML, the Web server need only stream the contents of the file to the Web browser. If the requested file is a JSP page, however, the Web server cannot simply stream its contents because Web browsers cannot render JSP syntactic elements. The Web server must first *interpret* the JSP page to generate additional dynamic HTML content before streaming the interpreted document back to the browser. The JSP specification calls the server-side Web process that manages streaming JavaServer Pages the JSP *container*.

The JSP Container

The Java 2 Enterprise Edition (J2EE) defines several containers, including the JSP container, a servlet container, and an Enterprise JavaBeans container. A container, in object-oriented parlance, is a class or component that organizes other classes or components. The J2EE specifications exceed this simple meaning. J2EE containers provide the total runtime environment within which enterprise components live and act. They manage the lifecycle of components and provide various services to the components. Additionally, they coordinate interactions between the components and the larger runtime environment.

J2EE containers cannot perform properly unless developers write software components that conform to programming conventions dictated by the containers. Developers must implement these conventions because the containers assume them at various times in a component's life cycle. The specifications often call such agreements between containers and application software *contracts,* to emphasize their importance. The containers enforce such contracts by requiring application software to implement particular Java interfaces.

Each J2EE container provides services to the components for which it bears responsibility. The JSP container translates JavaServer Pages into Java servlet code, and then compiles and loads the result into the servlet container. It also coordinates the relationship between the servlet container and the compiled JavaServer Pages. The servlet container provides the runtime environment for Java servlets.

JSP Stages

The first time a browser requests a JSP page, the following happens:

1. It interprets the JSP page.
2. It generates a Java servlet.
3. It compiles the generated servlet into Java bytecode using a standard Java compiler packaged with the JSP container.
4. It loads the servlet into the Java virtual machine (JVM) of the servlet container.
5. It invokes the *service* method of the generated servlet.

Figure 2-1 shows how it works.

If a browser application subsequently requests the same JSP page, the JSP container need only perform Step 5, unless the JSP page has changed since the last invocation. When a JSP page changes, the JSP container must revisit all five steps before streaming back a response. Steps 1 through 4 explain why JavaServer Pages take slightly longer to return responses the first time browsers request them.

Hint

You can overcome this first time compilation cost either by precompiling the application JavaServer Pages prior to deployment or by using the precompilation protocol specified in the JSP 1.1 specification, Section 3.4. Apache supplies the *jspc* program to precompile your application, and Tomcat supports the precompilation protocol. You use the protocol by appending `?jsp_ precompile=true` to your JSP request like this: `http://localhost:8080/Book/jsp/ScriptingElements.jsp?jsp_precompile=true`. This causes the JSP container to compile the page without executing it.

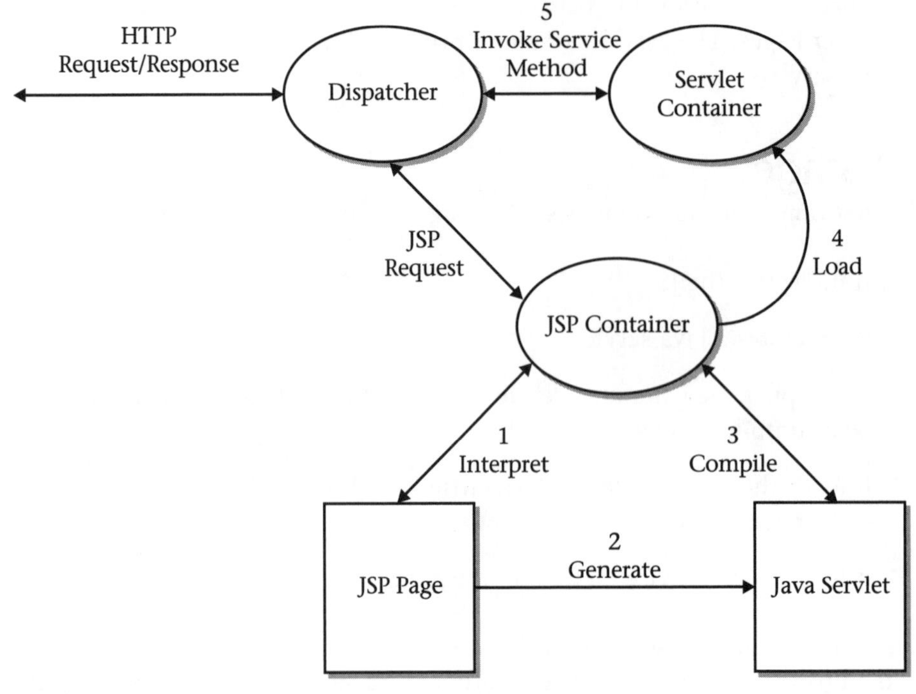

Figure 2-1 Stages in the life cycle of a JSP page

JSP Scope

The birth of a JSP page begins with a request, but the life cycle of some Java objects it creates span multiple requests. Sometimes the JSP container creates these objects implicitly (described in Module 4). You can also create Java objects using JSP actions (described in Modules 5 and 6). Finally, you can create such objects directly in a JSP script (described in Module 3). All such objects have a *scope* attribute defining *where* a reference to that object is available and *when* the container removes the object.

The JSP container supports four different scopes:

- **page** You can reference objects with *page scope* only within the JSP page that creates them. The JSP container removes all such objects after the JSP page returns a response or forwards the request to another page.

- **request** You can access objects with *request scope* from any page processing the same request. Often a page may forward a request to another page so that multiple pages process the same request. All such pages can access objects in request scope. The container removes such objects after the request completes.
- **session** You can access objects with *session scope* from any page sharing a session with that of the page that created the objects. The container removes such objects when the associated session ends.
- **application** You can access objects with *application scope* anywhere in the same Web application. The JSP container removes objects with application scope when it reloads the servlet context, usually when the server restarts.

Note

A Web application bundles servlets, JavaServer Pages, and other resources into a package you can deploy and run on multiple containers from multiple vendors. A Web application maps directly to a servlet context that provides an isolated environment for the application. The Java interface *javax.servlet.ServletContext* describes the services in this context. For example, you might associate this URL root with an application context in your Web server: `http://localhost/Book`. The servlet container creates a single *ServletContext* object associated with this context. Any JSP page referenced by a URL that starts with "`/Book`" (the *context path*) can access this *ServletContext* object.

1-Minute Drill

- What is a JSP container?
- What are the stages when a JSP page is first loaded?
- What are the scopes for the objects in a JSP page?

- A JSP container is a process that translates JavaServer Pages into Java servlet code and then compiles and loads the generated Java bytecode into the servlet container.
- The stages are (1) interpretation of the JSP page, (2) generation of the servlet, (3) compilation of the servlet, (4) loading of the servlet into the servlet container, and (5) invocation of the servlet *service* method.
- The scopes are page, request, session, and application.

JSP Constructs

A chart of all JSP constructs organized into categories can help orient you. Figure 2-2 shows the organizational chart of all JSP constructs. We explain these constructs in the next several modules. You can use this chart to track your progress through the modules.

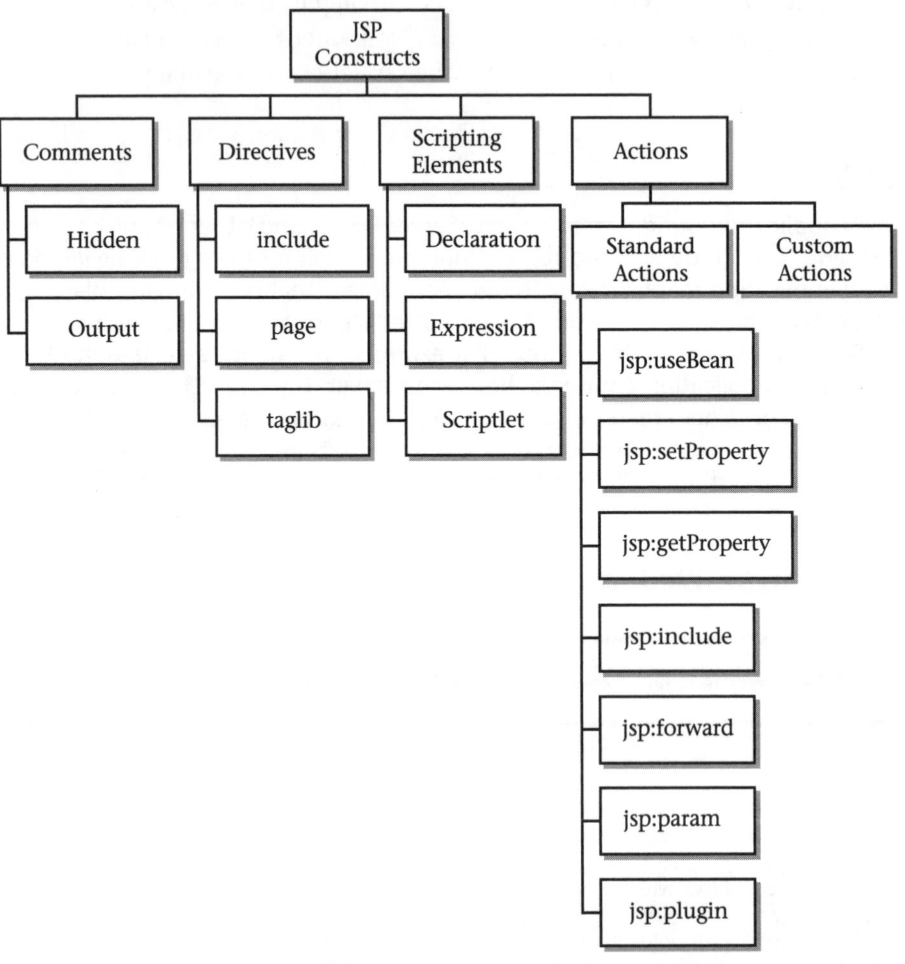

Figure 2-2 Organizational chart of all JSP constructs

Bird's-Eye View of a Complete JSP Page

Have you heard the story of the blind men and the elephant? This old fable from India describes six blind men interpreting their separate experiences of an elephant. One man touches the tail and calls the elephant a rope. Another touches the tusk and calls the elephant a spear. A third touches the trunk and calls the elephant a snake. The other three make similar misinterpretations. The story illustrates how limited perceptions lead to false understanding. To avoid a false understanding of JavaServer Pages, we provide a bird's-eye view of a complete sample JSP page containing most of the elements. Consult this picture as we work our way through the different modules:

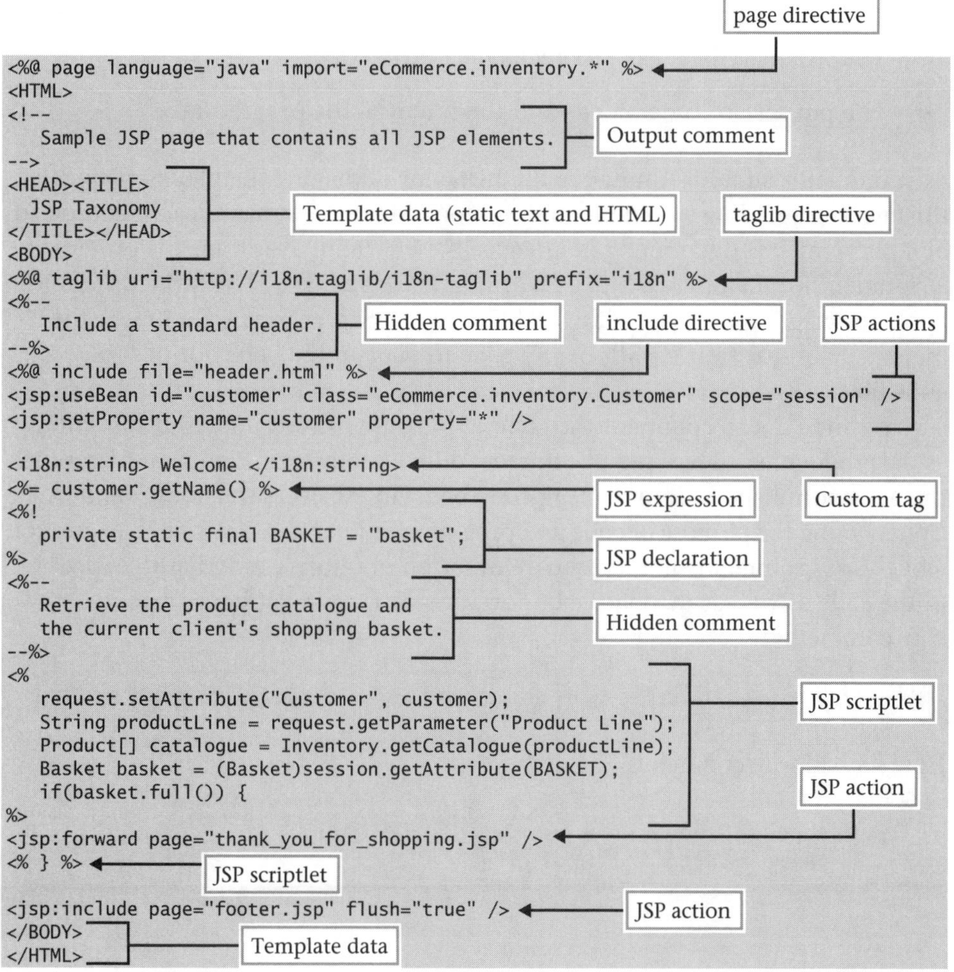
page directive
<%@ page language="java" import="eCommerce.inventory.*" %>
<HTML>
<!--
Sample JSP page that contains all JSP elements.
-->
Output comment
<HEAD><TITLE>
JSP Taxonomy
</TITLE></HEAD>
<BODY>
Template data (static text and HTML)
taglib directive
<%@ taglib uri="http://i18n.taglib/i18n-taglib" prefix="i18n" %>
<%--
Include a standard header.
--%>
Hidden comment
include directive
JSP actions
<%@ include file="header.html" %>
<jsp:useBean id="customer" class="eCommerce.inventory.Customer" scope="session" />
<jsp:setProperty name="customer" property="*" />
<i18n:string> Welcome </i18n:string>
<%= customer.getName() %>
JSP expression
Custom tag
<%!
private static final BASKET = "basket";
%>
JSP declaration
<%--
Retrieve the product catalogue and
the current client's shopping basket.
--%>
Hidden comment
<%
request.setAttribute("Customer", customer);
String productLine = request.getParameter("Product Line");
Product[] catalogue = Inventory.getCatalogue(productLine);
Basket basket = (Basket)session.getAttribute(BASKET);
if(basket.full()) {
%>
JSP scriptlet
JSP action
<jsp:forward page="thank_you_for_shopping.jsp" />
<% } %>
JSP scriptlet
<jsp:include page="footer.jsp" flush="true" />
JSP action
</BODY>
</HTML>
Template data

JSP Comments

Every programming language, whether C/C++, Java, Visual Basic, or JavaServer pages, must support comments. A comment in a document or program serves to clarify the content of that document or program. Comments do not add processing overhead to programs because compilers and interpreters ignore them.

Using Comments

While comments often clarify programs, you should use them with discretion. The most useful comments provide a natural language explanation of two things:

- The summary behavior of blocks of code
- The purpose of code blocks and the intent of the programmer

Comments should summarize the behavior of major code blocks. Typically, this means providing a documentation block for each class and each method in object-oriented programming languages like C++ and Java. It means providing a comment for major code blocks within methods as well. The same principles apply to scripting languages like HTML and JavaServer pages. Comment the major sections of your HTML or JSP page to explain the behavior of these code blocks.

You should also comment the general purpose of code and your intentions as the programmer. This kind of comment differs subtly from comments describing the behavior of code. Commenting code behavior answers the question *how*. Commenting the purpose of code and programmer intentions answers the question *why*. A *why* comment should prepare other programmers for what to expect in the code as well as its relative importance. For example, here's a good *why* comment:

```
/* Create a directory of all users */
```

Here's a bad *why* comment:

```
/* Loop through the user's array and add each
   user entry to the lookup table
*/
```

The first comment is *good* because it supplies the reason for the code. The second comment is *bad* because it states how the code works—which the code itself already describes.

Some programmers use comments for purposes other than summarizing code behavior and programmer intentions. Here is a kind of rogue's list of other common uses for comments:

- Programmers may use comments to state what code does in words other than the code itself.
- Sometimes programmers use comments to explain tricky or clever code.
- Occasionally, programmers comment individual lines of code as a natural language expression of their algorithm.

This list of comment usage is dubious. Let's address each point in this list.

You should never repeat in a comment what the code states. If a comment of this type seems useful, the code probably lacks clarity (e.g., badly named variables, confusing formatting, or an over-engineered solution). This kind of usage can actually obscure programs and raise the risk that comments and code will diverge. Typically, programmers maintain code better than they maintain comments. In some ways, this is like commenting on an English text using French. The French text is unlikely to clarify the English text and may even obscure it.

Commenting clever code makes a little more sense. When you must use clever code, you should comment the reasons. For example, "real-world" optimizations sometimes require exploitation of features or techniques that you would otherwise avoid. You should comment these optimizations so that another programmer does not inadvertently remove them, perhaps in the name of *elegant* programming. Such comments really help explain the intentions of the programmer. You should realize, however, that good excuses for clever code are rare and even dangerous. The infamous Y2K problem was a space optimization addressing a temporary limitation of existing technology that eventually cost the computer industry billions of dollars to correct.

You should not comment individual lines of code to document your algorithms. You should gather all such comments into a summary comment at the beginning of the entire code block. These summary comments should focus on the reasons for the algorithm, rather than the implementation in your code. Such comments are clearer and easier to find than a collection of comments scattered throughout code. On the other hand, you should comment data declarations because such annotations provide useful information about the role of data in the code.

Following are some common-sense rules for specifying comments regardless of the programming language:

- Comments should focus on intention and purpose—*why,* not *how.*
- Comments should summarize code and introduce it, not restate it.
- Comments should clarify, not compete with, code. The code documents a program, script, or JSP page best.
- Comments should never state the obvious.
- Write comments with care. Inaccurate or misleading comments never help.
- Strive for consistency when commenting. Keep comment location, format, and content consistent.

With these rules-of-thumb in mind, let's take a look at how you can specify comments in a JSP page.

JSP Comment Types

In the discussion of the JSP life cycle, you saw that JavaServer Pages involve two documents: the JSP page and the HTML it generates. Correspondingly, JSP supports two types of comments:

- Comments documenting the source JSP page
- Comments destined for the generated HTML document

Comments Documenting the Source JSP Page

Some comments document the source JSP page. The specification calls these comments *hidden comments* because browser clients cannot view them in the generated document. The JSP container strips out such comments when generating the HTML it sends to the browser. A hidden comment has this form:

```
<%– anything but a closing —%> ... «—%>
```

That is, you can place anything into a hidden comment but the close tag for hidden comments.

Hidden comments should normally explain behavior of the JSP page and not the generated HTML. Following is an example of a good hidden comment in our bird's-eye view sample:

```
<%--
   Retrieve the product catalogue and
   the current client's shopping basket.
--%>
```

Comments Destined for the Generated Document

Just as you should comment JavaServer Pages, you should comment the generated HTML. The JSP specification calls comments that are meant to be displayed in the generated document *output comments*. An output comment has this form:

<! – – *comments* – –>

You might recognize that JSP output comments share the same format as comments in Extensible Markup Language (XML) and HTML documents. Unlike hidden comments, which the JSP container ignores, the JSP container treats output comments as static text that it includes in the generated document. Unlike HTML or XML comments, the JSP container will interpret JSP expressions (described more fully in Module 3) inside an output comment. This means that the power of JavaServer Pages to generate dynamic Web content extends even to the content of output comments. For example, consider this comment line:

```
<!-- This page was created on <%= new java.util.Date() %> -->
```

This comment generates the following HTML line by executing the Java code between the `<%=` tag and the `%>` tag:

```
<!-- This page was created on Sat Dec 02 17:51:34 EST 2000 -->
```

Note

Output comments exist because browsers let you view the source of a Web page. Such code sharing is common, but it seems a stretch to expect Web developers to comment generated pages for the sake of such sharing. You should follow your own instincts and tendencies toward altruism when deciding how much to use output comments.

1-Minute Drill

- What is the difference between a *why* comment and a *how* comment? Which should you use more often?
- What are the two types of JSP comments and when would you use them?

JSP Directives

A JSP page can send messages to its container instructing the container to perform actions on its behalf. The specification calls such messages *directives*. JSP 1.1 directives use the following general format:

```
<%@ directive { attr="value" }* %>
```

That is, a directive starts with a `<%@` tag; specifies a directive name; includes zero or more attributes, each specified as a name-value pair; and ends with a `%>` tag. Directives in a JSP page do not produce any output in the generated document. They ask the JSP container to perform certain services for the JSP page. The JSP 1.1 specification supports three types of directives:

- include
- page
- taglib

Let's look at each directive.

- Comments that describe the purpose of the code and the intentions of the programmer are *why* comments. Comments that merely document code behavior are *how* comments. You should use why comments.
- The two types of JSP comments are hidden comments and output comments. You use hidden comments to document the behavior of the JSP page. You use output comments to document the behavior of the generated HTML.

The include Directive

Programmers break complex problems into smaller pieces to simplify the problems they must solve. Software applications are among the most complex problems people solve, so all modern software technologies, including JavaServer pages, support partitioning of software into smaller pieces, or *modules*. Software modules provide several advantages:

- Solving simpler problems encourages cleaner solutions.
- You can independently create and test each module.
- Because large problems tend to break into similar smaller problems, modularity improves software re-use.

The JSP container supports modularized development with two *include* mechanisms:

- include directive
- include action

We explain the include directive here and discuss the include action in Module 5.

The include directive instructs the JSP container to include a specified resource at the location where the directive appears. A resource can be any static page or another JSP page. If you include a file, usually an HTML or a JSP page fragment, the JSP container substitutes the bytes of this file *in place* for the directive. You specify the location for retrieving the resource using a *relative URL* (see RFC 2396, `http://www.ietf.org/rfc/rfc2396.txt`).

Relative URLs

Recall from Module 1 that an HTTP URL has the general form:

`http://`*origin-server[:port]/[path [?query]]*

The relative URL specification strips this to one of these forms:

- **net path** *//origin-server[:port]/[path[?query]]*
- **absolute path** */path[?query]*
- **relative path** *path [?query]*

Here are some examples:

- **net path** `//localhost:8080/examples/jsp/num/numguess.jsp`
- **absolute path** `/examples/jsp/num/numguess.jsp`
- **relative path** `examples/jsp/num/numguess.jsp`

Although the relative URL specification describes all three forms, the JSP specification supports only the last two of these forms. The JSP specification calls the absolute path form of URL (the form beginning with a slash [/]) a *context-relative path.* It calls the relative path form (without the beginning /) a *page-relative path.*

The JSP container interprets *context*-relative paths by concatenating the relative URL that you provide to a base URL provided by the *ServletContext* object (provided to the servlet container by the Web server):

context URL + relative URL

The JSP container interprets page-relative paths by concatenating the relative URL that you provide to a base URL consisting of the URL for the current JSP page minus the page name:

JSP page URL - JSP page name + relative URL

For example, we might declare a Tomcat Web server context like this:

```
<Context path="/examples"
   docBase="webapps/examples"
</Context>
```

These lines declare that the base URL for the `/examples` context is the following:

```
%TOMCAT_HOME%/webapps/examples
```

The JSP container then converts a context-relative path like this:

```
/jsp/num/numguess.jsp
```

to this:

```
%TOMCAT_HOME%/webapps/examples/jsp/num/numguess.jsp
```

Alternately, if we include a page-relative path like this:

```
hello.html
```

in `numguess.jsp`, the JSP container converts the path to this:

```
%TOMCAT_HOME%/webapps/examples/jsp/num/hello.html
```

Using the include Directive

The include directive takes this general form:

```
<%@ include file="relative URL"" %>
```

For example, assume that the following include directive appears in a JSP page called `Inventory.jsp`:

```
<%@ include file="header.html" %>
```

At translation-time, the first time the JSP container references `Inventory.jsp`, the container substitutes the HTML contents of `header.html` for the include directive. In this respect, it behaves very differently than the jsp:include action, which includes pages at request time.

The included resource could be another JSP page. In that case, the JSP container inserts the included JSP page into the parent JSP page before translating the combined JSP page into a single Java servlet. Here's an example of a JSP page that includes a second JSP page:

```
<html>
<head><title>Parent</title></head>
<body>
My favorite cousins are: <br>
<%@ include file="Children.jsp" %>
</body>
</html>
```

The included file, `Children.jsp`, looks like this:

```
Sarah whose age as of <%= new java.util.Date() %> is 12. <br>
Jenny whose age as of <%= new java.util.Date() %> is 9. <br>
Sam whose age as of <%= new java.util.Date() %> is 5.
```

After the inclusion and before the translation, the new `Parent.jsp` looks like this:

```
<html>
<head><title>Parent</title></head>
<body>
My favorite cousins are: <br>
Sarah whose age as of <%= new java.util.Date() %> is 12. <br>
Jenny whose age as of <%= new java.util.Date() %> is 9. <br>
Sam whose age as of <%= new java.util.Date() %> is 5.
</body>
</html>
```

The output of the combined `Parent.jsp` would be something like this:

```
My favorite cousins are:
Sarah whose age as of Sat Dec 02 19:18:53 EST 2000 is 12.
Jenny whose age as of Sat Dec 02 19:18:53 EST 2000 is 9.
Sam whose age as of Sat Dec 02 19:18:53 EST 2000 is 5.
```

The Limits of the include Directive

The include directive helps you develop modular JavaServer Pages by enabling you to break a JSP page into multiple parts, each part potentially reusable by another JSP page. Such modularity can support standardization of page elements like headers and footers. By splitting the header and footer out of the main JSP page, multiple JavaServer Pages can include them, thereby establishing a standard look and feel and reducing the size of each separate page. However, this kind of modularity is limited. Let's look at some of the limitations of the include directive.

The container doesn't reload included pages. A JSP developer usually iterates through multiple versions on the way to developing a final JSP page. The JSP 1.1 specification defines a mechanism to notify JSP containers whenever you modify a JSP page it has loaded. This enables the containers to recompile and reload modified pages automatically. Unfortunately, this notification mechanism fails for included files. In our previous example, if we modify the included file `Children.jsp`, the container will not reload our modified JSP page until we restart the servlet container and delete the generated servlet.

You can load only static files using the include directive. Static includes barely qualify as modular because they display only a minimal level of *cohesion*—the degree to which the contents of a module belong together. The content of a static include is cohesive only in the sense that you can load this content into more than one JSP page. The header or footer for a group of pages, for example, includes a collection of intrinsically unrelated HTML lines. Their cohesiveness consists solely in the fact that multiple HTML pages share these same lines.

The include directive binds included content to a page at translation time. In general, such early binding in software architectures limits flexibility. At the one end of the flexibility spectrum, developers may *hard-code* bindings as literal values when writing code, say by inserting HTML for the page header and footer rather than by using an include directive. At the other end of the spectrum, developers may bind content to pages at runtime using queries to data sources. Static includes lie between these, but closer to the hard-coded end. The JSP container helps overcome such inflexibility by allowing you to postpone translation until request time. This causes a noticeable performance pause the first time you request a page prior to its translation.

The include directive can lead to incomprehensible JavaServer Pages. JavaServer Pages get confusing when you overuse include files or when include files contain Java or JavaScript code. If you use such fragments, you must exercise care to keep these code fragments as self-contained and cohesive as possible. You could perversely split any part of any page into a separate disjoint fragment that, when included, could generate a legal JSP page. You should avoid including Java or JavaScript code fragments because you can include code better using JSP actions or custom tag libraries.

1-Minute Drill

- What is the syntax of an *absolute path* and a *relative path* in a relative URL?
- Define *context-relative* path and *page-relative* path.
- What are some problems with using the include directive?

Project 2-1: include Directive Test

Using relative URLs in an include directive is often tricky. This project illustrates how to identify a JSP resource using a relative URL.

Step-by-Step

1. Make sure that you have installed Tomcat, following the instructions in Appendix B.
2. Create a new context in your Tomcat installation named `Book`.
3. Create a subdirectory under `%TOMCAT_HOME%/webapps` named `Book`.
4. Edit the file `%TOMCATE_HOME%/conf/server.xml` and locate the *ContextManager* element identified by the tags `<ContextManager>` and `</ContextManager>`. Insert a new `<Context>`element between those tags. Your line should look like this:

```
<Context path="/Book"
         docBase="webapps/Book" >
</Context>
```

   This line states that your context has the virtual path `/Book` mapped to the real path `%TOMCAT_HOME%/webapps/Book`.

Note

Adding the context element to `server.xml` is optional for applications deployed in the `%TOMCAT_HOME%/webapps` directory, but it's still a good practice.

- The syntax for an absolute path is */path[?query]*. The syntax for a relative path is *path[?query]*.
- A *context-relative* path and a *page-relative* path are the names given by the JSP specification to absolute paths and relative paths in URLs.
- The include directive fails to recompile included pages, it lacks cohesion, it binds at translation time, and it leads to confusing JavaServer Pages.

5. Start (or restart) the Tomcat servlet container. (Tomcat requires this step to refresh its contexts.)

6. Create two subdirectories under `%TOMCAT_HOME%/webapps/Book` named `jsp` and `html`.

7. Copy the following text into a file called `includeTest.jsp` under `%TOMCAT_HOME%/webapps/Book/jsp`:

```
<HTML>
<HEAD><TITLE> Include Test </TITLE></HEAD>
<BODY>
I should see this <br>
<%@ include file="/html/insert.html" %>
<br><br>
If I don't, then the URL is not working...
</BODY>
</HTML>
```

8. Copy the following text into a file called `insert.html` and save it under `%TOMCAT_HOME%/webapps/Book/html`:

```
right below the line that reads: "I should see this"
```

9. Start a Web browser and enter the following URL: **`http://localhost:8080/Book/jsp/includeTest.jsp`**.

10. You should see the following in your browser:

```
I should see this
right below the line that reads: "I should see this"

If I don't, then the URL is not working...
```

What do we illustrate here? In the parent JSP `includeTest.jsp`, we specified an include directive that had a relative URL of `/html/insert.html`. Because the URL begins with a slash (/) character, the JSP container considers it a context- relative path. Because the document root of our context is `%TOMCAT_HOME%/webapps/Book`, the container looks for `insert.html` under the *`html`* subdirectory in our document root.

Here are some additional exercises for industrious readers.

- **Exercise 1** Without moving the included file `insert.html`, edit `includeTest.jsp` and modify the URL in the include directive into a page-relative path (i.e., without a starting / character). You should reload your JSP page and there should be no problems locating the included file.

- **Exercise 2** Modify the "I should see this" line in the file `insert.html` to this:

```
<H2> right below the line that reads: "I should see this" </H2>
```

That is, enclose its contents using the HTML element `H2`. Now reload the file `includeTest.jsp`. You might expect to see the contents of the included file in bigger, bold font, but you will not. Why didn't your change take effect? How would you make it take effect?

The page Directive

As you might expect, the page directive provides attributes for the JSP page. Attributes defined in a `page` directive apply to the JSP page and all included static files, whether these get included via the include directive or the jsp:include action. The JSP specification calls the JSP page source file and its included files a *translation unit*.

Page directives follow this general format:

`<%@ page` *[attribute="value"]** `%>`

As the syntax illustrates, a page directive contains zero or more attribute-value pairs. The attribute names and their respective behaviors are well defined in the specification. Here's a sample:

```
<%@ page import="java.util.*, com.myclasses.*", buffer="15kb" %>
```

This page directive states that this JSP page file imports classes from two Java packages, *java.util* and *com.myclasses*. It directs that a 15KB buffer should be used to handle output from this JSP page file.

You can insert an unlimited number of page directives into a JSP translation unit, even if it is a single JSP page file. These directives can appear anywhere in any file in the translation unit.

Tip

A good programming convention is to specify a single page directive at the very beginning of the JSP page file. This helps those who read your code find all attributes that apply to the page.

Attributes of the page Directive

Table 2-1 provides the list of attributes you can configure in a page directive.

We briefly describe each attribute in the next few sections.

language The language attribute specifies the scripting language used by the page. JSP 1.1 supports only the default language Java, so you need not specify this attribute. Nevertheless, you should specify it because your JSP container vender may support other languages (perhaps JavaScript). The specification implies that JSP will support additional scripting languages in later releases. If you set the language attribute, you set it like this:

```
<%@ page language="java" %>
```

extends The extends attribute specifies the parent class of the generated servlet. Generally, the JSP container extends the generated servlet from a default class. Advanced JSP developers can use this attribute to create custom parent classes for their JavaServer Pages. Such parent classes must implement the Java interface, *HttpJspPage*. Here's an example:

```
<%@ page extends="myPackage.ExampleHttpSuper" %>
```

Attribute	**Possible Values**
language	`java`
extends	*fully qualified class name*
import	*import list*
session	`true` *or* `false`
buffer	`none` *or size*`kb`
autoFlush	`true` *or* `false`
isThreadSafe	`true` *or* `false`
info	*information text*
errorPage	*URL for error page*
isErrorPage	`true` *or* `false`
contentType	*content type information*

Table 2-1 page Directive Attributes

Question: When would you create custom parent classes for a JSP page?

Answer: Your Web application might require certain methods or variables for a whole collection of JavaServer Pages. For example, you might create a Web application where a collection of JavaServer Pages must draw the same standard user interface elements. You could write a custom Java class that provides a set of utility functions such as *drawTable, drawComboBox, drawMenu,* and *drawButton*. You could then use the extends attribute to derive your generated JavaServer Pages from this drawing class. By extending your JavaServer Pages from this custom Java class, you've made these functions available to any Java code in your JavaServer Pages.

Question: How do you write such a class so that the servlet container and JSP container can use it?

Answer: When we explained the JSP life cycle, we mentioned that a JSP page is converted into a servlet by the JSP container the first time a client requests the JSP page. The JSP specification calls the generated class the *JSP page implementation class*. The specification defines two Java interfaces or contracts this generated class must implement: *javax.servlet.Servlet* and *javax.servlet.jsp.HttpJspPage*. (More precisely, the generated class needs to implement only the *HttpJspPage* interface because *HttpJspPage* extends the *JspPage* interface that in turn extends the *Servlet* interface.) Normally, the container provider supplies a parent class that satisfies this contract, and the page implementation class simply extends this. You can provide your own parent class and use the extends attribute to load it instead of the parent class provided by the container provider.

Question: Why do you call the interfaces *contracts*?

Answer: The JSP container and the Java class that implements the JSP page must communicate using a certain method-calling protocol. If the Java class fails to implement the methods, the JSP container cannot call them and therefore cannot provide container services. The Java class guarantees that it supports the protocol by implementing the methods in the interfaces. In this sense, the interfaces act as a contract between the JSP container and the generated servlet.

Question: **Should you avoid supplying such a custom parent class for your JavaServer Pages?**

Answer: Several reasons argue against writing your own parent class for the Java servlets generated from JavaServer Pages. First, the specification puts the onus on the developer of this custom class to conform to the contracts. JSP containers need not check for conformance. Second, the JSP container can make certain decisions while generating the servlet from the JSP page to improve performance. It is restricted from making such decisions if you force it to extend from your custom class. Third, you can create custom behavior more easily and more explicitly using custom actions. (We describe this in Module 6.)

import The import attribute lets you specify a Java import declaration—i.e., a comma-separated list of fully qualified Java type names or Java package names followed by the `.*` character sequence. If you insert multiple page directives in a JSP translation unit, *import is the only attribute that you can specify multiple times*. You must specify any Java class you intend to use that is not part of the default set of imported packages. The default set of imported Java classes includes *java.lang.**, *javax.servlet.**, *javax.servlet.jsp.**, and *javax.servlet.http.**. Here is an example:

```
<%@ page import="java.util.Date,
     java.text.SimpleDateFormat,
     com.myclasses.*"
%>
```

session The session attribute provides the means to specify whether your JSP page participates in an HTTP session. You should set this attribute to its default value, `true`, if your JSP page uses the *HttpSession* object, so that the container makes available the implicit variable *session*. Otherwise, you should set it to `false`. This example illustrates setting the session attribute:

```
<%@ page session="false" %>
```

Tip

As we described in Module 1, HTTP is stateless. This means that the protocol does not carry any client state between successive client requests. Nevertheless, servlets and JavaServer Pages supply other mechanisms to preserve a client's state across multiple requests. We call this preservation of a client's state a *session.* Java servlets provide an *HttpSession* object to store and retrieve session information. If you do not use the *HttpSession* object in your JSP page, set the session attribute to `false` because the session object is large and consumes memory resources.

buffer The buffer attribute sets the buffering model and buffer size for the *JspWriter* object referenced by the implicit JSP variable *out*.

Note

As we discuss in Module 4, the JSP container creates several implicit objects that it provides to the JSP developer. The *JspWriter* object and the *Httpsession* object are just two of these implicit objects.

When you specify the buffering value as `none`, the generated servlet does no buffering and passes output written to the *out* variable directly to the *PrintWriter* object provided by the *ServletResponse* object. When you set a buffer size, the *JspWriter* provides character buffering, which can improve performance. Unlike the *PrintWriter* object, the *JspWriter* throws *IOExceptions.* The default buffer size is 8KB. Here is an example:

```
<%@ page buffer="12kb" %>
```

autoFlush The autoFlush attribute determines the behavior of the *JspWriter* object when you use buffering. A value of `true` causes the container to flush the buffer automatically when it fills. A value of `false` causes an *IOException* instead. You cannot set the value to `false` when you set the buffer attribute to `none`. Generally, you set both the buffer and autoFlush attributes in the same page directive, like so:

```
<%@ page buffer="12kb" autoFlush="true" %>
```

Ask the Expert

Question: When would you set the autoFlush attribute in a page directive to `false`?

Answer: The autoFlush attribute is a flag to the *JspWriter* object telling it either to automatically flush the buffer or throw an error when the buffer fills. Web clients accessing your JSP page might not be able to deal with a partially constructed stream of data. You can ensure that you send the correct and complete stream of data to the client by setting autoFlush to `false`. After setting autoFlush to `false`, you receive a fatal error notification if the buffer fills before you send all the data.

isThreadSafe The isThreadSafe attribute indicates whether a JSP page is *reentrant* or not. Reentrant code must guarantee that it synchronizes all shared data. The JSP container behaves differently depending on the value of this attribute. If you set the value of the attribute to `true`, the container may dispatch multiple simultaneous requests to the generated servlet. If you set the value of the attribute to `false`, the container dispatches requests one at a time. The container sets the default value to `true`, so you should be careful to synchronize all shared data. Here is an example:

> **Hint**
> Setting isThreadSafe to `false` causes the container to add *implements SingleThreadModel* to the declaration of the generated servlet.

```
<%@ page isThreadSafe="false" %>
```

info The info attribute sets information that can be retrieved using the *Servlet.getServletInfo()* method. Generally, this method returns information such as author, version, and copyright. Here is an example:

```
<%@ page info="Author: Joe Blow; version:1.0" %>
```

errorPage The JSP container provides a simple one-stop, catchall, error-handling mechanism. Whenever an exception occurs in your JSP page, if the JSP page has no catch block for that exception, the container automatically forwards control to a URL that you specify using the errorPage attribute.

Ask the Expert

Question: Why not set the isThreadSafe attribute to `false` and not worry about synchronizing any shared data?

Answer: One of the biggest problems facing today's Internet technologies is providing *high availability*. High availability refers to the ability of your Web site to respond to client requests without interruptions (i.e., it rarely rejects or starves client requests). You probably remember the last time you were frustrated by network traffic that prevented you from accessing a Web site. When you set isThreadSafe to `false`, you force the JSP container to dispatch requests serially to your JSP page and thereby reduce the availability of your Web site. When you set isThreadSafe to `true` and synchronize access to shared resources, your JSP page can service multiple simultaneous requests and you thereby improve the availability of your site.

Tip We simplify a little here. The Servlet 2.2 specification allows for containers to implement a servlet pool for servlets that implement the *SingleThreadModel* (i.e., when the JSP page sets isThreadSafe to `false`). This helps maintain service availability even when using the single threaded model.

Question: If I set the isThreadSafe attribute to `false`, should you still worry about synchronizing any data?

Answer: Yes, you should. You should synchronize every mutable resource that is not unique to a specific request. For example, you should synchronize static fields and any objects with session or application scope.

This URL must reference another JSP page. This example sets the error page to `majorError.jsp`:

```
<%@ page errorPage="/mywebsite/errors/majorError.jsp" %>
```

Tip

The JSP container provides the exception object to the error page by setting it as an attribute of the *ServletRequest* object. You can access it in the error page using the *exception* implicit object.

isErrorPage The isErrorPage attribute indicates whether you intend that a page be the target of another page's exceptions. If you set the value to `true`, the *exception* implicit object variable is set and the container will set its value to the exception object from the offending JSP page. If the value is set to `false`, the JSP container does not set the exception variable *exception*. The default value is `false`. You set the attribute like this:

```
<%@ page isErrorPage="true" %>
```

contentType The contentType attribute sets the mime type and, optionally, the character encoding of the response by the JSP page. The default type is *text/html*. The default character encoding is *ISO-8859-1*. These defaults apply to standard HTML responses using Western European character sets. Here is how you set this attribute:

```
<%@ page contentType="text/html; ISO-8859-1" %>
```

errorTesting.jsp
errPage.jsp

Project 2-2: page Directive Test

In this project, we illustrate a simple error-handling mechanism for JavaServer Pages.

Step-by-Step

1. Ensure that you correctly installed the Tomcat servlet container and have it running.

2. Copy the following text into a file named `errorTesting.jsp` in the `Book` context you defined in Project 2-1.

```
<%@ page errorPage="errPage.jsp" %>
<HTML>
```

```
<HEAD><TITLE> Simple error testing </TITLE></HEAD>
<BODY>
<%!
   String nullString = null;
%>
<%-- Intentionally invoking a NullPointerException --%>
The length of the nullString is <%= nullString.length() %>
</BODY>
</HTML>
```

3. Copy the following text into another file named `errPage.jsp` in the same directory as `errorTesting.jsp`:

```
<%@ page isErrorPage="true" %>

Uncaught exception <%= exception %> has been encountered!
```

4. Start a Web browser and load the JSP page `errorTesting.jsp`. Your URL should look something like this:
`http://localhost:8080/Book/ errorTesting.jsp`.

You should see the following output in your browser:

```
Uncaught exception java.lang.NullPointerException has been encountered!
```

You probably realize that we intentionally coded `errorTesting.jsp` to throw the *java.lang.NullPointerException* by invoking the *length* function on a null *java.lang.String* reference. When the exception was thrown, the JSP container checked for an error page registered for this JSP page. Because we registered *errPage.jsp* as our error page, the container immediately forwarded control to it.

The taglib Directive

As you have seen, JavaServer Pages use tags to specify page elements. You can extend the set of tags that the JSP container can interpret by using a *tag library*. In a sense, tag libraries extend the JSP language itself, since you associate actions with the expanded set of tags. You can consider one whole class of JSP elements, JSP actions, built-in tag libraries. We consider tag libraries and actions so important that we devote two modules to them. In Module 5, we address standard actions (built-in tag libraries). In Module 6, we explain custom actions using tag libraries.

The general format of a taglib directive looks like this:

```
<%@
taglib
uri="URI To Tag Library"
prefix="tag prefix"
%>
```

You identify the tag library using a Uniform Resource Identifier (URI). This URI may be either an absolute URI or a relative URI, just like those we described. The URI specifies the location of a *tag library descriptor* (TLD), which defines the custom tags supported by the tag library. The prefix attribute specifies the tag prefix for those custom tags.

Note

The JSP specification also supports use of the *web.xml* deployment descriptor (we describe this in Appendix B) to map the directive's URI to an actual URI and location. If you specify a relative URI in the descriptor, you can use a taglib tag in the deployment descriptor to map this virtual URI into an actual location in the context of the deployed Web application.

Let's demonstrate the taglib directive with an example. Assume that you have defined two custom tags for your tag library:

- `<simple>`
- `<complex>`

A possible taglib directive might then look like this:

```
<%@ taglib uri="http://www.mywebsite.com/SearchTags.tld" prefix="search" %>
```

In our example, the directive informs the JSP container that this JSP page references custom tags using the prefix "search" and that these custom tags are defined in the TLD located at `http://www.mywebsite.com/SearchTags.tld`. Because the tag library supports both a simple and complex tag, a JSP page could use these tags like this:

```
<search:simple> .... </search:simple>
.....
<search:complex> .... </search:complex>
```

A JSP page can include any number of taglib directives as long as you provide a unique prefix for each. The prefix, as you can guess, scopes the tag library within the page. You can provide any unique string as the prefix. While a taglib directive can appear anywhere in the JSP page file, all custom tags requiring that directive must follow it.

1-Minute Drill

- What is the *only attribute* in a page directive that you can repeat in a JSP page?
- What are the *packages* that the JSP container imports by default?
- Why would you use the *session* attribute in the page directive?
- What does the taglib directive do?

- You can repeat only the import attribute.
- The packages are *java.lang, javax.servlet*, *javax.servlet.jsp,* and *javax.servlet.http*.
- You would use the session attribute to indicate whether your JSP page participates in an HTTP session.
- It declares a library of custom actions.

Mastery Check

1. What is wrong with this comment declaration?

```
<!-- This variable stores the JSP page context. --!>
```

2. What is the problem with this comment declaration?

```
<%-- This page was forwarded from <%= sourcePage %>. --%>
```

3. Your Web master has requested that you show a standard logo and a standard title at the top of each JSP page in your Web site. How would you do this without duplicating this information in each JSP page?

4. What packages do these page directives import?

```
<%@ page import="java.util.Vector"errorPage="/myError.jsp" %>
<%@ page import="com.mycorp.classes.*, java.util.*, java.text.*" %>
```

5. Is there a problem with the JSP page declarations shown here?

```
<%@ page import="java.util.Hashtable" "errorPage=/myError.jsp" %>
<%@ page errorPage="/myError.jsp" %>
```

Mastery Check

6. Can you use a Java class in your JSP page before you specify the page directive that imports it?

____

____

7. Is this taglib directive valid?

```
<%@ taglib uri="http://www.mywebsite.com/mytags" prefix="" %>
```

____

____

8. Must you specify the taglib directive for your custom tags before you specify them in a JSP page?

____

____

Module 3

JSP Elements: Scripting Elements

The Goals of This Module

- Learn the various scripting elements
- Understand how the container translates scripting elements
- Understand the limits of scripting elements

You saw in Module 2 how JSP comments let you clarify your intentions in a JSP page, while JSP directives help you configure the JSP container. Now you'll learn about JSP scripting elements that let you insert Java code directly into your JavaServer Pages. The ability to insert Java code into a JSP page has been the most important factor driving the popularity of JSP programming.

The Three Scripting Elements

The JSP 1.1 specification describes three types of scripting elements:

- declarations
- expressions
- scriptlets

The JSP 1.1 specification supports only Java versions of these scripting elements. In Module 2, you learned about the page directive with its language attribute. This directive provides the means for eventual support of other languages.

Generally, you use declarations to define variables, although you can also use them to declare methods, inner classes, or any valid Java construct at the class level. You can insert any valid Java expression into a JSP expression. JSP scriptlets insert working fragments of Java code into a JSP page; these code fragments differ in scope from JSP declarations and, unlike JSP expressions, need not end up as arguments to output statements.

All the scripting elements begin with `<%` and end with `%>`. Declarations and expressions distinguish themselves from each other and from scriptlets by the use of a special character that follows the initial `<%`. Declarations use the exclamation point character (`!`), while expressions use the equal sign character (=), and scriptlets use no special character. The general formats for the three elements are shown here:

```
<%! declaration(s) %>
<%= expression %>
<% scriptlet %>
```

All three formats specify different ways to insert Java code into the generated servlet. It's instructive to look at an example, so let's do that next.

How the Container Translates JSP Scripting Elements

Consider this simple JSP page that includes all three scripting elements plus some static HTML:

```
<%-- Sample JSP that contains all
     JSP scripting elements.
--%>
<%@ page language="java" %>
<%@ page buffer="8kb" %>
<%@ page isThreadSafe="false" %>
<%@ page import="ScriptingElements" %>

<HTML>
<HEAD><TITLE>
  JSP Scripting Elements
</TITLE></HEAD>
<BODY>

<%-- declaration --%>
<%! public String date = null; %>

<%– declaration (method) –%>
<%! public int factorial(int j) {
      if(j == 0)
         return 1;
      return j * factorial(j-1);
    }
%>

<%– scriptlet –%>
<% date = (new java.util.Date()).toString(); %>

<%– expression –%>
The date today is: <%= date %>

</BODY>
</HTML>
```

The Apache Tomcat JSP container translates this JSP page into a Java source file similar to the following:

```
package jsp;
import javax.servlet.*;
import javax.servlet.http.*;
import javax.servlet.jsp.*;
import javax.servlet.jsp.tagext.*;
import java.io.PrintWriter;
import java.io.IOException;
import java.io.FileInputStream;
import java.io.ObjectInputStream;
import java.util.Vector;
import org.apache.jasper.runtime.*;
import java.beans.*;
import org.apache.jasper.JasperException;
import ScriptingElements;

public class jspse2_jsp_0 extends HttpJspBase
                          implements SingleThreadModel {
   public String date = null;
   public int factorial(int j) {
      if(j == 0)
         return 1;
      return j * factorial(j-1);
   }

   static {
   }

   public jspse2_jsp_0( ) {
   }

   private static boolean _jspx_inited = false;
   public final void _jspx_init() throws JasperException {
   }

   public void _jspService(HttpServletRequest request,
                           HttpServletResponse response)
        throws IOException, ServletException {

      JspFactory _jspxFactory = null;
      PageContext pageContext = null;
      HttpSession session = null;
```

```
      ServletContext application = null;
      ServletConfig config = null;
      JspWriter out = null;
      Object page = this;
      String  _value = null;
      try {
         if (_jspx_inited == false) {
            _jspx_init();
            _jspx_inited = true;
         }

         _jspxFactory = JspFactory.getDefaultFactory();
         response.setContentType("text/html;charset=8859_1");
         pageContext = _jspxFactory.getPageContext(this,
                                                    request,
                                                    response,
                                                    "", true,
                                                    8192,
                                                    true);
         application = pageContext.getServletContext();
         config = pageContext.getServletConfig();
         session = pageContext.getSession();
         out = pageContext.getOut();

         out.write("\r\n");
         out.write("\r\n\r\n<HTML>\r\n<HEAD>");
         out.write("<TITLE>\r\n  JSP Scripting Elements\r\n");
         out.write("</TITLE></HEAD>\r\n<BODY>\r\n\r\n");
         out.write("\r\n");
         date = (new java.util.Date()).toString();
         out.write("\r\n\r\n");
         out.write("\r\nThe date today is: ");
         out.print( date );
         out.write("\r\n\r\n</BODY>\r\n</HTML>\r\n");
      } catch (Exception ex) {
         if (out.getBufferSize() != 0)
            out.clearBuffer();
         pageContext.handlePageException(ex);
      } finally {
         out.flush();
         _jspxFactory.releasePageContext(pageContext);
      }
   }
}
```

Implicit object initialization

Page-level directive (buffer size)

Static HTML

JSP scriptlet

JSP expression

As the code listing shows, Tomcat translates JSP scripting elements almost verbatim into Java source file equivalents. The implementation details of the generated servlet, most obviously the specific class name, are vendor specific. The JSP specification describes the structure of a generated servlet class but says that translation into this structure need not be "performed literally." The flexibility of vendors is limited, however, because they must implement functionality required by the specification and follow the syntax of the scripting language, which today is Java. For example, the specification requires support for the import attribute in the page directive. In Java, you must implement this using an import statement. Import statements must precede declaration of the class itself.

Tomcat generates the servlet in four sections:

- **Page-level syntax and configuration elements** JSP directives
- **Member declarations** JSP declarations
- **Implicit object initializations** JSP container objects
- **Main body for _jspService_** JSP scriptlets and expressions

The container translates page directives into page-level syntax and configuration elements. For example, it translates this directive

```
<%@ page import="ScriptingElements" %>
```

into this import statement:

```
import ScriptingElements;
```

Similarly, this directive

```
<%@ page isThreadSafe="false" %>
```

adds this implements clause

```
implements SingleThreadModel
```

to the class declaration.

The container translates JSP declarations into Java declarations of member variables and methods.

The JSP container generates an initialization and a main section as part of the *_jspService* method. The container initializes implicit objects in the initialization section of the *_jspService* method. We discuss implicit objects in Module 4.

The container translates static HTML (*template data*) and JSP expressions into *out.write* or *out.print* statements and puts these statements in the main section of the *_jspService* method.

Finally, the container translates JSP scriptlets into Java code fragments and puts them in the main section as well.

1-Minute Drill

- What are the three scripting elements described in the JSP 1.1 specification?
- What programming languages do JSP 1.1 scripting elements support?
- What are the four sections of a generated servlet?

JSP Declarations

Declarations explicitly define the entities you use in a program. Both the JSP specification and Java require the declaration of variables as well as methods and other advanced Java constructs. Here again is the general syntax for a JSP declaration:

```
<%! declaration(s) %>
```

You can insert as many JSP declarations into a JSP page as you want. You can also insert as many Java declarations into a JSP declaration as you want. Here is an example of a JSP declaration:

```
<%! public String date = null;
    public String name = "Shakespeare";
%>
```

As you will see, JSP declarations distinguish themselves primarily by inserting Java code at the class level rather than in the *_jspService* method.

- JSP 1.1 scripting elements include declarations, scriptlets, and expressions.
- In JSP 1.1, scripting elements support only the Java programming language. Proprietary implementations may support additional scripting languages such as JavaScript.
- A generated servlet has four sections: page-level syntax and configuration elements, member declarations, implicit object initializations, and a main area for static HTML and scriptlet translations.

Variables in a JSP Declaration

When you declare a variable in Java, you implicitly assign it a *scope*. For example, when you declare a variable within a code block (i.e., between curly braces) you implicitly give it *block scope*. Variables with block scope live and die within the execution of the code block. Likewise, if you declare a variable in a method, you implicitly assign it *method scope*. Variables with method scope exist only within the life span of the method call. Similarly, when you declare a member variable of a class, you implicitly give it *object scope*. Variables with object scope exist within the life span of the class instance or object that declares them. If you declare a variable to be static (using the `static` keyword), you implicitly assign it *class scope*. The JVM creates class variables the first time it loads the declaring class and destroys them only when the class is unloaded, usually when the JVM shuts down.

The following code illustrates the different Java scopes:

```
public class ScopeExample {
   public static int classScope = 1;      // Class scope
   public int objectScope = 2;            // Object scope
   public void myMethod() {
      int methodScope = 3;                // Method scope
      if (objectScope != methodScope) {
         int blockScope = 4;              // Block scope
      }
   }
}
```

When you declare variables using JSP declarations, you give them either object scope or class scope in the generated Java class, depending on whether you use the `static` keyword in your declaration. As you saw in the earlier example, all such variables end up in the declarations section of the generated servlet. A semicolon (`;`) should be used to terminate all variable declarations, just as it must for any Java declaration.

Methods in a JSP Declaration

All Java methods have either class or object scope. This means that you must declare them as either static or non-static. You can access static methods even if you never instantiate the class in which you declare them. Conversely, you access non-static methods only from an object instance of the class.

The JSP container translates all JSP method declarations into Java declarations of methods in the generated servlet class. You use the keyword `static` to give these methods class rather than object scope. Here's an example:


```
<%!
    public static int factorial(int j) {
       if(j == 0)
         return 1;
       return (j * factorial(j-1));
    }
    public String func() {
       return ("Inside function func()");
    }
%>
```

This example declares two methods: the static method *factorial* and the non-static method *func*. The first has class scope and the latter class object scope.

Declarations of Advanced Java Features

You can use declarations to insert advanced Java features into the generated servlet for a JSP page. For example, the following JSP declaration creates an inner Java class for a generated servlet:

```
<%! class InnerClass {
       public String count(int a) {
          return("InnerClass(" + a + ")");
       }
    }
%>
```

Your JSP page can then declare and use the inner class. Here is a use of our crude inner class:

```
<%-- Example using an inner class --%>
<% int j;
   InnerClass innerClass = new InnerClass();
   for (j = 0; j < 5; j++) {
%>
    <%= innerClass.count(j) %><BR>
<%}%>
```

The output in the browser looks something like this:

```
InnerClass(0)
InnerClass(1)
InnerClass(2)
InnerClass(3)
InnerClass(4)
```

1-Minute Drill

- A Java variable can have what four scopes?
- What scopes can a variable declared in a JSP declaration have?
- What scopes can a method in a JSP declaration have?
- An inner class in a JSP declaration has what scope?

More About JSP Declarations

You should take special note of a few points when using JSP declarations.

JSP declarations result in Java code with object or class scope.

JSP declarations can access variables in object or class scope only. They cannot reference implicit objects such as the *JspWriter* object, which have method scope and are available only in the *_jspService* method. Hence, the following code fragment causes a compilation error:

```
<%! public void foo() {
        out.println("Trying to cheat!!");
%>
```

Error: *out* object out of scope!

To correct such code you must convert it to a scriptlet rather than a declaration, like so:

```
<%    out.println("Trying to cheat!!");
%>
```

Correct: *out* object in scope!

- Java variables can have one of four scopes: block scope, method scope, object scope, and class scope.
- A JSP declaration can have one of two scopes: object scope and class scope.
- A JSP method can have one of two scopes: object scope and class scope.
- An inner class declared by a JSP declaration has object scope. You cannot declare a class `static`, so an inner class cannot have class scope.

Ask the Expert

Question: Consider the page directive and the extends attribute that were described in Module 2. What is the difference between declaring methods in a custom base class using the extends attribute versus declaring methods directly in the JSP page using JSP declarations?

Answer: When you create a custom base class for JavaServer Pages, any JSP page can extend it and take advantage of the methods declared in it by using the extends attribute of the page directive. On the other hand, by defining your own base class, you bypass the built-in base class provided by vendors. This may be useful at times, but in general doing this is not wise. Vendors can build in various optimizations in the base class they provide that you forfeit if you use your own base class.

If you declare methods directly in the JSP page using JSP declarations, only that JSP page can use those methods. A JSP declaration can provide a handy way to declare utility methods (and inner classes) for a specific JSP page.

JSP actions and custom tag libraries provide a more elegant approach than using custom base classes or JSP declarations. We explain these techniques in Modules 5 and 6.

JSP declarations must declare variables before using them. This code produces an error because it uses *y* before defining *y*:

```
<%!
    int x = y + 1;   <---- Error: y not yet defined!
    int y = 0;
%>
```

The correct code declares *y* first:

```
<%!
    int y = 0;
    int x = y + 1;   <---- Correct: y defined first!
%>
```

You can use variables in JSP pages before you declare them. Because JSP declarations have class or object scope, while expressions and scriptlets have method scope, the following code is legal, even though it uses *x* before declaring it in the JSP page:

```
The value of x is <%= x %>
<%! int x = 5; %>
```

This is legitimate code because the JSP container translates declarations as member variables of the generated servlet, but the container translates scriptlets and expressions as Java code fragments in the *_jspService* method.

Caution

We do not, in any way, recommend using variables in JSP pages before you declare them. It confuses readers without adding any useful optimization.

Synchronize variables declared in JSP declarations or use a page directive to set the isThreadSafe attribute to false. As you've seen, variables in a JSP declaration have object or class scope. JavaServer Pages run as servlets and servlets are multi-threaded by default. When you don't set the isThreadSafe attribute to `false`, multiple clients will likely share the same servlet instance and simultaneously access its member variables. These threads could trample each other by performing unsynchronized modifications to the member variables. Let's look at an example:

```
<%! Inventory inventory = new Inventory(); %>   ← JSP declaration
<% if(inventory.isFull()) {
       inventory.removeExcess();                 ← JSP scriptlet
   }
%>
```

In this example, the variable *inventory* has object scope. The scriptlet checks the status of the inventory and updates it if it was full. The code fragment in the scriptlet is executed by multiple threads, each servicing a different user. Since all these threads access the same *inventory* variable, they could step on each other when attempting to check the variable's status or updating it. One possible solution might be to use the *synchronize* keyword to serialize access to *inventory*. Here's how you do this:

```
<%! Inventory inventory = new Inventory(); %>
<% synchronized(this) {
      if(inventory.isFull()) {
         inventory.removeExcess();
      }
   }
%>
```

Synchronize access

3

1-Minute Drill

- When a JSP declaration contains an initializer, when and how many times is the initializer invoked?
- Can I use JSP variables in my JSP page before they are declared? Why?

JSP Expressions

Every programming language supports expressions. Here is the general syntax for a JSP expression:

```
<%= Java expression %>
```

The most basic JSP expression is a literal or variable. For example, the following is a valid JSP expression:

```
<%= 2 %>
```

You construct slightly more complex JSP expressions from operands and operators that you concatenate according to well-defined language rules. Here is a JSP example:

```
<%= 1 + 2 %>
```

- The JSP container invokes the initializer only once, when the JSP page is first loaded.
- Yes. JSP variables have object or class scope, so the JSP container creates and initializes them the first time it loads the JSP page. Hence, they are already available when the container invokes the *_jspService* method at request time.

In this example, the numbers 1 and 2 act as operands for the addition (+) operator. You build complex expressions by joining simpler expressions. For example, let's multiply our first simple expression by 4:

```
<%= (1 + 2) * 4 %>
```

We used parentheses in this more complex example. In JSP expressions, as in every modern programming language, parentheses dictate evaluation precedence. In this case, we evaluate the sub-expression (1+2) first. Then we multiply the result by 4.

Programming languages also define an *evaluation order* for operators. A thorough understanding of the evaluation order can sometimes allow you to omit parentheses. For example, the following code fragment evaluates to 9:

```
<%= 1 + (2 * 4) %>
```

We could remove the parentheses here, since Java gives precedence to the multiplication operator (*) over the addition operator (+):

```
<%= 1 + 2 * 4 %>
```

Why bother omitting the parentheses, however, when they make your intention so much clearer?

Tip

You should always use parentheses to explicitly state evaluation precedence for expressions. Remember that code is your first form of documentation.

Expressions can include variables and method calls. For example, this code uses the factorial method described earlier, and it evaluates to 12:

```
<% int a = 4; %>
<%= (1 + factorial(2)) * a %>
```

All expressions, however complex, evaluate to a single result or value. JSP pages rely on the *JspWriter* object for output of JSP expressions. This object takes any Java expression result, coerces it into a String type, and prints it to the response buffer. The upshot is that you can use any legal Java expression as the argument to a JSP expression. Here are some examples of JSP expressions:

```
Today's date is: <%= new java.util.Date() %>
<TD> <%= product.getSKU() %> </TD>
<INPUT TYPE=hidden NAME=<%= "UPDATE" %>
      VALUE="/jsp/Inventory.jsp">
```

As the examples illustrate, you can use JSP expressions anywhere in your JSP page where you would normally use a `String`. In the first line above, a JSP expression occurs as a continuation of regular text. In the second line, a JSP expression occurs as the contents of an HTML table cell. In the third line, a JSP expression provides the value for an HTML form element's attribute.

JSP expressions follow these rules:

- The contents of the JSP expression must be a *complete* Java expression.
- The contents of a JSP expression must be a *single* Java expression.
- You must *not* terminate Java expressions with a semicolon (unlike JSP declarations).

Ask the Expert

Question: What are some examples of legal Java expressions that might appear in a JSP expression?

Answer: The Java Language Specification mentions several categories of expressions. The simplest Java expressions (the specification calls these *primary expressions*) include literal values (e.g., `1`, `3.0`, or `true`) and parenthesized expressions (e.g., `(2 + 4)`). More complex expressions include such Java constructs as assignments (e.g., `a = 4`), class instance creation (e.g., `new java.util.Date()`), array creation (e.g., `new byte[10]`), and method calls (e.g., `someVar.doIt()`).

More About JSP Expressions

Keep in mind a couple of important summary points when using JSP expressions.

JSP expressions generate Java code with method scope. The JSP container translates JSP expressions into Java code that it inserts into the *_jspService* method of the generated servlet. Since this code appears inside the *_jspService* method, it can access any code created by JSP declarations, which have object or class scope. JSP expressions can also access container variables like *out*, the implicit *JspWriter* object, since the JSP container declares and initializes these implicit objects in the *_jspService* method (i.e., JSP expressions and implicit objects share the same code scope).

The JSP container evaluates the contents of all JSP expressions at request time. *Request time* occurs every time a client accesses a given JSP page. You saw that the container translates a JSP page into a servlet that includes the *_jspService* method. The JSP container calls this method whenever any client accesses the page. The *_jspService* method includes a Java equivalent for each JSP expression in your page. For example, a statement that looks like this in a JSP page

```
The factorial of 5 is: <%= factorial(5) %>
```

might be translated and inserted into the *_jspService* method as Java expressions that look like this:

```
out.print("The factorial of 5 is: ");
out.print(factorial(5));
```

1-Minute drill

- What types of Java expressions can you use in a JSP expression?
- When does the JSP container evaluate JSP expressions?

- You can use any legal Java expression in a JSP expression. The *JspWriter* object coerces all such Java expressions into a `String` and prints the result to the response buffer.
- The container evaluates JSP expressions at request time.

JSP Scriptlets

JSP 1.1 scriptlets support most Java constructs that you can legally express in a Java method. The JSP container translates JSP scriptlets into Java code that it inserts into the *_jspService* method of the generated servlet. Here is the general form of a JSP scriptlet:

```
<% scriptlet %>
```

Now let's look at how JSP scriptlets express some of the major types of Java statements.

Variables in Scriptlets

You can declare variables in scriptlets, just as you can in JSP declarations. However, while JSP declarations create member variables having class or object scope, JSP scriptlet declarations create *local variables* with method scope or less. Consider the following declarations:

```
<%! int a = 0; %>
<% int b = 0; %>
```

The first declares a member variable, and the second declares a local variable in the *_jspService* method.

This difference in scope becomes more important when you realize that servlets are multithreaded by default. If you declare member variables using JSP declarations, you should probably use the *isThreadSafe* page directive and set it to `false` to ensure that only one HTTP request at a time accesses your translated JSP page. Alternatively, you can synchronize access to these variables. Generally, you should avoid declaring member variables in JavaServer Pages, because safeguarding access to such variables is usually not worth the trouble. Local variables are naturally thread-safe because each invocation of the *_jspService* method gets a copy of these variables.

Expressions in Scriptlets

You can use JSP scriptlets to insert Java expressions into the *_jspService* method of the translated servlet. The JSP container converts such expressions into their Java equivalents. This differs significantly from JSP expressions in that the container converts each JSP expression into an argument for a *print* call by the *JspWriter*. For example, the container translates this JSP expression

```
<%= 1 + 2 %>
```

into this print call

```
out.print(1 + 2);
```

But the container converts this scriptlet

```
<% int anInt = 1 + 2; %>
```

into this code fragment:

```
int anInt = 1 + 2;
```

You can also use conditional Java expressions in JSP scriptlets. The following code illustrates their use:

```
<% String name = "JSP: A Beginner's Guide"; %>
<% String myBook = (name != null) ? name : "Unknown"; %>
The book's name is: <%= myBook %>
```

As the examples illustrate, when you use an expression in a JSP scriptlet, it must be either part of a larger expression or a valid Java statement. You saw earlier that this is not true of a JSP expression, which becomes an argument to a *print* method call.

Conditionals in Scriptlets

Java supports two kinds of conditional statements: `if/else` statements and `switch` statements. You can declare both using JSP scriptlets. Let's examine an `if/else` statement declared in a JSP fragment:

```
<% String greeting = "hello!";
   if (true) {
%>
      Say <%= greeting %>
<% }  else %>
      Say no greeting!
```

First scriptlet with `if`

Second scriptlet

Notice that when you mix Java code with static HTML in your conditionals you must use multiple scriptlets, one for each part of the conditional. Notice also that the braces in the first part of the conditional are required, because the container actually generates multiple Java statements from the single JSP line:

```
Say <%= greeting %>
```

The three statements our Tomcat container generated are shown here:

```
out.write("\r\n\tSay:  ");
out.print( greeting );
out.write("\r\n");
```

The `else` clause needed no braces because the JSP line

```
Say no greeting!
```

is static text (template data) for which the container generates the single Java code line:

```
out.write("\r\n\tSay no greeting!.\r\n");
```

The Tomcat container generates *write* calls for static text and HTML and *print* calls for Java expressions.

The second Java conditional type is the `switch` statement. The same principles apply to `switch` statements as to `if/else` statements. That is, it takes multiple JSP scriptlets to express a Java `switch` statement when that

Hint

It is good programming practice to enclose all conditional blocks within braces, even if the block contains only a single statement. Braces clearly identify the conditional blocks and make the code more readable and less error prone.

statement mixes template data (static text or HTML) with it Java code. Consider this JSP fragment:

```
<% switch (1) {
   case 0: { %>
      The value is: 0!<BR>
<%    break;
   }
   case 1: { %>
      The value is 1!<BR>
<%    break;
   }
   default: { %>
      The value is undefined!
<%    break;
   }
} %>
```

First scriptlet with `switch`

Second scriptlet

Third scriptlet

Fourth scriptlet

Here again, the braces are necessary because the code blocks in our conditional include both static text and Java code.

Iteration in Scriptlets

JSP scriptlets also support *iteration*, including `for` loops, `while` loops, and `do/while` loops. Consider this `for` loop:

```
<TABLE BORDER="2">
<% for (int i = 0; i < 7; i++) { %>
      <TR>
         <TD> Row <%=  i %> </TD><BR>
      </TR>
<% } %>
</TABLE>
```

First scriptlet with `for`

Second scriptlet

This code creates an HTML table with one column and seven rows. Each cell displays a label with the cell's row number. It includes two scriptlets:

```
<% for (int i =0; i < 7; i++) { %>
```

and

```
<% } %>
```

The second scriptlet is simply the closing brace character (`}`). Using constructs in this way lets you generate dynamic tables easily.

JSP scriptlets can also insert the other Java iteration constructs, the `while` and the `do/while` statements. For example, here's our JSP fragment coded as a `while` loop rather than a `for` loop:


```
<TABLE BORDER="2">
<% int i = 0;
   while (i < 7) { %>
      <TR>
         <TD> Row <%=  i %> </TD><BR>
      </TR>
<%    i++;
   } %>
</TABLE>
```

First scriptlet with `while`

Second scriptlet

Finally, here is our JSP fragment coded as a `do/while` loop:

```
<TABLE BORDER="2">
<% int i = 0;
   do { %>
      <TR>
         <TD> Row <%=  i %> </TD><BR>
      </TR>
<%    i++;
   } while (i < 7); %>
</TABLE>
```

First scriptlet with `do/while`

Second scriptlet with `while` expression

Advanced Java Features in Scriptlets

JSP scriptlets can declare advanced Java constructs like local and anonymous *inner classes*. Inner classes are classes that are included either as members of other classes, locally within a block of statements, or anonymously within an expression. Inner classes declared explicitly in a JSP scriptlet are local inner classes since they occur within the *_jspService* method and are therefore local to this method. Inner classes that are declared within an instance creation expression (a `new` expression) inside a JSP scriptlet are anonymous inner classes (also called anonymous classes). For more information about inner classes, please refer to `http://java.sun.com/products/jdk/1.1/docs/guide/innerclasses/index.html`.

Local Inner Classes in Scriptlets

Consider the following JSP fragment:

```
<B>The read/write files are:</B><BR>
<% class MyFileFilter implements FilenameFilter {
       public boolean accept(File dir, String name) {
           File file = new File(name);
           return (file.canRead() && file.canWrite());
       }
   }

   File file = new File(".");
   String[] fileList = file.list(new MyFileFilter());
   for (int i = 0; i < fileList.length; i++) {
%>
<%= fileList[i] %> <BR>
<% } %>
```

This fragment results in a local class declaration in the *_jspService* method of the generated servlet. We use it to display all the files the servlet can open for both read and write access.

When you declare inner classes using JSP scriptlets, these inner classes follow the standard restrictions imposed on any Java inner class inside a method. For example, these inner classes can access only local variables in the *_jspService* method that you declare `final`.

Anonymous Classes in Scriptlets

JSP scriptlets can also declare anonymous classes. In Java, anonymous classes supply a shorthand means to declare a *non-reusable* object type. For example, consider this JSP fragment:

```
<B>The read/write files are:</B><BR>
<% File anonFile = new File(".");
   String[] anonFileList = anonFile.list(new java.io.FilenameFilter() {
      public boolean accept(File dir, String name) {
         File curFile = new File(name);
         return (curFile.canRead() && curFile.canWrite());
      }
   });
```

Parent is a Java interface

```
    for (int i = 0; i < anonFileList.length; i++) {
%>
        <%= anonFileList[i] %> <BR>
<%  } %>
```

This fragment declares a class with no class name. Instead, the fragment declares the class using its Java interface, java.io.FilenameFilter. Since anonymous classes have no name, you cannot reuse them, as you can other inner classes.

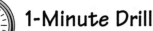

1-Minute Drill

- Can you insert any and every legal Java code fragment into a JSP scriptlet?
- What is the scope of a variable declared in a JSP scriptlet?
- When is a JSP scriptlet executed?

Exceptions in Scriptlets

You can throw custom exceptions and enclose them in `try/catch` scriptlets. Here is how such a construction might look:

```
<% try { %>
   some code
   throw new CustomException("message");
<% }
   catch (CustomException ex) {
%>
      <%= ex.getLocalizedMessage() %>
<% } %>
```

CustomException can be thrown here.

You can also throw exceptions that you do not catch. The *_jspService* method encloses the Java code it derives from JSP scriptlets and JSP expressions in a `try/catch` block. You can throw any exception sub-classed from

---

- No. A JSP scriptlet can contain only Java code that you can legally include in a method.
- Variables declared in a JSP scriptlet have method scope or less.
- The JSP container executes a JSP scriptlet at request time.

java.lang.Exception and the container will catch it and pass it to a handler method. Here is the catch block generated by the Tomcat container:

```
catch (Exception ex) {
   if (out.getBufferSize() != 0)
      out.clearBuffer();
   pageContext.handlePageException(ex);
}
```

By default, the *handlePageException* method used by Tomcat displays a stack dump. In Module 2, you learned about a page directive attribute that allows you to modify this default behavior. If you set the errorPage attribute, the *handlePageException* method forwards control to the HTML or JSP page that you specify as the value for that attribute.

More About JSP Scriptlets

You should consider a few important points when using JSP scriptlets.

JSP scriptlets generate Java code with method scope. JSP scriptlets, like JSP expressions, generate Java code with method scope. This means they can access any variables or methods defined by JSP declarations, as well as container objects like the implicit *JspWriter* object. The code scope for JSP scriptlets determines the syntactically valid Java you can use in them. The fact that scriptlets end up in the *_jspService* method of the generated servlet means you cannot declare member variables or member methods in JSP scriptlets. If you think you need such java constructs, you must define them in JSP declarations.

You should prefer using JSP scriptlet variables to JSP declarations. Variables declared in JSP scriptlets are local to the *_jspService* method, so they are naturally thread-safe local variables. Whenever possible, perhaps always, you should prefer using such local variables to JSP declarations. This greatly simplifies ensuring the thread-safety of your JavaServer Pages.

Question: If I should prefer using JSP scriptlet variables to JSP declarations, when would I ever use JSP declarations for variables?

Answer: Remember that the JSP container evaluates JSP scriptlets at request time. This means that the container creates and destroys any variable defined in a JSP scriptlet every time a client requests the JSP page. Sometimes your JSP page may require read-only variables, initialized once and unchanged thereafter. These might be good candidates for a JSP declaration since you need not create, initialize, and destroy them in every request. You should declare all such variables `final`.

JSP scriptlets are error prone and can obscure program logic. Java constructs that mix HTML and static text typically require multiple JSP scriptlets. This mixture of static HTML and Java code for conditionals, loops, and other program constructs is powerful and useful, but using the mixture can get confusing. For example, it is easy to leave out braces, the semicolon (`;`) character terminating a Java statement, parentheses, and many other important Java syntax elements. Text editors and Integrated Development Environments (IDEs) typically simplify such chores by automatically flagging unmatched parentheses or braces, or even by suggesting syntax elements. If you do not own a text editor or IDE for JSP page development, conventions and consistency can help simplify your burden.

When you mix Java and HTML, you can obscure program logic. One of the frequently stated advantages of JavaServer Pages is that they allow you to pull HTML out of servlet code, thereby reducing the confusion caused by a host of print statements. Adding too much Java code to a JSP page, however, can create just as much confusion. Heavy use of Java constructs such as `if/else` and `switch` statements can obscure even pure Java programs. Intersperse HTML tags and static text into such constructs and the picture can get grim. Instead, you should try to pull most Java code out of the JSP page and encapsulate it in helper JavaBeans. (We describe such encapsulation techniques in Modules 5 and 6.)

Expense.java
ExpenseReport.java
ExpenseReport.jsp

Project 3-1: Scripting Elements

This project illustrates the use of all three scripting elements in a JSP page. The project requires you to display a household expense report. The JSP page displays a dynamic list of household expenses, each of which include the following information:

- Date
- Category
- Description
- Amount

Your goal is to produce a well-formatted HTML table of these expenses.

Step-by-Step

1. Download the Java files for this project from `http://www.osborne.com`.
2. Compile the Java files `Expense.java` and `ExpenseReport.java`. Be aware that the Java files belong to a package named *scripting*.
3. Create the directory hierarchy `WEB-INF/classes/scripting` under the `Book` context in your Tomcat installation.
4. Move the class files that were created in step 2 under `%TOMCAT_HOME%/webapps/Book/WEB-INF/classes/scripting`. The JSP container automatically loads all class files located under the `WEB-INF/classes` sub-directory for a given application context. Since all your Java files are in the `scripting` package, create the subdirectory `scripting` under `WEB-INF/classes` and put your class files in this directory.
5. Quickly examine the two Java files to gain an understanding of their purpose. The Java files serve only to provide the dynamic content. The class *Expense* in `Expense.java` is a JavaBean that contains all information for a single household expense. The class *ExpenseReport* in `ExpenseReport.java` maintains a static list of all expenses for the month of January. Your goal in this project is to present this list of expenses to form your report in a JSP page.
6. Create an empty JSP page file named `ExpenseReport.jsp` under `%TOMCAT_HOME%/webapps/Book/jsp`.
7. Begin the JSP page by importing the classes that you might need using the page directive. First, import the Java files that you just built. In addition, import the JDK *java.util* package. Enter the first line as shown here:

```
<%@ page import="scripting.*, java.util.*" %>
```

3

8. Notice that the expense amount in `Expense.java` is encoded as a double. For uniformity, present each expense amount as a *String* with exactly two decimal places with padded zeros in the end. Define a method that will perform this conversion and include it as a JSP declaration, as shown here:

```
<%-- Declare Utility methods and variables --%>
<%!
  public String getStringifiedValue(double value) {
        String subval = "0.00";
      if (value > 0.0) {
         subval = Double.toString(value);
         int decimal_len = subval.length() -
(subval.lastIndexOf('.') + 1);
         if(decimal_len > 1)
           subval = subval.substring(0,
subval.lastIndexOf('.') + 3);
         else
           subval += "0";
      }
      return subval;
  }
%>
```

9. Now you're ready to insert some HTML. Enter the basic HTML tags that start every JSP page, like this:

```
<HTML>
<HEAD><TITLE> Scripting Elements Demo </TITLE></HEAD>
<BODY>
```

10. Retrieve the expense report so that you can start laying it out in the JSP page. Use the following scriptlet:

```
<%
   ExpenseReport rpt = ExpenseReport.getReport();
%>
```

11. Print a title for your table and take advantage of a JSP expression to print the month associated with this expense report, as shown here:

```
<H1> Expense Report for: <%= rpt.getMonth() %> </H1>
```

12. Create an HTML table with the first row containing headers that name the types of information in each table column. Enter the table like this:

```
<%-- Draw Table of all Expenses --%>
<TABLE WIDTH=650 CELLSPACING="0" CELLPADDING="3" BORDER="1">
<%-- Draw title bar --%>
```

```
<TR>
    <TD WIDTH=10% BGCOLOR="#ECA613"> <B>Date</B> </TD>
    <TD WIDTH=25% BGCOLOR="#ECA613"> <B>Category</B> </TD>
    <TD BGCOLOR="#ECA613"> <B>Description</B> </TD>
    <TD WIDTH=8% BGCOLOR="#ECA613"> <B>Amount</B> </TD>
</TR>
```

13. Retrieve the expense list (maintained as a *java.util.List*) for your report and iterate through it, inserting each expense into the HTML table. Each iteration retrieves a new expense. Enter this JSP scriptlet:

```
<%-- Draw data --%>
<%
   List expenses = rpt.getExpenses();
   for(int i=0; i<expenses.size(); i++) {
      Expense e = (Expense)expenses.get(i);
%>
```

14. Use JSP expressions to retrieve and print the various components of each expense. Use the utility method *getStringifiedValue*, defined earlier in the JSP declaration, to print your expense amount in a consistent format. The following JSP fragment performs these steps. Enter them in your JSP page:

```
<TR>
   <TD ALIGN=left> <%= e.getDate() %> </TD>
   <TD ALIGN=left> <%= e.getCategory() %> </TD>
   <TD ALIGN=left> <%= e.getDescription() %> </TD>
   <TD ALIGN=right> <%= getStringifiedValue(e.getAmount()) %> </TD>
</TR>
```

15. To close the loop, use another JSP scriptlet, as shown here:

```
<%
   }
%>
```

16. Close the HTML table, and then add these closing HTML tags:

```
</TABLE>
</BODY>
</HTML>
```

17. Save your file and load it in a Web browser using the URL: `http://localhost:8080/Book/jsp/ExpenseReport.jsp`. Make sure that Tomcat is running when you access this URL. You should see a page that looks like Figure 3-1.

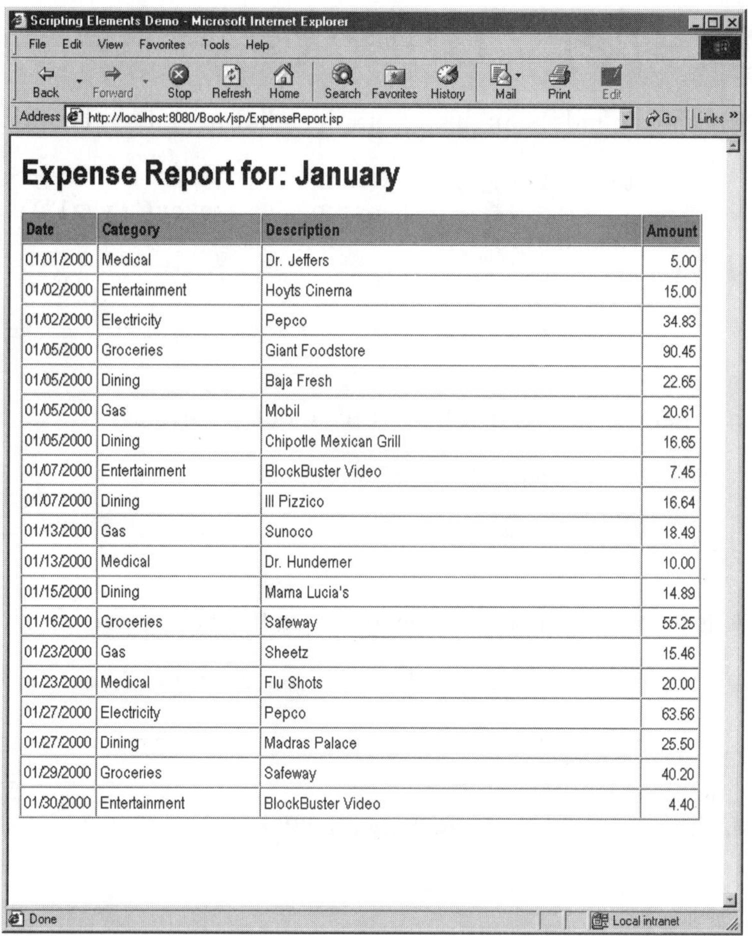

Expense Report for: January

Date	Category	Description	Amount
01/01/2000	Medical	Dr. Jeffers	5.00
01/02/2000	Entertainment	Hoyts Cinema	15.00
01/02/2000	Electricity	Pepco	34.83
01/05/2000	Groceries	Giant Foodstore	90.45
01/05/2000	Dining	Baja Fresh	22.65
01/05/2000	Gas	Mobil	20.61
01/05/2000	Dining	Chipotle Mexican Grill	16.65
01/07/2000	Entertainment	BlockBuster Video	7.45
01/07/2000	Dining	Ill Pizzico	16.64
01/13/2000	Gas	Sunoco	18.49
01/13/2000	Medical	Dr. Hundemer	10.00
01/15/2000	Dining	Mama Lucia's	14.89
01/16/2000	Groceries	Safeway	55.25
01/23/2000	Gas	Sheetz	15.46
01/23/2000	Medical	Flu Shots	20.00
01/27/2000	Electricity	Pepco	63.56
01/27/2000	Dining	Madras Palace	25.50
01/29/2000	Groceries	Safeway	40.20
01/30/2000	Entertainment	BlockBuster Video	4.40

Figure 3-1 Household expense report

Make sure that you carefully examine the JSP page generated by this project. Note how the page intersperses static HTML with JSP elements. Using too many JSP elements in a JSP page makes the page hard to read and difficult to maintain. But the goal in this project is simply to illustrate the various JSP scripting elements.

Mastery Check

1. Can you find the problem with the following JSP declaration?

```
<%! public String foo() {
        String val = request.getParameter("MyVal");
        return val;
%>
```

____

____

2. What problem does this JSP declaration illustrate?

```
<%! String request = "my request"; %>
```

____

____

3. Is there a problem with the following JSP expression?

```
This page was accessed: <%= counter.getNumTimes(); %>.
```

____

____

4. What do you see in the following JSP fragment that is cause for worry?

```
<%! Basket basket; %>
<%
   basket = (Basket)session.getAttribute("BASKET");
   if(basket.full()) {
%>
```

____

____

5. Is there a better option for the situation in question 4?

____

____

Mastery Check

6. Is there anything wrong with the following scriptlet?

```
<%
   if(basket.isEmpty()) {
        return basket;
   }
%>
```

7. Consider the following scriptlet. Do you see any problems with the way it has been declared?

```
<%
   class LocalClass {
     public String getName() {
        return request.getParameter("Name");
     }
   }
%>
```

8. Would the following scriptlet function as you intended?

```
<% if(time.before9AM() && time.after6PM()) %>
         Sorry, our office hours are <%= officeHours %>
```

Module 4

Implicit Objects

The Goals of This Module

- Get familiar with the various implicit JSP objects
- Understand the Java classes that the implicit objects represent
- Understand how to use implicit objects in JavaServer Pages

One of the advantages of writing Web applications in the context of the Java servlet and JSP containers is that these containers provide services to the applications. JavaServer Pages expose these services through implicit objects that are available for use by JSP page developers.

The JSP 1.1 specification requires that JSP scripting languages support a common set of *implicit* objects. The objects are implicit in the sense that you need not declare them before you use them. We mentioned implicit objects several times in Modules 2 and 3. For example, in Module 3 we described how JSP expressions and scriptlets could access the *JspWriter* object *out*. In this module, we provide a detailed list of each implicit object and describe each object's uses.

In JSP 1.1, because the only JSP scripting language is Java, each of the implicit objects maps to a specific Java class or interface. In our discussion, we use the variable name and object type more or less interchangeably. Table 4-1 lists the implicit objects and their Java types.

Variable Name	Java Type	Description	JSP Scope
request	A protocol-dependent subtype of *javax.servlet.ServletRequest*; for the HTTP protocol, *javax.servlet.HttpServletRequest*	Provides preparsed HTTP requests	request
response	A protocol-dependent subtype of *javax.servlet.ServletResponse*; for the HTTP protocol, *javax.servlet.HttpServletResponse*	Encapsulates HTTP response	page
pageContext	*javax.servlet.jsp.PageContext*	Encapsulates vendor-specific features; provides convenience methods to access information from multiple scopes and retrieve other implicit objects; supplies *forward*, *include*, and *handlePage Exception* methods	page

Table 4-1 Implicit Objects Available in JavaServer Pages

Variable Name	Java Type	Description	JSP Scope
session	*javax.servlet.http.HttpSession*	Provides mechanism for tracking clients across multiple service requests	session
application	*javax.servlet.ServletContext*	Provides a set of methods to access Web server information and to write messages to the servlet log file	application
out	*javax.servlet.jsp.JspWriter*	Encapsulates means to write into the HTTP response buffer	page
config	*javax.servlet.ServletConfig*	Supplies initialization parameters to the JSP page and access to the *ServletContext*	page
page	*javax.servlet.jsp.HttpJspPage*	A synonym for "this" in the page body	page
exception	java.lang.Throwable	The uncaught *Throwable* passed to an error page	page

Table 4-1 Implicit Objects Available in JavaServer Pages *(continued)*

The request Variable

The *request* variable provides access to the information supplied in client requests. The Java servlet container packages this information as an object with a protocol-dependent subtype of *javax.servlet.ServletRequest*. For our purposes, the protocol is HTTP, so the default object is of type *javax.servlet.HttpServletRequest*. It has request scope, which means the servlet container creates it at request time and destroys it when the request is complete. This also means that the same request object is available to all JavaServer Pages that service a given HTTP request.

The *request* implicit variable is a formal argument to the *_jspService* method of the generated servlet. The code fragment that follows, taken out of a servlet generated by the Tomcat JSP container, shows this argument:

The *request* implicit object is a formal argument

```
public void _jspService(HttpServletRequest request,
                        HttpServletResponse response)
       throws IOException, ServletException
```

request Services

The *request* variable, through the *HttpServletRequest* object it references, provides the following types of services to JavaServer Pages:

- Access to request parameters
- Management of attributes in request scope
- Retrieval of cookies
- Access to request headers
- Access to request line elements
- Access to security information
- Access to internationalization information

Access to Request Parameters

The *HttpServletRequest* object contains information populated from the URI query string for the current JSP page and possibly URL-encoded data posted from an HTML form. The servlet container provides this information as a list of Java *String* objects representing parameter names and values. The convenience methods *getParameter*, *getParameterNames*, and *getParameterValues* in the *request* object retrieve this information. The following JSP scriptlet code fragment prints the parameters in a request.

```
<H3>Parameters in this request:</H3>
<% java.util.Enumeration e =
      request.getParameterNames();
   while (e.hasMoreElements()) {
```

```
      String paramName = (String)e.nextElement();
      String[] paramValues =
         request.getParameterValues(paramName);
%>
      <BR>Parameter:  <%= paramName %>
      Values:
<%    for (int i = 0; i < paramValues.length; i++) {
%>
         <%= paramValues[i] %>
<%    }
   }
%><BR>
```


If you access the JSP page containing the preceding fragment with the URI query string `x=5&y=joe&y=larry`, your browser would display the following results:

> **Parameters in this request:**
> Parameter: x Values: 5
> Parameter: y Values: joe larry

You use parameters to capture and transfer user input between pages in a Web workflow. Usually you post such data from an HTML form. Consider the following HTML fragment:

```
<FORM METHOD="post" ACTION="paramRequest.jsp">
Please enter your name:
<INPUT TYPE=text SIZE=25 NAME="name"><BR>
Please enter your age:
<INPUT TYPE=text SIZE=3 NAME="age"><BR>
Please enter your Date of Birth (MM/DD/YYYY):
<INPUT TYPE=text SIZE=11 NAME="dob"><BR><BR>
<INPUT TYPE=submit VALUE="Go">
</FORM>
```

Figure 4-1 shows the form with sample data as entered by the user.

Assume that `paramRequest.jsp`, the `ACTION` in our form, prints the parameter names and values (like the code we listed earlier). When you submit the form, the JSP container loads `paramRequest.jsp`, which then prints the three parameters, "name", "age", and "dob", along with whatever values you entered into the `INPUT` text fields. Figure 4-2 shows sample output.

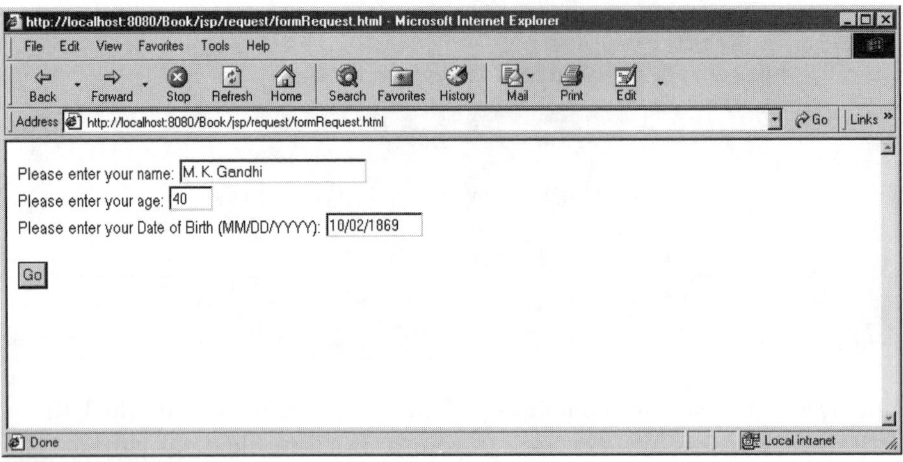

Figure 4-1 Basic HTML form with user input

Note

The servlet container automatically extracts parameters from query strings and form data and stores them in the *HttpServletRequest* object. There are no set methods that a JSP developer can invoke to store parameters as information in a request.

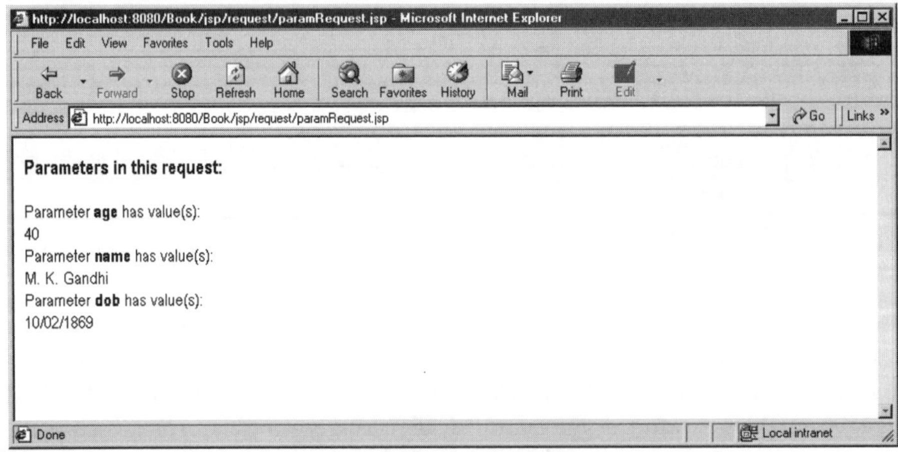

Figure 4-2 Output of form submission

Table 4-2 lists the methods provided by the *request* variable to access parameters and parameter values.

Management of Attributes in Request Scope

Attributes are objects you explicitly store in the *HttpServletRequest* object. Attributes allow a JSP developer to pass information between JSP pages and servlets. Unlike parameters, which are always Java *String* objects, attributes can be any Java type. Only one attribute value may be associated with a given attribute name.

Consider a source JSP page that includes the following JSP fragment:


```
<% request.setAttribute("Current Date",
                        new java.util.Date());
%>
<%@ include file="AttributeDestination.jsp" %>
```

In this fragment, we store a *Date* object under the name "Current Date." The JSP page, `AttributeDestination.jsp`, can then retrieve and print the object like this:

```
<% java.util.Date date = (java.util.Date)
     request.getAttribute("Current Date"); %>
Current Date is: <%= date %>
```

The output looks like this:

Current Date is: Sun Feb 11 21:12:13 EST 2001

Method Signature	Use
`String getParameter (String parameterName)`	Returns the value of a request parameter as a *String*, or null if the parameter does not exist
`java.util.Enumeration getParameterNames()`	Returns an enumeration of *String* objects containing the names of the parameters contained in this request
`String[] getParameterValues (String parameterName)`	Returns an array of *String* objects containing all of the values the given request parameter has, or null if the parameter does not exist

Table 4-2 Methods to Access Request Parameters

Note

The Java Servlet specification 2.2 recommends using the package naming convention suggested in the Java Programming Language Specification for attribute names. For more information on the package naming conventions, refer to section 6.8 of the Java Language Specification available at `http://java.sun.com/docs/books/jls/first_edition/html/index.html`. The specification reserves attribute names beginning with the prefixes `java.` and `javax.`, `sun.`, and `com.sun.`

The attribute management methods provided by the *request* variable are shown in Table 4-3.

Retrieval of Cookies

The *request* object contains the *getCookies* method to obtain an array of cookies that are present in the request. *Cookies* are data that is sent automatically from the client to the server on every request that the client makes. A common use of cookies is to send login or session identification information automatically from the client computer. The *getCookies* method signature is `javax.servlet.http.Cookie[] getCookies()`, which returns an array of all cookie names and values.

Access to Request Headers

As we described in Module 1, HTTP requests contain headers. The *HttpServlet Request* object provides methods to access the information sent in HTTP headers.

Method Signature	Use
`Object getAttribute (String name)`	Returns the value of the named attribute as an `Object`, or `null` if no attribute of the given name exists
`java.util.Enumeration getAttributeNames()`	Returns an enumeration containing the names of the attributes available to this request
`void removeAttribute (String attributeName)`	Removes an attribute from this request
`void setAttribute(String name, Object object)`	Stores an attribute in this request; the servlet container resets attributes between requests

Table 4-3 Methods to Manage Request Attributes

Consider the following JSP page fragment that retrieves header names and iterates through them while printing each header value:

```
<H3>Headers in this request:</H3>
<% int i = 1;
   java.util.Enumeration e =
      request.getHeaderNames();
   while (e.hasMoreElements()) {
      String name = (String)e.nextElement();
      String value = request.getHeader(name);
%>
      <B>Header <%= i++ + ": </B>" + name %>
               <%= value %></B><BR>
<% } %>
```

A sample run of a JSP page containing this fragment produces the following output:

Headers in this request:
Header 1: User-Agent Mozilla/4.0 (compatible; MSIE 5.5; Windows NT 5.0)
Header 2: Cookie JSESSIONID=xalkx8qnu1
Header 3: Accept */*
Header 4: Host wsolney.bellatlantic.net:8080
Header 5: Accept-Encoding gzip, deflate
Header 6: Accept-Language en-us
Header 7: Referer http://wsolney.bellatlantic.net:8080/Book/jsp
Header 8: Connection Keep-Alive

Table 4-4 lists the method signatures for accessing request headers.

Access to Request Line Elements

The *request* variable provides methods that help you determine information about the request line that led to the JSP page. Consider the following JSP page that we named `requestPathRequest.jsp`:

```
<B>Request Method:</B> <%= request.getMethod() %><BR>
<B>Request URI:</B> <%= request.getRequestURI() %><BR>
<B>Servlet Path:</B> <%= request.getServletPath() %><BR>
<B>Context Path:</B> <%= request.getContextPath() %><BR>
<B>Path Info:</B><%= request.getPathInfo() %><BR>
<B>Query String:</B><%= request.getQueryString() %>
```

4

Method Signature	Use
`java.util.Enumeration getHeaderNames()`	Returns an enumeration of *String* objects representing all the header names in the current request
`java.util.Enumeration getHeaders(String headerName)`	Returns an enumeration of *String* objects representing all the values for the named header
`String getHeader(String headerName)`	Returns the value of the named header as a *String*
`int getIntHeader(String headerName)`	Returns the value of the named header as an integer
`long getDateHeader(String headerName)`	Returns the value of the named header as a *long* representing a date

Table 4-4 Methods for Accessing Request Headers

When the JSP page was accessed using the URL `http://localhost:8080/Book/jsp/requestPathRequest.jsp?name=hello`, the output was as follows:

Request Method: GET
Request URI: /Book/jsp/requestPathRequest.jsp
Servlet Path: /jsp/requestPathRequest.jsp
Context Path: /Book
Path Info: null
Query String: name=hello

This maps to the following request line:

```
GET /Book/jsp/requestPathRequest.jsp?name=hello
```

As the output shows, you can express the relation between path elements using the equation:

requestURI = contextPath + servletPath + pathInfo

Table 4-5 lists the various methods for retrieving request line information.

Method Signature	Use
`String getMethod()`	Returns the name of the HTTP method with which this request was made; for example, `GET` or `POST`
`String getRequestURI()`	Returns the part of the request's URI between the protocol name and the query string in the first line of the HTTP request
`String getContextPath()`	Returns the portion of the request URI that indicates the application context of the request
`String getServletPath()`	Returns that part of the request URI that specifies the servlet or JSP page
`String getPathInfo()`	Returns any extra path information associated with the URL that follows the servlet path but precedes the query string
`String getQueryString()`	Returns the query string that follows the path part of the URI

Table 4-5 Request Line Methods

Access to Security Information

The *request* variable provides access to security attributes. For example, this line uses the *request* variable to determine whether the current request used a secure protocol like secure HTTP (HTTPS):

```
Uses secure protocol? <%= request.isSecure() %>
```

Note

HTTPS is a communications protocol that supports transmittal of encrypted information between browsers and supporting Web servers. The basis of the HTTPS protocol is the Secure Socket Layer (SSL) for encryption. If a request uses an SSL certificate, servlet containers must provide access to this certificate as an array of *java.security.cert.X509Certificate* objects. You retrieve this array from the request using a special attribute named *javax.servlet.request.X509Certificate.*

Table 4-6 lists some of the important security methods.

Access to Internationalization Information

Browsers can indicate to Web servers their preferred language by using an HTTP header called `Accept-Language`. The methods *getLocale* and *getLocales* in the

Method Signature	Use
`boolean isSecure()`	Returns `true` or `false` indicating whether this request used a secure protocol, such as HTTPS
`boolean isRequestedSessionIdFromCookie()`	A *boolean* indicating whether or not the session uses a cookie to manage the session id
`boolean isRequestedSessionIdFromURL()`	A *boolean* indicating whether or not the session uses URL rewriting to manage the session id
`boolean isRequestedSessionIdValid()`	Checks whether the requested session id is valid

Table 4-6 Methods for Accessing Security Information

request object allow a JSP developer to retrieve this information. The objects returned from these calls are of type *java.util.Locale*. These objects encapsulate a country and a language. Using this information, the JSP developer could respond with locale-specific responses. A simple example of this header's use is shown here:

```
<%@ page import="java.util.Locale" %>
<H1>
<% Locale requestedLocale = request.getLocale();
   if(requestedLocale.equals(Locale.US)) {
%>
      Hello! How are you?
<%
   } else if(requestedLocale.equals(Locale.FRANCE)) {
%>
      Bonjour! (Comment) ça va?
<%  } %>
</H1>
```

In our computer, where client requests send `en-us` (United States English) as the locale in the HTTP header, the output is

Hello! How are you?

The methods to access internationalization information from a request are shown in Table 4-7.

Method Signature	Use
`java.util.Locale getLocale()`	Returns the preferred *Locale* that the client will accept content in, based on the `Accept-Language` header
`java.util.Enumeration getLocales()`	Returns an enumeration of *Locale* objects indicating, in decreasing order starting with the preferred locale, the locales that are acceptable to the client based on the `Accept-Language` header

Table 4-7 Internationalization Methods

1-Minute Drill

- What is the source of the *request* implicit object?
- How do you use the *request* variable to retrieve request parameters?
- How do you store objects in request scope?
- How do you retrieve attributes in request scope?
- How can you tell whether your application is using a security protocol?

The response Variable

The *response* variable encapsulates all information returned to a client from a JSP page. It refers to an implicit object that is a protocol-dependent subtype of *javax.servlet.ServletResponse*. In the HTTP protocol, the implicit object has type *javax.servlet.http.HttpServletResponse*. As described in Module 1, an HTTP response consists of message headers and an optional message body. The *HttpServletResponse* object provides an elegant Java interface to set the components of the HTTP response.

- The *request* object is a parameter to the *_jspService* method in the generated servlet.
- You use the request variable to first retrieve parameter names and then to retrieve the values for each parameter.
- You use *request.setAttribute(String name, Object value)*.
- You use *request.getAttribute(String name)*.
- You call *request.isSecure()*.

The *HttpServletResponse* object has *page scope*, which means that it is valid only within the JSP page. As soon as the *_jspService* method returns, the response goes out of scope. Like the *request* variable, the *response* variable is a formal argument to the *_jspService* method of the generated servlet. The following code fragment, taken from a servlet generated by the Tomcat container, shows this argument.

The *response* implicit object is a formal argument

```
public void _jspService(HttpServletRequest request,
                        HttpServletResponse response)
      throws IOException, ServletException
```

response Services

The *response* object provides the following three services:

- Output buffering
- Setting response headers
- Redirecting resources

Let's look at each of these in detail.

Output Buffering

Buffering, as discussed in Module 2, can make transmission of content between server and client more efficient. The *HttpServletResponse* object enables buffer configuration in support of the *JspWriter* object. The *getBufferSize* method returns the current buffer size for the JSP page. The *setBufferSize* method allows the JSP page to set a preferred output buffer size for the body of the response. The actual buffer size that the container uses is at least as large as the size requested. If you set the buffer size, you must do so before writing content to the response. Otherwise, the JSP container will throw an *IllegalStateException*. For example, the following code causes an exception:

```
<%   out.println("Before setBufferSize()<BR>");
     response.flushBuffer();
     response.setBufferSize(16384);
     out.println("After setBufferSize()<BR>");
%>
```

This code, on the other hand, generally does not cause an exception:

```
<%   out.println("Before setBufferSize()<BR>");
     response.setBufferSize(16384);
     out.println("After setBufferSize()<BR>");
%>
```

The second code fragment does not flush its buffer (which sends output to the client) before setting the buffer size. If we turn buffering off first, as shown here, the second code fragment will also throw an exception:


```
<%@ page buffer="none" %>
<%  out.println("Before setBufferSize()<BR>");
    response.setBufferSize(16384);
    out.println("After setBufferSize()<BR>");
%>
```

Tip

If you modify the default buffer size (8K), you should make it your practice to set the buffer size before writing any output, whether it be static HTML or dynamic content.

A larger buffer allows you to write more content before sending anything to the client, thereby decreasing the number of network writes. A smaller buffer decreases server memory load and allows the client to start receiving data more quickly, but it increases the number of network writes.

Any content written to the client is said to be *committed*. This can be determined via the method *isCommitted*, which returns true or false. The *flushBuffer* method flushes the current content in the buffer immediately and sends it to the client. The *reset* method removes the current buffer content. You cannot call this method if the response buffer has already been committed. The following sample JSP fragment illustrates buffering:

```
The buffer size is: <%= response.getBufferSize() %> <BR>
Before flush... <BR>
Is the output committed? <%= response.isCommitted() %>  <BR><BR>
<% response.flushBuffer(); %>
After flush... <BR>
Is the output committed? <%= response.isCommitted() %>
```

When you execute this JSP page, Tomcat generates the following output:

```
The buffer size is: 8192
Before flush...
Is the output committed? false

After flush...
Is the output committed? true
```

As you can see, the default response buffer size is 8K. Our JSP page has not committed the response before the flush because 8K has not accumulated in the output buffer. This means that when we invoke the *isCommitted* method for the first time, nothing is committed even though we have written some output. When we explicitly flush the buffer, we send its contents to the client (even if the buffer is not full). This immediately commits the response buffer, as we see when we next invoke the *isCommitted* method.

The buffering methods provided by the *response* variable are listed in Table 4-8.

Setting Response Headers

A JSP page can set headers for the HTTP response using the *response* implicit variable. For instance, the following JSP page fragment sets the content type for the response to plain text:

```
<% response.setHeader("Content-Type", "text/plain");
%>
```

Tip

You must set headers before you send any content to a client. The container ignores headers set after the response is committed.

The ability to set the content type for a response is somewhat limited for JavaServer Pages compared to servlets, because the JSP container automatically retrieves the *JspWriter* using the *pageContext.getOut* method. The JSP specification requires that the JSP container make the *JspWriter* class available in the generated servlet for a JSP page as the *out* variable. Since this *JspWriter* is a wrapper around the *PrintWriter* retrieved from the response, the JSP container automatically retrieves the *PrintWriter*. The *PrintWriter* object can print only character-encoded output streams, so only the content types that can be written as character data can be set on a response.

Method Signature	Use
`int getBufferSize()`	Returns the actual buffer size used for the response; if no buffering is used, this method returns 0
`void setBufferSize(int size)`	Sets the preferred buffer size for the body of the response
`boolean isCommitted()`	Returns a boolean indicating whether the response has been committed; a committed response has already had its status code and headers written
`void reset()`	Clears any data that exists in the buffer, as well as clearing the status code and headers
`void flushBuffer()`	Forces any content in the buffer to be written to the client

Table 4-8 Methods for Managing Response Buffering

Table 4-9 shows header setting methods.

Ask the Expert

Question: Does the automatic retrieval of the *JspWriter* object mean you cannot use a JSP page to stream binary data?

Answer: The *Http.ServletResponse* object provides two different mechanisms to send output to a client. The *getWriter* method returns a *PrintWriter* object that can send character text to the client. The *getOutputStream* method returns a *ServletOutputStream* that can write binary data to the client. You can use only one mechanism for a given response. You will get an *IllegalStateException* if you attempt to use both for the same response. In order to stream binary data, you must use the *ServletOutputStream*. Because the JSP container automatically retrieves the *PrintWriter* in the *_jspService* method, if you attempt to retrieve the *ServletOutputStream* in your JSP page, you will receive an *IllegalState Exception*. The upshot is that you cannot stream binary data from a JSP page.

Method Signature	Use
`void addHeader(String name, String value)`	Adds a response header with the given name and value .
`void setHeader(String name, String value)`	Sets a response header with the given name and value. If the header had already been set, the new value overwrites the previous one.
`void addDateHeader(String name, long date)`	Adds a response header with the given name and date-value. The date is specified in terms of milliseconds since the epoch.
`void setDateHeader(String name, long date)`	Sets a response header with the given name and date-value. If the header had already been set, the new value overwrites the previous one.
`void addIntHeader(String name, int value)`	Adds a response header with the given name and integer value.
`void setIntHeader(String name, int value)`	Sets a response header with the given name and integer value. If the header had already been set, the new value overwrites the previous one.
`boolean containsHeader(String name)`	Returns a boolean indicating whether the named response header has already been set.
`void setContentType(String type)`	Utility to set the content type header for the response.
`void setContentLength(int length)`	Utility to set the content length header for the response.
`void setLocale(`java.util.Locale locale)	Utility to set the locale header for the response.

Table 4-9 Methods for Setting Response Headers

Resource Redirection

A JSP page can redirect a client to a different Web resource (URL) using the *sendRedirect* method available through the *response* implicit variable. For example, examine the following JSP scriptlet:

```
<% response.sendRedirect("NewLocation.jsp"); %>
```

The scriptlet states that any request coming to this JSP page should be automatically redirected to the relative URL: `NewLocation.jsp`. The *sendRedirect* method sets the appropriate headers and content body to redirect the client to this new URL. The JSP container translates the relative path to a fully qualified URL.

Tip

This method causes a second client request that wipes out all request parameters. This means redirecting pages must reset their parameters in the URL to the new page.

A JSP page can also indicate an error situation using the *sendError* method on the *response* implicit variable. This method takes an error code and an optional error message that is returned to the client in the content body. For instance, examine the following JSP scriptlet:

```
<% response.sendError(500,
      "Fatal internal error has occured. Please check back
later!");
%>
```

The scriptlet redirects the client to an error page with the optional message in the content body.

Both the *sendRedirect* and *sendError* methods terminate the current request and response. If the response has already been committed to the client, these methods cannot be invoked. Redirections such as these should be used cautiously and only for abnormal (error) conditions.

Table 4-10 lists resource redirection methods.

Method Signature	Use
`void sendError(int sc, String msg)`	Sends an error response to the client using the specified status code and descriptive message
`void sendError(int sc)`	Sends an error response to the client using the specified status code
`void sendRedirect (String location)`	Sends a redirect response to the client using the specified redirect location URL. The URL could be relative

Table 4-10 Methods for Redirecting Requests

1-Minute Drill

- What is the source of the *response* implicit object?
- Can you stream binary data from a JSP page?
- What is the value of output buffering?
- How do you use the *response* implicit object to set the buffer size?
- When should you use the *response* object's *sendRedirect* method?

StreamRequest.html
StreamResponse.jsp
StreamError.jsp

Project 4-1: Streaming the Contents of a File

This project demonstrates how to stream the contents of a file that is located on the server to a client using a JSP page. The project begins with a static HTML page with a form that requests a filename and an optional MIME type. The goal of this project is to stream the contents of the specified file as the response.

Step-by-Step

1. Download the files for this project from `http://www.osborne.com`.
2. Drop the file `StreamRequest.html` under `%TOMCAT_HOME%/webapps/Book`.
3. Examine the contents of `StreamRequest.html`. It has a basic HTML form that contains two input text elements requesting the name of the file to be streamed and an optional MIME type. The MIME type is necessary only if the client browser has to specially handle the contents of the file. There are two standard action buttons at the end of the form, to RESET and SUBMIT the form. A JSP page called `StreamResponse.jsp` handles the submission of the form. This is the file that you should write.
4. Start the Tomcat JSP container.
5. Start the client browser and load the HTML file `StreamRequest.html`. Enter the URL `http://localhost:8080/Book/StreamRequest.html` for this. You should see the page as shown in Figure 4-3.

- The *response* object is an argument to the *_jspService* method of the generated servlet.
- No, because the JSP container automatically assigns a *JspWriter* to the out variable, which can only write character data.
- Output buffering can reduce the number of network writes, thereby improving overall performance.
- You use `response.setBufferSize(int sizeInbytes)`.
- You use *sendRedirect* for abnormal situations; for instance, when the location of a page changes.

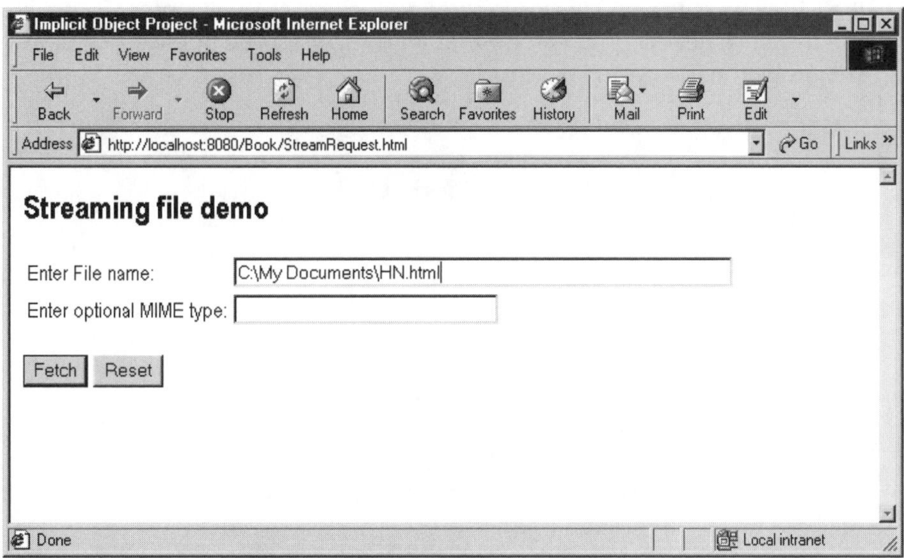

Figure 4-3 StreamRequest.html

6. Create an empty file `StreamResponse.jsp` and drop it under `%TOMCAT_HOME%/webapps/Book`.

7. Following our good programming practice of beginning the JSP page with the page directive, enter the following line in your JSP file:

```
<%@ page import="java.io.*" errorPage="StreamError.jsp" %>
```

8. Since we intend to open the file and print its contents to the response stream, we need to import the *java.io* package. A handy error page, `StreamError.jsp`, which you will be writing next, should universally handle all exceptions that occur in this page.

9. Fetch the parameters from the submitted form using the request implicit object as shown by this JSP scriptlet:

```
<%
    String filename = request.getParameter("File");
    String mime_type = request.getParameter("MIME type");
%>
```

10. If a MIME type was specified, we should specify it as the 'Content-Type' in the response header. You can do that with the response implicit object as shown by the following JSP scriptlet:

```
<%
    if((mime_type != null) && (mime_type.length() > 0)) {
       response.setHeader("Content-Type", mime_type);
    }
%>
```

11. Now, the file can be opened and each line in it can be output to the response stream using the out implicit object. Do this by entering the following JSP scriptlet:

```
<%
    String line = null;
    BufferedReader iread = new BufferedReader(new
FileReader(filename));
    while((line = iread.readLine()) != null) {
       out.write(line);
    }
    iread.close();
%>
```

12. Since we are done streaming the contents of the file, all that is left is coding the error handling JSP file, `StreamError.jsp`. If any exception occurred in our JSP page, control will be automatically redirected to our error file `StreamError.jsp` as specified in the page directive in the beginning.

13. Create an empty file `StreamError.jsp` under `%TOMCAT_HOME%/webapps/Book`.

14. Start with the page directive that indicates that this is an error JSP file using the isErrorPage attribute.

```
<%@ page isErrorPage="true" %>
```

15. Since it is registered as an error page, it automatically has access to the implicit object exception that holds the exception that caused redirection to this error page. So, use the exception object to print details of the exception. A sample is shown here:

```
<H3> Error occured: <%= exception.getMessage() %> </H3>
```

This project illustrates the use of three implicit objects—request, response, and exception—to stream the contents of a file. An important point to note in this project is that we use a *java.io.FileReader* to read the contents of our file. This uses a default character encoding to read the contents of the file and convert them into character text.

The *pageContext* Variable

The *pageContext* variable refers to a *javax.servlet.jsp.PageContext* object that provides access to vendor-specific features, operations across multiple scopes (page, request, session, and application), and a vendor-independent interface to convenience methods. The *PageContext* class is abstract, so JSP container vendors must extend it. The JSP container uses *PageContext* convenience methods to initialize other implicit objects. The idea is that a given vendor can supply a custom implementation for this object, possibly returning optimized versions of the other implicit objects and also supplying additional, vendor-specific methods. The *PageContext* object is retrieved using a creation method on the *javax.servlet.jsp.JspFactory* object, which is also an abstract class with a vendor-provided custom implementation.

Let's review the code Tomcat generates to initialize a generated servlet.

```
jspxFactory = JspFactory.getDefaultFactory();
response.setContentType("text/html;charset=8859_1");
pageContext =
   _jspxFactory.getPageContext(this,
                               request,
                               response,
                               "errorPage.jsp",
                               true,
                               8192,
                               true);
application = pageContext.getServletContext();
config = pageContext.getServletConfig();
session = pageContext.getSession();
out = pageContext.getOut();
```

When the JSP container starts, at initialization time, it typically registers its own *JspFactory* object implementation. At translation time, the JSP container follows these steps:

- At the start of the *_jspService* method in the generated servlet, the vendor-dependent implementation of the *JspFactory* is retrieved using the static method *JspFactory.getDefaultFactory*.
- The factory object's *getPageContext* method initializes and returns a vendor-dependent *PageContext* object.
- The servlet uses this object to retrieve several other implicit objects with mixed scope, including the *ServletContext* object, the *ServletConfig* object, the *HttpSession* object and the *JspWriter* object.
- The servlet assigns each of these objects to a local variable that JSP authors can use in expressions, scriptlets, and JSP actions (we describe actions in Modules 5 and 6).

Most of the implicit objects retrieved using pageContext are custom implementations providing vendor-specific optimizations or features. The JSP 1.1 specification gives special mention to the *JspWriter* object, *out*, as a candidate for optimization.

pageContext Services

The *PageContext* object provides four services:

- Access to multiple scopes
- Access to implicit objects
- Management of nested scopes
- Forward and include services

Access to Multiple Scopes

The pageContext variable supplies methods that provide uniform access to diverse scopes. Recall from Module 2 that the JSP container supports four different scopes. The *PageContext* object defines four constants representing these scopes:

- PageContext.PAGE_SCOPE
- PageContext.REQUEST_SCOPE
- PageContext.SESSION_SCOPE
- PageContext.APPLICATION_SCOPE

You can pass these constants to *PageContext* methods that set and get attributes in the different scopes. For example, this code sets an object in session scope.

```
CustomContext myContext =
   new CustomContext("Penguin");
pageContext.setAttribute("Large Bird",
   myContext, PageContext.SESSION_SCOPE);
```

This code retrieves the object:

```
CustomContext myContext = (CustomContext)
   pageContext.getAttribute("Large Bird",
      PageContext.SESSION_SCOPE);
```

Table 4-11 lists the different *PageContext* methods that provide access to diverse scopes.

Method Signature	Use
Object getAttribute (String name)	Returns the named object from page scope
Object getAttribute (name, int scope)	Returns the named object from the given scope
Object findAttribute (String name)	Returns the named object, searching the different scopes in this order: page, request, session, and application
java.util.Enumeration getAttributeNamesInScope (int scope)	Returns all the named objects in a given scope
int getAttributesScope (String name)	Returns the constant representing the scope of the named object
void removeAttribute (String name)	Removes the named object from page scope

Table 4-11 Access to Multiple Scopes

Method Signature	Use
`void removeAttribute (String name, int scope)`	Removes the named object from the given scope
`void setAttribute(String name, Object object)`	Registers the named object in page scope
`void setAttribute(String name, Object object int scope)`	Registers the named object in the given scope

Table 4-11 Access to Multiple Scopes *(continued)*

Access to Implicit Objects

As we described, the *PageContext* object provides access to other implicit objects. Table 4-12 lists the *PageContext* methods that return other implicit objects.

Management of Nested Scope

The *PageContext* object also supports management of nested output streams within tag libraries. The idea is to provide temporary buffers at each tag nesting level for those tag libraries that process *tag bodies*. Tag bodies are the page fragments between open and close tags. (As we describe in Module 6, not all

Method Signature	Use
`javax.servlet.jsp.JspWriter getOut()`	Returns the current value of the *out* variable
`Exception getException()`	Returns the current value of the *exception* variable
`Object getPage()`	Returns the current value of the *page* variable (`this`)
`javax.servlet.ServletRequest` getRequest()	Returns the current value of the *request* variable
`javax.servlet.ServletResponse getResponse()`	Returns the current value of the *response* variable
`javax.servlet.http.HttpSession` getSession()	Returns the current value of the *session* variable
`javax.servlet.ServletConfig getServletConfig()`	Returns the current *config* variable
`javax.servlet.ServletContext getServletContext()`	Returns the current *application* variable

Table 4-12 Methods for Retrieving Other Implicit Objects

tag libraries care about tag bodies.) The Tomcat JSP container generates code to push the current *BodyContent* object (a subclass of *JspWriter*) onto a stack and create a new one for the new tag body. It assigns this new *BodyContent* object to the *out* variable. This way, you can safely manipulate the content between nested tags. Later, as control passes out of nesting levels, Tomcat pops the temporary *BodyContent* off the stack and updates the previous *BodyContent* (now reassigned to the *out* variable) with revised content.

Since the JSP container generates code for handling buffers in different scopes, you as a JSP developer should not need to use the *PageContext* methods that support this effort. Table 4-13 lists the method signatures.

Forward and Include

You can use the *PageContext* object to forward control to another JSP page. The following JSP fragment tests the value of a variable to decide where to forward control:

```
<% if (nextPage.equals("Page1"))
      pageContext.forward("Page1.jsp");
   else
      pageContext.forward("Page2.jsp");
%>
```

The *forward* method replaces the current page with the forwarded page. The *PageContext* object also supports inclusion of pages. The following code includes a JSP fragment in the current page:

```
<% pageContext.include("PageFragment.jsp");
```

Method Signature	Use
`javax.servlet.jsp.JspWriter popBody()`	Returns the previous *JspWriter* saved by the matching *pushBody*, and updates the value of the *out* variable in the page scope attribute namespace
`javax.servlet.jsp.tagext.BodyContent pushBody()`	Returns a new *BodyContent* object, saves the current *JspWriter*, and updates the value of the *out* variable in the page scope attribute namespace

Table 4-13 Methods for Managing Nested Scope

Finally, the *PageContext* object supports redirection of exceptions to error pages. Generally, the JSP container handles this automatically because the *_jspService* method in the generated servlet traps all exceptions and redirects handling of the exceptions to *pageContext.handlePageException*. Table 4-14 lists the relevant method signatures.

1-Minute Drill

- What is the source of the *pageContext* implicit object?
- What implicit objects can *pageContext* retrieve?
- What attribute scopes can the *pageContect* object manage?
- What methods does the *pageContext* variable provide to pass control to another JSP page?

The *session* Variable

The *session* variable refers to the *javax.servlet.http.HttpSession* object, which encapsulates all information pertaining to a client's session. As we explained in Module 1, HTTP is stateless by design. Servlets and JavaServer Pages enhance this stateless architecture by providing several mechanisms that support session tracking. These mechanisms, briefly explained in the sections that follow, allow multiple client requests to share the same server state information.

URL Rewriting

URL rewriting adds session data to the end of every URL path for every request that participates in a given session. The servlet container then extracts this session data from the URL and associates the request with the correct session.

Installing Cookies

Installing a cookie as a persistent file on the client machine is perhaps the most popular method for tracking client sessions. The servlet container sends a

---

- The *pageContext* variable is set using a factory method called within the *_jspService* method of the generated servlet.
- The *pageContext* object can retrieve all the other implicit objects, including the *request, response, session, application, out, config, page,* and *exception* variables.
- The *pageContext* can manage attributes in *page, request, session,* and *application* scope.
- The *pageContext* variable supports both *forward* and *include* methods.

Method Signature	Use
`void forward(String relativeUrlPath)`	Forwards control to a different page
`void include(String relativeUrlPath)`	Includes another JSP page in the current page
`void handlePageException (java.lang.Exception e)`	Directs exceptions to the error page specified by the errorPage attribute of the page directive

Table 4-14 Forward and Include Methods

cookie containing a session identification token to the client, and the client returns this cookie on each subsequent request to the server. The server interprets this cookie and associates the request with the correct session.

SSL Sessions

The Secure Sockets Layer technology, used in the HTTPS protocol, provides a one-time only *master key* based upon a digital certificate handshake. Servlets and JavaServer Pages use this key to maintain session identity, and to encrypt and decrypt messages.

Note

We address JSP security programming in Module 8.

session Services

The *session* variable provides access to a *javax.servlet.http.HttpSession* object when the JSP page participates in a session. A client must explicitly *join* a session to participate in session tracking. JSP pages do this by default. As we mentioned in Module 2, however, you can use the session attribute in the page directive to disable participation in client sessions. You should generally do this if your JSP page does not need session information. The *session* implicit variable has session scope. This means that any JSP page that participates in the same session has access to the same *session* implicit variable. It goes out of scope when the servlet container terminates the client session. You should synchronize access to the *session* object in a multithreaded environment because multiple request threads could modify it simultaneously. The *HttpSession* object provides the following services:

- Attribute binding
- Management of session timeouts

Attribute binding

A JSP page can bind any object as a session attribute. The *HttpSession* object stores all attributes under unique names that you provide using the methods *getAttribute* and *setAttribute*. Here's a sample JSP fragment that illustrates their usage.

```
<% Date day = new Date();
   session.setAttribute("Today", day);
%>
<% Date today = (Date)session.getAttribute("Today");
%>
```

The method *removeAttribute* unbinds an object from the session. The method *getAttributeNames* returns all attribute names associated with this session. Table 4-15 lists the relevant methods for managing attributes in session scope.

Management of Session Timeouts

In a servlet and JSP architecture, the only way to ensure that client sessions terminate is by using timeouts. This is because Web clients do not explicitly

Method Signature	Use
`Object getAttribute(String attributeName)`	Returns the object bound with the specified name in this session, or null if no object is bound under the name
`java.util.Enumeration getAttributeNames()`	Returns an enumeration of *String* objects containing the names of all the objects bound to this session
`void setAttribute(String name, Object value)`	Binds an object to this session, using the name specified. If an object of the same name is already bound to the session, that object is replaced
`void removeAttribute(String name)`	Removes the object bound with the specified name from this session

Table 4-15 Managing Attributes in *session*

inform the server when they become inactive. In order to clean client resources stored in the *HttpSession* object, the servlet container sets a timeout window. When the inactive period exceeds the window, the container invalidates the *HttpSession* object and unbinds all its attributes.

Tip

The default timeout period is vendor specific. Tomcat's default timeout period is 30 minutes. To determine the default timeout period of a JSP container, create and load a JSP page that has this expression: `<%=session.getMaxInactiveInterval()%>`.

The *getMaxInactiveInterval* method returns the current inactive interval for the session. You can use the *setMaxInactiveInternal* method to modify the current inactive interval. The convenience method *getLastAccessedTime* returns the last time the session was accessed before the current request.

Table 4-16 lists all the useful methods that can be invoked via the *session* implicit variable.

1-Minute Drill

- What are three different ways to manage session identity?
- How are session attributes different from request attributes?
- How does the servlet container remove session objects?

startPage.html
redirect.jsp
HN.html
SP.html
PT.html
errorName.html
errorChoice.html

Project 4-2: URL Redirection and URL Includes

This project illustrates how one can use implicit objects in a JSP page to redirect or include other resources specified by a URL. Similar to the previous project, this starts with a static HTML page that contains an HTML form requesting user input. Depending on the input, a different page is included in the response. If

---

- Three mechanisms to do session tracking are URL rewriting, cookies, and secure HTTP using Secure Sockets.
- Session attributes maintain state across multiple requests by the same client, whereas request attributes are available only for a particular request.
- The servlet container sets a timeout. When the time expires, it invalidates the session object and unbinds all the *session* object's attributes.

Method Signature	Use
`long getLastAccessedTime()`	Returns the last time the client sent a request associated with this session, as the number of milliseconds since the epoch (midnight January 1, 1970, GMT)
`void setMaxInactiveInterval (int interval)`	Specifies the time, in seconds, between client requests before the servlet container will invalidate this session
`int getMaxInactiveInterval()`	Returns the maximum time interval, in seconds, that the servlet container will keep this session open between client accesses
`void invalidate()`	Invalidates this session and unbinds any objects bound to it

Table 4-16 Methods for Managing Session Life Cycle

there is an error in the user input, control is redirected to one of two different error pages.

Step-by-Step

1. Download the files for this project from `http://www.osborne.com`.
2. Drop the files `startPage.html`, `HN.html`, `SP.html`, `PT.html`, `errorName.html`, and `errorChoice.html` into the directory `%TOMCAT_HOME%/webapps/Book`.
3. Examine `startPage.html`. The page illustrates a News Service that contains an HTML form that has two input elements. The first requests the user name. The second is a selection element that requests the news topic. Each option in the selection element in `startPage.html` contains one of the coded values HN, PT, or SP that specify the HTML file (`HN.html`, `PT.html`, or `SP.html`) to be included in the response. At the end of the page, there are two action buttons to RESET and SUBMIT the form. The submission of the form is handled by the JSP page `redirect.jsp`, which is what you will write.
4. Start the Tomcat JSP container (if it is not already running).
5. Load the URL: `http://localhost:8080/Book/startPage.html`. You should see a page as shown in Figure 4-4.

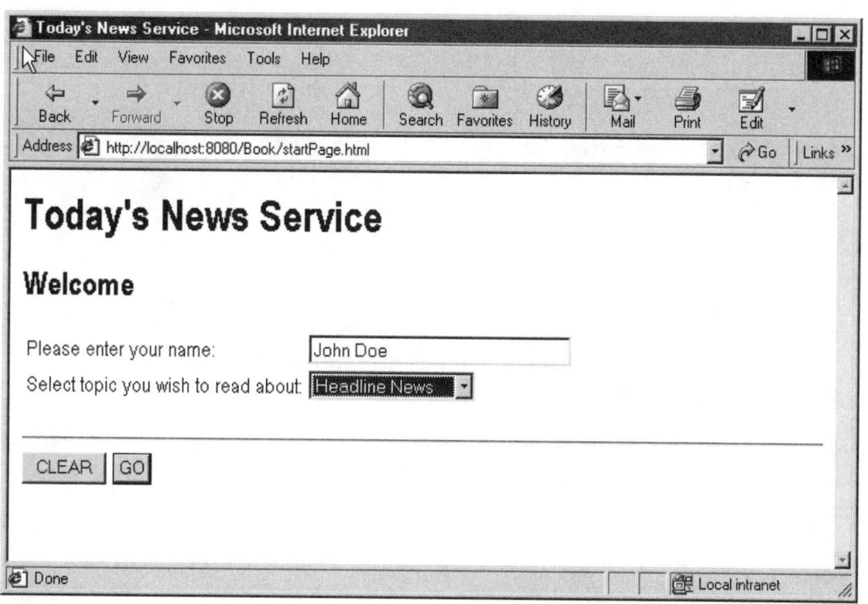

4

Figure 4-4 startPage.html

6. Create an empty file `redirect.jsp` under `%TOMCAT_HOME%/webapps/Book`.

7. The first thing to be done is to retrieve the user input. Enter the following JSP scriptlet that uses the request implicit object to retrieve the parameters of the submitted form—the user name and the topic selection.

```
<%
   String name = (String)request.getParameter("name");
   String choice = (String)request.getParameter("choice");
%>
```

8. Check the user input to see if there was any error. Two errors can happen: the user did not enter a name or the user did not make a topic selection. If the first error occurred, redirect the user to `errorName.html`. If the second error occurred, redirect the user to `errorChoice.html`. The following JSP scriptlet uses the *response* implicit object to perform these steps. Enter them in your JSP file.

```
<%
   if((name == null) || (name.length() == 0)) {
      response.sendRedirect("errorName.html");
   }
   else if(choice.equals("NONE")) {
      response.sendRedirect("errorChoice.html");
   }
%>
```

9. Remember that the URLs in the redirect calls are relative paths (they do not begin with a (/)). Hence, the HTML files `errorName.html` and `errorChoice.html` should reside in the same directory as `redirect.jsp` that we are currently working on.

10. Now that the error checking has been performed, print a standard welcome page for the user. A sample is shown here:

```
<h4> Hello <%= name %></h4>
Glad you could join us. Here's the news you requested.. <br>
<hr>
```

11. Use the *pageContext* implicit object to include the appropriate HTML file for the topic retrieved earlier. The JSP scriptlet that follows performs these steps. Enter it in your JSP file.

```
<%
   pageContext.include(choice + ".html");
%>
```

This project illustrates the use of methods in response and pageContext implicit objects to redirect or include resources from a JSP page. There are better ways than Java code in a JSP page to perform these operations, as we will see in the next module.

The *out* Variable

All data in a JSP page are written using the *javax.servlet.jsp.JspWriter* object that is referenced by the implicit variable *out*. *JspWriter* emulates the behavior of a *java.io.PrintWriter* except it throws *java.io.IOException* in all of its print methods whenever an I/O error occurs. If the JSP page is buffered (the default behavior), the *JspWriter* object also emulates a *java.io.BufferedWriter*. You enable or disable buffering using the buffer attribute in the page directive, as we described in Module 2. When buffering is enabled, there are two possible outcomes during a buffer overflow:

- It causes the buffer to be automatically flushed
- It causes a fatal error

The outcome is determined by the value of the autoFlush attribute in the page directive (as we described in Module 2).

The *out* variable is initialized and fetched from the *PageContext* object.

out Services

The two services provided by the *JspWriter* object are

- Managing response buffering
- Writing content

Let's look at each of them in detail.

Managing Response Buffering

A JSP page author can invoke the *clear* method to clear the contents of the buffer. This is similar to resetting the response stream to start from the beginning. This has the side effect of throwing an *IOException* if the response has already been committed. By contrast, an alternate method, *clearBuffer*, clears the *current* contents of the buffer and can be invoked even if content has already been committed to the client. The *out* variable also provides a *flush* method to explicitly write the current *JspWriter* buffer to the client. You can retrieve the current state of the buffer by using the *getRemaining* method. This method returns the number of bytes in the buffer. Table 4-17 lists the *out* variable's buffering methods.

Writing Content

The *JspWriter* object provides several methods to write content to the response buffer. *JspWriter* derives from *java.io.Writer*, which supplies a series of write methods. *JspWriter* itself supplies a series of *print* methods. For each *print* method, there is an equivalent *println* method that also inserts a line separator string after the requested data is printed into the response stream. The value of the

Method Signature	Use
`void clear()`	Clears the contents of the buffer
`void clearBuffer()`	Clears the current contents of the buffer
`void flush()`	Flushes the stream sending output to the client
`void close()`	Closes the stream, flushing it first
`int getBufferSize()`	Returns the size of the buffer in bytes
`int getRemaining()`	Returns the number of bytes unused in the buffer
`boolean isAutoFlush()`	Returns a boolean indicating whether this *JspWriter* is auto-flushing or throwing *IOExceptions* on buffer overflow conditions

Table 4-17 Buffering Methods Provided by the *out* Variable

line separator string is obtained from the system property `line.separator` and need not always be the single newline character (`\n`). One interesting print method prints any *Object* by retrieving the *String* produced by the *String.valueOf(Object)* method and writing it into the response stream.

Ask the Expert

Question: When would one use the implicit variable *out*? Can't you just use static text and JSP expressions?

Answer: The variable *out* can conveniently print to the response stream inside a JSP scriptlet without breaking the scriptlet. Consider this JSP code fragment:

```
<% /* For each category of expenses... */
   Iterator iter = splits.keySet().iterator();
   while(iter.hasNext()) {
      String cat = (String)iter.next();
      Total t = (Total)splits.get(cat);
      int percent = (int)((t.value()/grand_total) * 100);
%>
     <TR>
     <TD><%= cat %> (<%= percent %>%) </TD>
```

```
     <TD>    </TD>
<%-- Draw colored bar for this category. --%>
<%
     for (int i=0; i<100; i++) {
       if (i <= percent) {
%>
          <TD BGCOLOR="<%= colorForCategory(cat)
%>"> </TD>
<%
       } else {
%>
<%-- Fill with white spaces afterward --%>
          <TD BGCOLOR="white"> </TD>
<%
       }
     }
%>
     </TR>
<%-- Draw space between category bars --%>
     <TR><TD HEIGHT="5" colspan=101></TD></TR>
<%
   }
%>
```

This code fragment draws table rows and table cells in an HTML table with dynamic data. There are various conditional statements in between. This code is very hard to read, since there are HTML statements interspersed with Java code. Every time an HTML statement needs to be introduced, the current JSP scriptlet block needs to be closed and restarted after the HTML prints are complete. For situations like this, it might be better to use the *out* variable to print the HTML. Consider the same example, but this time we print the HTML statements using the *out* variable.

```
<% /* For each category of expenses... */
   Iterator iter = splits.keySet().iterator();
   while(iter.hasNext()) {
      String cat = (String)iter.next();
      /* Grab the total-expense for this category. */
      Total t = (Total)splits.get(cat);
      /* Calculate percentage for this category
         to the grand-total.
```

```
        */
        int percent = (int)((t.value()/grand_total) * 100);
        out.println("<TR>");
        out.println("<TD>" + cat + "(" + percent + ") </TD>");
        out.println("<TD>    </TD>");
        /* Draw colored bar for this category. */
        for (int i=0; i<100; i++) {
           if (i <= percent) {
               out.println("<TD BGCOLOR=" +
                      colorForCategory(cat) + "> </TD>");
        } else {
           /* Fill with white spaces afterward */
           out.println("<TD BGCOLOR=white> </TD>");

          }
       }
       out.println("</TR>");
       /* Draw space between category bars */
       out.println("<TR><TD HEIGHT=5 colspan=101></TD></TR>");
    }
%>
```

You might argue that the second version is itself hard to read, but it is certainly more readable than the first version. The second version has only one JSP scriptlet and all the Java code is bundled together, so code readability is slightly improved.

You might also use the *out* variable for debugging. In normal Java code, when you want to print an exception stack trace, you simply invoke the *printStackTrace* method on the exception. In a JSP development environment, the standard error stream will go to the JSP container console, if one exists. It doesn't show on your browser client as you might expect. If you want the exception to be visible to the browser client, you must invoke *printStackTrace* passing a *java.io.PrintWriter* argument. You obtain a *PrintWriter* by wrapping the *JspWriter* object with a *PrintWriter* as shown in this code fragment:

```
The exception stack trace is: <BR>
<PRE><% exception.printStackTrace(
      new java.io.PrintWriter(out));
%></PRE>
```

Table 4-18 lists some of the useful print methods in the *JspWriter* referenced by the out implicit variable.

- What is the difference between *out.clear* and *out.flush*?
- When should you use the *out* variable?

The *application* Variable

The *application* variable provides access to the *javax.serlvet.ServletContext* object. We mentioned the *ServletContext* in Module 2 when we described JSP scopes. We described how each Web application is rooted at a specific path within a Web server. In Project 2-1, you defined an application context for the Tomcat Web server by inserting the following lines into Tomcat's *server.xml* file:

```
<Context path="/Book"
   docBase="webapps/Book">
</Context>
```

These lines tell Tomcat to map all requests that start with /Book (the *context path*) to absolute paths starting at http://<server-host>/webapps/Book. In addition, Tomcat (and all other servlet containers) will route every servlet request mapped to this path to a single instance of *ServletContext*.

Note

The Servlet Specification, v.2.2, asserts that there can be only one instance of *ServletContext* per application within a single Java virtual machine (JVM). Web applications can be distributable (i.e., hosted on more than one physical machine, Web server, or JVM), and in such cases, more than one *ServletContext* will handle the same application context.

- The *clear* method purges all content written into the output buffer, while the *flush* method writes it to the client.
- The *out* variable can be useful in scriptlets and in support of debugging.

Method Signature	Use

`void print(boolean b)`
`void print(char c)`
`void print(int i)`
`void print(long l)`
`void print(float f)`
`void print(double d)`
`void print(char[] s)`
`void print(String s)`
	Prints the relevant variable's value to the output stream, converting the value into bytes according to the platform's default character encoding

`void print(Object obj)`	Prints an object. The string produced by the *String.valueOf(Object)* method is translated into bytes according to the platform's default character encoding

`void println(boolean x)`
`void println(char x)`
`void println(int x)`
`void println(long x)`
`void println(float x)`
`void println(double x)`
`void println(char[] x)`
`void println(String x)`
	Prints a relevant type to the output stream and then inserts a line separator string. The line separator string is defined by the system property line.separator, and is not necessarily a single newline character ('\n')

`void println(Object x)`	Prints an object and then inserts a new line

Table 4-18 Printing Methods Provided by the *out* Variable

Because all requests to a given application context share a single *ServletContext*, you can store application information in this object, which is accessible by every user from every servlet and JSP page in the context. You should always synchronize access to such information even if you set the isThreadSafe attribute in the page directive to be *false* in all your JavaServer pages. The isThreadSafe attribute only serializes access to a specific JSP page. It does not prevent simultaneous access by different JSP pages to objects stored in the application context.

application Services

The *ServletContext* object provides five services:

- Access to application initialization parameters
- Management of application context attributes

- Support for resource abstraction
- *RequestDispatcher* methods
- Utility methods

Access to Initialization Parameters

The *ServletContext* object (referenced by the *application* variable) provides access to application context attributes. This is useful for associating setup information with a given application. For example, you can use initialization parameters to provide a database hostname that every servlet client and JSP page can use to connect to a database and retrieve application data. You assign these parameters to servlets when you deploy them using a deployment tool or by modifying a configuration script. Tomcat uses the `web.xml` file in the `WEB-INF` directory under the application context directory for this purpose. For example, we could add a `host` initialization parameter to our `/Book` application context with the following lines:

```
<web-app>
   <context-param>
      <param-name>host</param-name>
      <param-value>madeline</param-value>
   </context-param>
</web-app>
```

You can access these initialization parameters in your JSP page using code similar to this:

```
<%@ page import="java.util.Enumeration" %>
<% Enumeration enum =
      application.getInitParameterNames();
   while (enum.hasMoreElements()) {
      String name = (String)enum.nextElement();
      String value = application.getInitParameter(name);
%>
      <%= name + ": " + value%><BR>
<% } %>
```

Table 4-19 lists the method signatures for accessing application context initialization parameters.

Method Signature	Use
`String getInitParameter (String name)`	Returns the value of a named initialization parameter
`java.util.Enumeration getInitParameterNames()`	Returns an enumeration of all the defined application initialization parameters

Table 4-19 Application Context Initialization Parameters

Management of Application Context Attributes

The *ServletContext* object also helps you cache and manage attributes with application scope. For example, suppose you build a *SecurityManager* class to track all active users and cache security attributes for each user. You should cache this object in application scope to ensure consistency and general availability. You can do this in a JSP page like this:

```
<% synchronized(SecurityManager.class) {
      SecurityManager secMgr = new SecurityManager();
      application.setAttribute("SecurityManager", secMgr);
   }
%>
```

Any other JSP page can then retrieve the *SecurityManager* object like this:

```
<% synchronized(SecurityManager.class) {
       SecurityManager secMgr = (SecurityManager)
               application.getAttribute("SecurityManager");
   }
%>
```

The ServletContext object also provides methods to remove attributes and to list all attribute names. Table 4-20 lists the method signatures for managing application attributes.

Support for Resource Abstraction

The *ServletContext* object supports direct access to Web resources in the static document hierarchy based upon a relative URL. You do this by using the *getResource* or *getResourceAsStream* method. This can be useful when you want

Method Signature	Use
`Object getAttribute(String name)`	Returns a named attribute from the *ServletContext*
`void setAttribute(String name, Object object)`	Sets a named attribute into the *ServletContext*
`java.util.Enumeration getAttributeNames()`	Returns an enumeration of all attributes stored in the *ServletContext*
`void removeAttribute(String name)`	Removes a named attribute from the *ServletContext*

Table 4-20 Managing Application Attributes

to read a resource and need to know its complete path. The idea seems to be to define an abstract interface to resources. This allows servlet and JSP container vendors to implement advanced search mechanisms similar to Java class loaders. Depending upon their goals, servlet and JSP container vendors could support reading URLs out of JAR files, or they could map the relative URLs you supply to another Web server, a database server, or an Enterprise JavaBeans service. Tomcat, however, simply appends the relative path to the context root for the application, much like the *getRealPath* method. The following code prints the same path using *getResource* and *getRealPath*:

```
<% URL url =
      application.getResource("/");
%>
getResource(lPATH): <%= url.getPath() %><BR>
getRealPath(lPATH): <%= application.getRealPath("/") %>
```

Rather than a *URL* object, the *getResourceAsStream* method returns an *InputStream* object for reading the content of the resource:

```
InputStream in = application.getResourceAsStream("/");
```

It functions as a handy shortcut for this code fragment:

```
<% URL url =  application.getResource("/");
   InputStream in = url.openStream();
%>
```

Table 4-21 lists the method signatures for managing resources.

Method Signature	Use
`java.net.URL getResource (String path)`	Provides an abstraction layer for retrieving application resources
`java.io.InputStream getResourceAsStream(String path)`	Opens an *InputStream* for reading a Web resource

Table 4-21 Managing Resources

RequestDispatcher Methods

The *RequestDispatcher* methods provide for the flow between servlets in a Web application. This is central to any significant Web application based on servlet and JavaServer Pages technology. Any given servlet can use a *RequestDispatcher* to redirect or forward control to another servlet, JSP page, or HTML page.

The *ServletContext* object provides two ways to get a *RequestDispatcher*, the *getNamedDispatcher* and *getRequestDispatcher* methods. Both methods wrap a *RequestDispatcher* object around a Web resource, the former around a named servlet, the latter around a relative URL.

You give a name to servlets when you deploy them. Tomcat requires you to do this in the `web.xml` file in the `WEB-INF` directory for the application context. We discuss `web.xml` in detail in Appendix C. These lines, for example, name the *snooper* servlet:

```
<servlet>
   <servlet-name>snooper</servlet-name>
   <servlet-class>SnoopServlet</servlet-class>
</servlet>
```

Once you name a servlet, JavaServer Pages can create a *RequestDispatcher* to forward the current request to the named servlet. The following JSP scriptlet forwards to the *snooper* servlet:

```
<% out.clear();
   RequestDispatcher rd =
      application.getNamedDispatcher("snooper");
   rd.forward(request, response);
%>
```

Notice that we clear the current contents of the output buffer prior to forwarding control to the snooper servlet. Care should be taken to ensure that the response is not committed and is empty before the *forward* method is called on the *RequestDispatcher*. A forward call after a committed response results in an *IllegalStateException*. The Servlet Specification, v2.2, states that if there is any output in the response buffer that has not been committed, it must be cleared prior to invoking the target servlet's *service* method.

Caution

We have noticed that Tomcat (version 3.2.1) does not clear the output of the response buffer prior to forwarding. In fact, it stacks the response and prints it after the output of the forwarded servlet is printed. A safe bet is to explicitly clear the output buffer prior to invoking the forward method.

You can use the *RequestDispatcher* to include resources rather than forwarding to them. The following JSP scriptlet includes the response of the snooper servlet inside the current JSP page.

```
<% out.flush();
   RequestDispatcher rd =
      application.getNamedDispatcher("snooper");
   rd.include(request, response);
%>
```

Notice that we flush the current contents of the output buffer prior to including the snooper servlet. The flush is necessary to ensure that the current contents of the output buffer shows up prior to the output from the snooper servlet. In contrast, we should clear the current contents of the output buffer if we did not want them in the output at all.

Caution

In Tomcat (version 3.2.1), if we did not include the flush, the effect is like stacking response buffers for the current JSP page and the snooper servlet. That is, the response buffer from the snooper servlet will appear in the browser output prior to that from our JSP page. The Servlet Specification, v2.2, does not state what the behavior should be in this situation. So, it is a good practice to flush or clear the output buffer prior to invoking the include method.

The second way to get a *RequestDispatcher* uses the *getRequestDispatcher* method, which identifies the Web resource via a URL path. Here is the code for this second approach:

```
<% out.clear();
   RequestDispatcher rd =
      application.getRequestDispatcher("/snooper");
   rd.forward(request, response);
%>
```

Notice that we call the *snooper* servlet using a path rather than its name. In Tomcat, the path can also be specified as a servlet mapping element in the `web.xml` file when the servlet is deployed. The following lines, for instance, register the URL to servlet mapping for snooper.

```
<servlet-mapping>
        <servlet-name> snooper </servlet-name>
        <url-pattern> /snooper </url-pattern>
</servlet-mapping>
```

You can use the *RequestDispatcher* returned by *getRequestDispatcher* to include Web resources into your JSP page. Here is an example:

```
<% out.flush();
   RequestDispatcher rd =
      application.getRequestDispatcher("/snooper");
   rd.include(request, response);
%>
```

When you include a resource, you can use the *out* variable both before and after the inclusion. This means the following code is legal:

```
<B>Hello!</B>
<% out.flush();
   RequestDispatcher rd =
      application.getRequestDispatcher("/snooper");
   rd.include(request, response);
%>
<B>Goodbye!</B>
```

The response buffer works differently depending upon whether you flush or clear before calling the *include* method. If you flush first, the JSP container writes existing output first, then the included content, then anything you write to the response buffer after the inclusion. If you clear the response buffer before doing your include, then the JSP container writes the included content, followed by anything you write after the inclusion. Table 4-22 lists the method signatures.

Utility Methods

The *ServletContext* object provides various utility methods. For example, it lets you log messages to the servlet log file. Tomcat's servlet log file, `servlet.log`, resides in `%TOMCAT_HOME%/logs/`. Here's how you log a message to this file:

```
<% application.log("test log message"); %>
```

This log results in the following log message:

```
2001-02-26 08:38:47 - path="/Book" :test log message
```

Notice that the log message includes the date, the application context, and the message itself. You can optionally log an exception with your message. By doing so, you cause a stack trace to be logged after your log message. Here's how you add a stack trace to the log message:

```
<% application.log("test log message",
                   new Exception("stack trace"));
%>
```

Table 4-23 lists the utility methods you might use.

Method Signature	**Use**
`javax.servlet.RequestDispatcher getNamedDispatcher(String name)`	Returns a *RequestDispatcher* identified by the given name
`javax.servlet.RequestDispatcher getRequestDispatcher(String path)`	Returns a *RequestDispatcher* identified by the given path within the scope of the *ServletContext*

Table 4-22 Request Dispatching Methods

Method Signature	Use
`void log(String message)`	Logs a message to the servlet log file
`void log(String message, Throwable throwable)`	Logs a message and a stack trace to the servlet log file
`String getMimeType (String file)`	Returns the MIME type of the specified file. For example, a text file will return `text/plain`. The MIME type is determined by the configuration of the servlet container and may be specified in a Web application deployment descriptor (`web.xml` file)
`String getRealPath(String virtualPath)`	Returns a *String* containing the real file system path for a given virtual path
`String getServerInfo()`	Returns a String containing information about the servlet container in which the servlet is running. This will include at least the container name and version number
`int getMajorVersion()`	Returns the major version of the Java servlet container. For containers supporting version 2.2, this method returns `2`
`int get MinerVersion()`	Returns the minor version of the Java servlet container. For containers supporting version 2.2, this method returns `2`

Table 4-23 Utility Methods

1-Minute Drill

- How does a JSP page retrieve application initialization values?
- How do you cache an object in application scope?
- What are the methods that the *application* object provides to retrieve a dispatcher?
- How do you log a message to the servlet log file?

- First, the JSP page calls *application.getInitParameterNames*. Then it calls *application.getInitParameter* for each parameter name.
- You cache an object in application scope by calling: *application.setAttribute.*
- The application implicit object provides *getNamedDispatcher* and *getRequestDispatcher.*
- You log a message to the servlet log file by calling: *application.log(String message)* or *application.log(String message, Throwable ex).*

The *config* Variable

The *config* variable provides access to the *javax.servlet.ServletConfig* object for a given servlet or JSP page. This object encapsulates initialization parameters as well as a couple of utility methods. The most interesting of these are the initialization parameters. You can provide initialization parameters to servlets and JavaServer Pages in the `web.xml` file for the application context.

Suppose you create a JSP page called `config.jsp` with this code fragment:

```
<% java.util.Enumeration e =
      config.getInitParameterNames();
   while (e.hasMoreElements()) {
      String paramName = (String)e.nextElement();
      String param =
         config.getInitParameter(paramName);
%>
      <BR>Parameter:  <%= paramName %>
         Value: <%= param %>
<% } %><BR>
```

You can assign this JSP page a logical name in the application context's `web.xml` file. The assignment might look like this:

```
<servlet>
   <servlet-name>config</servlet-name>
   <jsp-file>/jsp/config.jsp</jsp-file>
   <init-param>
      <param-name>host</param-name>
      <param-value>madeline</param-value>
   </init-param>
</servlet>
```

Here we assign our JSP page the logical name *config* and specify its relative URL. Then we start defining parameter name-value pairs. We complete the association with a `<servlet-mapping>` tag:

```
<servlet-mapping>
   <servlet-name>config</servlet-name>
   <url-pattern>/config</url-pattern>
</servlet-mapping>
```

In this web.xml fragment we specify that we will access the config JSP page using the URL /config. Now, when we access the JSP page we get this result:

Parameter: host Value: madeline

Table 4-24 lists the signatures for the *ServletConfig* object.

1-Minute Drill

- What is the primary use of the *config* variable?
- How do you name a JSP page?

The *page* Variable

The *page* variable is an implicit variable available in JSP scriptlets and expressions that corresponds to the instance of the JSP page's implementation class processing the current request. As we saw in Module 2, the JSP page implementation class is automatically generated when the JSP page is executed for the first time. When the scripting language is Java, the page variable is simply a synonym for the 'this' reference.

page Services

The page implicit variable provides two kinds of services:

- Contractual services
- Access to servlet information

Contractual Services

As we explained in Module 2, the page implementation class must implement the *javax.servlet.jsp.HttpJspPage* interface to satisfy the contract between the JSP container and the JSP page author. This interface mainly defines the contractual methods *jspInit*, *_jspService*, and *jspDestroy* that a JSP container would invoke. These methods are off-limits to the JSP page author.

- The primary use of the *config* variable is to retrieve initialization values for named JavaServer Pages.
- You name a JSP page the same way you name a Servlet. You name the JSP page in the application's web.xml file using a <servlet> element.

Method Signature	Use
`String getInitParameter (String name)`	Retrieve the name initialization parameter
`java.util.Enumeration getInitParameterNames()`	Retrieve an enumeration of all the initialization parameter names
`String getServletName()`	Retrieve the name of the current servlet or JSP page
`ServletContext getServletContext()`	Retrieve the servlet context for the current servlet or JSP page

Table 4-24 Methods Provided by the *config* Variable

4

Access to Servlet Information

The *HttpJspPage* interface extends *JspPage* that in turn extends *javax.servlet.Servlet* interface. This provides a couple of useful functions *getServletConfig* and *getServletInfo* that a JSP page author might invoke via the *page* implicit variable.

Table 4-25 shows these method signatures.

The page implicit variable is not typically used by JSP page authors.

The *exception* Variable

The *exception* variable provides access to exceptions inside error JSP pages declared using the errorPage attribute of the page directive (as we described in Module 2). The *_jspService* method traps exceptions thrown inside a JSP page, then redirects them either to a default page or to a declared error JSP page. The variable is not

Method Signature	Use
`javax.servlet.ServletConfig getServletConfig()`	Get the current *config* variable
`String getServletInfo()`	Returns information about the servlet, such as author, version, and copyright

Table 4-25 Useful Methods in page

available in any page that you do not declare to be an error page. A page is declared as an error page using the isErrorPage attribute of the page directive.

exception Services

Table 4-26 lists the methods available using the *exception* variable.

Method Signature	Use
`java.lang.String getLocalizedMessage()`	Creates a localized description of this Throwable
`java.lang.String getMessage()`	Returns the error message associated with this Throwable
`void printStackTrace()`	Prints the backtrace of the Throwable to the standard error stream
`void printStackTrace(java.io.PrintStream)`	Prints the backtrace to the specified print stream
`void printStackTrace(java.io.PrintWriter)`	Prints the backtrace to the specified print writer

Table 4-26 Useful Methods in exception

Mastery Check

1. List the implicit objects.

2. In what sense are the implicit objects implicit?

3. Which implicit object provides access to the application context? Which provides access to the request parameters?

4. Why does the JSP container provide a factory method to create the *pageContext* object?

5. Why cannot JavaServer Pages stream binary content?

6. How does a JSP page developer pass information from one request to another?

7. What are the different ways to pass control from one JSP page to another?

Mastery Check

8. What are some different ways to track sessions in servlets and JavaServer Pages?

9. Why would you want to track sessions in a JSP application?

10. What is the purpose of the *exception* implicit object?

Module 5

Standard Actions

The Goals of This Module

- Understand JSP actions
- Learn the standard actions
- Use standard actions effectively

In Modules 2 and 3, we described how to embed Java code in JavaServer Pages using JSP directives, declarations, expressions, and scriptlets. In Module 4, we described implicit objects, which give you direct access to Java servlet and JSP classes that you can use in declarations, expressions, and scriptlets. Some portray this ability to embed Java code in JavaServer Pages as their fundamental advantage over pure servlet programming when generating dynamic Web pages. We have already suggested, however, that complex applications that embed large segments of Java code in JavaServer Pages create code that is no less confusing than servlets that print large segments of static HTML. A monolithic mix of static HTML and Java in a JSP page is no better than a monolithic mix of Java and Java print statements in a servlet. A cleaner encapsulation of Web functionality in Web components is needed. JSP actions encourage such encapsulation by moving both static HTML and Java code out of the JSP page and replacing them with declarative tags.

JSP Actions

JSP actions associate code handlers with special JSP tags. These tags, based on the Extensible Markup Language (XML) specification, have two possible formats:

```
<prefix:tagName [attr="value"]* > tagBody </prefix:tagName>
<prefix:tagName [attr="value"]* />
```

The first format includes the start tag, zero or more tag attributes, a tag body, and an end tag that includes the prefix and tag name. The second format includes a start tag, zero or more tag attributes, and an end tag that is just the two-character sequence (/>). This second format is exactly equivalent to the first format with an empty tag body. When the JSP container encounters these special tags as it interprets a JSP page, it invokes the associated handler.

Standard Actions Versus Custom Actions

The JSP specification requires all conforming JSP containers to support a *standard* set of JSP actions as well as a mechanism for developing custom actions (tag libraries). We describe standard actions in this module and describe custom actions in Module 6. All standard actions use the reserved prefix "jsp." Table 5-1 lists the complete set of standard actions required by the JSP 1.1 specification.

Standard Actions	Description
<jsp:useBean>	Locates or instantiates a JavaBean with the specified name and scope
<jsp:setProperty>	Sets a property value or values in a JavaBean
<jsp:getProperty>	Gets the property value of a JavaBean
<jsp:include>	Includes a static file or sends a request to a dynamic file
<jsp:forward>	Forwards a client request to an HTML file, JSP file, or servlet for processing
<jsp:param>	Provides name/value information for other JSP actions
<jsp:plugin>	Downloads plug-in software to the browser and generates browser-specific tags to execute an applet or a bean
«<jsp:params>»	Used by «<jsp:plugin>» to encapsulate a list of «<jsp:action>» tags.
«<jsp:fallback>»	Used by «<jsp:plugin>» to supply an alternate HTML response when a plug-in fails to load.

Table 5-1 Standard Actions in JSP 1.1

Tag Attributes

The JSP container initializes actions using *tag attributes*. Tag attributes supply named values as arguments to the tag handler. All attributes are specified as name-value pairs using the assignment character (=) and enclosing the value in single (') or double (") quotes:

attribute-name="attribute-value" or

attribute-name='attribute-value'

Usually you specify values as some literal value or as a direction for some specific operation based upon the action type (such as instantiation of a Java object). For example, you might specify a name attribute like this:

```
name="myName"
```

In this case, you use the untranslated *String* value "myName" *as is*. You might specify a Java class to instantiate like this:

```
class="book.myBean"
```

In this case, the value "book.myBean" names a Java class to instantiate.

You can also specify some attributes using a JSP expression for the value. In Module 6, we describe how you enable and disable such attributes for custom actions. Here we list the standard actions that support such attributes. The general format is:

attribute-name="<%= *scriptlet-expr* %>" or

attribute-name='<%= *scriptlet-expr* %>'

Such attributes are distinguished by the ability to calculate their value at request time rather than page translation time.

You can use JSP expressions only for attribute values, not attribute names. When a JSP expression is the value of an attribute, it must appear in single or double quotes with no static text (including spaces) between the quotes and the expression. For example, the following use of the `<jsp:param>` action causes an error:

```
<jsp:param name="foo"
           value='  <%= request.getAttribute("bar") %>   ' />
```

The cause of the error is the extra space between the quotes and the JSP expression. Finally, an attribute value can take only a single JSP expression between the quote marks.

Table 5-2 shows the standard actions that support specification of values as JSP expressions.

The id Attribute

The `id="`*name*`"` attribute/value tuple has special meaning to conforming JSP containers. Two traits distinguish it from other attributes:

Action Type	**Attributes**
<jsp:setProperty>	value and beanName
<jsp:include>	page
<jsp:forward>	page
<jsp:param>	value

Table 5-2 Attributes of Standard Actions That Accept JSP Expressions

- You cannot use the same name for two different ids in the same translation unit (i.e., JSP page).
- The name is typically used to store a Java object that is accessible by that name using the *pageContext* variable, and to expose a variable by that name in the declaring scope.

For example, consider the <jsp:useBean> action. A typical use might look like this:

```
{
   <jsp:useBean id="shoppingCart" class="com.gb.shoppingCart" />
   <%= shoppingCart.getCustomerName() %>
}
```


The handler for this tag will create or find an object of the type identified by the class attribute and associate it with a Java variable *shoppingCart*. The first of the traits we mentioned would make the following code fragment illegal because it uses the same name for two distinct ids:

```
{
   <jsp:useBean id="shoppingCart" class="com.gb.shoppingCart" />
   <%= shoppingCart.getCustomerName() %>
   <jsp:useBean id="shoppingCart" class="com.gb.avancedShoppingCart" />
}
```

The second trait means that even after the variable *shoppingCart* goes out of scope (after the close brace), the object still exists and can be retrieved using the *pageContext* variable.

The scope Attribute

The scope attribute also has a special meaning to conforming JSP containers. Recall that JavaServer Pages can participate in four different scopes and life cycles:

- **Page** Accessible from and sharing the life cycle of the *PageContext* object
- **Request** Accessible from and sharing the life cycle of the *HttpServletRequest* object
- **Session** Accessible from and sharing the life cycle of the *HttpSession* object

- **Application** Accessible from and sharing the life cycle of the *ServletContext* object

When you use the `scope="page|request|session|application"` attribute/value tuple in conjunction with the `id` attribute, you associate a namespace and life cycle with the object having the specified id.

1-Minute Drill

- What is a JSP action?
- What types of actions does the JSP 1.1 specification support?
- What is the purpose of tag attributes?
- What tag attributes have a special meaning to the JSP container?

The <jsp:useBean> Action

One way to move most Java processing out of the JSP page is to encapsulate it in a JavaBean. A `<jsp:useBean>` action associates a JavaBean instance in a given scope with an id and a scripting variable sharing the same id. Its basic operation is to first seek an existing object using the id and scope; if it cannot find an object with the specified id in the specified scope, it attempts to create a new instance using the other attributes.

By moving the Java processing out of the JSP page itself and into a JavaBean, you also make it possible to reuse this functionality in other JSP pages. You can do this by using the `<jsp:useBean>` action to supply a local name to an object originally defined elsewhere.

There are two variants of the `<jsp:useBean>` action. If the `<jsp:useBean>` tag has no body, its syntax is:

```
<jsp:useBean id="name"
scope="page|request|session|application"
                                        typeSpec />
```

- A JSP action associates a Java handler with an XML tag. The JSP container invokes the handler when it processes the tag.
- The JSP 1.1 specification supports standard and custom tags. Standard tags all use the "jsp" prefix.
- Tag attributes initialize and supply arguments to the tag handler.
- The id and scope attributes have a special meaning to the JSP container.

```
typeSpec ::= class="className" |
             class="className" type="typeName" |
             beanName="beanName" type="typeName" |
             type="typeName"
```

The <jsp:useBean> action can also include a *tag body*. For example, you might want to insert the <jsp:setProperty> action to initialize the JavaBean. If the tag has a body, its syntax is:

```
<jsp:useBean id="name"
             scope="page|request|session|application"
            typeSpec >

             tagBody
</jsp:useBean>
```

5

Attributes and Usage Rules

Table 5-3 lists the set of attributes that you can supply to the <jsp:useBean> tag.

Processing Steps

The <jsp:useBean> action follows these steps:

Attribute	Usage Rules
id	The name of the object instance and the name of the scripting (Java) variable referring to the object. The name is case sensitive
scope	The scope of the object. The default is `page` scope
class	The fully qualified name of the (Java) class that defines the implementation of the JavaBean. If the `type` attribute is not specified, the `class` attribute must be specified. If the `beanName` attribute is specified, you cannot specify the `class` attribute
beanName	The name of the JavaBean as required by `java.beans.Beans.instantiate()`. That is, it must be of the form "a.b.c" or the form "a/b/c.ser." If the `class` attribute is specified, you cannot specify the `beanName` attribute
type	The type of scripting variable. This can be the same as the object, a superclass of the object or a Java interface implemented by the object. If the `class` attribute is not specified, the `type` attribute must be specified

Table 5-3 Attributes of the <jsp:useBean> Action

1. Search for an existing object with the given id and scope.
2. Define a Java variable using the given id in the current Java scope with the specified `type`, if given, or the specified class, if type is not specified.
3. If the object is found, initialize a Java variable in the current Java scope as a reference to the object. Cast the reference as specified by the type attribute if supplied, or according to the class attribute, if type is not supplied. If the cast fails, throw a *ClassCastException*. Ignore any tag body. This completes processing for the current tag.
4. If an object with the specified id and scope is not found and neither the `class` nor `beanName` attributes were specified, throw an *InstantiationException*. This completes processing for the current tag.
5. If an object with the specified id and scope is not found, and the class attribute was provided, attempt to instantiate the specified class. (The Tomcat JSP container uses the *java.beans.Beans.instantiate* method to do this.) The class cannot be abstract and must define a public, no-args constructor (i.e., a constructor with an empty argument list). If the instantiation succeeds, define a scripting variable referring to the object in the specified scope using the specified id. Proceed to step 7. If the instantiation fails, throw an *InstantiationException*.
6. If an object with the specified id and scope is not found, and the beanName attribute was provided, then invoke the *java.beans.Beans.instantiate* method, passing the *ClassLoader* used by the servlet and the beanName attribute as arguments. If the method succeeds, define a scripting variable referring to the object in the specified scope using the specified id. Proceed to step 7. If the instantiation fails, throw an *InstantiationException*.
7. If the `<jsp:useBean>` element has a nonempty tag body, process the body. The scripting variable is available within the scope of the body. Template text (static text and HTML), scriptlets, and actions are evaluated. This completes processing for the current tag.

Figure 5-1 shows a flow chart of this process.

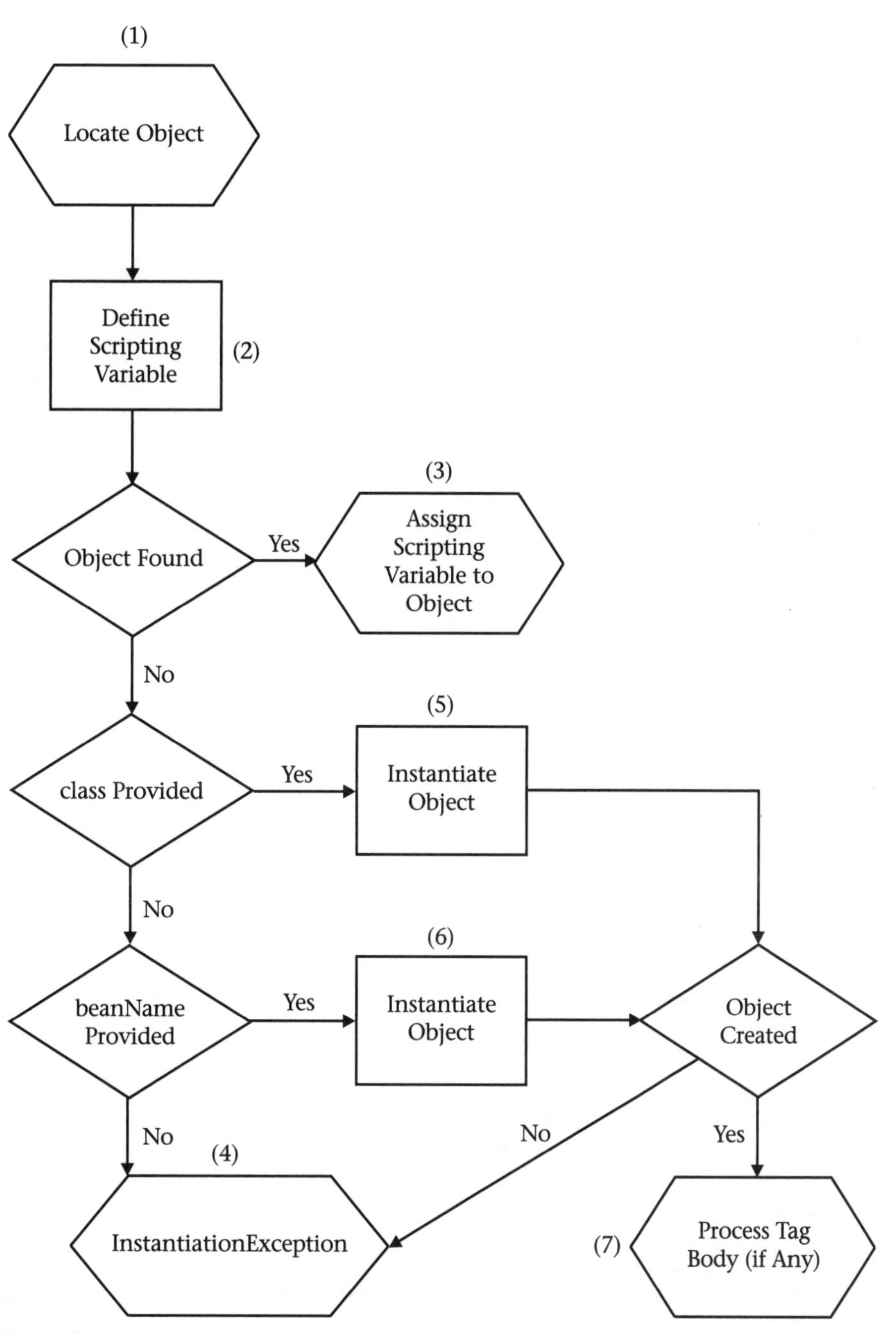

Figure 5-1 <jsp:useBean> process flow chart

Using <jsp:useBean>

Suppose you define a JavaBean called "HelperBean." Here is the code for the *HelperBean* class:

```
public class HelperBean {
   private int intProperty = -1;
   private String stringProperty = null;

   public HelperBean() {}

   public void setIntProperty(int value) {
      intProperty = value;
   }

   public int getIntProperty() {
      return intProperty;
   }

   public void setStringProperty(String value) {
      stringProperty = value;
   }

   public String getStringProperty() {
      return stringProperty;
   }
}
```

Next, suppose you want to use this class in a JSP page. Here's sample code to set and get properties from *HelperBean*:

```
<%-- import HelperBean class --%>
<%@ page import="HelperBean" %>

<%-- declare HelperBean --%>
<jsp:useBean id="myHelperBean"
             class="HelperBean" >
</jsp:useBean>

<%-- use property setter methods in JSP scriptlets --%>
<% myHelperBean.setIntProperty(25);
   myHelperBean.setStringProperty("Hello!");
```

```
%>

<%-- use property getter methods in JSP expressions --%>
Value of int property is:
   <%= myHelperBean.getIntProperty() %><BR>
Value of string property is:
   <%= myHelperBean.getStringProperty() %>
```

Tip

Notice that in Tomcat you must first use a page directive to import the Java class implementing *HelperBean*. The specification does not require this import using a page directive, but Tomcat does.

5

Now suppose you want to use this object in another JSP page or another client request. You can store this object in session (also request or application) scope using the scope attribute like this:

```
<%-- declare HelperBean --%>
<jsp:useBean id="myHelperBean"
             class="HelperBean"
             scope="session">
</jsp:useBean>
```

Then you can retrieve the object from any other page and assign it to a local variable using the `<jsp:useBean>` action again:

```
<jsp:useBean id="myHelperBean"
             type="HelperBean"
             scope="session" >
</jsp:useBean>
```

Then you can call methods on the object using the local reference:

```
<%-- use property getter methods in JSP expressions --%>
Value of int property is:
   <%= myHelperBean.getIntProperty() %><BR>
Value of string property is:
   <%= myHelperBean.getStringProperty() %>
```

Notice that the attribute name used for creating the object using the original `<jsp:useBean>` action must match the id name specified in the second `<jsp:useBean>` tag.

Finally, suppose the *HelperBean* class implements an interface, say the *StringProperty* interface, that might look like this:

```
public interface StringProperty {
   public String getStringProperty();
}
```

Since you can assign an object to any interface declaration that it implements, you could then retrieve the stored object like this:

```
<jsp:useBean id="myHelperBean"
             scope="session"
             type="StringProperty" >
</jsp:useBean>
```

If you did so, though, you could use only the *getStringProperty* method, since the *getIntProperty* method is not declared in the *StringProperty* interface.

Ask the Expert

Question: **Why would you want to declare a type attribute for `<jsp:useBean>` that is not the same class as the JavaBean?**

Answer: A universally acknowledged principle of good software design is to keep implementation details as private as possible. This is an aspect of what is sometimes called *information hiding*. When you define an interface for a helper JavaBean and require clients of the bean to interact with the interface, you isolate the client from any specific implementation of the interface—you hide the details of the implementation. By enforcing such a software contract with an interface definition, your implementation can change or your JSP page can use multiple different implementations based upon request-time conditions, without requiring changes or custom coding in the JSP page.

1-Minute Drill

- What is the purpose of the <jsp:useBean> action?
- What are the forms of the <jsp:useBean> tag?
- Does the <jsp:useBean> action always create an instance of the desired bean?

The <jsp:setProperty> Action

5

The <jsp:setProperty> action sets the values of properties in JavaBeans. Normally you define these beans using the <jsp:useBean> action. For example, you can define a *HelperBean* instance just as we did in the previous section:

```
<%-- import HelperBean class --%>
<%@ page import="HelperBean" %>

<%-- declare HelperBean --%>
<jsp:useBean id="myHelperBean"
             class="HelperBean" >
</jsp:useBean>
```

Then you can set the *intProperty* value on this *HelperBean* instance like this:

```
<%-- Set property on JavaBean --%>
<jsp:setProperty name="myHelperBean"
                 property="intProperty"
                 value="42"
/>
```

The JSP container uses standard Java introspection to discover properties, property names, property types, and the getter and setter methods. The use of Java introspection means that naming conventions are critical. If you specify a property name as “intProperty,” the JavaBean must support a property setter method named “setIntProperty.”

- The <jsp:useBean> action associates a JavaBean with a scripting variable, an id, and a JSP scope.
- The <jsp:useBean> tag can be used with or without a tag body.
- No. The <jsp:useBean> action can be used to provide a local name and scripting variable for a bean instance created earlier, possibly in a different JSP page.

The syntax of the `<jsp:setProperty>` tag is:

```
<jsp:setProperty name="beanName" propExpr />

propExpr::= property="*"|
        property="propertyName"|
        property="propertyName"param="parameterName" |
        property="propertyName"value="propertyValue"|
propertyValue::= string | JSP expression
```

Attributes and Usage Rules

Table 5-4 lists the set of attributes that you can supply to the `<jsp:setProperty>` tag.

Ask the Expert

Question: Must you use a **`<jsp:useBean>`** action to define the JavaBean denoted by the **`<jsp:setProperty>`** tag?

Answer: The JSP 1.1 specification suggests this, but the Tomcat JSP container implementation does not enforce it. Tomcat requires only that the named bean instance be present as an attribute of the *PageContext* object. In other words, using Tomcat, you can use the `<jsp:setProperty>` tag to set properties on any JavaBean stored in the current *PageContext* object. For example, the following code has the same effect as using the `<jsp:useBean>` action:

```
<%-- import HelperBean class --%>
<%@ page import="HelperBean" %>

<%-- Create JavaBean and store in PageContext --%>
<% HelperBean myHelperBean = new HelperBean();
   pageContext.setAttribute("myHelperBean", myHelperBean);
%>

<%-- Set property on JavaBean --%>
<jsp:setProperty name="myHelperBean"
                 property="intProperty"
                 value="42"
/>
```

Attribute	Usage Rules
name	The name of the JavaBean instance as defined by a `<jsp:useBean>` tag. The bean instance must contain the property, and you must declare the bean using a `<jsp:useBean>` tag prior to setting any properties
property	The name of the bean property whose value you want to set
param	The name of the HTTP request parameter whose value you want to assign to a bean property
value	The value to assign to a specified property. This value can be either a *String* constant or a request-time JSP expression

Table 5-4 Attributes of the <jsp:setProperty> Action

The Two Variants of <jsp:setProperty>

The `<jsp:setProperty>` action has two variants, the first assigning values from HTTP request parameters, the second assigning values directly using *String* constants or JSP expressions.

Assigning Property Values Using HTTP Request Parameters

Usually request parameters come from a Web form. Consider the following simple HTML form that sets two parameters named "intProperty" and "stringProperty":

```
<FORM METHOD=GET ACTION="/Book/jsp/setProperty.jsp">
    Integer Property: <INPUT TYPE=TEXT NAME="intProperty"><BR>
    String Property: <INPUT TYPE=TEXT NAME="stringProperty"><BR><BR>
    <INPUT TYPE=SUBMIT>
</FORM>
```

Figure 5-2 shows how this form looks in a Web page.

You can assign the two request parameters to a JavaBean with a single use of the `<jsp:setProperty>` tag:

```
<jsp:setProperty name="myHelperBean"
                 property="*"
/>
```

When you set the property name to an asterisk (`*`), the tag iterates over the current *HttpServletRequest* parameters, matching parameter names and values to property setter names and value types. Since in this case you do not specify

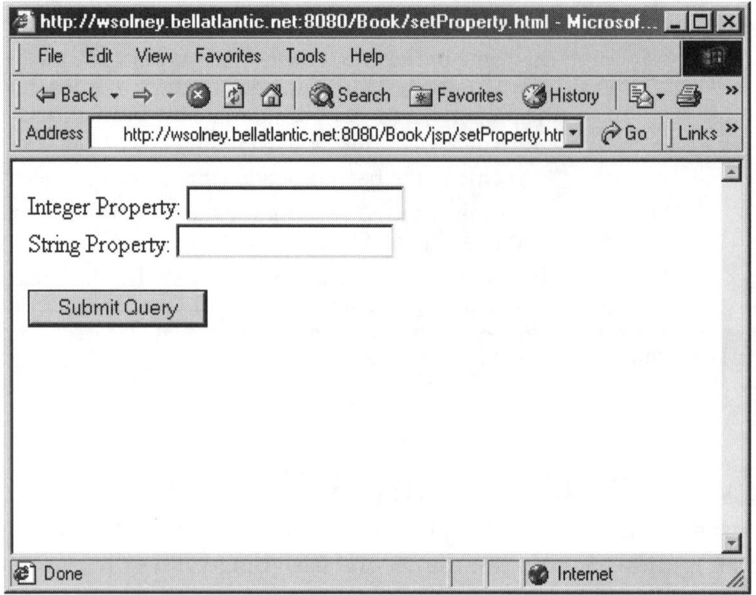

Figure 5-2 Simple form that sets two request parameters

parameter names, the tag assumes that parameter names match property names, and uses Java introspection to assign values. This means if the parameter name is "intProperty," the JavaBean must have a *setIntProperty* method.

Caution

In Tomcat, if the value of a request parameter is the empty string (" "), the property setter is not called. This has the unfortunate side-effect that you cannot set a text field in an HTML form back to a blank value when you use (`*`) as the property name with `<jsp:setProperty>`.

You can also set property values individually. The following lines set each property in the *HelperBean* instance:

```
<jsp:setProperty name="myHelperBean" property="intProperty" />
<jsp:setProperty name="myHelperBean" property="stringProperty" />
```

When you do not specify the parameter name, the tag assumes that the parameter name is the same as the property name. You can also specify the parameter name like this:

```
<jsp:setProperty name="myHelperBean"
                 property="intProperty"
                 param="intProperty"
/>
<jsp:setProperty name="myHelperBean"
                 property="stringProperty"
                 param="stringProperty"
/>
```

Although these lines specify the same param and property names, when you specify the parameter name it can differ from the property name.

The only type of values you can assign from request parameters are those that can be converted from *String* literals. Table 5-5 shows the legal assignments.

Assigning Property Values Using String Constants and JSP Expressions

Besides assigning values using HTTP request parameters, you can use the `<jsp:setProperty>`action to assign *String* constants or JSP expression results to JavaBean properties. As with request parameters, the only legal assignments using *String* constants are those specified in Table 5-5. Here are some examples using *String* constants to assign values to the *HelperBean* instance:

```
<%-- Assign integer property --%>
<jsp:setProperty name="myHelperBean"
                 property="intProperty"
                 value="22"
/>

<%-- Assign String property --%>
<jsp:setProperty name=myHelperBean"
```

Property Type	**Conversion from String Value**
`boolean` or `Boolean`	`Boolean.valueOf(`*String*`)`
`byte` or `Byte`	`Byte.valueOf(`*String*`)`
`char` or `Character`	`Character.valueOf(`*String*`)`
`double` or `Double`	`Double.valueOf(`*String*`)`
`int` or `Integer`	`Integer.valueOf(`*String*`)`
`float` or `Float`	`Float.valueOf(`*String*`)`
`long` or `Long`	`Long.valueOf(`*String*`)`
`String`	`String`

Table 5-5 Legal Property Assignments from HTTP Request Parameters

```
                   property="stringProperty"
                   value="Hello"
/>
```

The ability to assign the results of JSP expressions to properties adds two powerful features to the `<jsp:setProperty>` action:

- The ability to calculate values at request time
- The ability to assign any Java type to properties

For example, suppose we want to assign the current date and time to a property. If you add a new string property to our *HelperBean*, then you can calculate and store the current date and time as a *String* like this:

```
<jsp:setProperty name="myHelperBean"
                 property="stringDate"
                 value='<%= new Date().toString() %>'
/>
```

You can also store the current date and time as a *java.util.Date* object. You simply add a *Date* property to the *HelperBean* instance, then set its value like this:

```
<jsp:setProperty name="myHelperBean"
                 property="currentDate"
                 value='<%= new Date() %>'
/>
```

The <jsp:getProperty> Action

Corresponding to the `<jsp:setProperty>` action that sets properties on a JavaBean, the `<jsp:getProperty>` action gets properties from a JavaBean, converts them to a *String*, and places them in the output buffer. The conversion to a *String* works just as it does in JSP expressions. This means the tag calls the *toString* method on object types and directly converts primitive types. The syntax of the `<jsp:getProperty>` action is:

```
<jsp:getProperty name="name"
property="propertyName" />
```

Attributes and Usage Rules

Table 5-6 lists the attributes of the `<jsp:getProperty>` tag.

Attribute	Usage Rules
`name`	The name of the JavaBean instance as defined by a `<jsp:useBean>` tag. The bean instance must contain the property, and you must declare the bean using a `<jsp:useBean>` tag prior to setting any properties
`property`	The name of the bean property whose value you want to print

Table 5-6 Attributes of the <jsp:getProperty> Action

Using <jsp:getProperty>

The `<jsp:getProperty>` action functions as an alternative to calling a property getter inside a JSP expression. For example, the following two JSP fragments have equivalent results:

```
The value of intProperty is: <%= myHelperBean.getIntProperty() %><BR>
The value of stringProperty is: <%= myHelperBean.getStringProperty() %><BR>
```

and:

```
The value of intProperty is:
   <jsp:getProperty name="myHelperBean" property="intProperty"/><BR>
The value of stringProperty is:
   <jsp:getProperty name="myHelperBean" property="stringProperty"/><BR>
```

Ask the Expert

Question: There doesn't seem to be much difference between using `<jsp:getProperty>` and using a JSP expression. Why would I use `<jsp:getProperty>`?

Answer: The easiest answer is that `<jsp:getProperty>` requires no knowledge of Java. Page designers can use standard actions like `<jsp:useBean>`, `<jsp:setProperty>`, and `<jsp:getProperty>` without understanding Java and Java properties. This answer is weak, however, since JSP/XML syntax can get as complicated as Java syntax.

A better reason down the road is that the tags are theoretically language independent. The JSP specification anticipates other JSP scripting languages than Java.

1-Minute Drill

- What role do the `<jsp:setProperty>` and `<jsp:getProperty>` actions play?
- Why would you use the `<jsp:setProperty>` and `<jsp:getProperty>` actions rather than just use JSP scripting elements?

The <jsp:include> Action

The `<jsp:include>` action lets you include static HTML, the output from servlets and the output from other JavaServer Pages into the current JSP page. You specify these resources using a relative URL such as those we described in Module 2. An included JSP page can write to the *JspWriter* object (*out*) but cannot set headers or call any methods that affect response headers (the same constraints as those imposed on servlets included using a *RequestDispatcher* object). For example, you cannot call methods like *setCookie*.

If the page output is buffered then the output buffer is flushed prior to the inclusion of the resource. Request processing resumes in the calling JSP page after processing of the included resource.

The `<jsp:include>` action has two forms. The simplest form does not set any parameters prior to the inclusion. Its syntax is:

```
<jsp:include page="relativeURL" flush="true" />
```

The more complex form supports setting of parameters using the `<jsp:param>` action (which we describe later in this module). Its syntax is:

```
<jsp:include page="relativeURL" flush="true" >
      [<jsp:param ... /> ]*
</jsp:include>
```

Both forms require use of the flush attribute, even though the JSP 1.1 specification supports only `true` as the value for this attribute.

Note

The JSP 1.2 specification removes this restriction.

- The `<jsp:setProperty>` and `<jsp:getProperty>` actions manage setting and getting properties on JavaBean instances created and declared using `<jsp:useBean>`.
- The `<jsp:setProperty>` and `<jsp:getProperty>` actions require no knowledge of Java.

Question: Is there any relation between the *pageContext.include* method and the `<jsp:include>` action?

Answer: Yes, they have the same semantics and constraints. The Tomcat JSP container implements the `<jsp:include>` action by generating a call to *pageContext.include*.

Attributes and Usage Rules

Table 5-7 lists the attributes of the `<jsp:include>` tag.

5

Using <jsp:include>

The `<jsp:include>` action provides a simple way to decompose large JavaServer Pages into smaller pieces. Such decomposition provides several advantages, among them the ability to create layout templates for Web sites. To illustrate, you can define a page template using HTML tables where a `<jsp:include>` action provides the contents for each cell. Consider this simple example:

```
<TABLE BORDER="2">
    <TR><TD> <jsp:include page="Cell1.jsp" flush="true" />
    </TD></TR>
    <TR><TD> <jsp:include page="Cell2.jsp" flush="true" />
    </TD></TR>
</TABLE>
```

This use of the `<jsp:include>` action works but provides few advantages over embedding URLs directly into the table definition. Consider an alternate implementation of the template that takes advantage of the ability

Attribute	Usage Rules
`page`	A relative URL specifying the resource to include. The URL can be calculated as the result of a JSP expression
`flush`	Mandatory attribute with a value of `true` in JSP 1.1

Table 5-7 Attributes of the <jsp:include> Action

of the <jsp:include> action to calculate the value of the page attribute at request time:

```
<TABLE BORDER="2">
   <TR><TD>
   <jsp:include
         page='<%= request.getParameter("Cell1") %>'
         flush="true" />
   </TD></TR>
   <TR><TD>
   <jsp:include
         page='<%= request.getParameter("Cell2") %>'
         flush="true" />
   </TD></TR>
</TABLE>
```

With this new implementation of the table template, you can create pages that simply define the values of *Cell1* and *Cell2*, then include the template. Each such page reuses the same template code. For example, you can create a JSP page that does exactly what our first example did:

```
<jsp:include page="pageTemplate.jsp" flush="true" >
     <jsp:param name="Cell1" value="Cell1.jsp" />
     <jsp:param name="Cell2" value="Cell2.jsp" />
</jsp:include>
```

The difference is that in our second example any JSP page can reuse the template simply by specifying values for the request parameters.

Tip

Notice that we used the <jsp:param> action to define the values of the *Cell1* and *Cell2* variables. This action adds these parameters to the request parameters of the included JSP page. That is why we could use the *request* implicit object to retrieve their values.

The <jsp:forward> Action

A <jsp:forward> action provides for the runtime dispatch of the current request to a static HTML page, a servlet or another JSP page. Unlike a <jsp:include> action, it terminates the execution of the current page.

The *request* object is adjusted according to the value of the page attribute used in the <jsp:forward> action. The original request parameters get passed to the new resource. You can add additional parameters using the <jsp:param> action. The action has two forms. If no parameters are added using the <jsp:param> action, the syntax is

```
<jsp:forward page="relativeURL" />
```

If you add parameters, the syntax is

```
<jsp:forward page="relativeURL" >
      [<jsp:param ... /> ]*
</jsp:forward>
```


Attributes and Usage Rules

Table 5-8 lists the attributes of the <jsp:forward> tag.

Using <jsp:forward>

Why use this action since it seems to just send you to another page with nothing written to the output buffer? In fact, if you try to write anything out and the page is either unbuffered or flushed prior to executing the <jsp:forward> action, the JSP container will throw an *IllegalStateException*.

One reason to use it is to separate processing activity from display activity. You can calculate parameter values in the first JSP page, then forward to a new page that displays content based on these calculated parameters.

1-Minute Drill

- What is the difference in processing scope between <jsp:include> and <jsp:forward>?
- Can you write out content prior to use of the <jsp:include> action?
- Can you write out content prior to use of the <jsp:forward> action?

- The <jsp:include> action returns processing back to the calling JSP page; the <jsp:forward> action does not.
- Yes. You can flush output to the response buffer both before and after use of the <jsp:include> action.
- No. The <jsp:forward> action will throw an *IllegalStateException* if you try to write to the response buffer prior to its use.

Attribute	Usage Rules
page	A relative URL specifying the resource to forward to. The URL can be calculated as the result of a JSP expression

Table 5-8 Attributes of the <jsp:forward> Action

The <jsp:param> Action

The `<jsp:param>` action provides name/value information. We have already showed its use in the `<jsp:include>` and `<jsp:forward>` actions. It can also be used in the `<jsp:plugin>` action. When used with `<jsp:include>` or `<jsp:forward>`, the included or forwarded page sees the original *request* object augmented by the new parameters. The `<jsp:param>` action has no effect when used independently of these other actions.

If you specify new values for existing parameter names, the newer values take precedence. The only value types you can specify with the `<jsp:param>` action are those listed in Table 5-5. You can calculate these values using a JSP expression.

The scope of the new parameters is the `<jsp:include>` or `<jsp:forward>` action. In other words, in the case of the `<jsp:include>` action, the new parameters do not apply when the include returns.

The syntax of the `<jsp:param>`action is:

```
<jsp:param name="name" value="value" />
```

Attributes and Usage Rules

Table 5-9 lists the attributes of the `<jsp:param>` tag.

Attribute	Usage Rules
name	The parameter name
value	The parameter value

Table 5-9 Attributes of the <jsp:param> Action

CartItem.java
header.html
footer.html
ShoppingCart.jsp
ShoppingCartTemplate.jsp
ResultPage.jsp

Project 5-1: A Simple Shopping Cart

This project shows you how to build some elements of an online shopping cart using several of the JSP actions we have described. The pages display a list of grocery items and calculate the cost of the items you select.

Step-by-Step

1. Download the files for this project from `http://www.osborne.com`.

2. Compile the file `CartItem.java`.

3. Move the class file created in step 2 into `%TOMCAT_HOME%/webapps/Book/WEB-INF/classes`.

4. Examine `CartItem.java`. Its purpose is to store an item's name, the count of the item purchased, and the price of the item.

5. Move the downloaded JSP and HTML files into `%TOMCAT_HOME%/webapps/Book/jsp`.

6. Examine `ShoppingCartTemplate.jsp`. This JSP page provides a standard format for `ShoppingCart.jsp` and `ResultPage.jsp`. The format consists of a header page, a table of shopping cart items, and a standard footer.

7. It first imports the Java class `CartItem`:

```
<%@ page import="CartItem" %>
```

8. Then it uses the `<jsp:include>` action to insert a standard header, `header.html`:

```
<%-- include header --%>
<jsp:include page='<%= request.getParameter("header") %>'
             flush="true" />
```

9. Next it inserts a table of shopping cart items. It uses request parameters to supply values for the table caption and the form action. It retrieves cart items from the *session* variable (*HttpSession*).

```
<%-- insert table caption --%>
<CENTER><H2><%= request.getParameter("tableCaption") %></H2>

<%-- create an HTML form including a table of items --%>
<FORM METHOD="post" ACTION='<%= request.getParameter("action") %>' >
<TABLE WIDTH=450 CELLSPACING="0" CELLPADDING="0" BORDER="1">
```

5

```
<%-- the first row is the table headings --%>
<TR>
    <TD WIDTH=5% BGCOLOR="#ECA613"> <B>SKU#</B></TD>
    <TD BGCOLOR="#ECA613"> <B>Item Name</B></TD>
    <TD WIDTH=5% ALIGN=center BGCOLOR="#ECA613" > <B>Pounds</B></TD>
    <TD WIDTH=25% BGCOLOR="#ECA613"> <B>Price/Lb. (US $)</B> </TD>
</TR>
<%- loop through each cart item display the item number,
     the item name, an editable count field and a price
     per item field
--%>
  <% int count = 0;
     CartItem item = null;
     double total = 0.0;
     while ((item = (CartItem)
             session.getAttribute("item" + count)) != null)
     {
%>
<TR>
    <TD> <%= count %> </TD>
    <TD> <%= item.getItemName() %> </TD>
    <TD> <INPUT TYPE=text SIZE=6 MAXLENGTH=6
         NAME='<%= "item" + count %>'
         VALUE=<%= item.getNumItems() %>>
    </TD>
    <TD ALIGN=right> $<%= item.getPricePerItem() %> </TD>
</TR>

<%- calculate the running total spent -%>
<%    total += (item.getNumItems() * item.getPricePerItem());
      count++;
     }
%>

<%- display total -%>
<TR>
    <TD COLSPAN=4 align=right BGCOLOR="#ECA613"><B>
     Total: $<%= total %> </B></TD>
</TR>
</TABLE>

<%- create table for action buttons -%>
<TABLE WIDTH=450 CELLSPACING="0" CELLPADDING="0" BORDER="0">
<TR>
    <TD ALIGN=left><INPUT TYPE=submit NAME=Page VALUE=Update></TD>
    <TD ALIGN=right><INPUT TYPE=reset VALUE="Reset"></TD>
</TR>
</TABLE>
</FORM>
</CENTER>
```

10. Finally, `ShoppingCartTemplate.jsp` inserts a standard footer using the `<jsp:include>` action:

```
<%-- include standard footer --%>
<jsp:include page='<%= request.getParameter("footer") %>'
             flush="true"
/>
```

11. Once you have a template, other JavaServer Pages can use it as a layout tool. Let's see how this works in `ShoppingCart.jsp`. First, it imports the `CartItem` class using a page directive. Then, it declares two shopping cart items using the `<jsp:useBean>` action, setting the item name and price per item values using the `<jsp:setProperty>` action:

5

```
<%@ page import="CartItem" %>

declare two shopping cart items -->
<jsp:useBean id="item0" class="CartItem" scope="session" >
     <jsp:setProperty name="item0"
          property="itemName" value="Carrots" />
     <jsp:setProperty name="item0"
          property="pricePerItem" value=".34" />
</jsp:useBean>

<jsp:useBean id="item1" class="CartItem" scope="session" >
     <jsp:setProperty name="item1"
          property="itemName" value="Red Peppers" />
     <jsp:setProperty name="item1"
          property="pricePerItem" value="2.49" />
</jsp:useBean>
```

12. Then, `ShoppingCart.jsp` forwards control to the template page. Notice that it uses the `<jsp:param>` action to add request parameters required by `ShoppingCartTemplate.jsp`.

```
<%-- forward control to the template page --%>
<jsp:forward page="ShoppingCartTemplate.jsp" >
     <jsp:param name="header" value="header.html" />
     <jsp:param name="tableCaption" value="Produce Purchases" />
     <jsp:param name="action" value="ResultPage.jsp" />
     <jsp:param name="footer" value="footer.html" />
</jsp:forward>
```

13. Now access your JSP page using this URL: `http:/localhost:8080/Book/jsp/ShoppingCart.jsp`. The result is a page that looks like Figure 5-3 when displayed.

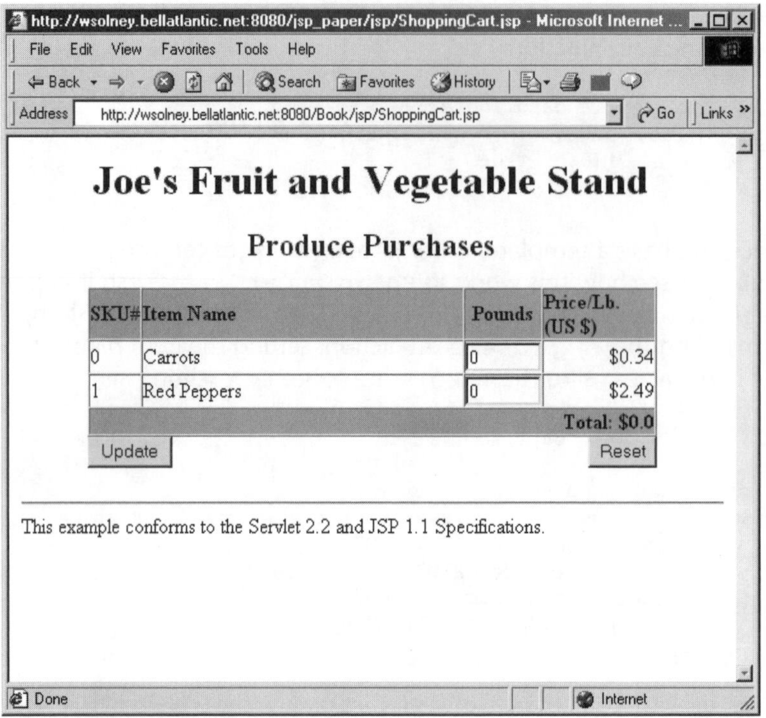

Figure 5-3 ShoppingCart.jsp display

14. Now let's create a second JSP page that also uses the template page. In `ShoppingCart.jsp`, the action we specified was `ResultPage.jsp`. Let's create that page.

15. Create a file called `ResultPage.jsp` in `%TOMCAT_HOME%/webapps/Book/jsp`. Then add a page directive to import the `CartItem` class:

```
<%@ page import="CartItem" %>
```

16. Next, use the `<jsp:useBean>` action to create scripting variables for the JavaBeans we declared in `ShoppingCart.jsp` and set values in the beans using request parameters supplied by the form we created in `ShoppingCartTemplate.jsp`:

```
<%-- retrieve the two shopping cart JavaBeans --%>
<jsp:useBean id="item0" class="CartItem" scope="session" />
```

```
<% item0.setNumItems(Integer.parseInt(request.getParameter("item0"))); %>

<jsp:useBean id="item1" class="CartItem" scope="session" />
<% item1.setNumItems(Integer.parseInt(request.getParameter("item1"))); %>
```

17. Finally, forward control to the template while supplying request parameters using the `<jsp:param>` action:

```
<%-- forward control to the template --%>
<jsp:forward page="ShoppingCartTemplate.jsp" >
     <jsp:param name="header" value="header.html" />
     <jsp:param name="tableCaption" value="Produce Purchases" />
     <jsp:param name="action" value="ResultPage.jsp" />
     <jsp:param name="footer" value="footer.html" />
</jsp:forward>
```


18. Notice that in our example we forward control from `ResultPage.jsp` back to `ResultPage.jsp`. This allows you to modify the number of pounds of each item you purchase. You could add an additional button in the template to forward control to a check-out page. This might modify `ShoppingCartTemplate.jsp` with the following lines:

```
<%-- create table for action buttons --%>
<TABLE WIDTH=450 CELLSPACING="0" CELLPADDING="0" BORDER="0">
<TR>
    <TD ALIGN=left><INPUT TYPE=submit NAME="Page" VALUE="Update"></TD>
    <TD ALIGN=left><INPUT TYPE=reset VALUE="Reset"></TD>
    <TD ALIGN=right><INPUT TYPE=submit NAME="Page" VALUE="Checkout"></TD>
</TR>
</TABLE>
```

19. In step 18 we added a checkout button. To use the value of this button, you must add the lines similar to these to `ResultPage.jsp`. You should insert them after setting the JavaBean properties and before forwarding to `ShoppingCartTemplate.jsp`:

```
<%-- check for checkout --%>
<% String submit = request.getParameter("Page");
   if (submit.equals("Checkout")) {
%>
      <jsp:forward page="Checkout.jsp" />
<% } %>
```

20. The whole page would then look like this:

```
<%@ page import="cart.CartItem" %>

<%-- retrieve the two shopping cart JavaBeans --%>
```

```
<jsp:useBean id="item0" class="CartItem" scope="session" />
<% item0.setNumItems(Integer.parseInt(request.getParameter("item0"))); %>

<jsp:useBean id="item1" class="CartItem" scope="session" />
<% item1.setNumItems(Integer.parseInt(request.getParameter("item1"))); %>

<%-- check for checkout --%
><% String submit = request.getParameter("Page");
   if (submit.equals("Checkout")) {
%>
       <jsp:forward page="Checkout.jsp" />
<% } %>

<%-- forward to template --%>
<jsp:forward page="ShoppingCartTemplate.jsp" >
     <jsp:param name="header" value="header.html" />
          <jsp:param name="tableCaption" value="Produce Purchases" />
          <jsp:param name="action" value="ResultPage.jsp" />
     <jsp:param name="footer" value="footer.html" />
</jsp:forward>
```

The <jsp:plugin> Action

The `<jsp:plugin>` action supports generation of HTML to include Java applets in a JSP page. It also inserts a URL to download the JavaSoft Java applet plugin software (if necessary) that allows the applet to run inside the browser.

The `<jsp:plugin>` tag is replaced by either an HTML `<object>` or an HTML `<embed>` tag, as appropriate, and is written to the response output stream. The syntax of the `<jsp:plugin>` action is:

```
<jsp:plugin
        type="bean|applet"
        code="classFile"
        codebase="objectCodeBase"
        [ align="alignment" ]
        [ archive="archiveList" ]
        [ height="height" ]
        [ hspace="hspace" ]
        [ jrevision="jrevision" ]
        [ name="componentName" ]
        [ vspace="vspace" ]
        [ width="width" ]
        [ nspluginurl="url" ]
        [ iepluginurl="url" ] >
        [ <jsp:params>
```

```
                [ <jsp:param name="paramName"
                             value="paramValue" /> ]+
            </jsp:params> ]
          [ <jsp:fallback> anyArbitraryText </jsp:fallback> ]
</jsp:plugin>
```

Attributes and Usage Rules

Table 5-10 lists the attributes of the `<jsp:plugin>` tag.

Attribute	Usage Rules
`type`	Identifies the type of component—either a JavaBean or an applet
`code`	Same as HTML 4.0 specification for applets. The *filename* (not URL) of the object class
`codebase`	Same as HTML 4.0 specification for applets. Use it to specify the URL of the storage location for the applet classes
`align`	Same as HTML 4.0 specification for applets. As with the HTML `<img>` tag, you can position the object with respect to its surrounding text
`archive`	Same as HTML 4.0 specification for applets. A URL identifying a *.jar* file holding the Java classes for the object
`height`	Same as HTML 4.0 specification for applets. Defines the height of the object's display area
`hspace`	Same as HTML 4.0 specification for applets. The size of empty space between the object and surrounding text
`jrevision`	Identifies the specification version number of the Java Runtime Environment (JRE) the component requires. (The default is "1.1")
`name`	Same as HTML 4.0 specification for applets. A unique name for this instance of the Java object. Allows this object to share information with other objects
`vspace`	Same as HTML 4.0 specification for applets. Vertical empty space between object and surrounding text
`title`	Same as HTML 4.0 specification for applets. An object title used by IE (not Netscape)
`width`	Same as HTML 4.0 specification for applets. Defines the height of the applet's display area
`nspluginurl`	URL where the JRE plug-in can be downloaded for Netscape Navigator. The default URL is implementation dependent
`iepluginurl`	URL where the JRE plug-in can be downloaded for Internet Explorer (IE). The default URL is implementation dependent

Table 5-10 Attributes of the <jsp:plugin> Action

Mapping an Applet to a <jsp:plugin>

One way to get an understanding of how to use the <jsp:plugin> action is to convert an existing applet to a plugin object. Here's how you specify a very simple demonstration applet supplied by JavaSoft with JDK 1.3 (slightly modified):

```
<applet code="Blink.class" width=300 height=100>
   <param name=lbl
          value="This is the next best thing to sliced bread!">
  <param name=speed value="4">
  alt="Your browser understands the &lt;APPLET&gt;
       tag but isn't running the applet, for some reason."
</applet>
```

This applet code maps into a `<jsp:plugin>` action like this:

```
<jsp:plugin type="applet" code="Blink.class" width=300 height=100>
     <jsp:params>
          <jsp:param name="lbl"
                value="This is the next best thing to sliced bread!" />
          <jsp:param name="speed" value="4" />
     </jsp:params>
     <jsp:fallback>Your browser isn't running the applet for some reason.
     </jsp:fallback>
</jsp:plugin>
```

1-Minute Drill

- What is the purpose of the `<jsp:plugin>` action?
- How do you specify parameters to the object inserted by the `<jsp:plugin>` action?

Ask the Expert

Question: Since the mapping between the HTML **`<applet>`** tag and the **`<jsp:plugin>`** action is so close, why would you prefer the JSP tag?

Answer: The best reason to use the `<jsp:plugin>` action is that it ensures that you are using the correct version of the Java Virtual Machine (JVM) for your applet. It also helps shelter you from changes to the HTML specification.

- The `<jsp:plugin>` action inserts an HTML `<object>` or `<embed>` tag into the response stream.
- You specify parameters to the object using the `<jsp:params>` and `<jsp:param>` actions.

SimpleMenuApplet.java
SimpleMenu.jsp
SimpleMenuTarget.jsp
SimpleMenu.gif

Project 5-2: Inserting a Menu Applet

This project illustrates use of the `<jsp:plugin>` action by walking through steps to insert a menu into a JSP page.

Step-by-Step

1. Download the files for this project from `http://www.osborne.com`.
2. Compile the file `SimpleMenuApplet.java`.
3. Move the class compiled in step 2 into `%TOMCAT_HOME%/webapps/Book/applets`.
4. Move `SimpleMenu.gif` into `%TOMCAT_HOME%/webapps/Book/images`.
5. Move `SimpleMenuTarget.jsp` into `%TOMCAT_HOME%/webapps/Book/jsp`.
6. Create a file in `%TOMCAT_HOME%/webapps/Book/jsp` named `SimpleMenu.jsp` and add a page directive to import the `SimpleMenuApplet` class:

```
<%@ page import="SimpleMenuApplet" %>
```

7. Use a JSP scriptlet to create the data for your menu. Notice that the (`!`) character separates menu labels from menu actions and that you use the `MAIN` keyword to specify a new browser page. You specify menu nesting using braces (`{}`). Finally, the (`-`) character specifies a separator.

```
<%-- create data string defining menus items and URLS --%>
<% String menuData =
      "{Search   {Search Page!SimpleMenu.jsp}" +
      "{-}" +
      "{Advanced Search!SimpleMenuTarget.jsp}" +
      "{Simple Search!SimpleMenuTarget.jsp}}" +
      "{Logout!SimpleMenuTarget.jsp!MAIN}";
%>
```

8. Now add these lines to insert the menu:

```
<%-- create SimpleMenuApplet --%>
<jsp:plugin type="applet"
            code="SimpleMenuApplet"
            codebase="/Book/applets"
            width="250"
            height="50"
            jreversion="1.3"
```

5

```
>
    <jsp:params>
        <jsp:param
            name="font"
            value="SansSerif"
        />
        <jsp:param
            name="fsize"
            value="12"
        />
        <jsp:param
            name="image"
            value="/Book/images/SimpleMenu.gif"
        />
        <jsp:param
            name="data"
            value='<%= menuData %>'
        />


    </jsp:params>
    <jsp:fallback>
        <B>Unable to start plugin!</B>
    </jsp:fallback>
</jsp:plugin>
```

Now access the menu using this URL: `http://localhost:8080/Book/jsp/SimpleMenu.jsp`. Make sure Tomcat is running first. You should see a page that looks like Figure 5-4.

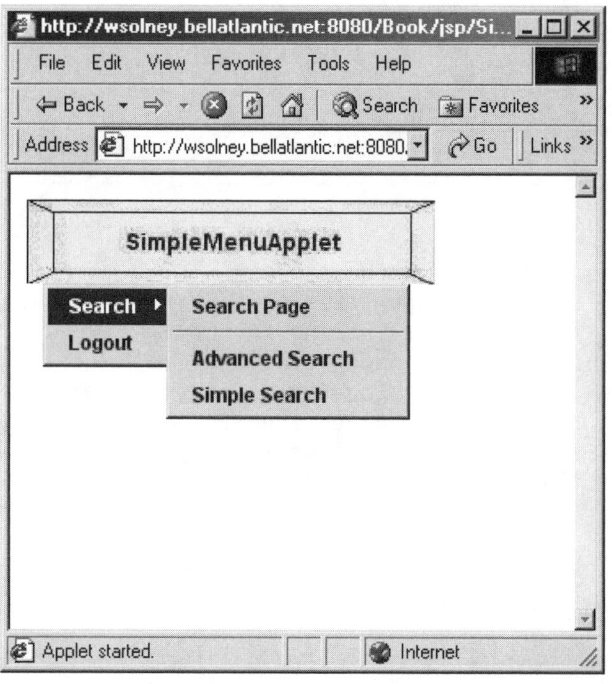

Figure 5-4 SimpleMenuApplet

Mastery Check

1. What is the error in this use of <jsp:useBean>?

```
<jsp:useBean id="myHelperBean"
             scope="session"
             type="StringProperty" >
<jsp:setProperty name="myHelperBean"
                 property="stringProperty"
                 value="The String Property" />
The String property value is:
   <jsp:getProperty name="myHelperBean"
                    property="stringProperty"/>
```

2. How do you set a login name property of type *String* on a helper JavaBean using a request parameter?

3. What is the constraint on the Java property types you can initialize using the <jsp:setProperty> action?

4. What attributes of standard actions can take a JSP expression as their value?

5. Why would you use a JSP expression to set the value of an attribute?

6. How do you create a JSP page template using the <jsp:include> action?

Mastery Check

7. What `<jsp:plugin>` attributes map directly into HTML tags?

8. What JSP tags can qualify the behavior of the `<JSP:plugin>` tag?

9. Why can't you print output to the JSP response buffer prior to using the `<jsp:forward>` action?

10. What is the purpose of the `<jsp:param>` action?

Module 6

Tag Libraries

The Goals of This Module

- Understand the value of custom tags
- Understand how custom tags work
- Know how to implement custom tags
- Package a set of custom tags into a tag library

In Module 5, we described the standard actions defined by the JSP specification. This module explains how to write your own actions to augment standard actions and thereby extend the JSP scripting language. Such custom tags add so much power and design flexibility that you can arguably consider them the most important feature provided by JavaServer Pages.

Why Define Custom Tags?

Custom tags, also called *custom actions*, *tag extensions*, or *tag libraries*, provide a JSP page author a specialized sublanguage to insert dynamic functionality into the JSP page. Such libraries separate business logic from presentation detail more cleanly than other JSP constructs such as scriptlets, expressions, declarations, and implicit objects. By encapsulating some well-defined abstract functionality into a single library, tag libraries provide a single point to extend, test, and correct business logic. This clean separation also makes them easier to maintain. Let's look at an example to understand their value. Consider the following static HTML form. It computes simple or compound interest and accumulated balance for a given principal amount and interest rate over a period of years:

```
<HTML>
<HEAD><TITLE>Accumulated Compound Interest Calculator </TITLE> </HEAD>
<BODY>
<H2> Interest Calculator </H2>
<FORM METHOD="POST" ACTION="jsp/InterestCalc.jsp">
<TABLE>
<TR>
  <TD> Please enter principal ($) </TD>
  <TD> <INPUT NAME="principal" TYPE=text SIZE=10>
</TR>
<TR>
  <TD> Please enter interest (%) </TD>
  <TD> <INPUT NAME="rate" TYPE=text SIZE=10>
</TR>
<TR>
  <TD> Please enter # years </TD>
  <TD> <INPUT NAME="years" TYPE=text SIZE=10>
```

```
</TR>
<TR>
  <TD> <input TYPE=radio name=itype VALUE=Simple> Simple </TD>
  <TD> <input TYPE=radio name=itype VALUE=Compound> Compound </TD>
</TR>
<TR>
  <TD><INPUT TYPE=submit VALUE="Submit"></TD>
  <TD><INPUT TYPE=reset  VALUE="Reset"></TD>
</TR>
</TABLE>
</FORM>
</BODY>
</HTML>
```

Figure 6-1 shows the HTML page.

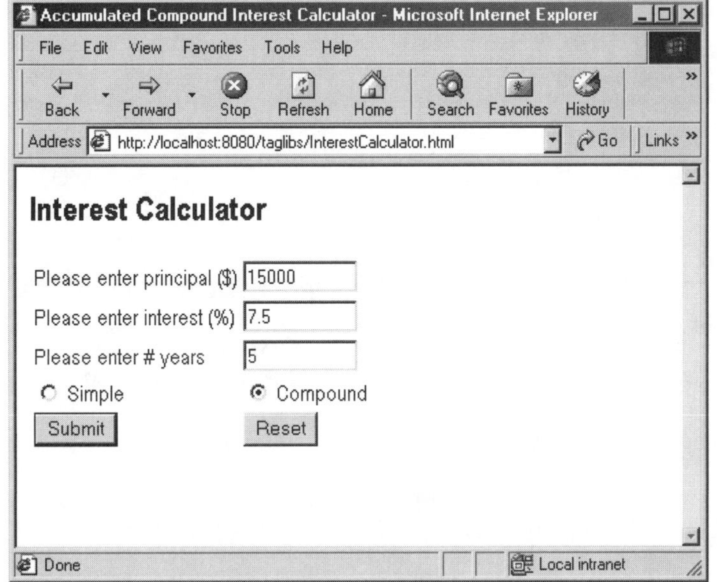

Figure 6-1 Interest Calculator HTML

As you can see, the JSP page `jsp/InterestCalc.jsp` handles the form submission. Here is the implementation of this JSP page using JSP scriptlets and expressions:

```
<HTML>
<HEAD><TITLE> Interest Results </TITLE></HEAD>
<BODY>
<%!
  public String getStringifiedValue(float value) {
   String subval = "0.00";
   if (value > 0.0) {
     subval = Float.toString(value);
     int decimalLen = subval.length() -
                     (subval.lastIndexOf('.') + 1);
     if(decimalLen > 1)
       subval = subval.substring(0,
                      subval.lastIndexOf('.') + 3);
     else
       subval += "0";
   }
   return subval;
  }
%>
<%
    float principal =
          Float.parseFloat(request.getParameter("principal"));
    float rate   =
          Float.parseFloat(request.getParameter("rate"));
    int years = Integer.parseInt(request.getParameter("years"));

    String itype = request.getParameter("itype");
%>
<H2> <%= itype %> Interest Results </H2>
<TABLE CELLSPACING="0" CELLPADDING="3" BORDER="1">
<TR>
  <TD> <B>Year</B> </TD>
  <TD> <B>Principal</B> </TD>
  <TD> <B>Interest</B> </TD>
  <TD> <B>Cumulative Balance</B> </TD>
</TR>
<%
```

```
    float balance = principal;
    float interest = 0;
    for(int i=1; i<=years; i++) {
      interest = principal * (rate/100);
      balance += interest;
%>
<TR>
  <TD> <%= i %> </TD>
  <TD> <%= getStringifiedValue(principal) %> </TD>
  <TD> <%= getStringifiedValue(interest) %> </TD>
  <TD> <%= getStringifiedValue(balance) %> </TD>
</TR>
<%
      if(itype.equals("Compound")) {
         principal = balance;
      }
    }
%>
</TABLE>
</BODY>
</HTML>
```

This JSP page does four things:

1. It retrieves the parameters (principal, interest rate, number of years, and interest type) from the *request* object.
2. It iterates through each year.
3. It computes the interest and accumulates the balance for each year.
4. It lays out the principal, interest, and accumulated balance for each year in a table row.

You must insert Java code into all four steps. A JSP declaration also inserts a convenience method that formats floating-point values. The presence of this much Java code makes the page hard to read. If a Web designer must make some layout changes involving pure HTML (such as changing a column width or adding a logo), that designer would find it hard to distinguish HTML code from the Java code.

6

Now consider the same problem handled by a different JSP page, `TaglibInterestCalc.jsp`, that produces exactly the same results:

```
<%@taglib uri="/interest-taglib" prefix="sample" %>
<HTML>
<HEAD><TITLE> Interest Results </TITLE> </HEAD>
<BODY>
<sample:readInterestType/>
<H2> <%= interestType %> Interest Results </H2>
<TABLE CELLSPACING="0" CELLPADDING="3" BORDER="1">
<TR>
  <TD> <B>Year</B> </TD>
  <TD> <B>Principal</B> </TD>
  <TD> <B>Interest</B> </TD>
  <TD> <B>Cumulative Balance</B> </TD>
</TR>
<sample:calcInterest yearName="numYear"
                     principalName="principal"
                     interestName="interest"
                     balanceName="balance" >
  <TR>
      <TD> <%= numYear %> </TD>
      <TD> <%= principal %> </TD>
      <TD> <%= interest %> </TD>
      <TD> <%= balance %> </TD>
  </TR>
</sample:calcInterest>
</BODY>
</HTML>
```

Several things distinguish this JSP page from the previous one. The most obvious difference is that apart from some JSP expressions, this JSP page is devoid of Java code. Consequently, it is also far smaller than the previous JSP page.

Second, there is a taglib directive at the top of this JSP page. Taglib directives identify the tag libraries that a JSP page uses and associate a namespace prefix for each library's tags. (We described the taglib directive in Module 2). The `interest-taglib` supports two custom tags: `<sample:readInterestType>` and `<sample:calcInterest>`.

The first one has an empty body, and the second encloses an HTML table row. Our JSP page has so little Java code because we hide it behind the implementation of these two actions.

Third, the absence of the Java code simplifies reading HTML elements in the page. A Web designer can easily modify the HTML in this JSP page. More importantly, someone without knowledge of Java could write this JSP page.

Finally, by encapsulating Java code in a tag library we made it possible to enhance, test, and correct this code without modifying the JSP page itself. For example, if we wanted to compute a completely different interest type, perhaps applying a variable interest rate, we could add it to the tag library without touching any JSP page using the library.

Figure 6-2 shows the output from this JSP page.

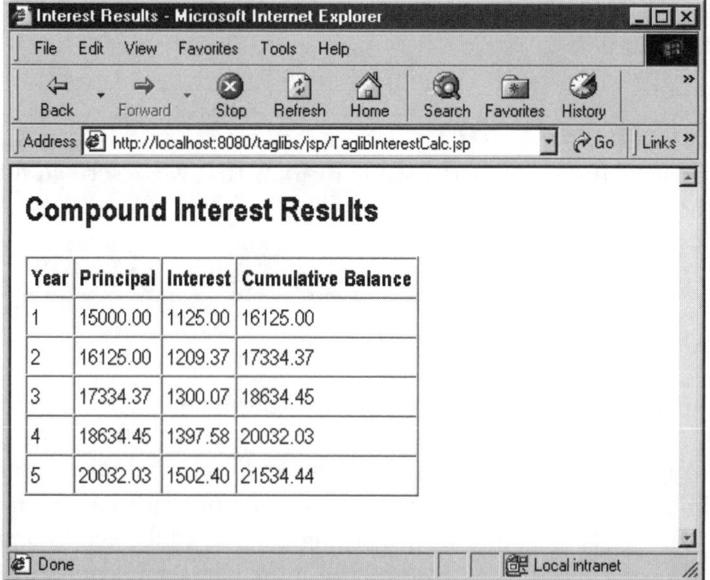

Year	Principal	Interest	Cumulative Balance
1	15000.00	1125.00	16125.00
2	16125.00	1209.37	17334.37
3	17334.37	1300.07	18634.45
4	18634.45	1397.58	20032.03
5	20032.03	1502.40	21534.44

Figure 6-2 Output page for interest calculation

1-Minute Drill

- What are other names for custom tags?
- How do custom tags make a JSP page easier to maintain?

Elements of a Tag Library

Tag libraries have four elements:

- The definition of the custom action (i.e., the tags)
- The taglib directive
- The tag library descriptor
- The tag handlers

Tag Library Formats

Custom tags have the same two possible formats that we described for standard actions in Module 5. Here are the formats:

<prefix: tagName [attr="value"] > tagBody </prefix: tagName>*

<prefix: tagName [attr="value"] />* or

<prefix: tagName [attr="value"] ></prefix:tagName>*

The first format is an action with a tag body. The body includes all text between the start tag and the end tag. The second format is an action without a body. You can specify an empty body by using a start tag followed by an immediate end tag or by using a single tag that ends with the character sequence slash–close angle bracket (/>).

Custom tags can appear in any JSP page, and the JSP container interprets them at request time, just as it does standard actions. A tag library is a collection of custom tags that encapsulate some coherent set of functionality useful to JSP pages.

- Other names for custom tags are tag libraries, custom actions, and tag extensions.
- Custom tags remove Java code from a JSP page, thereby making enhancements to dynamic functionality independent of the JSP page.

The taglib Directive

A taglib directive in a JSP page informs the JSP container that this JSP page uses a tag library, uniquely identified by a URI, and associates a prefix that distinguishes usage of the actions in the library. Here is the syntax of a taglib directive, reproduced from Module 2:

```
<%@
   taglib
   uri="URI To Tag Library"
   prefix="tag prefix"
%>
```

The URI specifies the location of a *tag library descriptor*, which defines the custom tags supported by the tag library. The prefix attribute specifies the tag prefix for those custom tags.

The Tag Library Descriptor

A tag library descriptor (TLD) is an Extensible Markup Language (XML) document that describes the tag library. A JSP container uses the taglib directive to identify the location of the TLD. It then parses the descriptor and gets a comprehensive description of each custom action in that tag library. You can find the official *document type definition* (DTD) for TLD files at `http://java.sun.com/j2ee/dtds/web-jsptaglibrary_1_1.dtd`.

Note

The details of XML and the definition of a DTD are beyond the scope of this book. The basic point you should note is that you define JSP tag extensions using XML in a way defined by another document, the DTD for tag library descriptors. XML is itself a tagging language, and a DTD defines the valid tags for a given use of XML. Once you finish this module, you should be able to define a TLD without a deep understanding of either XML or DTD documents.

Table 6-1 lists the various elements of a TLD document and their formal syntax.

Element	Syntax	Required Element?	Description
taglib	`<!ELEMENT taglib (tlibversion, jspversion?, shortname, uri?, info?, tag+)>`	Required	The document root
tlibversion	`<!ELEMENT tlibversion (#PCDATA)>`	Required	The version of the tag library implementation
jspversion	`<!ELEMENT jspversion (#PCDATA)>`	Optional	The version of the JSP specification this tag library requires. The default is 1.1
shortname	`<!ELEMENT shortname (#PCDATA)>`	Required	A simple, default short name. A JSP page-authoring tool might use this to create names with mnemonic value
uri	`<!ELEMENT uri (#PCDATA)>`	Optional	The public URI that uniquely identifies this version of the tag library
info	`<!ELEMENT info (#PCDATA)>`	Optional	An arbitrary text description for this tag library
tag	`<!ELEMENT tag (name, tagclass, teiclass?, bodycontent?, info?, attribute*)>`	Required	The definition for a custom action. There can be several of these in a TLD file
name	`<!ELEMENT name (#PCDATA)>`	Required	Unique name for the action
tagclass	`<!ELEMENT tagclass (#PCDATA)>`	Required	The tag handler class implementing the *javax.servlet.jsp.tagext.Tag* interface

Table 6-1 Elements of a Tag Library Descriptor

Element	Syntax	Required Element?	Description
teiclass	`<!ELEMENT teiclass (#PCDATA)>`	Optional	A Java class providing additional information for the action implementing the interface *javax.servlet.jsp.tagext.TagExtraInfo*
bodycontent	`<!ELEMENT bodycontent (#PCDATA)>`	Optional	Hint to the JSP container on how to interpret the body of this action. The possible values are: `tagdependent`—The tag handler interprets the body of the action so the container should not `JSP`—The body of the action contains elements using the JSP syntax and the container should interpret it `empty`—The body must be empty The default value is `JSP`
info	`<!ELEMENT info (#PCDATA)>`	Optional	Optional description for the action
attribute	`<!ELEMENT attribute (name, required?, rtexprvalue?)>`	Optional	The definition for an attribute of an action
name	`<!ELEMENT name (#PCDATA)>`	Required	Distinguishing name for the attribute

Table 6-1 Elements of a Tag Library Descriptor *(continued)*

Element	Syntax	Required Element?	Description
required	`<!ELEMENT required (#PCDATA)>`	Optional	Defines whether the attribute is required or optional. Possible values are: `true` | `false` | `yes` | `no` The default is `false`, indicating the attribute is optional
rtexprvalue	`<!ELEMENT rtexprvalue (#PCDATA)>`	Optional	Defines if an attribute can take JSP expressions as its value. In other words, the JSP container can calculate the value of the attribute at request time in contrast to a static value determined at translation time. Possible values are: `true` | `false` | `yes` | `no` The default is `false`, indicating the attribute takes only static values

Table 6-1 Elements of a Tag Library Descriptor *(continued)*

Here is the TLD describing the `interest-taglib` we used in our calculator JSP:

```
<?xml version="1.0" encoding="ISO-8859-1" ?>
<!DOCTYPE taglib PUBLIC
   "-//Sun Microsystems, Inc.//DTD JSP Tag Library 1.1//EN"
   "http://java.sun.com/j2ee/dtds/web-jsptaglibrary_1_1.dtd">
<taglib>
   <tlibversion>1.0</tlibversion>
   <jspversion>1.1</jspversion>
   <shortname></shortname>
   <tag>
      <name>readInterestType</name>
      <tagclass>sample.ReadRequestTag</tagclass>
      <teiclass>sample.ReadRequestTEI</teiclass>
      <bodycontent>empty</bodycontent>
      <info> Extracts request parameters </info>
```

```
   </tag>
   <tag>
      <name>calcInterest</name>
      <tagclass>sample.InterestCalcTag</tagclass>
      <teiclass>sample.InterestCalcTEI</teiclass>
      <bodycontent>JSP</bodycontent>
      <info>
       Iterative tag that calculates interest (compound or simple)
      </info>
      <attribute>
         <name>yearName</name>
         <required>true</required>
         <rtexprvalue>false</rtexprvalue>
      </attribute>
      <attribute>
         <name>principalName</name>
         <required>true</required>
         <rtexprvalue>false</rtexprvalue>
      </attribute>
      <attribute>
         <name>interestName</name>
         <required>true</required>
         <rtexprvalue>false</rtexprvalue>
      </attribute>
      <attribute>
         <name>balanceName</name>
         <required>true</required>
         <rtexprvalue>false</rtexprvalue>
      </attribute>
   </tag>
</taglib>
```

6

Here are the most important points you should note about this TLD:

1. The TLD defines two custom tags: `readInterestType` and `calcInterest`. You declare a custom action between the `<tag>` start tag and the `</tag>` end tag.

2. The TLD declares Java classes that implement the functionality of the library between the `<tagclass>` start tag and the `</tagclass>` end tag. In this case, *sample.ReadRequestTag* implements the functionality of the `readInterestType` action, while *sample.InterestCalcTag* implements the functionality of the `calcInterest` action.

3. The TLD declares other Java classes between the `<teiclass>` start tag and the `</teiclass>` end tag. These classes are *TagExtraInfo* classes, and you use them to define additional scripting variables for your JSP page.

4. The TLD declares an `empty` body for the `readInterestType` action. In contrast, it declares a body for the `calcInterest` action. You declare use of a tag body between the `<bodycontent>` start tag and the `</bodycontent>` end tag.

5. The TLD defines four attributes for the `calcInterest` action: `yearName`, `principalName`, `interestName`, and `balanceName`. The TLD declares all these attributes and specifies that you cannot provide their values as request-time JSP expressions. You define attributes between the `<attribute>` start tag and the `</attribute>` end tag.

6. Tag attribute definitions require a tag body consisting of three additional tags: `<name>`, `<required>`, and `<rtexprvalue>`. These specify, respectively, the name of the attribute, whether the attribute is required or optional, and whether a JSP page can provide the attribute value as a JSP expression.

1-Minute Drill

- What are the four elements in a tag library?
- What is the difference between the two forms of a custom action?
- What is the purpose of a *taglib* directive?
- What is the purpose of a tag library descriptor?

Tag Handlers

Tag handlers implement the programmatic behavior of JSP actions. You specify tag handlers for custom tags using the `<tagclass>` element in a tag library descriptor. When the JSP scripting language is Java, the tag handler is a JavaBean component that implements a Java interface. The Java interface enforces the

---

- The four elements of a tag library are the tags, the taglib directive, the tag library descriptor, and the tag handlers.
- One format contains a body, and the other does not.
- A *taglib* directive informs the JSP container that this JSP page uses a tag library identified by a URI.
- A tag library descriptor describes the custom tags in the tag library.

runtime protocol between the JSP container and the handler. You can use either of two Java interfaces to define tag handlers:

- *javax.servlet.jsp.tagext. Tag* Defines the protocol for a simple tag handler that is not interested in manipulating its body
- *javax.servlet.jsp.tagext. BodyTag* Extends *javax.servlet.jsp.tagext.Tag* to give a tag handler access to the tag body

Communications between the JSP container and the tag handler illustrate a callback pattern.

Note

The callback pattern requires an association between an event and an event handler. When the event occurs, a runtime execution engine (in this case, the JSP container) calls the event handler, possibly passing additional information about the event.

As it encounters various tags in a JSP page, the JSP container invokes the associated methods defined by the tag interfaces. Figure 6-3 illustrates this protocol.

Default Tag Handler Properties

The JSP container must initialize all tag handlers with certain properties. The container sets these properties using JavaBean property setter methods. The container automatically sets the following properties on tag handlers:

- The *PageContext* object that, as we explained in Module 4, provides access to vendor-specific features, operations across multiple scopes, and a vendor-independent interface to convenience methods
- The parent tag handler for the enclosing action
- The *BodyContent* object that provides access to evaluated tag bodies. This property is set only if the TLD indicates that the tag handler will manipulate the tag body.

Tag Attributes

The start tag for a custom action can contain attribute assignments of the form `attr="value"`. Attributes customize the behavior of an action by initializing custom properties on a tag handler. For instance, in our action

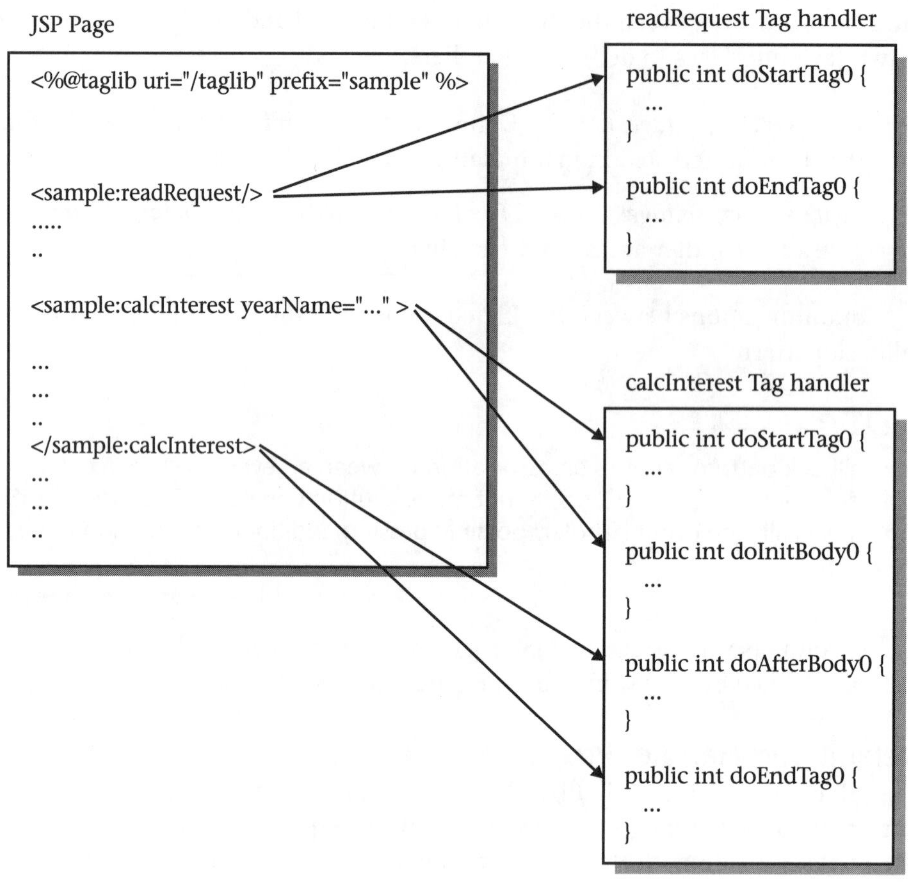

Figure 6-3 Protocol between the JSP container and a tag handler

`<sample:calcInterest>`, we exposed four attributes: `yearName`, `principalName`, `interestName`, and `balanceName`. We specified these in the tag library descriptor using the `<attribute>` element, as shown here.

```
<attribute>
   <name>yearName</name>
   <required>true</required>
   <rtexprvalue>false</rtexprvalue>
</attribute>
```

```
<attribute>
   <name>principalName</name>
   <required>true</required>
   <rtexprvalue>false</rtexprvalue>
</attribute>
<attribute>
   <name>interestName</name>
   <required>true</required>
   <rtexprvalue>false</rtexprvalue>
</attribute>
<attribute>
   <name>balanceName</name>
   <required>true</required>
   <rtexprvalue>false</rtexprvalue>
</attribute>
```

The tag handler must define a JavaBean property for every attribute defined in the TLD. This means they must provide property setter methods that follow the naming requirements of a JavaBean. For example, the tag handler must provide a *setBalanceName* method to match the TLD attribute `balanceName`. The JSP container automatically invokes the setter methods when it encounters the start tag in a JSP page. The code fragment that follows shows these setter methods in our tag handler:

```
public void setPrincipalName(String principalName) {
   this.principalName = principalName;
}
public void setInterestName(String interestName) {
   this.interestName = interestName;
}
public void setYearName(String yearName) {
   this.yearName = yearName;
}
public void setBalanceName(String balanceName) {
   this.balanceName = balanceName;
}
```

Tag handler properties can have any Java type. If you provide the value for an attribute using a *String* (either an *HttpServletRequest* parameter or a *String* constant), the property must have one of the types listed in Table 6-2. The conversion column states how the JSP container converts a *String* value to the appropriate type.

6

Property Type	Conversion on *String* value
boolean or Boolean	Result of *java.lang.Boolean.valueOf(String)*
byte or Byte	Result of *java.lang.Byte.valueOf(String)*
char or Character	Result of *java.lang.Character.valueOf(String)*
double or Double	Result of *java.lang.Double.valueOf(String)*
int or Integer	Result of *java.lang.Integer.valueOf(String)*
float or Float	Result of *java.lang.Float.valueOf(String)*
long or Long	Result of *java.lang.Long.valueOf(String)*
String	String

Table 6-2 Tag Attribute Property Types You Can Provide Using a String Conversion

If you provide the attribute value using a JSP expression, the JSP container calculates its type at request time and makes no automatic conversion from type *String*. The type of the return value in the JSP expression should match the type of the property in the tag handler. For example, consider the action that follows:

```
<% java.util.Map items = Cart.getItems();  %>
<sample:purchase cart="<%= items %>" />
```

In the example, the custom action has an attribute named `cart` that has a value of type *java.util.Map*. This means that the tag handler for this action should have a setter method like the following:

```
public void setCart(java.util.Map map) {
   this.map = map;
}
```

Ask the Expert

Question: Is there any particular order in which attributes are set for a custom action?

Answer: The specification does not require a particular order, but Tomcat evaluates attributes in the order that you specify them in the tag library descriptor (TLD), *not* in the order that you provide them to the custom action. You must consider this if your tag relies on an attribute order. For example, consider this TLD fragment specifying a simple iterator tag:

```
<tag>
   <name>for</name>
   <tagclass>sample.ForTag</tagclass>
   <teiclass>sample.ForTagTEI</teiclass>
   <bodycontent>JSP</bodycontent>
   <info> A simple iteration tag </info>
   <attribute>
      <name>counter</name>
      <required>true</required>
      <rtexprvalue>false</rtexprvalue>
   </attribute>
   <attribute>
      <name>initial</name>
      <required>false</required>
      <rtexprvalue>false</rtexprvalue>
   </attribute>
   <attribute>
      <name>final</name>
      <required>false</required>
      <rtexprvalue>false</rtexprvalue>
   </attribute>
```

```
    <attribute>
        <name>increment</name>
        <required>false</required>
        <rtexprvalue>false</rtexprvalue>
    </attribute>
</tag>
```

The TLD specifies the attribute order as: `counter`, `initial`, `final`, and `increment`. Now consider this possible validation step in our tag handler code:

```
public void setIncrement(int increment) throws JspTagException {
    if (((initialVal < finalVal) && (increment < 0)) ||
         ((initialVal > finalVal) && (increment > 0)))
        throw new JspTagException("Infinite Loop!");
        this.increment = increment;
}
```

This validation code checks for an infinite loop. It expects the attributes `initial` and `final` to be set before the attribute `increment`. If we had not specified them in the correct order in our TLD, this conditional check would produce invalid results.

In practice, your tags should avoid dependence upon such idiosyncrasies of the JSP container. When you introduce them, you exploit implementation decisions that the specification does not mandate. This means your code is inherently not portable, even across different versions of the same container.

1-Minute Drill

- What are the two tag handler interfaces?
- What are the default properties associated with a tag handler?
- What should the tag handler define for each attribute described in the tag library descriptor?

- The tag handler interfaces are *javax.servlet.jsp.tagext.Tag* and *javax.servlet.jsp.tagext.BodyTag*.
- The default properties for a tag handler are: the *PageContext*, the parent tag, and (if the tag handler implements *BodyTag*) the *BodyContent*.
- The tag handler should define a JavaBean property for each attribute.

The Tag Interface

The *javax.servlet.jsp.tagext.Tag* interface defines the basic protocol for all tag handlers. Table 6-3 lists the methods in the *Tag* interface.

The generated servlet for the JSP page first calls the *Tag* interface's property setter methods to initialize the basic properties *pageContext* and *parent*. Then the servlet initializes any additional properties that the TLD exposed as attributes. After initializing all the properties, the generated servlet invokes the main action methods. The *Tag* interface supports three main action methods: *doStartTag*, *doEndTag*, and *release*.

The doStartTag Method The generated servlet invokes the *doStartTag* method after initializing all properties. At this point, the generated servlet has not yet processed the tag body.

The return value of *doStartTag* indicates whether the generated servlet should process the tag body. The three possible return values are:

- `EVAL_BODY_INCLUDE` Process the body of the tag but do not allow the tag handler to manipulate it.
- `EVAL_BODY_TAG` Process the body of the tag and allow the tag handler to manipulate it through a new *BodyContent* object.
- `SKIP_BODY` Do not process the body of the tag.

Method signature	Description
`int doStartTag()`	Process the start tag
`int doEndTag()`	Process the end tag
`void release()`	Release the current instance of the tag handler
`Tag getParent()`	Get the immediate parent tag if one exists
`void setPageContext (PageContext pc)`	Set the current page context for this JSP page
`void setParent(Tag t)`	Set the current nesting tag for this Tag

Table 6-3 Methods in the *Tag* interface

Tag handlers that do not evaluate their tag body (if one exists) return `SKIP_BODY` from their *doStartTag* method. Tag handlers that permit a tag body but do not manipulate it return `EVAL_BODY_INCLUDE` from their *doStartTag* method. Such tag handlers must implement the *Tag* interface and cannot implement the *BodyTag* interface. A tag handler returns `EVAL_BODY_TAG` from its *doStartTag* method if it intends to manipulate its tag body. Such tag handlers *must* implement the *BodyTag* interface. At the end of this method, some new scripting variables may be available to the JSP page, depending upon the existence and behavior of an optional *TagExtraInfo* class.

The *doStartTag* method may throw a *JspException* to indicate an error.

The doEndTag Method The generated servlet invokes the *doEndTag* method after either skipping or processing the tag body. If the tag had a body and the tag's *doStartTag* method returned `EVAL_BODY_TAG`, the generated servlet will have processed the tag body at this point. The return value of this method indicates whether the generated servlet should evaluate the rest of the JSP page. The possible values are:

- EVAL_PAGE Continue to evaluate the rest of the JSP page.
- SKIP_PAGE Complete the request by skipping the rest of the JSP page.

At the end of this method, some new scripting variables may be available to the JSP page, depending upon the existence and behavior of an optional *TagExtraInfo* class.

The *doEndTag* method may throw a *JspException* to indicate an error.

The release Method The generated servlet invokes the *release* method after all invocations of the tag handler have completed. A tag handler should use this method to release any resources that it might be holding. For example, it should release any database or socket connections in this method.

The TagSupport Base Class The *javax.servlet.jsp.tagext.TagSupport* is a utility base class that simplifies development of new tag handlers. It implements the *Tag* interface and provides convenience getter and setter methods for basic properties. It makes the *PageContext* available as the data member *pageContext* and defines the methods *doStartTag* and *doEndTag* with empty bodies and default return values. The *doStartTag* method returns `SKIP_BODY`, and *doEndTag* returns `EVAL_PAGE`. Tag handler subclasses can override these methods with their own behaviors.

Table 6-4 lists the most useful methods provided by the *TagSupport* base class.

Method Signature	Use
`static Tag findAncestorWithClass (Tag, Class)`	Finds the instance of a given class that is closest to a given instance. This method uses the *getParent* method from the *Tag* interface
`public Tag getParent()`	Returns the *Tag* instance enclosing the current tag
`void setValue(String key, Object value)`	Stores a value associated with a key with this tag handler
`Object getValue(String key)`	Returns the value associated with the key
`java.util.Enumeration getValues()`	Returns an enumeration of all values associated with this tag handler
`void removeValue(String key)`	Removes the value associated with the key

Table 6-4 Useful Methods in the *TagSupport* Base Class

The BodyTag Interface

The *javax.servlet.jsp.tagext.BodyTag* interface extends *Tag* with methods to manipulate the body of an action. These methods act on the *bodyContent* property of the tag handler. Table 6-5 lists the methods in the *BodyTag* interface.

The tag handler totally controls how it handles the tag body. It can fetch it as a *String* and process it without ever sending it to the response buffer. It can send a modified *String* to the response buffer. Or, it can write out its body *as is* to the enclosing *JspWriter*.

The JSP container treats tag handlers that implement *BodyTag* the same as those that implement *Tag*, except that the *doStartTag* method must return either

Method Signature	Description
`void setBodyContent (BodyContent bc)`	Setter method for the *bodyContent* property
`void doInitBody()`	Prepares the handler for the body of the action. Invoked only once per action occurrence in a JSP page
`int doAfterBody()`	Performs any action after the evaluation of the body. This is reinvoked (after reevaluations of the body) as long as the return value of this method is EVAL_BODY_TAG

Table 6-5 Methods in the *BodyTag* Interface

SKIP_BODY or EVAL_BODY_TAG. It cannot return EVAL_BODY_INCLUDE. When *doStartTag* returns EVAL_BODY_TAG, the generated servlet automatically creates a new *BodyContent* object (a subclass of *JspWriter*) by invoking the *pushBody* method on the *PageContext* object. This object supports manipulation of the action's tag body. Then, the generated servlet sets the *BodyContent* object as a property on the tag handler object.

The *BodyTag* interface adds a single additional property: *bodyContent*. If the *doStartTag* method returns EVAL_BODY_TAG, the generated servlet invokes the setter method for the *bodyContent* property (*setBodyContent*) once, just before *doInitBody*. The servlet does not invoke this method if *doStartTag* returns SKIP_BODY.

The *BodyTag* interface adds two main methods to the *Tag* interface: *doInitBody* and *doAfterBody*.

The doInitBody Method The *BodyTag* interface adds a *doInitBody* method to the *Tag* interface. You use this method to initialize body handling, perhaps to get a database or network connection. If the *doStartTag* method returns `EVAL_BODY_TAG`, the generated servlet will invoke *doInitBody* once before entering a loop to process the tag body. The servlet does not invoke this method if *doStartTag* returns `SKIP_BODY`.

This method may throw a *JspException* to indicate an error.

The doAfterBody Method The *BodyTag* interface also adds a *doAfterBody* method to the *Tag* interface. The generated servlet invokes *doAfterBody* after each loop that processes the tag body. The servlet does not invoke this method if a custom action has no body or if *doStartTag* returns `SKIP_BODY`. If this method returns `EVAL_BODY_TAG`, the servlet begins a new evaluation of the body, followed by a new invocation of *doAfterBody*. If the *doAfterBody* method returns `SKIP_BODY`, the body evaluation loop exits and the generated servlet invokes the *doEndTag* method.

This method may throw a *JspException* to indicate an error.

The BodyContent Class The *javax.servlet.jsp.tagext.BodyContent* class is a subclass of *JspWriter* and is used to process tag bodies in custom actions. As we explained in Module 4, the *PageContext* maintains a stack of *BodyContent* objects, each representing the tag body for an action. As processing enters a given nesting level, the generated servlet for the JSP page pushes a new *BodyContext* object on the stack using the *pushBody* method. As processing leaves a given nesting level, it calls the *popBody* method on the *PageContext* object to retrieve the previous *BodyContent* object. Finally, it calls *popBody* to retrieve the original *JspWriter* object. Consider this example of nested tags:

```
<sample:top>  <-- BodyContent for top
   <sample:nested_level_1>  <-- BodyContent for nested_level_1
      <sample:nested_level_2>  <-- BodyContent for nested_level_2
         Regular text
      </sample:nested_level_2>
   </sample:nested_level_1>
</sample:top>
```

This nesting of tags requires three *BodyContent* objects, each representing a tag body at a given nesting level.

Manipulation of a *BodyContent* object is similar to manipulation of a *JspWriter*. The main difference is that unlike a *JspWriter*, the *BodyContent* object does not have a backing stream (connection to a client) into which you can flush the response buffer. The consequences are:

- The *BodyContent* object has an “unbounded” buffer.
- You cannot specify a `<jsp:include>` action in the body of a custom action, since this action automatically flushes the current buffer.

At any point while processing a tag body there can be multiple *BodyContent* objects in the stack maintained by the *PageContext* object. Each *BodyContent* maintains a reference to the previous or enclosing *BodyContent* and can retrieve it using the *getEnclosingWriter* method. The top-level *BodyContent* returns the reference to the original *JspWriter* (backed by the response stream). Each *BodyContent* can manipulate its own tag body using the methods shown in Table 6-6.

The BodyTagSupport Base Class The *javax.servlet.jsp.tagext.BodyTagSupport* utility class provides a base class for tag handlers that manipulate their tag bodies. It implements the *BodyTag* interface and provides default behavior. The return value of its *doStartTag* method is EVAL_BODY_TAG. The return value for its *doEndTag* is EVAL_PAGE. The return value for its *doAfterBody* is SKIP_BODY.

Method Signature	Description
`void clearBody()`	Clears the body. This cannot throw exceptions
`java.io.Reader getReader()`	Returns a reader into its contents after the JSP container has evaluated it
`String getString()`	Returns a String representing its contents after the JSP container has evaluated it
`void writeOut(java.io.Writer out)`	Writes all of its contents into the provided writer
`JspWriter getEnclosingWriter()`	Returns the enclosing writer

Table 6-6 Methods in the *BodyContent* Object

BodyTagSupport also provides convenience methods to retrieve the *BodyContent* object and the enclosing *JspWriter*. Table 6-7 describes these methods.

1-Minute Drill

- What are the three main action methods in the *Tag* interface?
- What is the purpose of the *TagSupport* class?
- What are the main methods in the *BodyTag* interface that manipulate the tag body?
- How many times does the generated servlet invoke the *doAfterBody* method on a tag handler that implements *BodyTag*?
- What is the size of the buffer for the *BodyContent* object?

Method Signature	Use
`BodyContent getBodyContent()`	Returns the BodyContent object for this tag
`JspWriter getPreviousOut()`	Returns the surrounding JspWriter for this tag

Table 6-7 Useful Methods in *BodyTagSupport*

- The action methods are *doStartTag, doEndTag,* and *release.*
- The *TagSupport* class is a utility base class that provides default behavior for a tag handler that implements the *Tag* interface.
- The main methods are *doInitBody* and *doAfterBody.*
- The generated servlet invokes *doAfterBody* method in a loop after every processing of the tag body until it returns `SKIP_BODY`.
- The *BodyContent* object has an "unbounded" buffer.

Life Cycle of a Tag Handler

Now that we've seen the details of the two tag handler interfaces, let's examine the life cycle of both types of tags. Figure 6-4 shows the generated servlet's invocation sequence for a simple *Tag* handler that does not process its body and a *BodyTag* handler that manipulates its body.

Here are the processing steps in the life cycle of tag handlers:

1. As the first block in Figure 6-4 illustrates, both simple and body tag handlers go through a creation and initialization step. First, the generated servlet sets the basic properties, *pageContext*, *parent*, on the tag handler. If the handler implements the *BodyTag* interface, the servlet also sets the *bodyContext* property. Then, the servlet sets all the custom property values by invoking the JavaBean property setter methods for each attribute.

2. If the handler is a simple *Tag* handler, the generated servlet invokes the *doStartTag* method and evaluates the return value. Otherwise, it jumps to Step 5.

3. If the return value from *doStartTag* is `EVAL_BODY_INCLUDE`, the generated servlet processes the tag body.

4. The generated servlet jumps to Step 11.

5. If the handler is a *BodyTag* handler, the generated servlet invokes the *doStartTag* method and evaluates the return value. If the return value is `SKIP_BODY`, it jumps to Step 11.

6. If the return value is `EVAL_BODY_TAG`, the generated servlet creates a new *BodyContent* object using the *pushBody* method and sets it on the tag handler using the *setBodyContent* method.

7. Next, the servlet invokes the *doInitBody* method.

8. The generated servlet processes the tag body using the *BodyContent* object. After processing the tag body, it invokes the *doAfterBody* method.

9. If the *doAfterBody* method returns EVAL_BODY_TAG, processing returns to Step 8. (This allows the tag handler to modify repeatedly the tag body.)

10. The generated servlet invokes the *popBody* method.

11. The generated servlet invokes the *doEndTag* method.

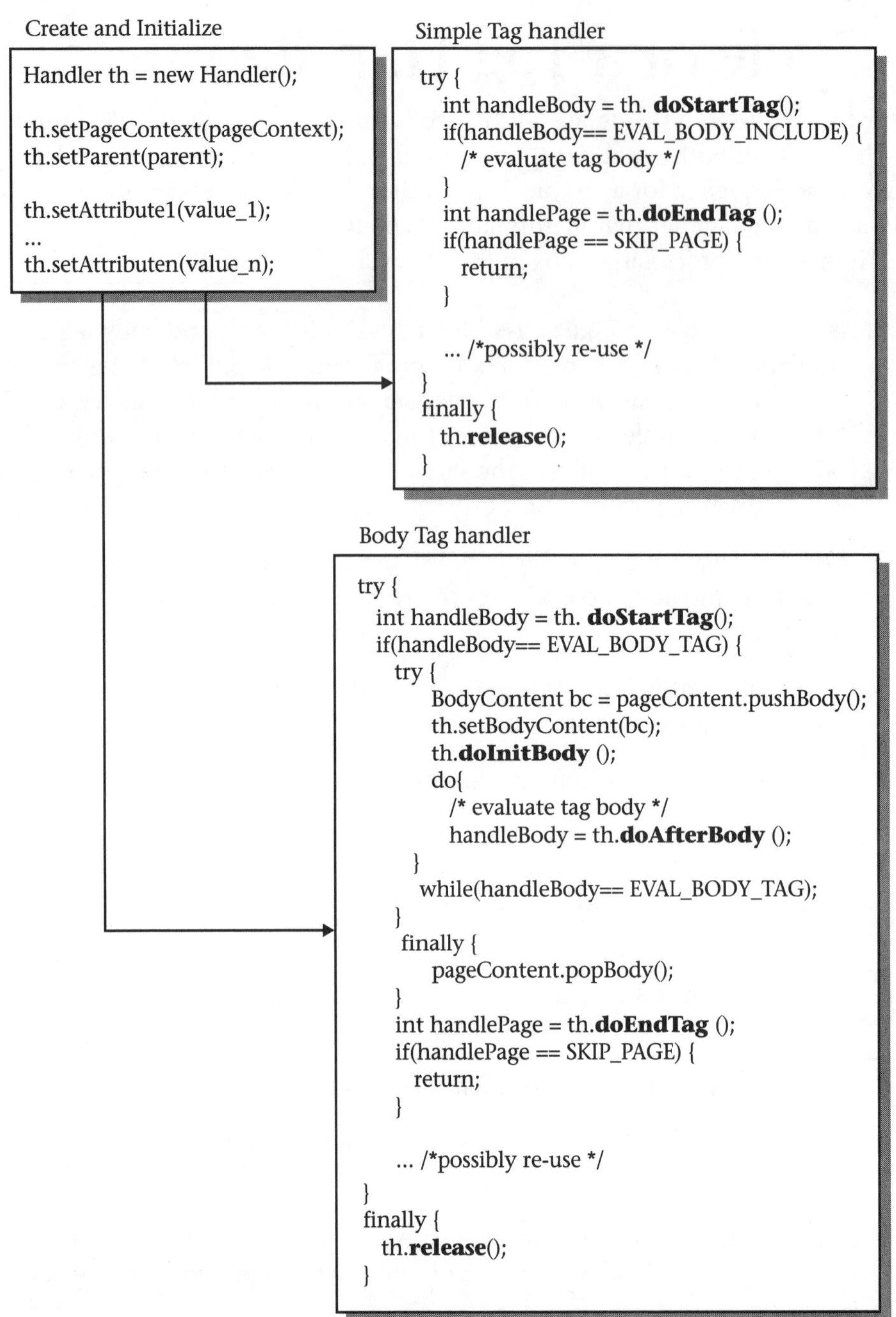

Figure 6-4 The invocation sequence for *Tag* and *BodyTag* handlers

12. If *doEndTag* returns SKIP_PAGE, the generated servlet ignores the rest of the current JSP page (i.e., the generated servlet immediately returns from its *_jspService* method after invoking the current tag handler's *release* method).

13. The generated servlet invokes the *release* method. This allows the tag handler to relinquish any resources that it might have established.

Note

The JSP 1.1 specification states that a JSP page can re-use tag handlers for multiple invocations of a custom action. In re-using the instances, the container could be smart about only initializing the attributes that might have changed. The Tomcat JSP container, version 3.2.1, does not re-use tag handlers but creates a new instance for each occurrence of a custom action.

1-Minute Drill

- What is the first step in the life cycle of a tag handler?
- What is the intent of a tag handler that returns `EVAL_BODY_INCLUDE` in the *doStartTag* method?
- When does the generated servlet invoke the *release* method on the tag handler?

Defining Scripting Variables

In Module 4, we described how the JSP container supports named implicit objects (scripting variables) for use by JSP scriptlets and expressions. We saw in Module 5 how a `<jsp:useBean>` standard action defines a JavaBean and makes it available as a scripting variable. The JSP 1.1 specification also supports the definition of named objects or scripting variables by custom tag libraries.

The TagExtraInfo Class

A custom action informs the JSP container about the scripting variables that it will define by extending the *javax.servlet.jsp.tagext.TagExtraInfo* abstract class.

- The generated servlet sets the basic properties *pageContext, parent,* and *BodyContent* (if the tag handler implements *BodyTag*).
- The tag handler returns this when it processes but does not intend to manipulate the body of the custom action.
- The generated servlet invokes the *release* method once all invocations on the tag handler are complete.

You specify this extended class in the TLD using the `<teiclass>` element. The JSP container invokes the *getVariableInfo* method on the provided *TagExtraInfo* class *at translation time*. This method provides information on each variable that the generated servlet must define *at request time* when it executes the custom action.

As we saw in Module 5 with the `<jsp:useBean>` action, the names of scripting variables are typically defined using static values that the JSP container processes at translation time. When the JSP container invokes the *getVariableInfo* method on our TagExtraInfo class, it passes a *javax.servlet.jsp.tagext.TagData* object that holds the [attribute, value] pairs it can discern at translation time. In our example, our custom action specifies four scripting variables whose names you provide as attributes to our action like this:

```
<sample:calcInterest yearName="numYear"
                     principalName="principal"
                     interestName="interest"
                     balanceName="balance" >
```

The JSP container provides these attributes and their values to our *TagExtraInfo* class using a *TagData* instance.

The *getVariableInfo* method returns an array of *javax.servlet.jsp.tagext.VariableInfo* objects. Each such object describes a scripting variable by providing its name, its type, whether the variable is new or not, and its scope. Here is the *TagExtraInfo* class for our custom action:

```
public class InterestCalcTEI extends TagExtraInfo {
   public VariableInfo[] getVariableInfo(TagData data) {
      VariableInfo info1 = new
         VariableInfo(
            data.getAttributeString("yearName"),
                                   "String",
                                   true,
                                   VariableInfo.NESTED);
      VariableInfo info2 = new
         VariableInfo(
            data.getAttributeString("principalName"),
                                   "String",
                                   true,
                                   VariableInfo.NESTED);
      VariableInfo info3 = new
         VariableInfo(
```

```
            data.getAttributeString("interestName"),
                                    "String",
                                    true,
                                    VariableInfo.NESTED);
        VariableInfo info4 = new
          VariableInfo(
            data.getAttributeString("balanceName"),
                                    "String",
                                    true,
                                    VariableInfo.NESTED);
        VariableInfo [] info = { info1, info2, info3, info4 };
        return info;
    }
}
```


Our *InterestCalcTEI* class defines four scripting variables. The first argument to the *VariableInfo* constructor provides the attribute name. You retrieve the value for the named attribute using the *TagData* object passed into the *getVariableInfo* method.

The second argument states the type of the variable *(String)*, while the third argument states whether the variable is new to the current JSP page (`true`).

The fourth argument defines the scope of the variable. Scripting variables have three possible scopes:

- `VariableInfo.NESTED` The scripting variable is available between the start tag and the end tag of the action that defines it.
- `VariableInfo.AT_BEGIN` The scripting variable is available from the start tag of the action that defines it until the end of the page.
- `VariableInfo.AT_END` The scripting variable is available after the end tag of the action that defines it until the end of the page.

All of our variables have `VariableInfo.NESTED` scope. Figure 6-5 illustrates the three scopes.

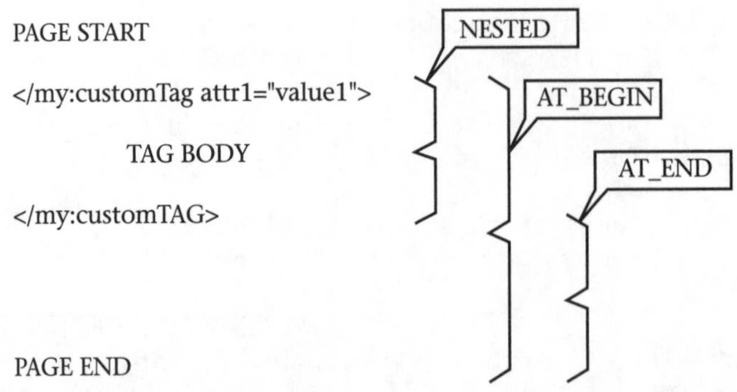

Figure 6-5 Scopes for scripting variables

The *TagExtraInfo* class also validates the attributes specified in a custom action. The JSP container invokes the *isValid* method at translation time. The method causes a translation time error if the *isValid* method returns `false`. Like the *getVariableInfo* method, the *isValid* method receives a *TagData* instance that contains all values for translation-time attributes. This permits the method to validate the values. Table 6-8 shows the two methods in *TagExtraInfo* that the JSP container invokes at translation time.

Defining the Scripting Variables

Tag handlers define scripting variables by storing them in the *pageContext* using the *setAttribute(name, value)* or *setAttribute(name, value, scope)* methods under

Method Signature	Description
`VariableInfo[] getVariableInfo(TagData)`	Returns an array of objects each describing a scripting variable defined by the custom action. The abstract class returns null
`boolean isValid(TagData)`	Validates translation-time attribute values. The abstract class returns true

Table 6-8 Methods Provided by *TagExtraInfo*

Question: How do you use a *TagExtraInfo* class to validate the attributes of a custom action?

Answer: You can specify attribute values for a custom action as static String values or as request-time JSP expressions. The TLD specifies whether an action can accept request time JSP expressions. If the attribute accepts only static values, you should validate attributes once, at translation time, instead of during every request, since this is more efficient. You can do translation-time validation by providing a *TagExtraInfo* class for your custom action and defining the *isValid* method on it. This method is invoked the when the JSP page is translated by the JSP container to generate the page implementation servlet. The method has access to a *TagData* object that encapsulates all translation-time [attribute, value] pairs. For example, this code fragment shows a *TagExtraInfo* class for a custom action that expects the attribute "isRequired" to have one of two values: `true` or `false`:

```
public class MyActionTEI extends TagExtraInfo {
   public boolean isValid(TagData data) {
      String val = data.getAttributeString("isRequired");
      return val.equals("true") || val.equals("false");
   }
}
```

If the attribute can accept request time JSP expressions as values, then you must validate it in every request. You can do this by validating the values in the tag handler and throwing a *javax.servlet.jsp.JspTagException* if there is a validation error. For example, the following code fragment shows a setter method for the attribute `name`. This code requires the attribute to have the value of either "cosmo" or "kramer":

```
public void setName(String name) throws JspTagException {
      if(!name.equals("cosmo") && !name.equals("kramer"))
         throw new JspTagException("Name has to be cosmo or kramer!");
      this.name = name;
   }
```

6

the exact name specified in the *TagExtraInfo* class. The JSP container creates a scripting variable under the name provided by the *TagExtraInfo* class and assigns it to the object stored under that same name in the *pageContext*. Let's look at our example to illustrate this.

Our custom action `<sample:calcInterest>` defined four scripting variables with the names: *numYear*, *principal*, *interest*, and *balance*. So, our tag handler must create these variables and store them using the *PageContext* object. This code fragment shows how you store them:

```
pageContext.setAttribute("numYear", value);
pageContext.setAttribute("principal", value);
pageContext.setAttribute("interest", value);
pageContext.setAttribute("balance", value);
```

The point in code to set these attributes depends on the scope of the scripting variable. The scope indicates what methods *may* affect the value of a scripting variable and thereby defines when a tag handler can set the value of the scripting variable. Table 6-9 describes the correct point to set these attributes.

1-Minute Drill

- What is the purpose of the *TagExtraInfo* class?
- What are the possible scopes for a scripting variable declared using a custom action?
- When does the servlet container examine the *TagExtraInfo* class?

- A custom action informs the JSP container about the scripting variables that it will define by extending the *TagExtraInfo* class.
- The possible scopes are: `VariableInfo.AT_BEGIN`, `VariableInfo.AT_END`, and `VariableInfo.NESTED`.
- The servlet container examines the *TagExtraInfo* class at translation time.

Scope	When to Set the Value
NESTED	After *doInitBody* and *doAfterBody* for a tag handler implementing *BodyTag*, and after *doStartTag* otherwise
AT_BEGIN	After *doInitBody*, *doAfterBody*, and *doEndTag* for a tag handler implementing *BodyTag*, and *doStartTag* and *doEndTag* otherwise
AT_END	After *doEndTag*

Table 6-9 Synchronization of Scripting Variables

The Recommended Convention for Defining Implicit Objects

The JSP specification advocates a particular style for defining implicit objects. It recommends building a tag library and adding an action called `<prefix:defineObjects />` that defines the desired implicit objects. The JSP page for such a setup might look like this:

```
<%@ taglib prefix="mySetup" uri="relativeURL" %>
<mySetup:defineObjects />
… start using the defined implicit objects …
```

The specification goes on to say that this convention requires no new machinery and makes the dependency of the objects on the custom action very explicit.

Ask the Expert

Question: Doesn't the recommended convention for defining scripting variables make it difficult to know what scripting variables it defines?

Answer: Yes, it does, since the tag itself gives no clue about the name or type of the implicit objects. We prefer the standard `<jsp:useBean>` action that specifies an `id` attribute and a Java class name or type attribute. The `<jsp:useBean>` action explicitly declares what scripting variables and object types are available for use by a JSP page.

DefineVars.jsp
web.xml
DefineVarTag.java
DefineVarTEI.java
deineVar.tld

Project 6-1: Defining Implicit Objects

This project illustrates construction of a custom action. Our goal is to create an action similar to the standard `<jsp:useBean>` action, but simpler. We use our custom action to define several scripting variables that we explicitly name and type.

Step-by-Step

1. Download the files for this project from `http://www.osborne.com`.

2. Move the JSP file `DefineVars.jsp` into `%TOMCAT_HOME%/webapps/Book/jsp`.

3. Examine `DefineVars.jsp`. We reproduce it here:

```
<%@page import="java.util.*, define.*" %>
<%@taglib uri="/taglib" prefix="tls" %>

<tls:defineVariable name="leader" type="String" />
<tls:defineVariable name="independenceDate" type="Date" />
<tls:defineVariable name="PI" type="Double" />

<TABLE WIDTH=400 CELLSPACING="0" CELLPADDING="3" BORDER="1">
<TR>
  <TD WIDTH=40%> <B> Leader </B> </TD>
  <TD> <%= leader %> </TD>
</TR>
<TR>
  <TD WIDTH=40%> <B> Independence Date </B> </TD>
  <TD> <%= independenceDate %> </TD>
</TR>
<TR>
  <TD WIDTH=40%> <B> PI </B> </TD>
  <TD> <%= PI %> </TD>
</TR>
</TABLE>
```

The JSP page imports relevant classes using a page directive. It then uses a taglib directive to import a tag library whose location is simply `/taglib`. The string "tls" will prefix all actions in this tag library. Then there are three invocations of the custom action `defineVariable`. This tag takes two attributes, the name and type of the scripting variable. After processing of the tags, the JSP page can access three implicit variables: a String named "leader", a Java Date named "independenceDate", and a Java Double named "PI". We use JSP expressions to print the values of these variables in an HTML table. Our goal in this project is to write the tag handlers and other relevant entities to make this JSP page work.

4. Create a file called `defineVar.tld` with these contents:

```
<?xml version="1.0" encoding="ISO-8859-1" ?>
<!DOCTYPE taglib PUBLIC
  "-//Sun Microsystems, Inc.//DTD JSP Tag Library 1.1//EN"
  "http://java.sun.com/j2ee/dtds/web-jsptaglibrary_1_1.dtd">
<taglib>
   <tlibversion>1.0</tlibversion>
   <jspversion>1.1</jspversion>
      <shortname></shortname>
   <tag>
      <name>defineVariable</name>
      <tagclass>define.DefineVarTag</tagclass>
      <teiclass>define.DefineVarTEI</teiclass>
      <bodycontent>empty</bodycontent>
      <info> A custom tag that defines scripting variables </info>
      <attribute>
         <name>name</name>
         <required>true</required>
         <rtexprvalue>false</rtexprvalue>
      </attribute>
      <attribute>
         <name>type</name>
         <required>true</required>
         <rtexprvalue>false</rtexprvalue>
      </attribute>
   </tag>
</taglib>
```

The TLD describes the custom tag named "defineVariable" to have the Java class *define.DefineVarTag* as its tag handler and *define.DefineVarTEI* as its *TagExtraInfo* class. The tag is required to have an empty body and it takes two attributes: `name` and `type`. Both attributes are required.

5. Place the file `defineVar.tld` under `%TOMCAT_HOME%/webapps/Book/WEB-INF`.

6. In the file named `web.xml` under `%TOMCAT_HOME%/webapps/Book/WEB-INF`, add the following XML fragment:

```
<taglib>
   <taglib-uri>/taglib</taglib-uri>
   <taglib-location>/WEB-INF/define_var.tld</taglib-location>
</taglib>
```

6

This XML fragment informs the JSP container that there exists a tag library that can be located using the URI "/taglib". The actual location of the tag library is relative to the root of the current application context (`%TOMCAT_HOME%/webapps/Book`). We explain Web application deployment and packaging in Appendix C.

7. Now, we need to write our *TagExtraInfo* class to inform the JSP container about the scripting variables created by our custom action. Create a file named `DefineVarTEI.java`. Start by importing the relevant classes.

```
package define;
import javax.servlet.jsp.tagext.*;
```

8. Define the class as shown here:

```
public class DefineVarTEI extends TagExtraInfo {
public VariableInfo[] getVariableInfo(TagData data) {
   VariableInfo info1
      = new VariableInfo(data.getAttributeString("name"),
                         data.getAttributeString("type"),
                         true,
                         VariableInfo.AT_END);
   VariableInfo [] info = { info1 };
      return info;
   }
}
```

Our class extends from *TagExtraInfo* and defines the method *getVariableInfo* that describes each scripting variable created by this custom action. Our custom action defines only one scripting variable on each invocation, although the variable has a different name and type on each invocation. Hence, the method *getVariableInfo* returns only one *VariableInfo* object. You can retrieve the values for the name and type attributes from *TagData,* which encapsulates all translation-time attribute values. We specify the scope `VariableInfo.AT_END`, indicating that the JSP page can use the variable following processing of the end tag for this custom action.

9. Finally, we need to write the tag handler. Create a Java file named `DefineVarTag.java`. Start by importing the relevant classes.

```
package define;
import javax.servlet.jsp.*;
import javax.servlet.jsp.tagext.*;
```

```
import java.io.*;
import java.util.Calendar;
import java.util.Date;
```

10. Since our custom action will have an empty body, our tag handler can just extend *TagSupport*. So add this line:

```
public class DefineVarTag extends TagSupport {
```

11. Define member variables for each attribute of our custom action and define JavaBeans setter methods for them as shown here:

```
private String name = null;
private String type = null;

public void setName(String name) {
   this.name = name;
}
public void setType(String type) {
   this.type = type;
}
```


12. Since we defined our scripting variables to have the scope of `VariableInfo.AT_END`, our scripting variables need to be available after the *doEndTag* method of our tag handler. So define *doEndTag* as follows:

```
public int doEndTag() throws JspException {
   if(name.equals("leader"))
      pageContext.setAttribute(name, "Mahatma Gandhi");
   else if(name.equals("independenceDate"))
      pageContext.setAttribute(name, constructDate());
   else if(name.equals("PI"))
      pageContext.setAttribute(name, new Double(3.1415));
   return EVAL_PAGE;
}
private Date constructDate() {
   Calendar c = Calendar.getInstance();
   c.set(1947, 7, 15);
   return c.getTime();
}
```

Since we invoke the custom action three times using different names in our JSP page, based on the name, we need to create a different scripting variables and store it in the *PageContext* object. The three variables also have different types. We could do additional checking on the type attribute to ensure that we create variables with the correct type.

13. Compile the Java file and move it to %TOMCAT_HOME%/webapps/Book/WEB-INF/classes/define.

14. Start the Tomcat JSP container.

15. Start a browser and access the JSP page using the URL: `http://localhost:8080/Book/jsp/DefineVars.jsp`. You should see a page as shown in Figure 6-6.

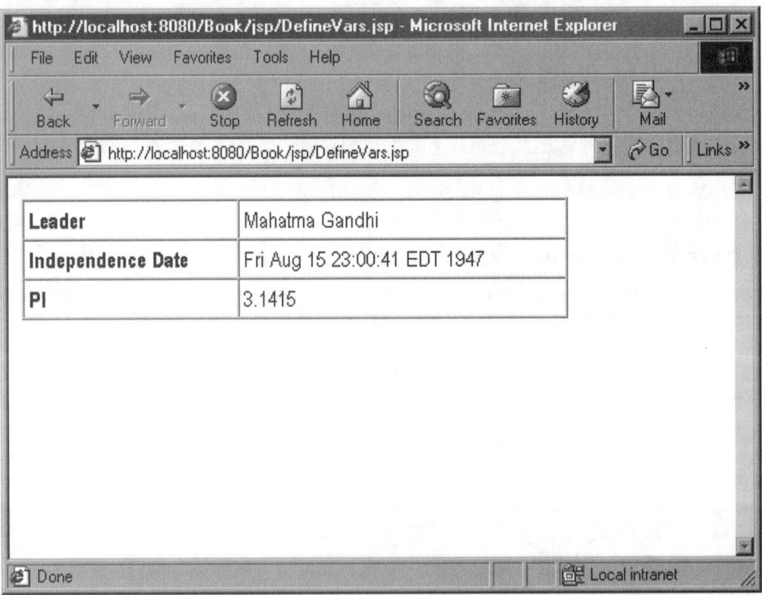

Figure 6-6 Defining implicit objects using tag libraries

Exchanging Data Between Actions and Tag Libraries

When you create a set of cooperating actions or tag libraries, you must also define how they share data. For example, one action might search a database and return a result set while a different action loops through such a result set to lay it out in an HTML table. The JSP specification recommends two mechanisms for sharing data between tag libraries:

- Object ids stored in global data
- Object scoping

Ids and the PageContext Object

The most popular mechanism for exchanging data between actions assigns data objects a name. That is, one action creates, names, and stores the object in a shared data area, while the second action uses the name to retrieve the object. For example, in the following JSP page fragment, the first action, `<x:foo>`, creates an object and gives it the name "myObject." The `<x:bar>` action then accesses the same object using its name:

```
<x:foo id="myObject" />
<x:bar ref="myObject" />
```

By explicitly identifying objects by name, the two actions advertise the cooperation between them. As we saw earlier, the JSP container maintains the mapping between the name and the actual object as an attribute in a shared data space, often the current *PageContext* object. The `<x:foo>` action calls the *setAttribute* method provided by the *pageContext* variable to store the object under the name "myObject". Then the `<x:bar>` action retrieves the object using the *getAttribute* method.

This method also works between tag libraries, whose actions can be included into the same JSP page. This method even works across JSP scopes because actions have access to other shared data spaces like the *HttpSession* object through the *PageContext* object. This means that the shared data space could be the *HttpSession* object as easily as the *PageContext* object.

The Runtime Stack

A second method uses object scoping to share data. For example, consider this code fragment:

```
<x:foo>
   <x:bar />
</x:foo>
```

In this fragment, the `<x:bar />` action nests within the `<x:foo>` action. Remember that all tag handlers share at least two basic properties: the current *pageContext* and the *parent* tag handler. So, the `<x:foo>` action can create and provide an access method to an object. The `<x:bar />` action can then access its parent and ask for that object by invoking the accessor method.

Let's examine a concrete example. Consider this code fragment:

```
<sample:account number="34404">
    <sample:withdraw amount="500" />
</sample:account>
```

Here is the tag handler for the `<sample:account>` action:

```
public class AccountTag extends BodyTagSupport {
   private int account = 0;
   public void setNumber(int number) {
      account = number;
   }
   public int getNumber() {
      return account;
   }
}
```

The `<sample:account>` tag handler stores the account number and provides access to it through the *getNumber* method. The tag handler for the `<sample:withdraw>` action can then extract this account number like this:

```
public class WithdrawTag extends TagSupport {
   private int amount = 0;
   public void setAmount(int amt) {
      amount = amt;
   }
   public int doStartTag() {
      AccountTag parent_tag = (AccountTag)getParent();
      int acctNumber = parent_tag.getNumber();
   }
}
```

WithdrawTag uses the *getParent* method in the *Tag* interface to fetch the enclosing tag handler and requests the account number directly from it.

The utility class *TagSupport* provides two useful facilities to support such implicit communication between actions:

- It provides a static method, *findAncestorWithClass*, that locates the closest ancestor of a given Java class, starting from a given tag handler instance.
- It maintains a *Hashtable* of *String* keys mapped to *Object* values and provides the methods *setValue*, *getValue*, *getValues*, and *removeValue* to manipulate it. So tag handlers that extend the *TagSupport* object can store and retrieve values from this *Hashtable*.

Tip

The *getParent* method can only retrieve the immediate parent. This means that a user who inadvertently encloses the innermost tag in another tag will break the innermost tag. It is better to use the *findAncestorWithClass* method, since this method works whatever the nesting level.

1-Minute Drill

- What are the two ways that custom tags can exchange data?
- What are the useful methods that the TagSupport utility base class provides to enable communication between tags?

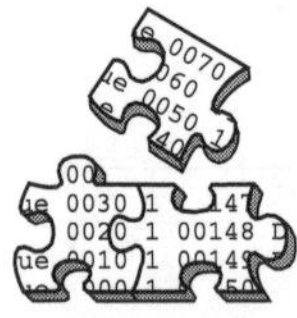

InsertTag.java
PutTag.java
GetTag.java
web.xml
template.tld
template.jsp
instance1.jsp
instance2.jsp
Inventory.html
Checkout.html
Sidebar.html
header.html
Main.html
logo.jpg

Project 6-2: A Template Using a Tag Library

In Module 5, we developed a simple template mechanism using the `<jsp:include>` standard action. We expand on that concept in this project to build a template mechanism for page layouts using custom tags. A template mechanism separates constant layout elements from elements that change with each page. Using templates, a Web designer can easily provide a consistent look-and-feel for all pages.

In this project, we also see actions communicating with each other using both the *pageContext* and the runtime stack.

Step-by-Step

1. Download the files for this project from `http://www.osborne.com`.
2. Move all the HTML files and the JSP files to the location `%TOMCAT_HOME%/webapps/Book/jsp`.
3. Move the JPG file `logo.jpg` to the location `%TOMCAT_HOME%/webapps/Book/images`.

   Examine the file `template.jsp`. The file is reproduced here:

```
<%@ taglib uri="/template" prefix="template" %>
<HTML>
<HEAD><TITLE>
   <template:get name="title" default="Hello" direct="true" />
</TITLE></HEAD>
<BODY>
   <TABLE WIDTH=650 BORDER=0>
   <TR>
      <TD COLSPAN=2>
```

- The two ways are:
  1. Named objects stored in global data accessed via pageContext
  2. Runtime stack based on Object scoping
- It provides the *findAncestorWithClass* method to locate the closest ancestor and provides utility methods on a *Hashtable* for storing and retrieving values.

```
            <template:get name="header" default="header.html" />
        </TD>
    </TR>
    <TR>
    <TD>
        <TABLE WIDTH=650 BORDER=1>
        <TR>
        <TD WIDTH=15%>
            <template:get name="sidebar" default="Sidebar.html" />
        </TD>
        <TD WIDTH=85%>
            <template:get name="main" default="Main.html" />
        </TD>
        </TR>
        </TABLE>
    </TD>
</TR>
</TABLE>
</BODY>
</HTML>
```


The JSP page produces a layout as shown in Figure 6-7. There are four dynamic elements representing four different regions on the page: title, header, sidebar, and main. Each region uses the custom action `<template:get>` to include a Web resource. You identify the included resource using the attribute `name`. You can also specify a default value using the attribute `default`. When the value is a *String* constant (e.g., the title), you indicate this by assigning `true` to the attribute `direct`. Otherwise, the value specifies a file (JSP page or HTML page).

4. Examine the file `instance1.jsp`. It is reproduced here:

```
<%@ taglib uri="/template" prefix="template" %>
<template:insert name="template.jsp">
    <template:put name="title" value="Inventory" />
    <template:put name="main" value="Inventory.html" />
</template:insert>
```

This JSP page defines its layout using `template.jsp`. It uses two custom tags, `<template:put>` and `<template:insert>`, the former nested within the latter. It assigns the *String* "Inventory" to the title and inserts the JSP file, `Inventory.html`, into the main region. The rest of the elements insert default values.

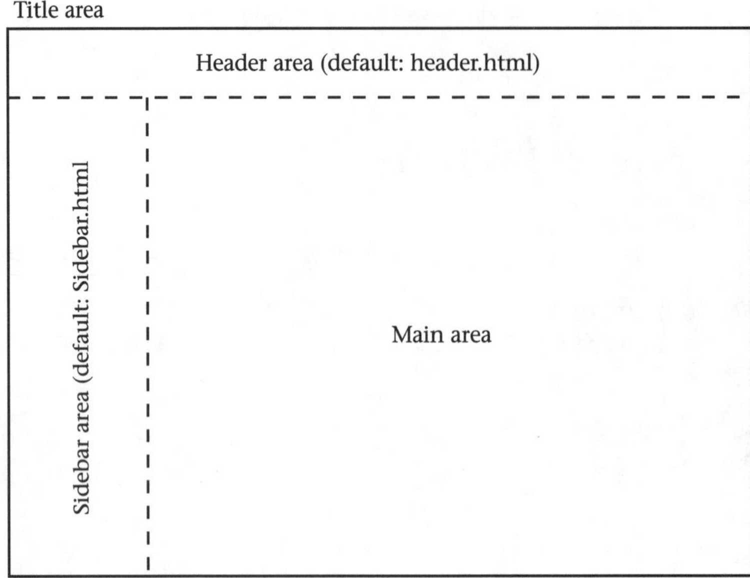

Figure 6-7 Template layout

5. Now examine the file `instance2.jsp`. We reproduce it here:

```
<%@ taglib uri="/template" prefix="template" %>
<template:insert name="template.jsp">
   <template:put name="title" value="Checkout" />
   <template:put name="main" value="Checkout.html" />
</template:insert>
```

   This JSP page also defines its layout using `template.jsp`. This time, our JSP page assigns the *String* "Checkout" to the title while it inserts the HTML file, `Checkout.html`, into the main region. The rest of the elements insert default values.

6. Let's define and implement the three custom tags `<template:put>`, `<template:get>`, and `<template:insert>`. Move the TLD, `template.tld`, to the location `%TOMCAT_HOME%/webapps/Book/WEB-INF`. Examine `template.tld` and be sure that you understand it.

7. Move the file `web.xml` to the location `%TOMCAT_HOME%/webapps/Book/WEB-INF`. Examine the file to see how we map the URI location `/template` to the TLD. We explained how you do this in Project 6-1.

Examine the tag handlers in order, starting with the one for the `<template:get>` action. It is shown here:

```
package template;
import javax.servlet.*;
import javax.servlet.jsp.*;
import javax.servlet.jsp.tagext.*;
import java.io.*;
public class GetTag extends TagSupport {
   private String name = null;
   private String deflt = null;
   private boolean isDirect = false;
   public void setName(String name) {
      this.name = name;
   }
   public void setDefault(String deflt) {
      this.deflt = deflt;
   }
   public void setDirect(boolean isdirect) {
      this.isDirect = isdirect;
   }
   public int doEndTag() throws JspException {
      String value =
         (String)pageContext.getAttribute(name,
                              PageContext.REQUEST_SCOPE);
      if(value == null) {
         value = deflt;
      }
      try {
         if (isDirect == true) {
            // write value as direct output to JspWriter
            pageContext.getOut().print(value);
         }
         else {
            // consider value as resource to be included
            pageContext.include(value);
         }
      }
      catch(IOException ioe) {
         throw new JspTagException("Get Tag: " + ioe);
      }
      catch(ServletException se) {
         throw new JspTagException("Get Tag: " + se);
      }
      return EVAL_PAGE;
   }
}
```

The `<template:get>` action does not require a tag body, so it extends the *TagSupport* utility class. It defines setter methods for its attributes: `name`, `default`, and `direct`. The attribute `name` indicates the name of the dynamic element in the template. The attribute `default` indicates its default value. The attribute `direct` indicates whether the element represents a *String* for direct output or a resource that needs to be included.

The action defines only the *doEndTag* method in the tag protocol. The method retrieves the values for the current dynamic element from the current *HttpServletRequest* object (using the *pageContext* variable). If the action fails to find the value in the *HttpServletRequest* object, it uses the attribute's default value. Depending on the boolean value of the attribute `direct`, the action prints the value as a direct string or includes the value as a resource using the *pageContext.include* method (that we explained in Module 4). Finally, it returns EVAL_PAGE to indicate to the generated servlet to process the rest of the JSP page.

8. Now, let's examine the tag handler for the `<template:put>` action. Here is the code:

```
package template;
import javax.servlet.jsp.*;
import javax.servlet.jsp.tagext.*;
import java.io.*;
public class PutTag extends TagSupport {
   private String name = null;
   private String value = null;
   public void setName(String name) {
      this.name = name;
   }
   public void setValue(String value) {
      this.value = value;
   }
   public int doEndTag() throws JspException {
      InsertTag parent = (InsertTag)getParent();
      parent.setEntry(name, value);
      return EVAL_PAGE;
   }
}
```

This tag handler also extends *TagSupport,* since it does not require a tag body. It then defines setter methods for its two attributes: `name` and `value`. Then, it defines the *doEndTag* method where it retrieves its parent tag, which happens to be *InsertTag,* and sends the values of *name* and *value* to the parent using the *setEntry* method. (This illustrates communication between actions based on implicit syntactic scoping.)

9. Finally, here is the tag handler for the `<template:insert>`:

```
package template;
import javax.servlet.*;
import javax.servlet.jsp.*;
import javax.servlet.jsp.tagext.*;
import java.io.*;
import java.util.*;
public class InsertTag extends BodyTagSupport {
   private String name = null;
   private Map entries = new HashMap();

   public void setName(String name) {
      this.name = name;
   }
   public int doAfterBody() throws JspException {
      Iterator iter = entries.keySet().iterator();

      // Set the template inputs as variables in pageContext
      while(iter.hasNext()) {
         String name = (String)iter.next();
         String value = (String)entries.get(name);
         pageContext.setAttribute(name, value, PageContext.REQUEST_SCOPE);
      }
      try {
         pageContext.forward(name);
      }
      catch(IOException ioe) {
         throw new JspTagException("Insert Tag: " + ioe);
      }
      catch(ServletException se) {
         throw new JspTagException("Insert Tag: " + se);
      }
      return SKIP_BODY;
   }
   public void setEntry(String name, String value) {
      entries.put(name, value);
   }
}
```

The `<template:insert>` action contains a tag body and is interested in manipulating it. Hence its tag handler extends the *BodyTagSupport* utility class. It stores the template filename (set as the value of the attribute `name`) using the *setName* method. It also maintains a *HashMap* of [name, value] pairs for each dynamic attribute the template sets.

The action defines only *doAfterBody*, which the generated servlet invokes after evaluating the body of the tag. Since the tag body contains the `<template:put>` actions, the generated servlet has already invoked the tag handlers for those `<template:put>` actions before it invokes the *doAfterBody* method. These handlers used the *setEntry* method (accessed through their parent reference) to store the [name, value] pairs in the *HashMap*. This means that when the generated servlet invokes the *doAfterBody* method, the *HashMap* already contains [name, value] pairs derived from `<template:put>` actions.

The *doAfterBody method* first sets each [name, value] pair as a *PageContext* attribute with request scope. Remember that this is necessary in order for the `<template:get>` action to retrieve it later. The default page scope is insufficient in this case because storage and retrieval of these attributes happen in different pages. Hence, we use request scope. Finally, *doAfterBody* forwards control to the template JSP page specified as the value of the attribute "name."

10. Compile the three Java files: `InsertTag.java`, `PutTag.java`, and `GetTag.java`. Move the class files to `%TOMCAT_HOME%/webapps/Book/WEB-INF/classes/template`.

11. Start the Tomcat JSP container.

12. Start a Web browser and enter the URL: `http://localhost:8080/Book/jsp/instance1.jsp`. You should see a Web page as shown in Figure 6-8.

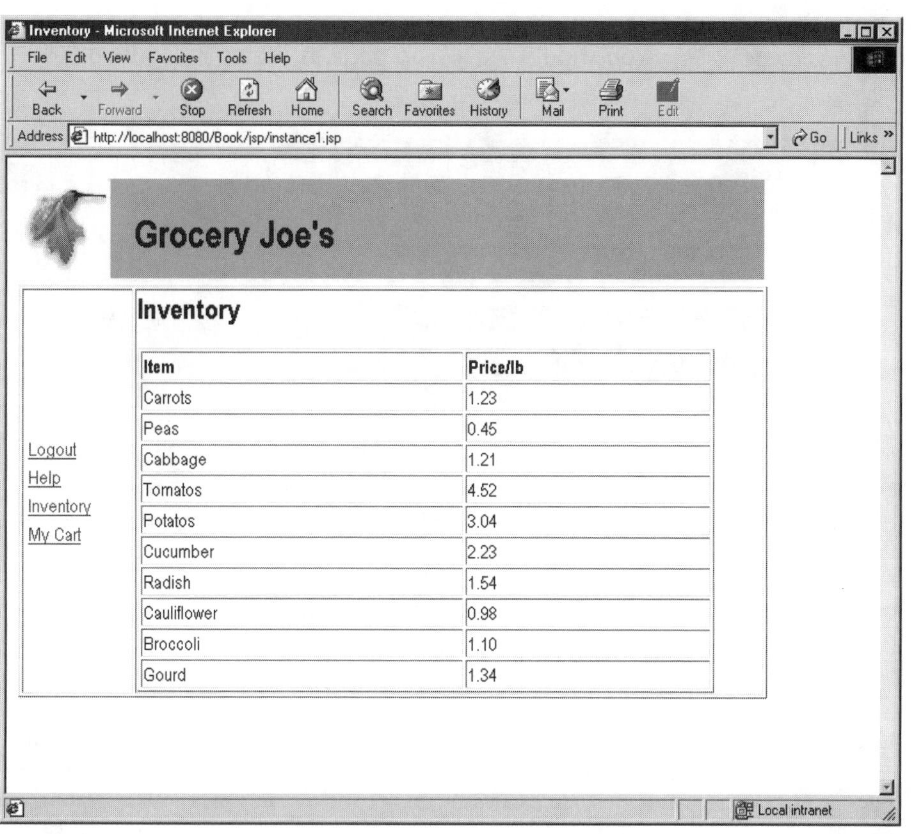

Figure 6-8 First use of the template

13. Now enter the URL: `http://localhost:8080/Book/jsp/instance2.jsp`. You should see a Web page as shown in Figure 6-9.

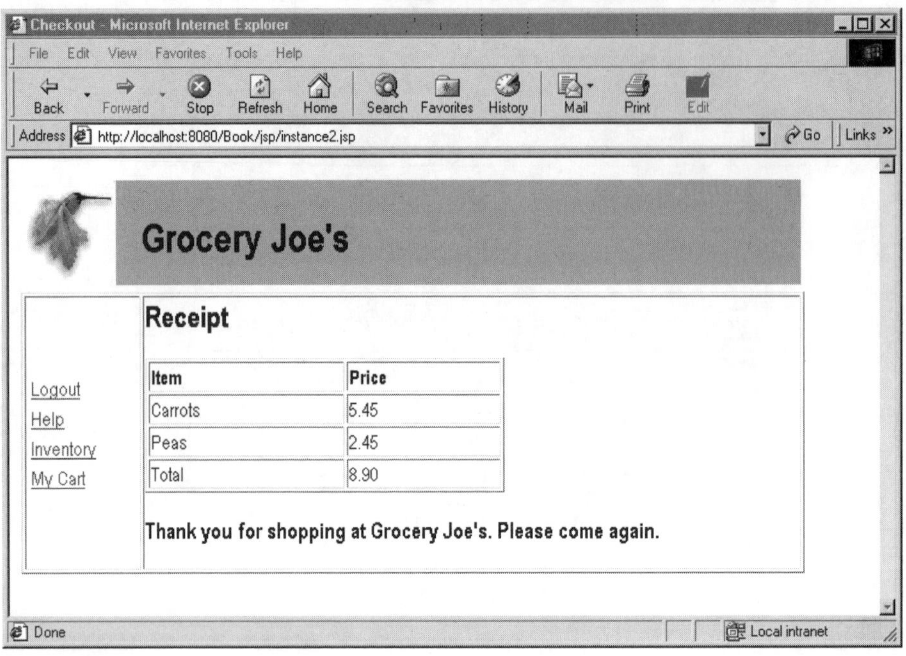

Figure 6-9 Second use of the template

Mastery Check

1. What advantages do custom tags provide JSP developers?

2. What are the main elements of a custom action or tag library?

3. What two types of tag interfaces can a tag developer implement?

4. Can a tag handler call the *pageContext.include* method in its *doAfterBody* method?

5. How does a tag library developer specify that you can provide the value of a tag attribute using a JSP expression?

6. What is the role of the *BodyContent* object?

7. What are the roles of the *TagExtraInfo* class?

Mastery Check

8. What are the two recommended ways to share data between custom actions?

9. What is the role of the tag library descriptor?

10. How do you specify the tag handler class for a custom action?

11. What is the role of the *release* method in the *Tag* interface?

12. When and how many times does the generated servlet call the *doInitBody* method? What is the purpose of the *doInitBody* method?

13. How does a custom action developer specify that a tag attribute is optional?

Part II

Building Real-World Applications

Module 7

JSP Architectures

The Goals of This Module

- Gain basic familiarity with software patterns
- Understand the basics of Java-based Web architectures
- Understand the architectural role of JavaServer Pages
- Understand how to apply software patterns to JSP programs
- Present a concrete application that will drive the discussion in Modules 8, 9, and 10

In Part I, you learned basic JSP syntax and techniques. Now in Part II, you will learn how to apply these foundations in the context of four "real-world" problems:

1. Designing Web application architectures
2. Implementing security mechanisms in JSP applications
3. Coordinating the flow of control (*web-flow*) within a Java-based Web application
4. Managing data in JSP applications

This module addresses the first of these topics, Web application architectures based upon JavaServer Pages.

We begin with a general discussion of software patterns, one of the more profound contributions to modern software design. Then, we describe architectural patterns and their importance to Web applications. Next, we describe a few of the more important software patterns applicable to JSP architectures. Finally, we describe an application that will guide our discussion in Part II.

Patterns in Application Development

Analysis patterns are a relatively recent application development tool. The so-called "Gang-of-Four" book (GoF)—Gamma, Helm, Johnson, and Vlissides, *Design Patterns: Elements of Reusable Object-Oriented Software*, (Addison-Wesley Publishing Company, 1995) acts as the de facto bible for pattern-based development. Its importance lies in the fact that it first named, categorized, and explained in a single book a fundamental set of object-oriented software design patterns. The term "pattern" and its application to software precedes the Gang-of-Four book, however, and has diverse roots. The early Smalltalk community and the ideas of a building architect, Christopher Alexander (Alexander, Ishikawa, Silverstein, Jacobson, Fikadahl-King, and Angel, *A Pattern Language*, Oxford University Press, 1977) were especially important. The general idea has been widespread in a variety of groups since the early 1990s.

The Idea of Patterns

The patterns community has proposed several different definitions of patterns. The GoF defined patterns as "a solution to a problem in a context" (GoF, p. 3). For the purposes of the book, GoF then restricted this definition to *communicating software objects and classes*. You need not, however, confine the idea of a pattern to software objects and classes. Another definition describes patterns as "an effective solution to an important design problem" (Mowbray and Malveau, *CORBA Design Patterns*, John Wiley & Sons, Inc., 1997, p. 6). Martin Fowler defines patterns this way: "A pattern is an idea that has been useful in one practical context and will probably be useful in others" (Fowler, *Analysis Patterns*, Addison-Wesley, 1997, p. xv).

Some recurring themes emerge from all the discussions of software patterns. The most important of these themes is that patterns name and explain solutions to recurring practical problems. They are a kind of notation for what good software designers have discovered about the best ways to solve a class of "real-world" problems that appear in a variety of software contexts. The key here is that patterns give a name to a solution and explain how to apply it. In this way, they supply both a vocabulary and a lesson. Sometimes the lesson is familiar and the name just helps you talk about it. This can be an incredibly effective way to communicate ideas that would otherwise require a drawing. At other times, the lesson helps you work through the distractions of a problem to identify its essential traits. A good pattern should play both roles, often at the same time.

A second important theme is that patterns are not academic inventions. Patterns are more like folklore than mathematical proofs. They are a kind of received wisdom from a community of problem solvers. Their genealogy in actual projects is important and distinctive. Their importance derives from the fact that they work—they are demonstrably useful.

A third theme is that while patterns emerge in a specific problem domain, they can sometimes cross multiple problem domains. Good patterns generally express something that you can apply elsewhere. They are idea factories.

1-Minute Drill

- Why does the "Gang-of-Four" book have such a high standing among developers?
- What do software patterns express about software design?
- In what sense are software patterns "idea factories"?

- The Gang-of-Four book first categorized and explained in a single book a fundamental set of object-oriented software design patterns.
- Software patterns express the best ways to solve a class of real-world problems that appear in a variety of software contexts.
- Software patterns are "idea factories" in the sense that they generally can be applied to multiple software domains.

The Utility of Patterns

Patterns are useful for several reasons. As we said, patterns provide names for solutions and by doing so provide a vocabulary for describing development projects. So long as your audience understands the language, your communication can be more precise at the same time that it is more concise.

Patterns teach good software design practices. Patterns identify recurring design problems and appropriate solutions to the problems. This means that a thorough understanding of patterns and their applicability helps developers better understand good software design practices. A good software design is more elegant, adaptable to change, and reusable.

Patterns facilitate debate about solutions, since patterns imply a problem context. If you attach a pattern to your problem, you effectively express your analysis of the problem. Someone else can debate this analysis with you, and the debate can further illuminate the problem.

By consciously using patterns (you might do so unconsciously, but this is not as helpful), you enrich your repertoire of applicable solutions. This can accelerate your ability to identify appropriate software solutions on future projects.

Patterns codify the wisdom of a community of developers. When you apply patterns appropriately, you have the security of knowing that other developers agree with the solution. This reduces the probability of inelegant, inflexible, or incorrect solutions.

1-Minute Drill

- How do software patterns facilitate communication about software designs?
- How do software patterns help educate programmers?
- Why does the application of a software pattern help validate a proposed design solution?

- Software patterns supply a vocabulary for typical solutions to software problems.
- Software patterns teach good programming practices because they identify and name recurring design problems and the best solutions to these problems.
- Software patterns codify the wisdom of a community of developers. When you apply a pattern, you increase the probability that other developers will agree with your solution.

Architectural Patterns

Information systems comprise several different types of architectures. Unfortunately, use of the term "architecture" is not always consistent. Without attempting to provide an exhaustive list of the many ways people use the term "architecture," we can identify four different aspects of software applications that you can meaningfully describe as architectures:

- Physical architecture
- System architecture
- Database architecture
- Application software architecture

Here, briefly, is what we mean by these different terms:

A *physical architecture* defines the hardware and network infrastructure on which an application runs. Every software application depends upon a physical architecture. For example, an application may require specific client machines running a Web browser, a Web server machine, and a database machine. In addition, there may be network cabling and hard disk requirements. The specification of the hardware and network requirements of an application and the specific interactions between these hardware components is what we mean by a physical architecture.

A *system architecture* defines the software infrastructure within which an application runs. Every software application presupposes such an infrastructure. For example, you typically must consider the network protocols and operating systems in order to deploy an application. Sometimes you must integrate applications with other applications. Integration of multiple applications is also part of the systems architecture.

A *database architecture* defines the data model for an application. There are many different ways to model any given application data, and database vendors provide different functional capabilities to support such definitions. You could lump database architectures under application software architectures (our next topic) because they lie on top of the system and physical architectures and because application developers typically define them. We separate them because there is a logical distinction between application data and the underlying data model that might implement the data representation. For example, if you implement the data model using XML, your model will have a very different architecture than one implemented using a relational database. Likewise, the architecture of a relational database will differ markedly from that of an object database.

An *application software architecture* defines the software elements of an application and the flow of data between them. This module focuses on application software architectures based on JavaServer Pages. Architectural patterns define the major high-level subsystems of an application and the roles they play in relation to each other.

Application Tiers

Architectural patterns fall into different types based upon the number of application *tiers* they define. The term "tiers" refer to the different parts of an application: presentation, domain definition, and data definition.

The *presentation* tier supplies the user interface and controls movement through the application. Human factors like perception, response times, and obviousness of function drive its requirements.

The *domain* tier models the semantics of the problem domain. For example, a banking application might have an internal representation of customer accounts. It would then model interactions with accounts by providing logic to make deposits and withdrawals.

The *data* tier models the requirements of information storage. The application must tailor such logic to the requirements of the underlying data storage mechanism. For example, if the storage mechanism is the file system, the data tier must supply methods to store and retrieve data from the file system. If the storage mechanism is a relational database, on the other hand, the data tier must supply logic to store and retrieve data from the database.

Based upon these tiers, the three basic types of applications are:

- **Single-tier** The application is monolithic and doesn't separate presentation from domain definition and data definition.
- **Two-tier** The application separates presentation and domain definition from data definition.
- **Three-tier** The application separates presentation, domain definition, and data definition into separate components.

Single-Tier Architectures

A *single-tier* application makes no attempt to separate the different logical parts of the application from each other. Modern software development relegates single-tier applications to small, command-line utilities and noninteractive batch processes. This, in no small part, is due to the advent of modern client-server systems (a form of two-tier architecture). Modern database systems were especially influential because they provide simplified data sharing between applications and improve scalability by allowing a separate allocation of hardware resources to the database.

Two-Tier Architectures

A *two-tier* architecture separates presentation and domain logic from data access logic. Database applications and simple Web applications, like all client-server systems, illustrate two-tier architectures. Many modern interactive applications illustrate a two-tier architecture, primarily because of the importance of sharing data. Figure 7-1 reproduces the figure we used in Module 1 to describe the client-server architecture.

Two-tier architectures are superior to single-tier architectures when shared data and centralized control and maintenance of data are important requirements (as they are for most business applications). They also have the advantage that they are relatively easy to understand and implement. But two-tier applications have disadvantages as well.

Two-tier architectures exploit the idea that applications should process data locally but store it in a shared, centralized server. But this is simplistic. For example, corporate applications must all process a shared data store in roughly the same way. If applications process all data locally, they must each duplicate this common business logic. To circumvent this duplication, modern databases support significant processing in the database using stored procedures. This encourages application developers to move common business logic into the database rather than duplicate

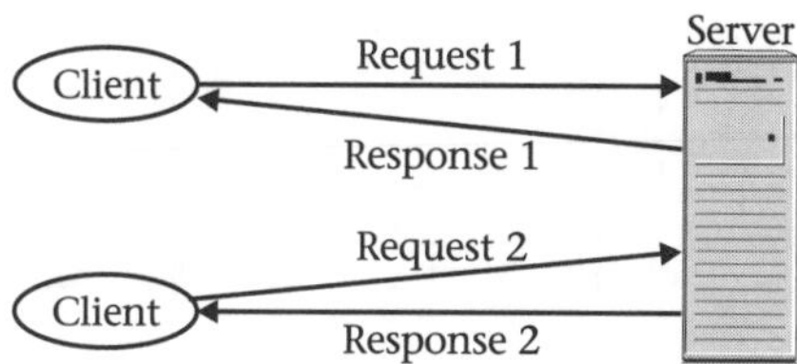

Figure 7-1 Clients request resources from centralized server

it in each application. But this solution is also problematic, since it breaks down any clean separation between application logic and data access logic. Further, stored procedures do not in general provide the same level of encapsulation and domain modeling support that modern object-oriented languages like C++ or Java provide. Some databases such as Oracle provide the ability to invoke Java code inside the database server. But often, the more business logic you stuff into the database, the more confusing your application becomes and the more obscure its connections to other applications. Stuffing business logic in the database also ties you to a particular database vendor, since there is no consistent support for or clear standardization of these techniques among database vendors.

Further, modern applications must sometimes access multiple databases. Two-tier applications must put the logic for managing multiple databases in the application tier, thereby migrating data access logic from the database to the application. Application developers must have intimate knowledge of which databases hold what data and the precise data model in each database. The likelihood is that physical data models do not map well to the domain model. This exacerbates the problem because applications must provide logic to do the mapping.

Three-Tier Architectures

A *three-tier* architecture separates presentation logic, domain logic, and data access logic into three different components. Figure 7-2 illustrates a typical three-tier architecture.

The primary advantage of the three-tier architecture is that it supports a cleaner separation and encapsulation of application functions. Presentation logic can

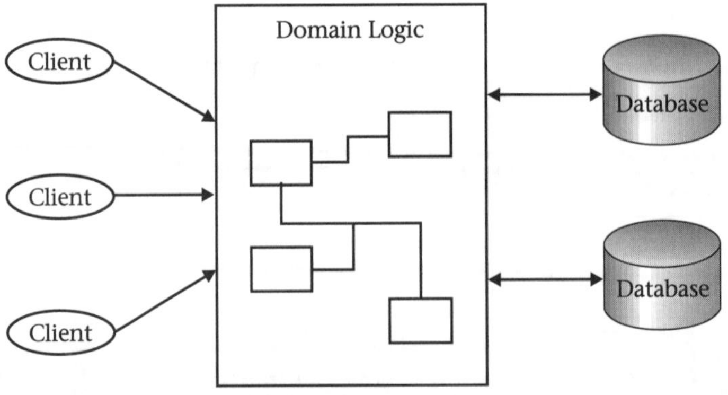

Figure 7-2 A typical three-tier architecture

address human factors requirements, while data access logic can address the structure of the physical data model and the capabilities of the database engine. Most importantly, the middle tier, the domain tier, can address and model the semantics of the business problem.

Another advantage of three-tier architectures is that you can move the domain tier off the client machine onto one or more server machines. The two-tier architecture made it possible to move the data tier off the client; the three-tier architecture expands upon this ability to allocate separate hardware to separate application functions. It is often the case that allocation of a layer of hardware to an application tier can greatly improve performance and scalability.

Ask the Expert

Question: Isn't a three-tier architecture simply better than single-tier or two-tier architectures? Would you ever implement any other kind of architecture?

Answer: The short answer is no! All other things being equal, the three-tier architecture scales better and is more flexible than single-tier or two-tier architectures. But there are many trade-offs. Three-tier architectures require an additional network layer that slows performance and makes support and troubleshooting more complex. Greater sophistication is required to implement three-tier architectures. As we described in Module 1, the network is never totally transparent, so issues of latency and reliability grow more troublesome in three-tier architectures.

The result is that you are better off modeling some applications as single-tier or two-tier applications. Desktop utilities, for example, never require three tiers. Workgroup applications are often more responsive and more intuitive when designed as two-tier applications rather than three-tier. Internet applications, on the other hand, are almost always better off if given three tiers rather than two. Internet applications can never predict precisely their potential load. In this case, you had better be cautious and program in maximum scalability and flexibility.

Splitting the Presentation Tier

A variation on two- and three-tier architectures splits the presentation tier into two parts: pure presentation logic and application logic. The former is responsible for user interface elements such as windows, menus, fonts, colors, screen positioning, and size. The latter bears no responsibility for user interface elements but mediates all interactions between the presentation elements and other tiers. In particular, it manages all accesses to the domain tier in three-tier architectures and to the data tier in two-tier architectures. The application logic hides the complexities of the other tiers from the presentation logic, presenting data to the presentation in exactly the form the presentation requires. Figure 7-3 shows this variation for a three-tier application.

1-Minute Drill

- What is an *application software architecture*?
- What are the different tiers of an application?
- What are the goals of a two-tier architecture?
- What are two advantages of three-tier architectures over two-tier architectures?
- Why would you sometimes split the presentation tier into pure presentation logic and application logic?

Web Application Architectures

Recall from Module 1 that the basic Web architecture is two-tier. The Web server functions as the data tier, serving up Web resources like HTML pages and images. The Web browser functions as the presentation tier, rendering user interfaces defined by the data itself (using HTML tags).

Client-side extensions to the Web browser do not in themselves change the basic two-tier character of a Web application. For example, a JavaScript or Java applet control providing a drop-down menu can greatly improve a user's experience

---

- An application software architecture defines the software elements of an application and the flow of data between them.
- The tiers of an application include: presentation, domain definition, and data definition.
- Two-tier architectures arose to share data among several applications and centralize control and maintenance of this data.
- Three-tier architectures cleanly separate business logic from presentation logic. They also improve scalability by supporting distribution of business logic onto separate physical machines.
- When you split the presentation tier into presentation logic and application logic, you can better isolate the complexities of the business and data logic tiers from pure presentation issues.

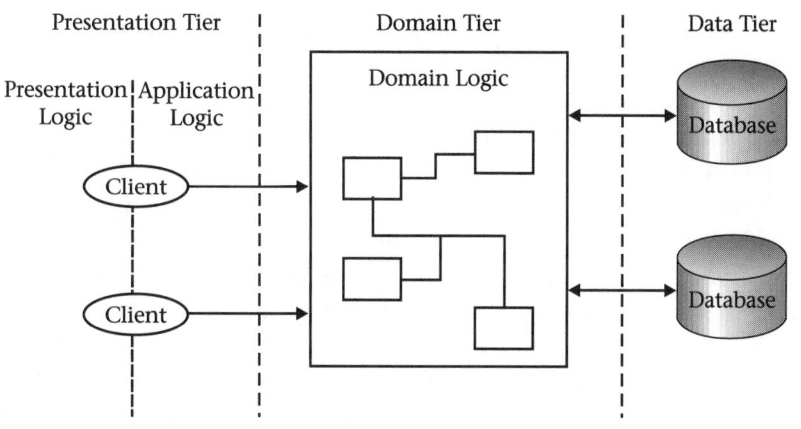

Figure 7-3 Separation of presentation and application logic

but does not separate the domain model from the presentation logic. Such client-side technologies merely add sophistication to the presentation tier.

Likewise, server-side extensions do not in themselves change the two-tier character of Web applications. For example, CGI programs can add sophistication to the physical data tier, extending the physical data model from simple Web pages to complex relational information. But this does not separate the domain model from the data tier. Figure 7-4 illustrates this two-tier Web architecture, including client and server extensions.

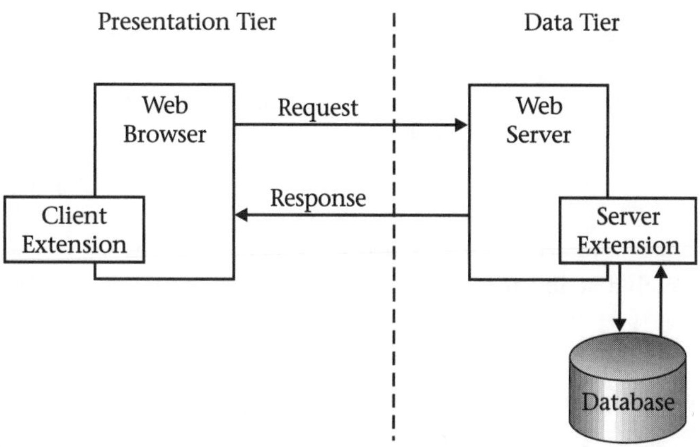

Figure 7-4 The basic Web application architecture

The ability of Web browsers to run plug-in COM components and Java applets means that you *can* add application tiers in the browser. A Java applet, for example, might implement a full-featured windowed application. It would then make sense to divide the presentation tier into presentation and application logic tiers. The problem with such client-side solutions is that they fatten up the client tier and, much like an operating system, use the browser merely as an application host. Microsoft's Active Desktop paradigm carries this architecture to an extreme, effectively converting the browser into an extension of the operating system.

Server extensions can also add tiers to Web applications, and this is the approach we take in Part II. The advantage of this approach over the client-side approach is that it takes full advantage of the browser as a *thin client*. Like the client-side approach, the server-side approach separates the presentation tier into presentation logic and application logic. Unlike the client-side approach, it distributes the two tiers across a network. The browser handles the presentation logic, while a Java servlet (or Active Server Page) handles the application logic. Figure 7-5 shows this server-side architecture.

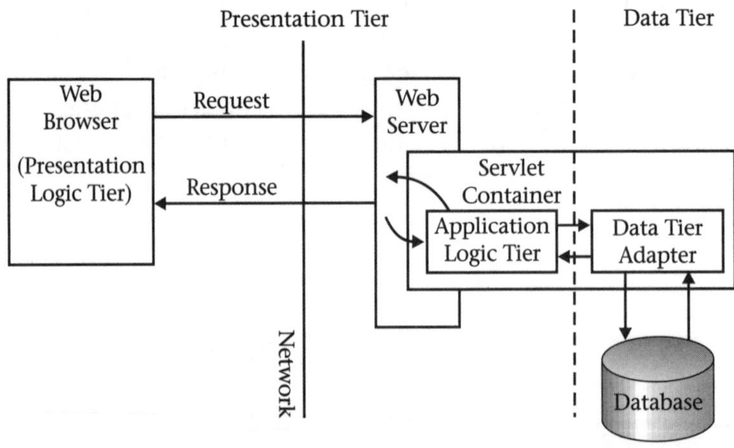

Figure 7-5 Web distribution of the two halves of the presentation tier

1-Minute Drill

- How many tiers are there in a basic Web architecture?
- Can you add tiers using client-side technologies?
- Can you add tiers using server-side technologies?

Object-Oriented Software Design Patterns

Applications implement different object-oriented software design patterns as well as embodying different architectural patterns. The difference between architectural patterns and object-oriented patterns is a matter of one's point of view. From a macro level, where one's interest is in the major subsystems of an application, architectural patterns apply. Object-oriented patterns apply when one focuses on software classes and objects and their interactions.

7

GoF is still the authority for basic object-oriented software design patterns. It classifies object-oriented design patterns into three basic types:

- **Creational patterns** Abstractions of the instantiation process
- **Structural patterns** Abstractions of object composition approaches
- **Behavioral patterns** Abstractions of communication between objects

This classification is useful because it helps provide a context for the role played by a set of objects in an application.

Creational patterns apply to the common ways applications use some objects to create other objects. *Structural* patterns apply to the ways in which applications

---

- The basic Web architecture has two tiers, the presentation and data tiers.
- Yes, both Java applets and COM controls can add tiers by splitting the presentation tier.
- Yes, using Java servlet technology or Active Server Pages (ASP), you can easily add tiers to the server side of an application.

compose larger software objects and object systems from smaller objects or object systems. *Behavioral* patterns apply both to the composition of objects and to the ways applications communicate and cooperate. As we lay out the application we describe in Part II, we will describe the relevant patterns and how they fit into this classification.

A few patterns are especially relevant to typical Web application architectures:

- Model-view-controller
- Mediator
- Command
- Strategy
- Bridge

Model-View-Controller

Figure 7-6 shows the model-view-controller (MVC) pattern, which partitions applications into separate data management (model), presentation (view), and control components.

The MVC pattern underlies most modern graphical user interfaces. You can also apply the MVC pattern to Web applications. The partitioning cleanly separates

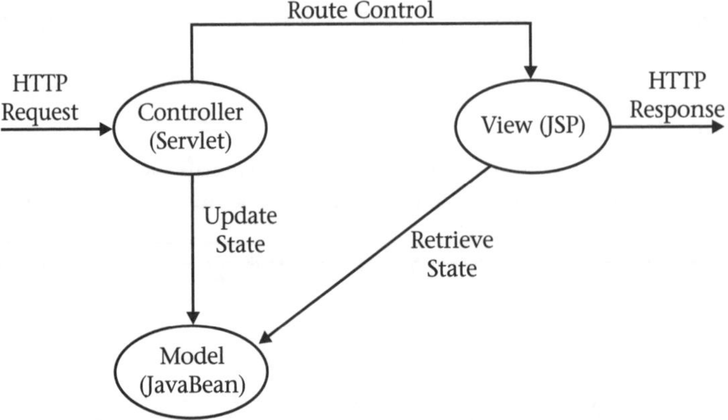

Figure 7-6 The model-view-controller pattern

control logic, data management, and presentation. It thereby encourages independent evolution and reuse of the separate components. It also makes better use of other patterns like the mediator, command, strategy, and bridge patterns. JavaServer Pages most appropriately implement the presentation part of a Web application. JavaBeans encapsulate the services that supply content to a Web site and simplify passing data between the components of the architecture. Servlets function best as controllers and mediators routing user requests and application messages, updating application data, and driving the application workflow.

The MVC pattern maps quite naturally into multitier architectural patterns. Figure 7-7 shows how two-tier architectures usually map the control part of the MVC pattern into the presentation sphere. This is a natural mapping when servlets implement the control logic because servlets generally reside in the presentation tier. Sometimes, however, three-tier architectures will map some or all of the control logic into the middle or business logic tier. Figure 7-8 shows this mapping.

An advantage of mapping control logic into the business logic tier is that systems often host this tier on a better, faster hardware platform than they provide for the presentation tier. A second advantage arises when control must cross multiple data tiers, perhaps because of legacy application integration. In this case, the complexity of the control logic makes such a mapping attractive.

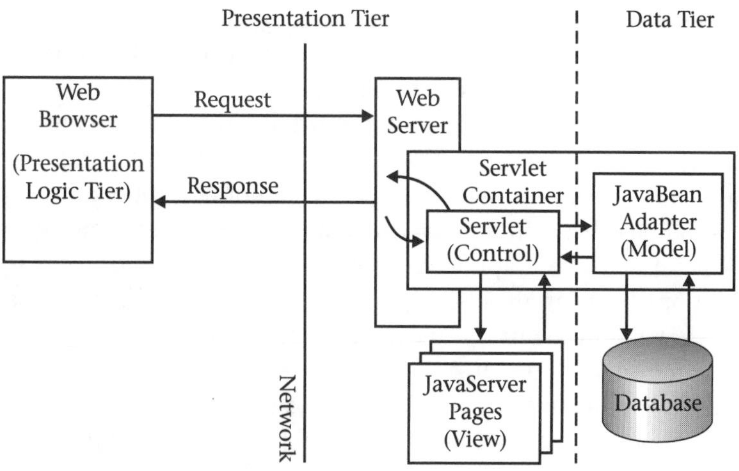

Figure 7-7 Mapping the MVC pattern onto a three-tier architecture

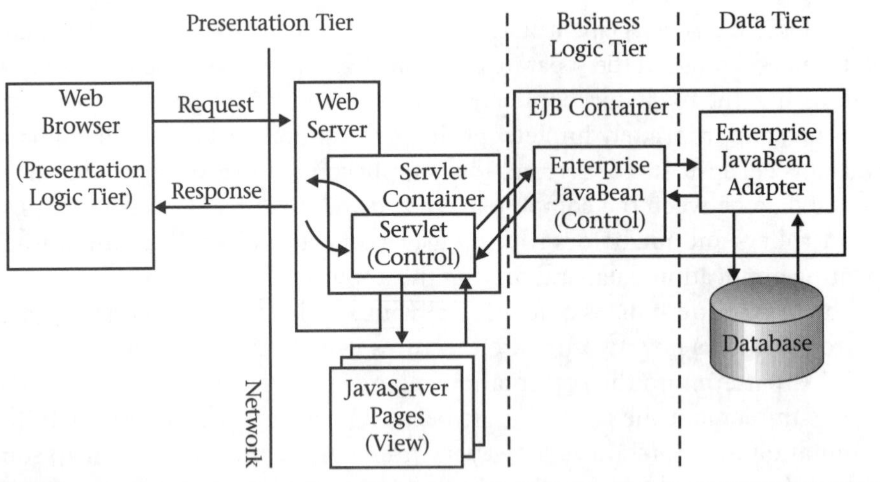

Figure 7-8 Mapping control logic into the business logic tier

Mediator

In JSP architectures, a servlet often functions as a *mediator*, routing requests and responses between business logic and presentation. GoF classifies the mediator as a behavioral pattern. This pattern controls interactions between software subsystems by encapsulating related functionality behind a manager object that separates messages with purely internal relevance from messages that must pass outward to other subsystems.

In the worst-case scenario, assuming mutual dependencies among all components, unmediated interactions can result in $n * (n - 1)$ communication paths, where n is the number of components. Of course, applications do not as a rule use all possible communication paths, so this scenario rarely happens. Nevertheless, in real-world applications enough dependencies occur to make communications between these components confusing and hard to manage. Figure 7-9 shows how arbitrary interactions between software components proliferate communication paths.

The mediator pattern dramatically reduces hard-coded communication paths between components and converts these dependencies to decision rules. Figure 7-10 shows how use of a mediator simplifies communication paths between software components.

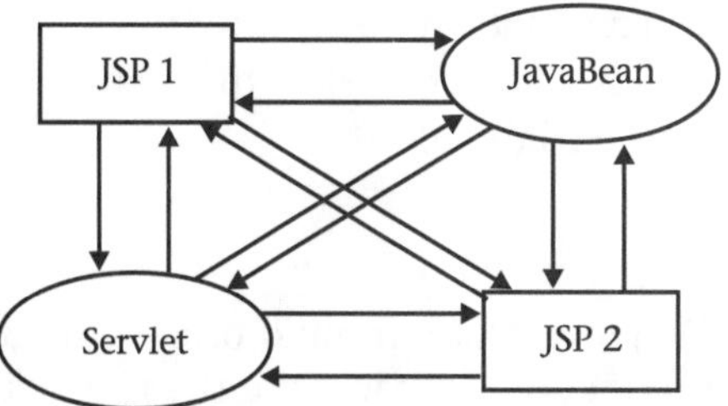

Figure 7-9 Unmediated communication paths

Mediators reduce the worst-case scenario (mutual dependencies among all components) to 2 * (n – 1), where n is the number of components. With 50 components, the worst case without a mediator requires 2450 communication paths, whereas with a mediator, only 98 are needed. Additionally, mediators provide a need-to-know architecture where a component need worry only about the messages it sends, not the message's destination.

Command

The *command* pattern wraps an operation in an object so that you can register it for execution by a different object. GoF classifies it as a behavioral pattern. The command pattern separates a specific operation from the object performing the operation. The obvious example is a window menu toolkit. Menu items must execute some operation, but the toolkit can't build this operation into the menu item because only the user of the menu knows what operation it must perform.

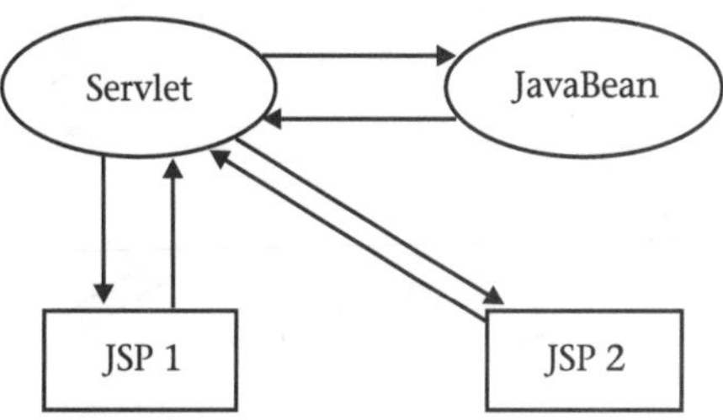

Figure 7-10 The mediator pattern

To use the toolkit, you encapsulate an operation in an object and register the object with the toolkit. Then when you select the menu item, the toolkit invokes the operation on the registered object.

Tip

You may have done X Window programming or in some other way have used function callbacks. Function callbacks are the procedural equivalent to the command pattern.

You can apply the command pattern to Web applications as well as window menus. There is an analogy between menu selections and Web application requests. Just as menu selections may launch windows or redraw existing windows, so a browser uses HTTP requests to launch new windows or display new pages. In an MVC architecture, a servlet typically acts as the router for this movement between Web pages. You can write custom Web applications that simply hard-code an application's web-flow. In that case, you embed decision logic in the controlling servlet. Figure 7-11 shows an MVC-based Web architecture that embeds decision logic in the controlling servlet.

Hard-coding works if you are never required to change the application control logic or the pages displayed. Suppose, however, that you must change the control

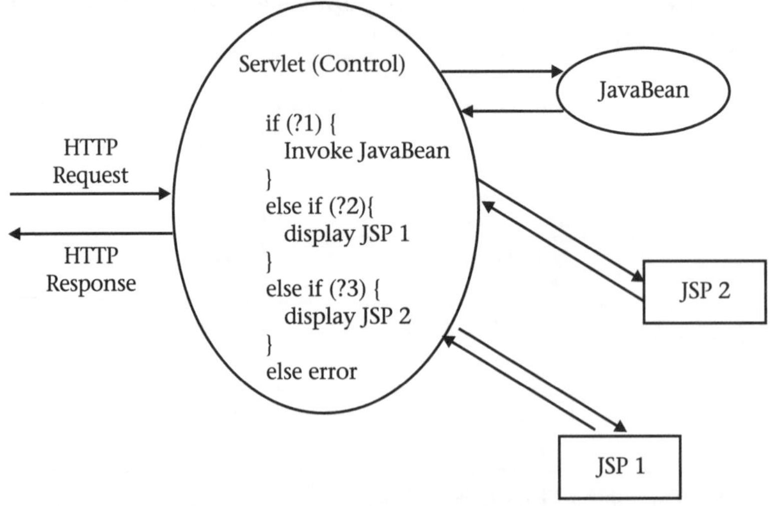

Figure 7-11 Controlling servlet without the command pattern

logic or the JavaServer Pages displayed, or even the path to the JavaServer Pages. In this approach, you must recompile and redeploy the servlet, because it compiles all these elements into the servlet. The command pattern helps you separate behavior from control logic. Figure 7-12 shows how.

In Figure 7-12, the command pattern encapsulates each action in its own Java object. This helps separate control logic from specific actions, even though the control logic remains embedded in the servlet. This separation allows you to change the path to a JSP page or the specific JavaBean or JSP page that the servlet invokes, without changing the servlet itself. Of course the control logic is still too restrictive, since the conditional logic remains in the servlet. A better approach would also separate control logic from the servlet body. This is the job of the strategy pattern.

Strategy

The *strategy* pattern defines a family of algorithms and encapsulates each algorithm in an object. GoF classifies the strategy pattern as a behavioral pattern. The purpose of the strategy pattern is to let the choice of algorithm vary independently from the objects that use them.

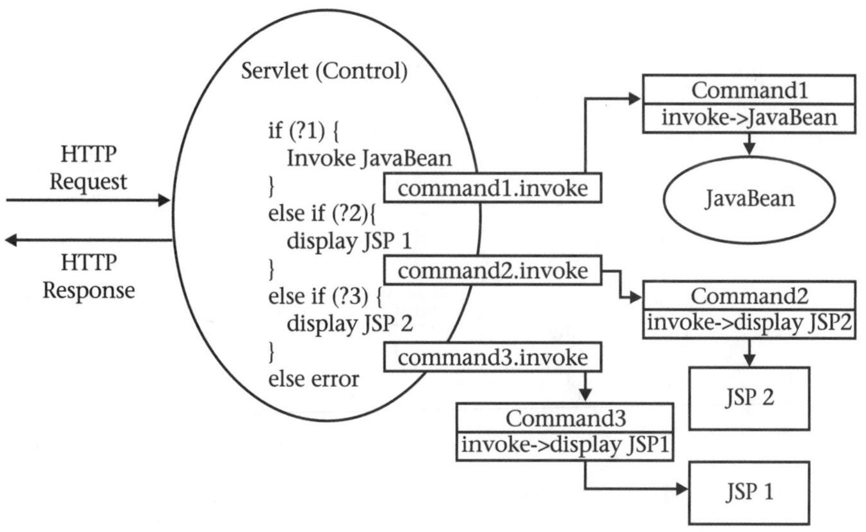

Figure 7-12 Use of the command pattern

The control servlet in a JSP architecture is essentially a router for an application web-flow. A toolkit for JSP development can use the strategy pattern to support flexible definition of families of such routers. You can consider each web-flow a strategy. Every Web application must then define its strategy. Given the strategy pattern, you can define new web-flows and add them to the family without modifying the servlet that uses them. Figure 7-13 shows this architecture.

Tip

You can create a strategy that is so general that you may not need to employ a pluggable model. For example, you might drive your logic by a command token. Your strategy could then use a lookup based upon the token to find the command to execute. This avoids the use of conditional logic altogether.

Bridge

The *bridge* pattern decouples an abstract interface from its implementations. Among other advantages, it insulates clients from any platform-specific or proprietary method signatures. The methods defined by a bridge may not match the methods defined by its implementations. Often it is less primitive, thereby raising the level

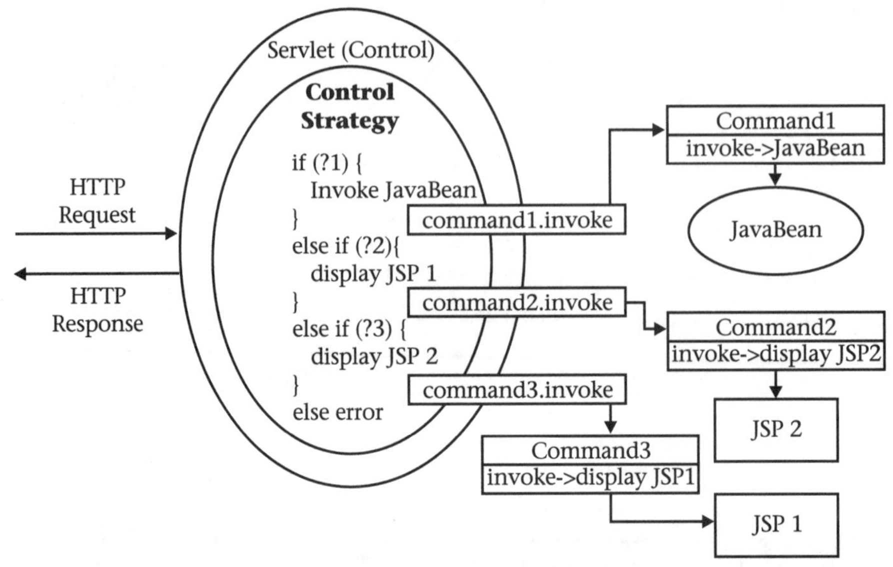

Figure 7-13 JSP architecture using the strategy pattern

of abstraction. GoF classifies the bridge as a structural pattern. The bridge pattern helps support a *pluggable* architecture—an architecture that supports multiple implementations of the same abstract functionality. It also supports independent extension of the abstraction and its implementation.

Figure 7-14 shows a possible realization of the bridge pattern in a JSP architecture. Notice that the bridge requires two participants, the abstraction object and a root-level implementation component. In Java, this root-level implementation component might be just a Java interface. It could also be an abstract class. The job of this part of the bridge is to define the interface for the different implementations. Notice also that the abstraction object holds a reference to an object to which it delegates operations. This reference has the same data type as the root-level implementation component. The bridge pattern also requires at least one concrete implementation.

The bridge pattern can play an important role in JSP architectures by helping an application support multiple implementations of its model. Why might you do this? Sometimes you cannot anticipate a customer requirement or you cannot dictate a specific technology. Sometimes you want to replace an existing technology with a newer technology. Sometimes you want to enter a new market space and find that the market requires a different implementation. 7

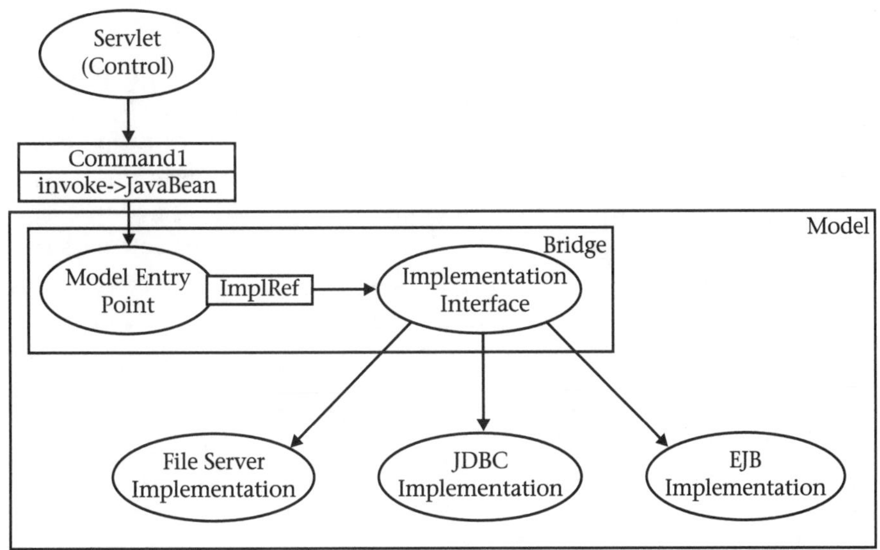

Figure 7-14 The bridge pattern

A common reason is that different customers require different levels of scalability. A workgroup in a publishing house can be satisfied with a file server–based model. A corporate-wide application for General Motors or Sony would want a more scalable implementation, possibly accessing a database using JDBC *behind* an Enterprise JavaBean (EJB) implementation.

1-Minute Drill

- What three types of software patterns did GoF identify?
- What is the MVC pattern?
- Can you map the MVC pattern onto multitier architectural patterns?
- Besides MVC, what are other important patterns for Java-based Web architectures?

Ask the Expert

Question: It seems like the command pattern, the strategy pattern, and the bridge pattern could use a configuration file that maps specific object classes to application roles. What role might such a configuration file play for each of these patterns?

Answer: The command pattern encapsulates a Web URL mapped to action tokens (conditions). A configuration file could provide the list of URLs and their associated action tokens. Similarly, the specific strategy pattern could be loaded at runtime based upon a configuration file setting. Finally, the bridge pattern depends upon loading a concrete implementation. You could specify the correct implementation class in a configuration file.

- GoF identified creational, structural, and behavioral patterns.
- The MVC pattern divides software objects into three roles: a controller, a view, and a model. The controller routes messages, the view manages the presentation, and the model manages application state.
- Yes, quite easily. For example, a two-tier architecture generally maps the controller and the view into the presentation tier, and the model into the data tier.
- Other important software patterns include: mediator, command, strategy, and bridge.

Enter.html
GalleryLayout.jsp
web.xml
galleryLayout-taglib.tld
Inventory.java
ControllerServlet.java
ImageItem.java
GalleryItem.java
Command.java
GalleryLayout.java

Project 7-1: Gallery Viewer

This project demonstrates the use of design patterns to develop a simple Web application including servlets and JavaServer Pages. The application presents a gallery view of images that are retrieved according to a selection from a catalog. The user can also modify the layout of the gallery.

The primary pattern that we wish to demonstrate in this project is the MVC pattern. You will see a clear separation between a servlet that acts as the controller, an Inventory class that serves as the model, and a JSP page that serves as the view. Command, mediator, and strategy design patterns are also relevant in this project.

Step-by-Step

1. Download the files for this project from `http://www.osborne.com`.
2. Create a new application context named "gallery" in Tomcat by inserting the following lines in the `server.xml` configuration file located under `%TOMCAT_HOME%/conf`.

```
<Context path="/gallery"
   docBase="webapps/gallery"
   crossContext="true"
   debug="0"
   reloadable="true"
   trusted="false" >
</Context>
```

3. Create a `gallery` directory under `%TOMCAT_HOME%/webapps`.
4. Create subdirectories `html`, `jsp`, `images`, and `WEB-INF` under the newly created `gallery` directory.
5. Create the subdirectories `summer` and `spring` under the `images` subdirectory.
6. Drop some sample images into the `summer` and `spring` subdirectories. To simulate a real situation, we recommend that you drop some images that show summer clothing into the `summer` subdirectory and spring clothing into the `spring` subdirectory. The idea here is to distinguish the retrieval of selective images based on user selection.
7. Move the JSP page file `GalleryLayout.jsp` into the `jsp` subdirectory.
8. Move the HTML file `Enter.html` into the `html` subdirectory.
9. Move the `web.xml` file into the `WEB-INF` subdirectory.

10. Create the subdirectories `tlds` and `classes` under `WEB-INF`.
11. Move the tag library descriptor file `galleryLayout-taglib.tld` into `WEB-INF/tlds`.
12. If you examine the HTML file `Enter.html`, you will notice that it contains a simple form with two select elements, one for choosing the catalog and the other for choosing the number of images per row in the gallery.
13. Pay particular attention to the hidden input element with the name "COMMAND" and value "GET_IMAGES":

```
<INPUT TYPE=hidden NAME="COMMAND" VALUE="GET_IMAGES">
```

    This element ensures that when you submit this form, the servlet controller will invoke the command identified by the tag GET_IMAGES.

14. The action for the form is named `/gallery/Controller`, which actually translates to the Java Servlet class *gallery.ControllerServlet*. We use the `<servlet>` and `<servlet-mapping>` tags to establish this mapping in the `web.xml` file. First we use a `<servlet>` tag:

```
<servlet>
   <servlet-name>Controller</servlet-name>
   <servlet-class>gallery.ControllerServlet</servlet-class>
/servlet>
```

    Then we use the `<servlet-mapping>` tag:

```
<servlet-mapping>
   <servlet-name>Controller</servlet-name>
   <url-pattern>/Controller</url-pattern>
</servlet-mapping>
```

    Note that the webapp DTD requires that all `<servlet>` tags must be grouped, all `<servlet-mapping>` tags grouped, and all `<taglib>` tags grouped. The tags must also appear in the `web.xml` file in this order: `<servlet>`, `<servlet-mapping>`, and `<taglib>`.

15. Now, let's examine the *ControllerServlet*. As the name suggests, this servlet functions as the controller in the MVC pattern. The controller is responsible for routing user requests and driving the application workflow. Here is the *ControllerServlet* class:

```
public class ControllerServlet extends HttpServlet {
   private Map commands = new HashMap();
```

```
private Inventory inventory = null;

public void init() throws ServletException {
   // initialize path
   ServletConfig config = this.getServletConfig();
   ServletContext context = config.getServletContext();
   String INVENTORY_ROOT = context.getRealPath("/images");

   // initialize inventory.
   inventory = new Inventory(INVENTORY_ROOT, "images/");

   // setup all commands.
   commands.put("GET_IMAGES", new GetImagesCommand());
}

public void doGet(HttpServletRequest req,
                  HttpServletResponse res)
   throws ServletException, IOException {
   doPost(req, res);
}

public void doPost(HttpServletRequest req,
                   HttpServletResponse res)
   throws ServletException, IOException {
   logmsg("doPost");
   // Fetch command-name from request
   String commandName = req.getParameter("COMMAND");
   // Fetch command from command-name
   Command c = (Command)commands.get(commandName);
   // handle command.
   c.handle(req, res);
}

private class GetImagesCommand implements Command {
   public void handle(HttpServletRequest req,
                      HttpServletResponse res)
      throws ServletException, IOException {
      logmsg("command->handle");
      String catalog = req.getParameter("CATALOG");
      String numRows = req.getParameter("ITEMS_PER_ROW");
      // Fetch images from catalog.
      Iterator images = inventory.getImagesFor(catalog);
      // Set data for view.
      req.setAttribute("IMAGES", images);
      req.setAttribute("ITEMS_PER_ROW", numRows);
```

7

```
            // Forward to the view.
            RequestDispatcher rd =
                req.getRequestDispatcher("/galleryViewer");
            rd.forward(req, res);
        }
    }

    private void logmsg(String s) {
        System.err.println("logmsg: " + s);
    }
}
```

16. The servlet maintains a *java.util.HashMap* that associates command strings with command objects. It also holds a reference to the *Inventory* class, which functions as the model in the MVC pattern.

17. The *init* method performs three critical acts:

- It determines the inventory root directory as a relative path from the application context. Normally, this need not be under the application context and could be fetched as an initial parameter to the application context specified in `web.xml`.
- It creates the *Inventory* class, initializing it with the inventory root directory as well as the URL root directory for the catalog of images.
- It establishes the command object *GetImagesCommand* that implements the *Command* interface as the handler for the command string, "GET_IMAGES". There can be any number of such command handlers for command strings. In a "real-world" setup, you might establish this kind of mapping by reading a configuration file, thereby removing any hard-coded dependencies.

18. When you post the HTML form, the servlet container transfers control to the *doPost* method of *ControllerServlet*. The *doPost* method retrieves the command string from the request (previously established in the HTML file via the hidden INPUT element as described earlier). It then uses the command string to retrieve the proper command object from its mapping table and invokes the handler method on the command object. This setup demonstrates both the mediator and command patterns. The controller servlet implements the mediator pattern, routing requests between elements. The source (the HTML file) merely sends a message (the command string) to the mediator and does not worry about who is handling the message. Notice that our routing algorithm is so general that we do not need to replace it (using a strategy pattern) to accommodate new applications. The destination, *GetImagesCommand,* is an implementation of the command pattern.

19. We implement *GetImagesCommand* as an inner class (so it can have access to the *Inventory* object). This might very well be a separate class. The *handle* method retrieves the request parameters and sends the selected catalog name to the model (*Inventory*) to retrieve its images. The *Inventory* object returns a *java.util.Iterator* to the list of images. This is stored in the request and sent to the URL `/galleryViewer`, which functions as the view in the MVC pattern. This URL maps to the JSP page file `GalleryLayout.jsp`. We establish this mapping in the `web.xml` file using this XML fragment to set a servlet name:

```
<servlet>
   <servlet-name>galleryViewer</servlet-name>
   <jsp-file>/jsp/GalleryLayout.jsp</jsp-file>
</servlet>
```

Then we use this XML fragment to map the name to a relative URL:

```
<servlet-mapping>
   <servlet-name>galleryViewer</servlet-name>
   <url-pattern>/galleryViewer</url-pattern>
</servlet-mapping>
```

7

20. Let's examine the *Inventory* class:

```
public class Inventory {
   private String inventoryDirRoot = null;
   private String inventoryURLRoot = null;

   public Inventory(String inventoryDirRoot,
                    String inventoryURLRoot) {
      this.inventoryDirRoot = inventoryDirRoot;
      this.inventoryURLRoot = inventoryURLRoot;
   }

   public Iterator getImagesFor(String catalog) {
      File dir = new File(inventoryDirRoot + "/" +
                          catalog);
      String[] fileList = dir.list(new ImageFilter());
      if((fileList != null) && (fileList.length > 0)) {
         List l = new ArrayList();
         for(int i=0; i<fileList.length; i++) {
            l.add(new ImageItem(inventoryURLRoot +
                                catalog + "/" +
                                fileList[i], fileList[i]));
         }
         return l.iterator();
```

```
        }
        return null;
    }

    class ImageFilter implements FilenameFilter {
        public boolean accept(File dir, String name) {
            return(((name.toLowerCase()).endsWith(".jpg")) ||
                     ((name.toLowerCase()).endsWith(".gif")));
        }
    }
}
```

21. The *Inventory* class functions as the model in our MVC pattern. It maps the catalog name to its physical location and retrieves images from it. The images in our simple application come from a named directory in the application context. In a real-world setup, they could be stored in a database and protected by a middle-tier application server.

22. The method *getImagesFor* retrieves the images for a catalog, stores them in a *java.util.ArrayList*, and returns an iterator to it. It examines the contents of the inventory root directory, filtering them for only the files with the extensions `.gif` and `.jpg`. The *ImageFilter* inner class does the filtering. The *getImagesFor* method returns a file in the directory only if *ImageFilter* returns `true` for it. The *ImageFilter* and its application in a directory listing is an example of the strategy pattern.

23. Here is the JSP page file `GalleryLayout.jsp`, that functions as the view in our MVC pattern:

```
<%@ page import="gallery.GalleryLayout" %>
<%@ page import="java.util.Iterator" %>
<%@ taglib uri="galleryLayout-taglib" prefix="gallery" %>
<HTML>
<HEAD><TITLE>Image Reader and Layout Test</TITLE></HEAD>
<BODY bgcolor="white" >
<FONT color="black" >
<%-- Layout the images in a gallery view --%>
<% String itemsPerRow =
      (String)request.getAttribute("ITEMS_PER_ROW");
   Iterator iterator =
      (Iterator)request.getAttribute("IMAGES");
%>
<gallery:layout
   images='<%= iterator %>'
```

```
    itemsPerRow='<%= itemsPerRow %>'
    width="5"
    borderWidth="10"
/>
</BODY>
</HTML>
```

24. As you see, we implement the gallery view as a custom tag `<gallery:layout>`. We pass the *Iterator* representing the list of images for the catalog and the number of items per row selected by the user. (We leave the details of this custom tag as an exercise for the reader.)

25. Compile all the Java source files—`GalleryLayout.java`, `GalleryItem.java`, `ImageItem.java`, `ControllerServlet.java`, `Command.java`, and `Inventory.java`—and drop the class files under the directory `%TOMCAT_HOME%/webapps/gallery/WEB-INF/classes`.

26. Restart Tomcat and load the HTML file using the URL: `http://localhost:8080/gallery/html/Enter.html`. You should see an HTML page as shown in Figure 7-15.

7

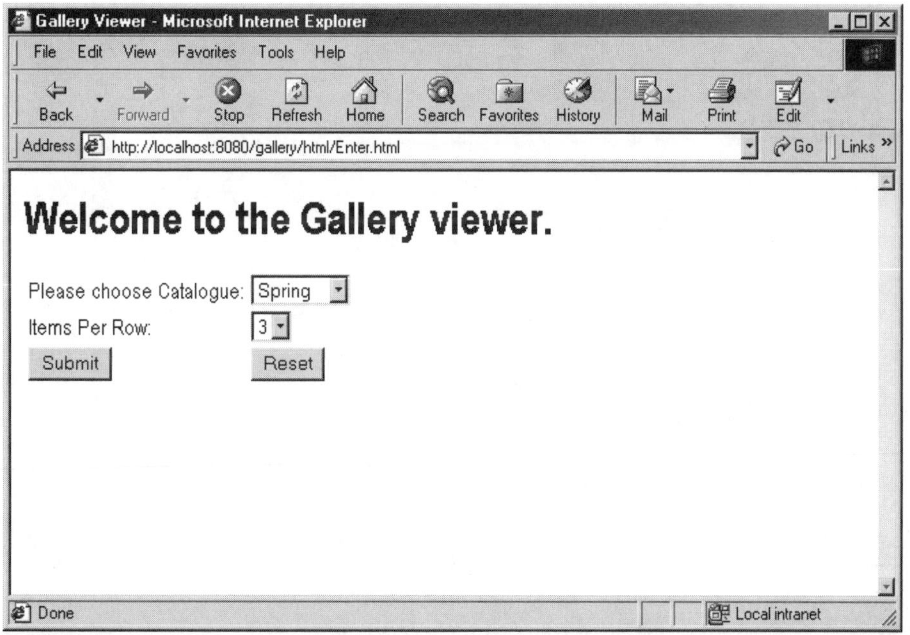

Figure 7-15 The input HTML page (Enter.html)

27. Select the catalog and also make a selection for the number of rows and submit the form. You should see a gallery view of the images for the selected catalog, as shown in Figure 7-16.

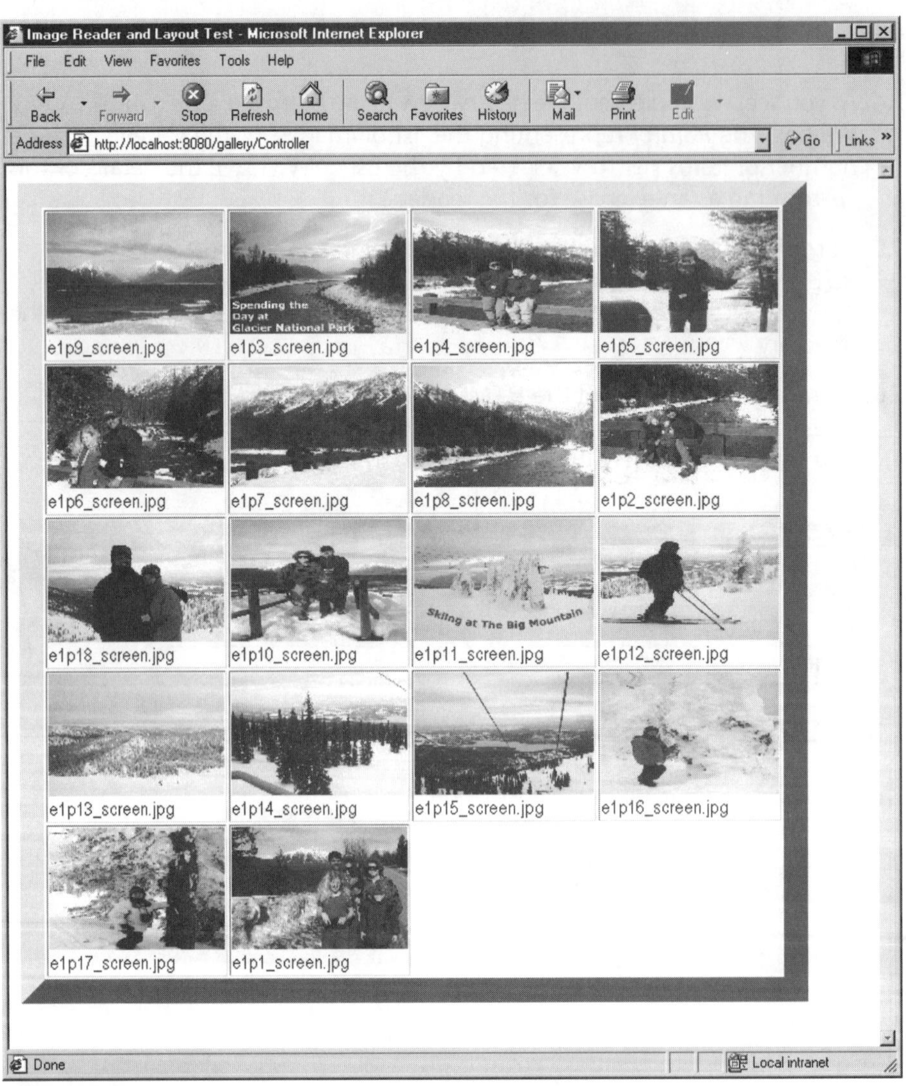

Figure 7-16 Gallery view (output from GalleryLayout.jsp)

The Application: A Family Center

The remaining modules in Part II illustrate the use of the design patterns we have described in an application called the "Family Center." The Family Center is similar to a workgroup environment over the Web, only it services an extended but close-knit family rather than a corporation. Our intention is to define an application complex enough to illustrate some typical "real-world" enterprise features. Before we dive into the details of this application, it is a good idea to develop its requirements. Such a requirements analysis, as you might be aware, is an integral part of software development. It sets broad requirements for what the application must implement.

An important first step in a requirements analysis develops a set of high-level use cases. Here is a list of use cases guiding development of our Family Center:

- A family member wishes to contact another family member.
- A family member wishes to update personal contact information.
- A family member wishes to consult a family calendar for family events.
- A family member wishes to post an event in the calendar inviting other members.
- A family member wishes to view photos of a family event.
- A family member wishes to make photos of an event available for viewing.
- A family member wishes to consult a bulletin board for messages.
- A family member wishes to post to a bulletin board.

One could think of many other use cases that a family center might satisfy. Our application, however, will limit itself to the listed use cases.

A perceptive reader might have noticed a pattern in the listed use cases. Each pair of use cases imply a common function. For example, the first two use cases concern contact information that we implement as an Address Book. The next two use cases concern the dates of family events that we implement as a Family Calendar. Similarly, the next two use cases deal with family photos that we implement as a Photo Album. Finally, the last two use cases concern ad hoc postings of family messages that we implement as a Bulletin Board. So our use cases suggest to us that our Family Center application should contain these four features:

1. Address Book
2. Family Calendar
3. Photo Album
4. Bulletin Board

Security

Our family center hosts confidential information over the Internet that only family members should view or modify. This means we must implement a security model to protect access to our Family Center. In Module 8, we discuss how to go about setting up simple user management to provide login and logout services that protect the Web site from malicious access.

Web-Flow

A well-designed application must be able to adapt to change. The chances are that we will one day want more services in our application, or will want to change the existing services. A rigid, inflexible web-flow would make such changes tedious or impossible. In Module 9, we discuss how we can build a flexible web-flow framework.

Repository

Our application requires a repository to store information. Since we are designing the application from scratch, we must also define the structure of our information. The structure of our information should model the requirements of our application, not necessarily the requirements of the storage technologies we use. We should de-couple our information model from any given storage implementation. This allows us to transparently change the actual physical repository without affecting our application. We describe this design in Module 10.

Note

You can download the complete application from the Osborne Web site.

Mastery Check

1. List three ways in which software patterns help develop quality applications.

____

____

2. How long have software patterns been part of the environment for software development?

____

____

3. What are some important themes that have emerged from the general discussion about software patterns?

____

____

4. What are some different types of information systems architectures and what are the respective roles tha t they play?

____

____

5. What are some advantages of three-tier architectures over two-tier architectures and in what contexts are such advantages important?

____

____

6. Why would a Web application architect choose the MVC pattern?

____

____

7. What is the purpose of the mediator pattern in a software architecture?

____

____

Mastery Check

8. Why would a Web application designer introduce the command pattern?

9. What is the purpose of the bridge pattern and why might this be important to Web application designers?

10. How does the strategy pattern work together with the command pattern to manage web-flow in a JSP architecture?

Module 8

JSP Security

The Goals of This Module

- Understand the basics of software security
- Become familiar with different approaches to Web application security
- Become familiar with servlet and JSP security mechanisms
- Create the security elements of our Family Center

In this module, we address JSP security architectures. The topic is complex and diverse, and we merely introduce it here. Application security attempts to protect information from illicit access or modification. Deployment-grade JSP applications that manage corporate or personal information must secure such information. We provide an overview of security basics and then present specific security procedures for JSP architectures and Java-based Web applications.

Basic Application Security

In general you must consider seven security services when building applications:

- **Authentication** Confirmation of identity
- **Integrity** Confirmation that a request arrived unmodified
- **Confidentiality** Protection of information
- **Authorization** Access control
- **Non-repudiation** Guarantee of authenticity
- **Availability** Guaranteeing responsiveness to messages
- **Auditing** Tracking user behavior

User authentication is the most fundamental of these security services. Let's look more closely at each of these services.

Authentication

Authentication is the process where a user convinces an application of his or her identity. Often applications authenticate users by requiring them to log in. When users log in, they must supply a valid username and user password. Operating systems like Windows or UNIX require a login, then associate a security record with the user that testifies to the identity of the user. That way the user need not log into other applications supported by the operating system. Some applications, however, require an additional login besides the operating system login. This is often the case, for example, when the application spans a local area network (LAN) or wide area network (WAN). A user's network identity may then differ from the identity credentials the user provided to the operating system. When the two can differ, the application cannot trust the security record supplied by the operating system and must require an additional login.

Applications may also function as users of other applications. For example, the model in a JSP architecture (as explained in Module 7) may access a database application that requires a user login. In this case, your application must log in either by using login credentials supplied by each user or by using its own credentials.

Security Domains and "Rings of Trust"

You can think of security as organized into different *security technology domains*, each domain enforcing security using its own technology mechanisms. For example, Web servers and operating systems typically use different technologies to enforce security. The term "security technology domain" in this sense refers to any grouping of functionality or resources controlled by a common security technology (such as a login).

You can also think of security as organized into different *security policy domains* or *realms*. A security policy domain is any grouping of functionality or resources controlled by a common security policy. The boundaries of such realms are often hard to discern, since they can overlap. Depending on the degree of security required, you can cluster domains into "rings of trust." Different "rings of trust" can be managed in the same technology domain (i.e., using the same technology mechanisms). Figure 8-1 shows passage through such a clustering of applications into low-, medium-, and high-security realms.

The idea behind the "rings of trust" model is that users *should* meet extra security requirements (often including additional logins) when they move from security realms clustered in less secure rings to security realms clustered in more secure rings. Realms within a ring share roughly the same security requirements. Security *breaches* arise when users gain access to realms in a ring requiring greater security using security credentials valid only for realms in ring requiring less security.

For example, database access is usually a realm with high security requirements. By comparison, an operating system's directory and file structure typically have lesser security requirements. Often an application will log into the database

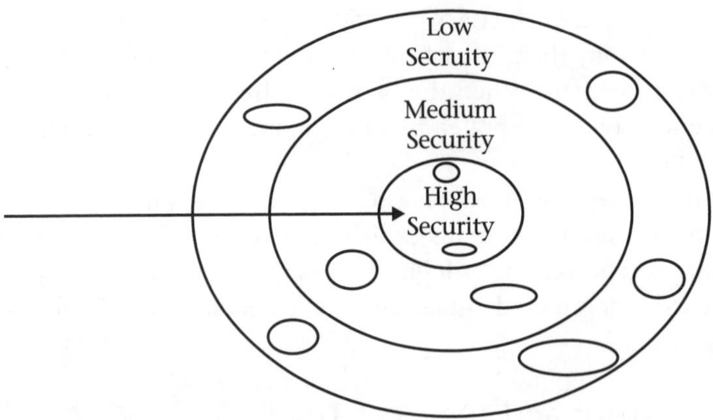

Figure 8-1 "Rings of Trust"

using an application-wide security identity, including an application username and password. If you store this application username and password on the file system, then you make it possible for users with access to the file system to retrieve database credentials. Such users can thereby gain access to the database using security credentials valid only for the lesser security requirements of the file system.

In practice, you cannot easily separate information technology functions into neat rings mapping to common security requirements. The "rings of trust" model is more a paradigm for analysis than a classification of security domains. The paradigm says that you should determine the relative levels of security requirements for information technology functions, then create security gateways or filters between functions with lower security requirements and functions with higher security requirements.

Network architectures for the Internet illustrate this paradigm well. Figure 8-2 shows such a network architecture.

In this network architecture, there are three "rings of trust": the Internet, which is not trusted, a DMZ network that is somewhat more trusted, and a corporate network that is most trusted.

Note

The term "DMZ" stands for "demilitarized zone." In network architectures, it refers to a network added between a protected network (i.e., protected by a firewall) and an external network (i.e., the Internet) in order to provide an additional layer of security. Another name for it is *perimeter network*.

In this network architecture, a router separates the wholly untrustworthy Internet from the DMZ, while a network firewall separates the DMZ network from the corporate network. All network traffic must pass through the router to get to the DMZ and through the firewall to get to the corporate network.

Figure 8-2 shows a network that separates the differing security levels well and manages effectively the movement from less secure rings to more secure rings. Suppose, however, that the depicted corporation decided to use the Network File System (NFS) to mount a hard drive hosted by a corporate machine on a machine in the DMZ. Either the corporation must then create

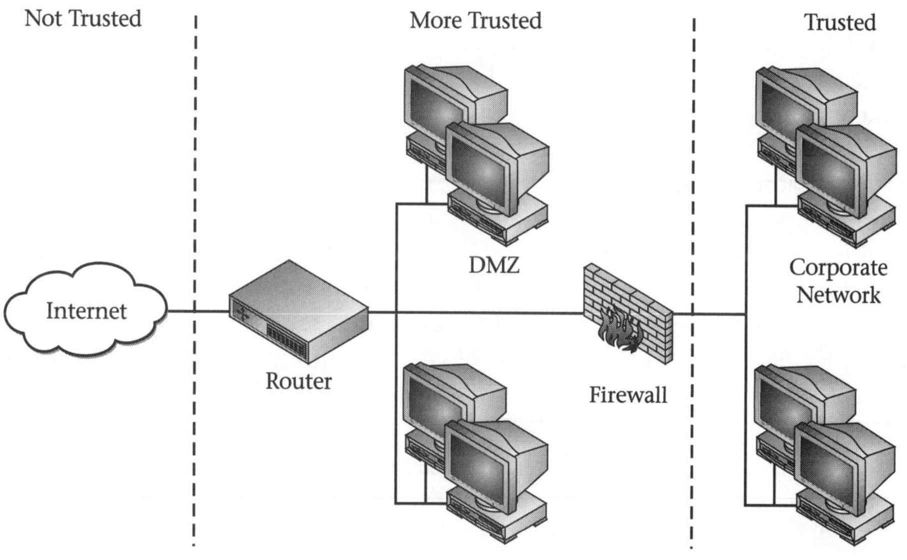

Figure 8-2 Internet network architecture

an entirely new network that bypasses the firewall or it must allow the NFS protocol to pass through the firewall. In either case, NFS then sets the security level for the entire realm, thereby circumventing the firewall.

1-Minute Drill

- What security services must you consider when designing a Web application?
- What is *authentication*?
- What is a "security technology domain"?
- What is a "security policy domain"?
- When does a security breach occur?

Authorization

Authorization is the process whereby an application enforces access restrictions or privileges associated with a known user. Typically, applications implement authorizations using Access Control Lists (ACLs). In such a scheme, a security service grants access to a requested resource by comparing the client's authenticated identity against a list of authorized clients. If the client has a record in the ACL with sufficient rights or privileges, the server grants the requested access to the client.

File systems are the most obvious example of a service that uses ACLs to authorize access. In Windows 2000, if you right-click any file, then view its security properties, you will see a dialog that looks similar to Figure 8-3.

Figure 8-3 shows four different access rights for files: `Modify`, `Read & Execute`, `Read`, `Write`. The name "Everyone" in Figure 8-3 simply says that

---

- You must consider at least seven services when designing a Web application: authentication, integrity, confidentiality, authorization, non-repudiation, availability, and auditing.
- Authentication refers to the process whereby a user convinces an application of his or her identity.
- A "security technology domain" is any grouping of functionality or resources controlled by a common security technology.
- A "security policy domain" is any grouping of functionality or resources controlled by a common security policy.
- A security breach occurs when credentials applicable in a less restrictive security realm in some way provide access to a more restrictive security realm.

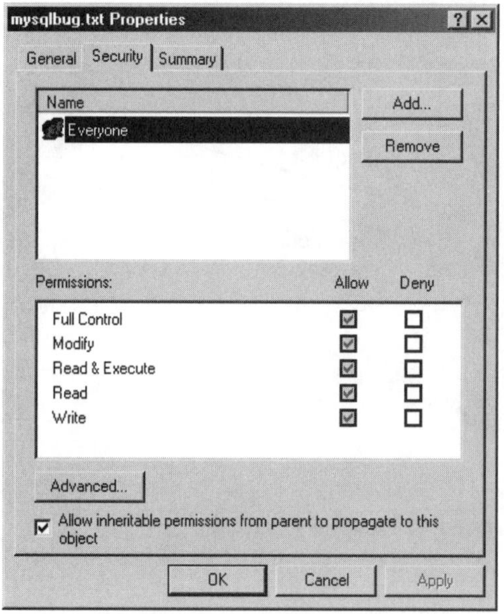

Figure 8-3 Use of Access Control List for Files

every user has the selected rights. The combination of an identity and selected rights is an ACL. An ACL grants a permission or set of permissions on a resource or class of resources to a list of users and groups.

Integrity

Message integrity refers to the process whereby an application confirms that messages sent from a user survived the transmission without modification in transit. If you can modify a message in transit, then you can *spoof* the recipient into inappropriate security decisions. Imagine you have access to someone's Internet communications with their online broker. By intercepting a message and modifying the response, you could spoof a person into providing his Social Security number (SSN) or credit card information. Figure 8-4 shows the problem. It shows a Web browser requesting a Web page from a spoofing site. The spoofing site then requests the real page from the real site. The real site returns the requested page. The spoofer rewrites the page and returns it to the

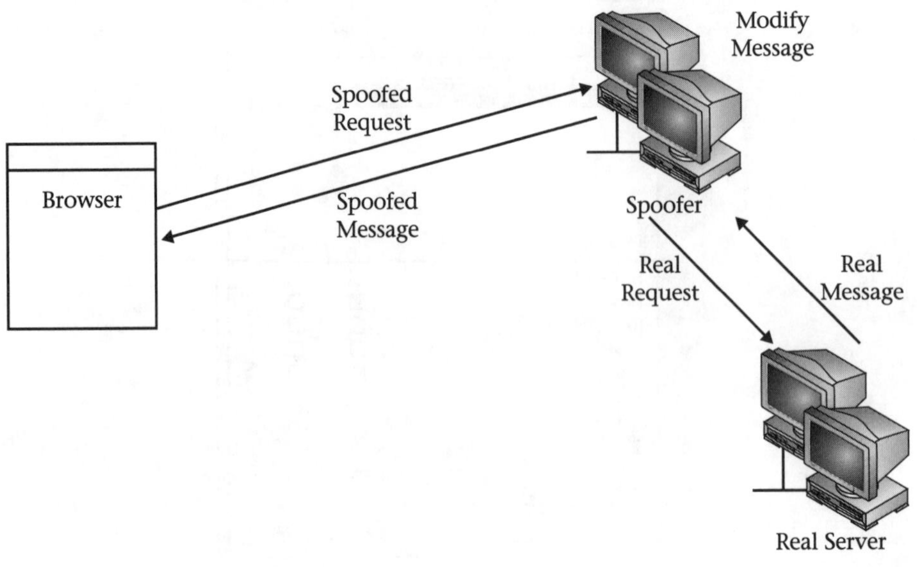

Figure 8-4 How a spoofer violates message integrity

Web browser. Throughout the process, the user never realizes that the spoofer is manipulating information for her own purposes.

The best way to guarantee message integrity is to store an encrypted *message digest* in the message. A message digest uses a hashing algorithm (i.e., a way to generate a binary signature for every binary input). Such hashes must have several traits:

- The input to the hash can be of any length.
- The output must have a fixed length.
- It must be difficult to guess or derive the input from the digest.
- It must be computationally impractical to find any two messages that hash to the same digest.

A security hash is better or worse depending upon the computational difficulty of circumventing the hash. A good hash function should make guessing or spoofing the input practically impossible. For example, consider a computer with petaflop (a million billion floating-point operations per second) speed (far faster than the fastest computer today). Given a hash that produces a 128-bit digest, and assuming you need 1000 floating-point operations per hash, you would need more than 10 million trillion years (worst case) to "discover" a message that hashes to a known value. To find two messages with the same digest, on the other hand, would require (worst case) only a little more than half a year.

Given these traits, both the sender and the receiver can perform the same hash on the same part of the message, and if the hashes match, they can have confidence that no one modified the message in transmission. Of course, this mechanism requires that the sender includes the entire message as input to the hash and then encrypts the resulting digest. If the sender hashes only part of the message, then the digest can only validate that part of the message as authentic. If the sender fails to encrypt the digest, then someone might modify the digest itself.

Tip

The most common hashes used for security purposes are the Secure Hash Algorithm (SHA) and MD5. The SHA algorithm produces a 160-bit "fingerprint" of its input (`http://www.itl.nist.gov/fipspubs/fip180-1.htm`). The MD5 algorithm produces a 128-bit "fingerprint" of its input (`http://www.cis.ohio-state.edu/cgi-bin/rfc/rfc1321.html`).

8

Confidentiality

Confidentiality ensures that no one inspects client messages during transmission. Encryption is the only guarantee of confidentiality. If an observer of the message cannot decrypt it, they cannot read it. Secure Sockets (SSL) are the dominant encryption technology providing confidentiality on the Internet.

Availability

Availability refers to the presence of a service on the network and its ability to respond to user messages. Many factors affect availability, including network traffic. Network traffic is the basis of so-called "denial of service" attacks against services. The idea behind such attacks is to make so many requests that the service is overwhelmed to the point of failure. The most common response to such attacks is to use routers or firewalls to filter out the sources of the attack messages. Generally, the number of attackers in a denial of service attack are very few, though they can be very hard to identify.

Hardware or software failures can also damage the availability of services. There are two approaches to resolving technology failures: redundancy of hardware and software or simplicity and rapidity of repair. The first provides alternate or backup responses when primary systems fail. The second enables administrators to locate and repair systems quickly when they fail.

Auditing

An *audit trail* tracks user activity in the application. When security breaches occur, an audit trail is often the only way to determine what happened. It may also provide the only clue to the identity of the attacker.

1-Minute Drill

- What is *authorization*?
- What is message *integrity*?
- What is *confidentiality*?
- What is a "denial of service attack"?
- Why might you audit user activity?

- The term "authorization" refers to the process whereby an application enforces access control over functionality or resources.
- The term "message integrity" refers to the confidence an application has that a user message survived transmission from the user without any modifications in transit.
- The term "confidentiality" refers to the confidence an application has that nobody inspected a user message during its transition from the user to the application.
- A denial of service attack tries to overwhelm an application with so many user messages that it can no longer respond (i.e., it becomes unavailable).
- You might audit user activity to determine the source of security breaches when they occur.

Web Authentication

There are a variety of technologies used for authentication in Web applications. We describe three:

- LDAP authentication
- Certificate-based authentication
- Web server–based authentication

LDAP authentication and certificate-based authentication have a general importance to many modern applications. Web server–based authentication works only with Web applications.

LDAP Authentication

Cooperative authentication schemes have an obvious utility in that they allow applications to share security information. For example, *network directory services* provide a centralized database of valid users and required authentication information. This means in effect that users can log in once to gain access to multiple applications. Such services have been available since the advent of local area networks (LANs) and the requirement to establish a network identity rather than just an identity on a single computer.

LDAP servers implement the Lightweight Directory Access Protocol (LDAP) to provide a generic directory service. An LDAP server stores information as entries in a tree structure. An object class defines each entry's type, including both required and optional attributes. A *distinguished name* (DN) uniquely identifies each entry. The format of the DN consists of the entry's label plus the path to the root of the tree. Figure 8-5 illustrates an LDAP directory.

Figure 8-5 shows three LDAP object classes: *Country*, *Organization*, and *Individual*. *Country* entries fill the first level in the LDAP hierarchy. These entries have a single required attribute, `c` (country). *Organization* entries fill the second level of the hierarchy. These entries have the single required attribute, `o` (organization). *Individual* entries fill the leaf notes of the hierarchy. These entries have two required attributes: `cn` (common name) and `sn`

8

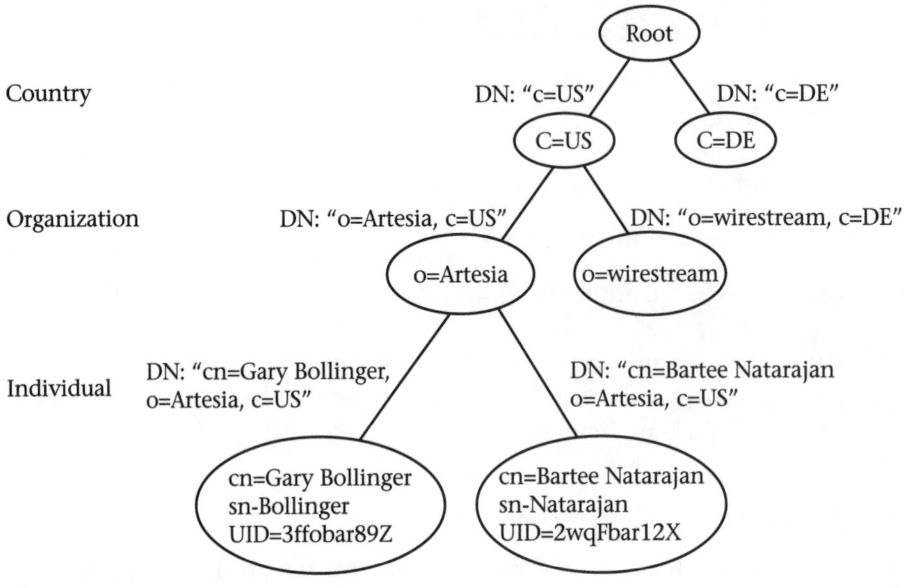

Figure 8-5 LDAP directory structure

(surname). They also have one optional attribute, `UID` (user id). Applications supply authentication information to the LDAP server in order to retrieve application attributes like `UID`.

Certificate-Based Authentication

Certificate-based authentication relies on X.509 security certificates. Like LDAP security schemes, certificate-based security schemes help centralize security information. Their primary advantage, however, is encryption. Such certificates use public-key/private-key encryption to establish identity. Let's look more closely at how this works.

Traditional message encryption relies on a common secret key known by both the sender and the receiver of the message. In this scheme (known as *secret key* or *symmetric cryptography*), the sender encrypts the message with the secret key and transmits the message. Then the receiver decrypts the message with the same secret key. This scheme works well when the sender and receiver share the same physical location, but it does not work so well over a widely distributed space like the World Wide Web. The problem is sharing the same key yet keeping it secret. The more people that share a secret, the less secret it becomes, and the harder it is to keep it secret. This problem of *key management* gave rise to *public key* schemes.

The idea behind public key schemes is to simplify keeping the secret by splitting encryption into two keys, one private and the other public. Users publish only their public key, keeping the private key secret. Private and public keys are large numbers that work in pairs to encrypt and decrypt digital signatures. The mathematics behind public-key/private-key encryption virtually guarantees that a private key cannot be "guessed" from a public key. Users encrypt messages using their private key and recipients of the message use the public key to decrypt them. Similarly, recipients encrypt return messages using the public key and users decrypt them using the private key.

An X.509 certificate stores an entity's identity and "signs" it digitally by encrypting some piece of data using the entity's private key (i.e., by creating a *digest*). A recipient of a "signed" message must decrypt the signature using the entity's public key. This can succeed only if the signature is valid, that is, if the client encrypted the signature using the matching private key. The entity alone knows the private key, so if decryption succeeds, the signature is valid and the entity is authenticated. Figure 8-6 shows how digital signatures authenticate entities.

8

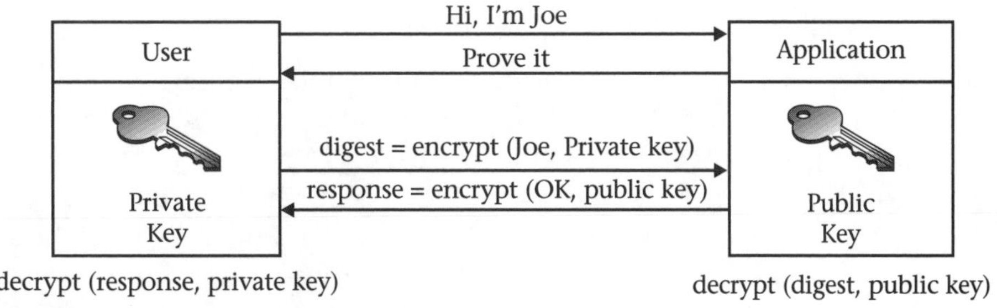

Figure 8-6 Digital certificate-based authentication

Certificates require *certificate authorities* (CAs) that vouch for the identity information stored in a certificate. The idea is that such authorities have legal liabilities that make their testimonies about certificates trustworthy. Anybody could set themselves up as a certificate authority, so the whole scheme depends upon the reputation of the authority. This means, in effect, that the key management problem in public key schemes has shifted from management of the secret key to management of the public key.

Note

Some of the better known certificate authorities are Verisign and Entrust. You can set yourself up as a certificate authority for development purposes using the **keytool** utility shipped with Java 2.

Currently Web browsers are the best-known users of security certificates. They use the certificates to enable the Secure Sockets Layer (SSL) protocol. Web sites also use certificates to identify themselves to browser users. Java programmers can embed certificate-based authentication in applications by using the *java.security.cert* package and purchasing an implementation of the abstract classes defined in this package from a vendor.

Ask the Expert

Question: I understand how these security certificates work, but why the odd name? What is the meaning of "X.509"?

Answer: The "X.509" certificate definition and recommendation is part of a series of X recommendations provided by the International Telecommunications Union and the International Standards Organization (ITU/ISO). The series also includes X.500, a comprehensive definition of a directory service similar to LDAP. (In fact, LDAP was "lightweight" explicitly in comparison to the X.500 directory service.) The X.509 certificate recommendation provided a way to attach secure signatures to X.500 directory service messages.

1-Minute Drill

- What is the advantage of using a network directory service to manage security?
- What is the primary advantage of using security certificates to manage security?

Web Server–Based Authentication

Every production-quality Web server provides some mechanism to control access to the resources it manages. Our example will be the Apache Web server (Apache). The HTTP/1.1 specification defines two forms of authentication, basic and digest. Apache supports both forms.

Similar to certificate-based authentication, basic and digest authentication use a form of challenge-response negotiation. Figure 8-7 illustrates this mechanism.

In a challenge-response negotiation, the client first requests access to a specific resource. If access to the resource is controlled, the security mechanism intercepts this request and returns an authorization error. For example, when using basic authentication the server might return an HTTP response header (Module 1) similar to this:

```
HTTP/1.1 401 Unauthorized
WWW-Authenticate: Basic realm="wsolney"
```

8

At this point, the browser will show a dialog box into which the user must enter credential information. The client can then respond with authorization credentials in a request header that uses base64 encoding to return the credentials. Here is an example:

```
Authorization: Basic base64-encoding-of(username:password)
```

If the client provides sufficient credentials, the security mechanism allows the request. If not, the security mechanism returns another authorization error. If authentication succeeds, the browser typically caches authentication information so that the client need not provide this authentication information again for the duration of the session.

- A network directory service like LDAP provides a centralized database of valid users enabling users to supply the same information to log into multiple applications.
- The primary advantage of security certificates is their ability to encrypt identity information.

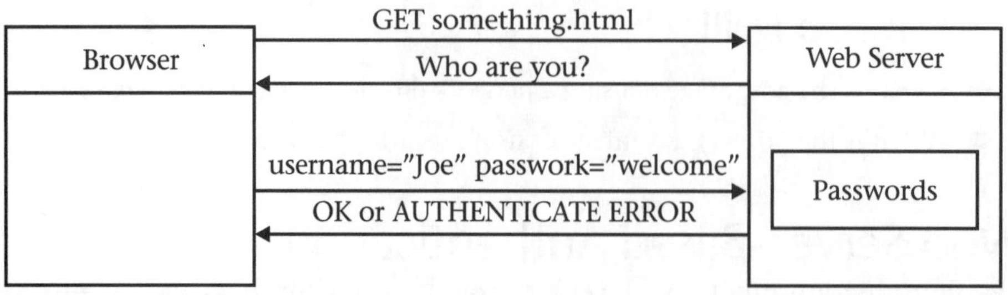

Figure 8-7 Challenge-response security mechanism

Ask the Expert

Question: What is base64 encoding? Is it a form of encryption?

Answer: Base64 encoding is a Multipurpose Internet Mail Extensions (MIME) specification for encoding any binary data in a printable character form (clear text) that is not humanly readable (i.e., viewable but not understandable as a language—`http://www.ietf.org/rfc/rfc1341.txt`). Its purpose was not so much to secure privacy as to ensure portability across different character encodings like standard US ASCII and the several variants of IBM's EBCDIC. It uses a 65-character subset of US ASCII, enabling each printable character to represent six bits of binary data.

Base64 encoding is a form of data marshaling, *not* a form of encryption. It enables reliable and portable transmission of data, but you can decode it as easily as you encode it. For this reason RFC 2617, which defines basic and digest authentication, asserts that basic authentication "is not a secure method of user authentication" unless enhanced with other authentication or encryption schemes (`http://www.cis.ohio-state.edu/cgi-bin/rfc/rfc2617.html#sec-4`).

Digest authentication adds one-way hashing of the credentials into a message digest (i.e., an irreversible encoding of the username and password in a non-readable form). This allows users to enter a username and password to authenticate themselves but not send these credentials in clear text across a network. Instead, the browser sends a digest (hash) of the credentials to the server. The server then authenticates the digest against a database of valid digests.

Caution

Unfortunately, some current browsers do not support digest authentication. Virata Corporation supplies an online test for browser support of digest authentication (`http://digest-test.agranat.com/`). When we tested two browsers, Internet Explorer 5.5 (IE) and Netscape 4.7.7 (Netscape), IE passed but Netscape did not.

The gravest weakness of digest authentication is that it provides no secure way to pass the digest to the server. The scheme is therefore open to identity "spoofing"—pretending to be someone other than oneself. A second problem is that the scheme provides no means to establish the initial arrangement between the user and the server of the correct digest for a given user.

1-Minute Drill

- What two forms of Web-based authentication does the HTTP/1.1 specification mandate?
- What is a *message digest*?
- What is basic authentication?

Configuring Apache Authentication

Using authentication, Apache provides user-level and group-level access control over Web resources. You must take several steps to configure Apache

- The HTTP/1.1 specification requires basic and digest authentication.
- A message digest is an irreversible encoding of information that makes it prohibitively expensive in time and resources to discover two messages with the same digest or to calculate a message that results in a given digest.
- Basic authentication requires a username and password but passes this information to a Web server in base64 clear text.

to support user-level and group-level access control using basic authentication. Here are the steps:

1. Define a realm of users.
2. Define a set of groups for the realm.
3. Create a password file for the realm and add records to it.
4. Create a group file and add users to groups.
5. Configure the server to use basic authentication and the password and group files for the realm.

An Apache *realm* is just a named set of Web resources under common access control. Such realms meet our own definition of security realms—any grouping of functionality or resources controlled by a common security policy. The Apache configuration documents recommend that you *not* put the password and group files under the document root (the starting point for browsing a Web site). If you put them under the document root, users could view them in their Web browsers, thereby compromising the security of these files.

In the Apache Server Version 1.3, on Windows platforms, the format of password file records is:

username:*password*

By default on Windows platforms, both the username and the password must be clear text (unencrypted) ASCII strings. This is because Apache statically compiles clear text authentication (`mod_auth`) into the server. You can confirm this default behavior by changing to the Apache `bin` directory and typing this in a console window:

```
\>Apache.exe -l
```

After doing so, you should see this output:

```
Compiled-in modules:
  http_core.c
  mod_so.c
  mod_mime.c
  mod_access.c
```

```
mod_auth.c
mod_negotiation.c
mod_include.c
mod_autoindex.c
mod_dir.c
mod_cgi.c
mod_userdir.c
mod_alias.c
mod_env.c
mod_log_config.c
mod_asis.c
mod_imap.c
mod_actions.c
mod_setenvif.c
mod_isapi.c
```

If you want to use password encryption, you must enable it by configuring `httpd.conf` to load the appropriate module. Here is a listing of the relevant fragment (formatting changed to fit on the page):

```
#LoadModule anon_auth_module
    modules/ApacheModuleAuthAnon.dll
#LoadModule dbm_auth_module
    modules/ApacheModuleAuthDBM.dll
#LoadModule digest_auth_module
    modules/ApacheModuleAuthDigest.dll
```

As you can see, Apache supports authentication of anonymous users (`anon_auth_module`), as well as authentication using a password file in the DBM database file format (using `crypt` encryption) or Berkeley DB format (`dbm_auth_module`). Finally, it also supports digest authentication (`digest_auth_module`). If you use any of these alternate forms of authentication, you must create the password file using the `htpasswd` utility with the appropriate options. Further, the Apache directives are different for each module. We describe Apache configuration using the default—clear text password authentication.

Here is an example of an Apache password file on Windows:

```
Gary:welcome
Bartee:goodbye
```

```
Mary: goodbye
Sandy:welcome
```

Notice that you specify each user and password pair on a single line followed by a line break.

The Apache group file is just as simple. Suppose we want two groups in our realm: `admin` and `default`. The group file would then have two lines looking like this:

```
admin:Gary Bartee
default:Mary Sandy
```

Notice that an Apache group file consists of lines giving a group name followed by the colon character (`:`) and a space-separated list of users in that group.

To configure the server to use the password and group files, you add a `<Directory>` block directive to the `httpd.conf` file. Apache uses such directives to configure the server. Apache block directives apply an enclosed set of Apache directives to operations on a directory and all the files and subdirectories in the directory. Here is an example of how you configure access control for a directory and all its files and subdirectories. In this example, we supply the absolute path to the controlled directory:

```
<Directory "E:/Apache/htdocs/controlled/wsolney">
   AuthType Basic
   AuthName "wsolney"
   AuthGroupFile "E:/Apache/login/wsolney/groups"
   AuthUserFile "E/Apache/login/wsolney/users"
   require valid-user
</Directory>
```


The `AuthType` directive specifies the authentication mechanism that Apache should apply. The value of this directive determines whether Apache will expect basic or digest authentication credentials from the client.

The `AuthName` directive specifies a name for the realm (i.e., the set of controlled directories and files).

The `AuthGroupFile` and `AuthUserFile` directives specify respectively the path to the user groups file and the path to the password file for the named realm.

The `require` directive in our example just says that any valid user can access the realm's controlled resources. With the `require` directive, you can restrict access in a variety of ways to different variations of users and groups. For example, suppose we want to restrict access to the `admin` group. We must then provide this `require` directive:

```
require group admin
```

Since the `<Directory>` directive lets you specify the path to the password and group files, different realms *could* (but need not) share the same database of users and groups. The `<Directory>` directive defines the realm and its security properties. The `require` directive restricts access to specific users and groups defined in some designated database of users and groups.

After you configure Apache to control resources, when you try to access those resources you will see a login screen like that shown in Figure 8-8.

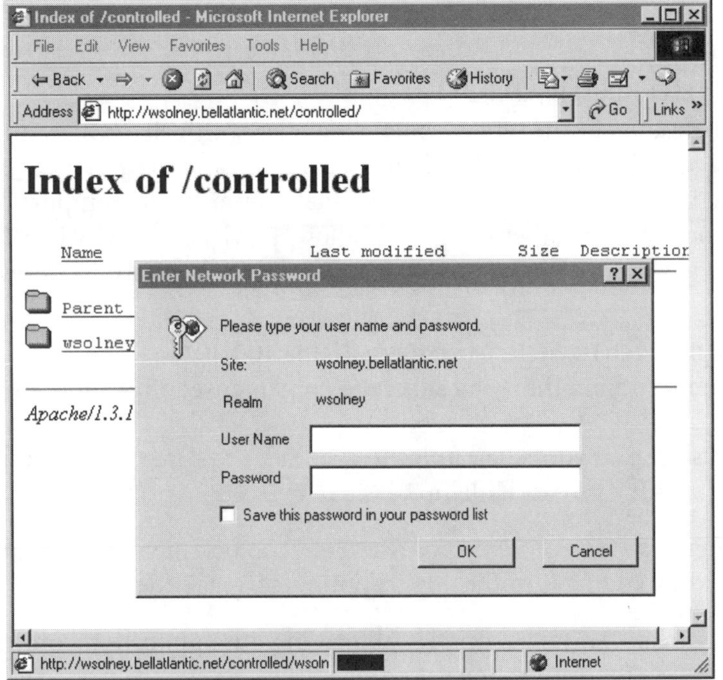

Figure 8-8 Browser login screen

8

Servlet Container Authentication

Servlet container authentication is relevant only to Servlet and JSP applications. The Servlet 2.2 specification either encourages or requires four authentication methods:

- Basic authentication is required.
- Digest authentication is encouraged.
- Form-based authentication is required.
- HTTPS client authentication is required.

Let's look at each of these methods.

Basic Authentication

Basic authentication by the servlet container works exactly like basic authentication in Web servers like Apache. The Servlet 2.2 specification requires all Java 2 Enterprise Edition (J2EE) compliant servlet containers to support basic authentication. Among other things, this allows servlet containers like Tomcat to function in a lightweight, stand-alone mode for use by Web site developers.

Configuring Tomcat for Basic Authentication

Basic authentication in the Tomcat servlet container requires three steps:

1. Add users, passwords, and roles to a `<tomcat-users>` block in the `tomcat-users.xml` file in %TOMCAT_HOME`%\conf`.
2. Configure a `<security-constraint>` block in your application context by adding it to the application's `web.xml` file.
3. Configure a `<login-config>` block in your application context by adding it to the application's `web.xml` file.

Configuring Users, Passwords, and Roles The Tomcat installation provides a few users and roles to support its examples. In the default `tomcat-users.xml` file, you find this `<tomcat-users>` block (formatting changed):

```
<tomcat-users>
   <user name="tomcat" password="tomcat"
         roles="tomcat"
   />
   <user name="role1"
         password="tomcat" roles="role1"
   />
   <user name="both"   password="tomcat"
         roles="tomcat,role1"
   />
</tomcat-users>
```

This `<tomcat-users>` block defines three users: "tomcat," "role1," and "both." All three users share the same password, "tomcat." The first user belongs to the role "tomcat," the second user belongs to the role "role1," and the third user belongs to both roles.

8

Configuring a <security-constraint> Block After adding users, you must configure a `<security-constraint>` block in your application's `web.xml` file. Tomcat provides an example application that configures security. You can find it in `%TOMCAT_HOME%\webapps\examples`. If you look at the `web.xml` for this application (in its `WEB-INF` directory), you find this `<security-constraint>` block (formatting changed):

```
<security-constraint>
   <web-resource-collection>   ← Specify the resources to protect
      <web-resource-name>Protected Area
      </web-resource-name>
      <!-- Define the context-relative URL(s)
              to be protected
      -->
      <url-pattern>/jsp/security/protected/*   ← Protected pages
      </url-pattern>
      <!-- If you list http methods, only
           those methods are protected
```

```
        -->
        <http-method>DELETE</http-method>
        <http-method>GET</http-method>
        <http-method>POST</http-method>
        <http-method>PUT</http-method>
    </web-resource-collection>
    <auth-constraint>
        <!-- Anyone with one of the listed
             roles may access this area
        -->
        <role-name>tomcat</role-name>
        <role-name>role1</role-name>
    </auth-constraint>
</security-constraint>
```

Protected HTTP methods

Roles with access to resources

This <security-constraint> block configures the example application context using two subelements: <web-resource-collection> and <auth-constraint>. The first subelement specifies the protected resources; the second specifies the user roles that can access the protected resources.

The DTD for web.xml files supports a third subelement: <user-data-constraint>. A <user-data-constraint> subelement specifies security constraints for the protocol between client and server. For example, consider this XML fragment:

```
<user-data-constraint>
    <transport-guarantee>INTEGRAL</transport-guarantee>
</user-data-constraint>
```

This fragment requires that the transport protocol for a request must guarantee its integrity. This means that the browser must submit the request in such a way that no one can alter it in transit. Other values can be NONE and CONFIDENTIAL. The NONE value, the default, imposes no constraints on the request transport. The CONFIDENTIAL value requires that the request transport guarantee that no one can read the request in transit. The values INTEGRAL and CONFIDENTIAL mean in practice using SSL as the request transport.

Configuring a <login-config> Block Finally, you must configure a <login-config> block for your application. Look again at the web.xml file for Tomcat's example application. You can find a <login-config> block that looks like this:

```
<login-config>
   <auth-method>BASIC</auth-method>
   <realm-name>Example Basic Authentication Area
   </realm-name>
</login-config>
```

The `<auth-method>` tag specifies the authentication method for servlets and JavaServer Pages in the same way that the `AuthType` directive configured the Apache Web server for authentication. Tomcat supports four valid values for this tag:

- BASIC
- DIGEST
- CLIENT-CERT
- FORM

The `<realm-name>` tag specifies the name of the security realm for servlets and JavaServer Pages in the same way that the `AuthName` directive configures the Apache Web server for realms. The `<realm-name>` tag can take any string as its value.

Digest Authentication

Digest authentication by the servlet container works like digest authentication in the Apache Web server. You configure Tomcat for digest authentication just as you configure it for basic authentication, except that you supply a different value to the `<auth-method>` tag. Here is what the `<login-config>` block for digest authentication looks like:

```
<login-config>
   <auth-method>Digest</auth-method>
   <realm-name>Example Basic Authentication Area
   </realm-name>
</login-config>
```

Servlet containers need not implement digest authentication to be J2EE compliant, though the specification recommends such support.

HTTPS Client Authentication

The servlet specification requires all conforming J2EE servlet containers to support HTTPS authentication. HTTPS provides the strongest form of authentication required by the servlet specification. The specification states that HTTPS authentication requires a public key certificate (PKC) as we described them earlier in this module.

Form-Based Authentication

None of the authentication schemes we have described so far allow you to create a custom "look and feel" for your login page. The browser login dialog looks unprofessional in a product and undesirable even in personal Web sites. Providing a custom "look and feel" for your login pages enhances the experience of your site. The Servlet 2.2 specification addresses this issue by requiring J2EE-compliant servlet containers to provide form-based authentication.

Form-based authentication allows you to provide a custom login page to servlet authentication mechanisms. If we return to the example security application in `%TOMCAT_HOME%\webapps\examples`, we see this XML fragment in the `web.xml` file (formatting changed):

```
<login-config>
   <auth-method>FORM</auth-method>
   <realm-name>Example Form-Based Authentication Area
   </realm-name>
   <form-login-config>
      <form-login-page>/jsp/security/login/login.jsp
      </form-login-page>
      <form-error-page>/jsp/security/login/error.jsp
      </form-error-page>
   </form-login-config>
</login-config>
```

As the fragment shows, form-based authentication adds a specification for a login page and error page to the `<login-config>` block.

The servlet specification provides specific instructions for the login form. The login form's method must be `POST`, and its action must be `j_security_check`. The form must also contain a username field named "j_username" and a password field named "j_password." Here is the page provided by the Tomcat security example (`$TOMCAT_HOME/webapps/examples/jsp/security/login/login.jsp`):

```
<HTML>
<BODY>
<H>Login page for examples</H1>

<FORM METHOD="POST" ACTION="j_security_check" >
 Username: <INPUT TYPE="text" NAME="j_username"><br>
 Password: <INPUT TYPE="password" NAME="j_password"><br>
 br>
 <INPUT TYPE="submit" VALUE="login" NAME="j_security_check">
</FORM>

</BODY>
</HTML>
```

When you access this example page, you get a Web page that looks like Figure 8-9.

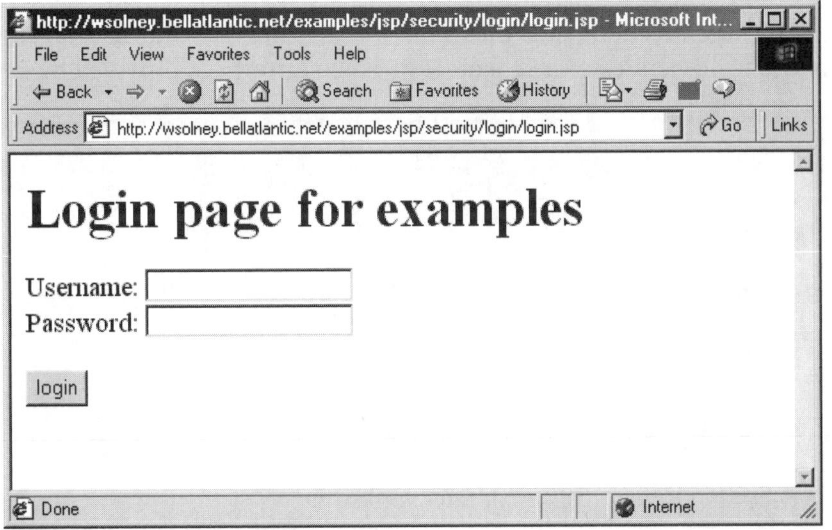

Figure 8-9 Login page for Tomcat security example

8

The servlet specification also dictates the steps that must occur when using form-based authentication. Here are the steps that occur when a user requests a protected Web resource:

1. The container returns the specified login form and stores the requested URL.
2. The client fills out the form.
3. The client posts the form back to the server.
4. The container uses the form fields to authenticate the user. If authentication fails, the container returns the specified error page to the client.
5. If authentication succeeds, the container checks to see if the authenticated principal's role has access to the requested URL (Web resource).
6. If the principal cannot access the Web resource, the servlet container returns the specified error page.
7. If the client has access, the container redirects the client to their requested URL.

The specification recommends that the error page provide information about the failure to authenticate the client. Here is the error page provided by the Tomcat example:

```
<html>
<head>
<title>Login Error</title>
</head>
<body bgcolor=white>

Login error -- please try <a href="login.jsp">again</a>.

</body>
</html>
```

Figure 8-10 shows what this error page looks like.

Form-based login passes the username and password in clear text (i.e., unencrypted) and provides no protection against spoofing. For these reasons, the servlet specification recommends additional protection such as HTTPS (HTTP over SSL) or security at the network level (e.g., IPSEC).

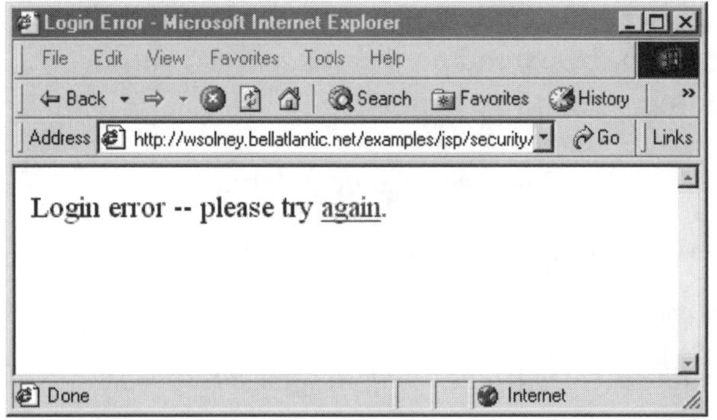

Figure 8-10 Error page for the Tomcat security example

Note

IPSEC stands for the Internet Protocol Security suite of standards. These standards include both authentication and encryption at the Internet Protocol (IP) level.

1-Minute Drill

- What types of authentication does the Servlet 2.2 specification require?
- In form-based authentication, what must the action of the form be?

8

Tomcat Security Interceptors

Tomcat provides an implementation of the Servlet 2.2 specification that allows developers to replace a default security handler with a custom security handler.

Caution

Tomcat interceptors are not portable to other servlet containers; this discussion assumes Tomcat 3.2.x.

- The Servlet 2.2 specification requires three form of authentication: basic, form-based, and HTTPS. It also recommends a fourth, digest authentication.
- In form-based authentication, the action of the form must be: `j_security_check`. There must also be username and password fields named `j_username` and `j_password`, respectively.

A security handler in Tomcat implements the Java interface *org.apache.tomcat.core.RequestInterceptor* by extending the *org.apache.tomcat.core.BaseInterceptor* class and overriding at least five methods:

- *public void setContextManager(ContextManager cm)*
- *public void contextInit(Context ctx)*
- *public void contextShutdown(Context ctx)*
- *public int authenticate(Request req, Response response)*
- *public int authorize(Request req, Response response, String roles[])*

The security interceptor's role is to authenticate the HTTP request before forwarding it to the requested resource (i.e., it intercepts the request). Figure 8-11 shows this interceptor architecture.

As we described earlier in this module, Tomcat's default security handler uses the `%TOMCAT_HOME%\conf\tomcat-users` file to specify users, passwords, and roles. There are a few reasons not to use the default security handling provided by Tomcat in any kind of production environment. For one thing, it stores passwords in clear text on the file system. For another reason, a simple text file is hard to manage when the number of users grows large. A third reason is that the default handler caches the authentication database in memory, needlessly consuming a precious resource. In order to strengthen Tomcat security mechanisms, you must use some other security interceptor.

Tomcat itself provides an alternate security interceptor: *org.apache.tomcat.request.JDBCRealm*.

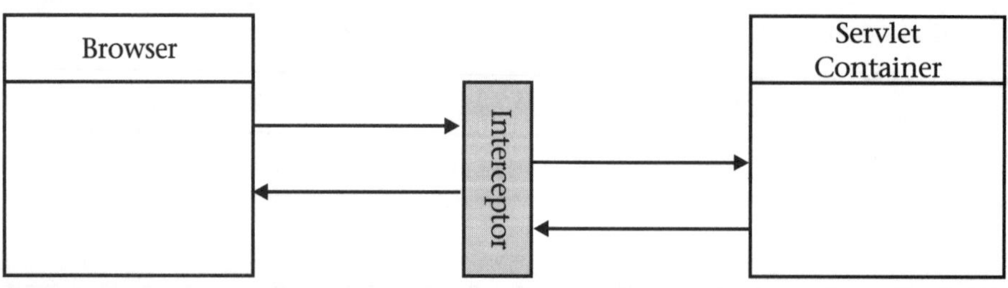

Figure 8-11 Interceptor architecture

Tip

You can find a "how to" discussion of the JDBC realm interceptor in `%TOMCAT_HOME%\doc\JDBCRealm.howto`.

This second interceptor allows you to authenticate and authorize resource requests using a database rather than a text file. In Tomcat's `server.xml` file, you must comment out the default realm and add lines configuring the JDBC realm. Here are the configuration lines specifying the default interceptor:

```
<!-- Check permissions using the simple
     xml file. You can plug more advanced
     authentication modules.
-->
<RequestInterceptor
 className="org.apache.tomcat.request.SimpleRealm"
 debug="0" />
```

To use the JDBC interceptor for MySQL, you should comment out these lines and add the following lines:

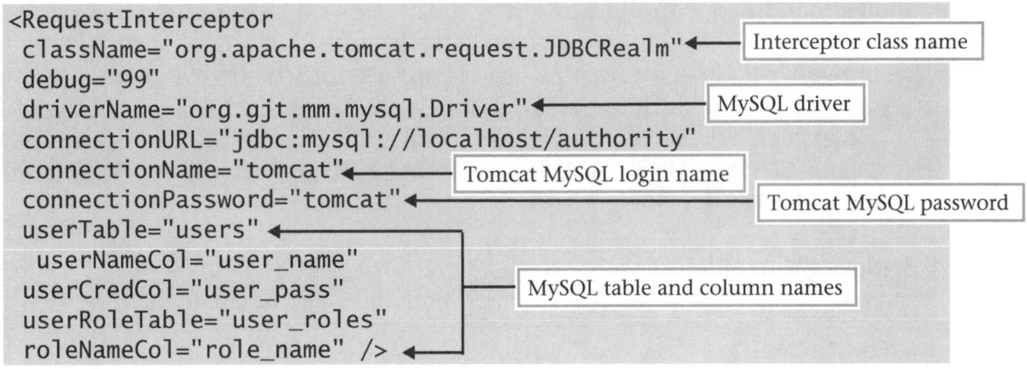

```
<RequestInterceptor
 className="org.apache.tomcat.request.JDBCRealm"
 debug="99"
 driverName="org.gjt.mm.mysql.Driver"
 connectionURL="jdbc:mysql://localhost/authority"
 connectionName="tomcat"
 connectionPassword="tomcat"
 userTable="users"
  userNameCol="user_name"
 userCredCol="user_pass"
 userRoleTable="user_roles"
 roleNameCol="role_name" />
```


8

web.xml
jspTest.jsp
error.jsp
login.jsp
CustomRealm.java

Project 8-1: A Custom Tomcat Security Interceptor

Tomcat interceptors implement a common pattern in network programming—the request interceptor pattern. The idea behind interceptors is that they can be loaded at runtime to extend or customize functionality without modifying or recompiling existing code. They generally act as filters qualifying the request, either by modifying it or rejecting it for security reasons. Sometimes interceptors simply track request activity, but generally they enforce some policy choice. Interceptors operate like callbacks. You register your interceptor, and at specific points in the runtime operation of the container, the container calls the interceptor methods.

Tomcat security interceptors authenticate and authorize requests for Web resources. In this project, we step through development of a custom security interceptor.

Step-by-Step

1. Download the **W**eb **AR**chive (WAR) `interceptor.war` containing the files for this project from `http://www.osborne.com`.

2. Move `interceptor.war` to `%TOMCAT_HOME%\webapps`.

3. Extract the interceptor application using the **jar.exe** utility:

```
\>jar.exe xvf interceptor.war
```

4. You should now see the `%TOMCAT_HOME%\webapps\interceptor` directory. Change to the `%TOMCAT_HOME%\webapps\interceptor\WEB-INF\src` directory and compile the file `CustomRealm.java`. Make sure you include `servlet.jar` and `webserver.jar` in your `CLASSPATH`.

```
\>set CLASSPATH=%CLASSPATH%;%TOMCAT_HOME%\lib\servlet.jar
\>set CLASSPATH=%CLASSPATH%;%TOMCAT_HOME%\lib\webserver.jar
\>javac.exe CustomRealm.java
```

5. Move the resulting class file (`CustomRealm.class`) into `%TOMCAT_HOME%\classes`. (You will probably need to create this directory.)

6. Edit `%TOMCAT_HOME%\conf\server.xml`. Comment out these lines:

```
<RequestInterceptor
   className="org.apache.tomcat.request.SimpleRealm"
   debug="0" />
```

7. The lines should now look like this:

```
<!--
<RequestInterceptor
```

```
    className="org.apache.tomcat.request.SimpleRealm"
    debug="0" />
-->
```

8. Immediately after the lines you commented out, add these lines:

```
<!-- Check permissions using CustomRealm -->
<RequestInterceptor
    className="CustomRealm"
/>
```

9. These changes configure Tomcat to use *CustomRealm* for authentication and authorization rather than *org.apache.tomcat.request.SimpleRealm.*
10. Now you must add some roles to the `web.xml` file. Change directories to `%TOMCAT_HOME%\webapps\interceptor\WEB-INF` and edit the `web.xml` file you find there.
11. In the `<auth-constraint>` block in `web.xml`, consider these lines:

```
<role-name>administrator</role-name>
<role-name>family</role-name>
```

12. With these lines, we added role-based access control over all requests that match the pattern: "/jsp/app/*". We have also defined the required roles to be "administrator" and "family."
13. Start `Tomcat` and enter the URL: `http://localhost:8080/interceptor/jsp/app/jsptest.jsp`.
14. You should now see the Web page shown in Figure 8-12.
15. Type this into the *Username* field: **Gary Bollinger**
16. Type this into the *Password* field: **user1**
17. After clicking the *login* button, you should see the Web page displayed in Figure 8-13.
18. What happened that required you to log in? When you requested the URL `http://localhost:8080/interceptor/jsp/app/jsptest.jsp`, the *CustomRealm* security interceptor redirected your request to the login page. When you entered a valid username and password, the container finally delivered the requested page.

19. Why did the container protect the page? The container protected it because the interceptor application's `web.xml` file specified protection for it. Here is a `web.xml` fragment that shows how protection is specified:

```
<web-resource-collection>
   <web-resource-name>Protected Area
   </web-resource-name>

   <!-- Define the protected URL(s) -->
   <url-pattern>/jsp/app/*</url-pattern>

   <!-- Define the protected HTTP methods -->
   <http-method>DELETE</http-method>
   <http-method>GET</http-method>
   <http-method>POST</http-method>
   <http-method>PUT</http-method>
</web-resource-collection>
```

Project 8-1 introduced the concept of Tomcat security interceptors. Such interceptors provide a way to provide servlet container-based custom login pages to applications. Now, in Project 8-2 we expand on these techniques.

Figure 8-12 Our login page

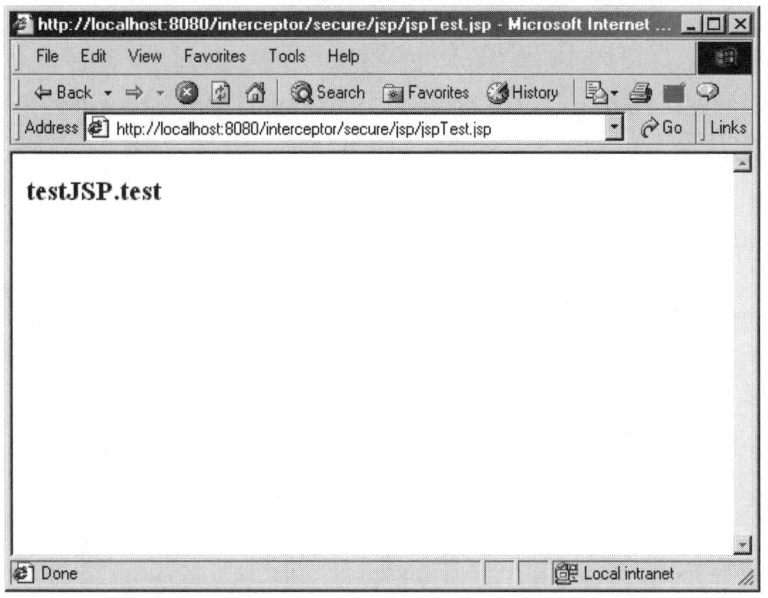

Figure 8-13 Result of logging in

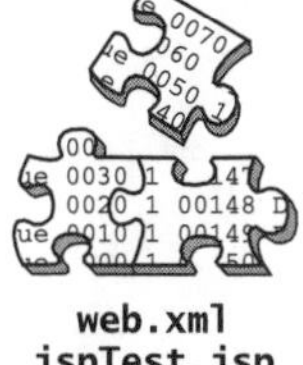

web.xml
jspTest.jsp
error.jsp
login.jsp
CustomRealm.java
Family.
jpg
bluepaper.gif
LoginError.jpg

Project 8-2: Enhancing Our Login Pages

We want our Family Center to be secure from non-relatives but also to present an attractive interface. To build it, we will expand on the project you just completed (we assume you did complete it). Since we have not yet developed the Family Center application code, we will install this enhanced approach in a "security" application context.

Step-by-Step

1. Download the **W**eb **AR**chive (WAR) `security.war` containing the files for this project from `http://www.osborne.com`.
2. Move `security.war` to `%TOMCAT_HOME%\webapps`.
3. Extract the WAR file:

```
\>jar.exe xvf security.war
```

4. You should see the `security` directory containing all the files for the security application.
5. Restart Tomcat.

6. Enter the URL:
   `http://localhost:8080/security/jsp/app/jsptest.jsp.`
7. You now see a more sophisticated login page. Figure 8-14 shows the new login page.
8. Type this into the *Username* field: **Gary Bollinger**
9. Type this into the *Password* field: **user13**
10. After clicking the *login* button, you should see the Web page displayed in Figure 8-15, which means your login failed. Substitute **user1** to correctly log in.

Figure 8-14 The Family Center login page

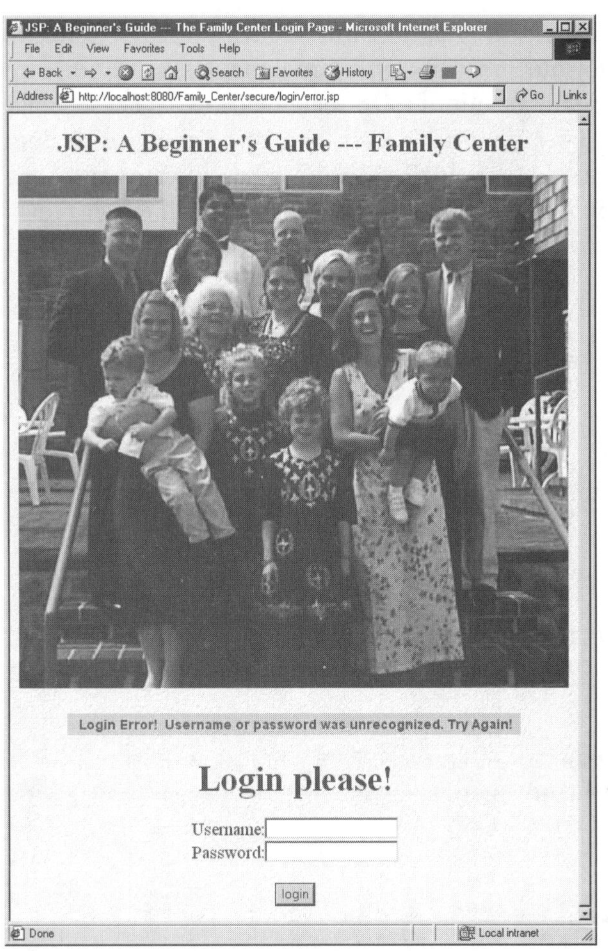

Figure 8-15 Family Center error page

Security is often the last thought when developing applications, partly because it is hard to demo to customers or bosses, partly because there seems no end to it. As a first step you must ask yourself, "How secure is secure enough?" A *security policy* is just an answer to this not so simple question. At its core a security policy just evaluates the degree of risk you are willing to take and assigns the technologies or persons responsible for assuring the security elements you choose.

There is no such thing as absolute security on a local network, much less the Internet. For our purposes, we want enough security that no one will access our site accidentally or out of misdirected curiosity. These goals dictate a login page requiring users to enter a username and password. It does not require more sophisticated technologies like digital certificates and SSL. If despite our login page people access our Web site, then we will either reevaluate the risk we want to take or accept the illicit access.

The Elements of Our Security Solution

Let's examine the elements of the security pages we have developed so far.

The Login and Login Error Pages

There is nothing especially sophisticated about our login page. We display a family picture and a login form derived from the Tomcat example. Here is the code:

```
<HTML>
<BODY BACKGROUND="../../../images/bluepaper.gif">
<TITLE>JSP: A Beginner's Guide ---
 The Family Center Login Page
</TITLE>
<CENTER>
<H2>JSP: A Beginner's Guide --- Family Center</H2>
<IMG src="../../../images/Family.jpg">
<H1>Login please!</H1>
<FORM METHOD="POST" ACTION="j_security_check" >
 Username:<INPUT TYPE="text" NAME="j_username"><BR>
 Password:<INPUT TYPE="password"
          NAME="j_password"><BR><BR>
         <INPUT TYPE="submit" VALUE="login"
          NAME="j_security_check">
</FORM>
</CENTER>
</BODY>
</HTML>
```

Required method

Required action

Required username field

Required password field

Our login error page (error.jsp) merely adds an error image after the image of the Family.jpg. So that HTML fragment looks like this:

```
<IMG src="../../../images/Family.jpg">
<BR>
<IMG src = "../../../images/LoginError.jpg">
```

The web.xml File

The web.xml file specifies access control for every page under %TOMCAT_HOME\webapps\security\jsp. It also specifies just two roles: administrator and family. (Eventually we want the family role to grant all family members *read* access to the site. The administrator role should grant *write* access as well. We must code this into the *CustomRealm*, however, and we won't do this except in the final version of the Family Center that we post on the Osborne Web site.) Here is the web.xml file. Notice that we name our security realm "Family Center":

```
<?xml version="1.0" encoding="ISO-8859-1"?>
<!DOCTYPE web-app
  PUBLIC "-//Sun Microsystems, Inc.//DTD
  Web Application 2.2//EN"
  "http://java.sun.com/j2ee/dtds/web-app_2_2.dtd">

<web-app>
   <security-constraint>
      <web-resource-collection>
         <web-resource-name>Protected Area
         </web-resource-name>
         <!-- Define the context-relative URL(s)
              to be protected -->
         <url-pattern>/jsp/app/*</url-pattern>
         <!-- If you list http methods, only
              those methods are protected -->
         <http-method>DELETE</http-method>
         <http-method>GET</http-method>
         <http-method>POST</http-method>
         <http-method>PUT</http-method>
      </web-resource-collection>
      <auth-constraint>
```

8

```
        <!- Anyone with one of the listed
             roles may access this area ->
        <role-name>administrator</role-name>
        <role-name>family</role-name>
     </auth-constraint>
  </security-constraint>

  <!- Form-based login ->
  <login-config>
     <auth-method>FORM</auth-method>
     <realm-name>Family Center</realm-name>
     <form-login-config>
        <form-login-page>/jsp/secure/login/login.jsp
        </form-login-page>
        <form-error-page>/jsp/secure/login/error.jsp
        </form-error-page>
     </form-login-config>
  </login-config>
</web-app>
```

The CustomRealm Security Interceptor

Our Family Center security interceptor (*CustomRealm*) extends the class *org.apache.tomcat.core.BaseInterceptor* and overrides five methods: *setContextManager*, *contextInit*, *contextShutdown*, *authenticate*, and *authorize*. Let's look at each of them to see how they work.

The *setContextManager* Method

The purpose of the *setContextManager* method is to store a local reference to Tomcat's instance of the *org.apache.tomcat.core.ContextManager* object. This object is the main entry point into the Tomcat servlet container. It acts as the execution controller and manager of application contexts as well as installed interceptors (including security interceptors). It is responsible for directing request processing including request parsing, *service* method invocation, and logging. Here is our code for *setContextManager*:

```
/**
 * Store a local reference to the ContextManager
 */
 public void setContextManager(ContextManager contextManager)
 {
```

```
    super.setContextManager(contextManager);
    this.contextManager = contextManager;
    System.out.println("CustomRealm.setContextManager()");
}
```

The *contextInit* Method

The purpose of the *contextInit* method in our interceptor is to initialize authentication and authorization information. We are going to "hard-code" some information for now (in Module 10, we show how to use a database to avoid hard-coding such values). Here is our code adding two families with two family members each:

```
/**
 * Initialize authentication and authorization
 * information for CustomRealm.
 */
public void contextInit(Context ctx)
    throws TomcatException
{
    if (!inited)
    {
        inited = true; // do it only once
      /*
        * set up roles database
        */
        userRoles = new HashMap();
        userRoles.put(GARY_BOLLINGER,
                      ADMINISTATOR);
        userRoles.put(BHARATHI_NATARAJAN,
                      ADMINISTRATOR);
        userRoles.put(MARY_BOLLINGER,
                      FAMILY);
        userRoles.put(SANDY_NATARAJAN,
                      FAMILY);
      /*
        * set up password database
        */
        userPasswords = new HashMap();
        userPasswords.put(GARY_BOLLINGER,
                          GARY_PASSWORD);
        userPasswords.put(BHARATHI_NATARAJAN,
                          BHARATHI_PASSWORD);
```

Hardcode user/role mappings

Hardcode user/password mappings

8

```
        userPasswords.put(MARY_BOLLINGER,
                          MARY_PASSWORD);
        userPasswords.put(SANDY_NATARAJAN,
                          SANDY_PASSWORD);
        System.out.println(
                "CustomRealm.contextInit()");
    }
}
```

The *contextShutdown* Method

The purpose of the *contextShutdown* method is to release any resources used by our interceptor before Tomcat shuts down. Our security interceptor does not need to release any resources. Here is the code:

```
/**
 * release any resources before Tomcat shuts down
 */
 public void contextShutdown(Context ctx)
    throws org.apache.tomcat.core.TomcatException
 {
    super.contextShutdown(ctx);
 }
```

The *authenticate* Method

The purpose of the *authenticate* method is to approve or deny access to the application on the basis of the identity of the user. This is the method that performs the most important security function of the application—restricting access to unwanted users. Let's examine this method more closely. Here is the annotated code:

```
/**
 * Use CustomRealm to authenticate user.
 */
 public int authenticate(Request req,
                         Response response)
 {
    int authValue = NOT_AUTHORIZED; //401 indicates error

    // extract login credentials from login.jsp
    HttpSession session = req.getSession(false);
    if (session == null)
```

```
        return authValue; // not OK since no session
    String username =
        (String)session.getAttribute("j_username");
    String password =
        (String)session.getAttribute("j_password");

    // authenticate the username and password
    if (username != null && password != null)
    {
        String userPwd =
            (String)userPasswords.get(username);
        if ((userPwd != null) &&
             (userPwd.equals(password)))
        {
            System.out.println(
                "CustomRealm.authenticate(" +
                username + ")");
            // set remote user name in request
            req.setRemoteUser(username);
            req.setUserPrincipal(
                new SimplePrincipal(username));
            authValue = OK; // 0 says authenticated
        }
    }
    return authValue;
}
```

Get username and password from login form

Get user password from hard-coded password database

Check password

Store authenticated user in container

The *authorize* Method

The purpose of the *authorize* method is to approve or deny access to application resources on the basis of the user's role. We have hard-coded some roles here, but as in the case of usernames and passwords, we will replace this with a database implementation in Module 10. The algorithm here is to get the user's role, then compare it against the roles we defined for the current resource (passed into *authorize* as a *roles* array). If there is a match, the user has access. Here is the code:

```
/**
 * Use CustomRealm to authorize user.
 */
public int authorize(Request req,
                     Response response,
                     String roles[])
```

```
{
   int authValue = NOT_AUTHORIZED; // 401

   // we stored username in authenticate
   String username = req.getRemoteUser();
   if (username != null)
   {
      String role = (String)userRoles.get(username);
      if (role != null)
      {
         System.out.println(
             "CustomRealm.authorize(" +
             username + ", " + role + ")");

         for (int i = 0;
              authValue != OK && i < roles.length; i++)
         {
            if (role.equals(roles[i]))
            {
               authValue = OK; // 0 says authorized
            }
         }
      }
   }
   return authValue;
}
```

Get current authenticated user from container

Get user's role

See if user's role gives access to current resources

The server.xml Configuration File

If you did not follow Project 8-1, you will have to configure the `server.xml` file in `%TOMCAT_HOME%\conf` to use the *CustomRealm* interceptor. In this case, review the project instructions. The servlet container can support only one security interceptor at a time, so you must be sure to comment out the *SimpleRealm* interceptor and add in the *CustomRealm* interceptor. Do not worry about the simplicity of our application so far. We begin to add functionality to the Family Center in Modules 9 and 10.

Mastery Check

1. Which of the security services addresses the problem of spoofing? What is spoofing?

2. What is a security interceptor? How do interceptors work?

3. Where do you configure the security realm in Tomcat?

4. Where do you configure the security realm in the Apache Web server?

5. Which of the security services do you consider most fundamental? What are your reasons?

6. What do "rings of trust" represent?

7. What are some reasons not to use the default security mechanism of `Tomcat`?

8. What kind of structure does an LDAP service give its repository?

Mastery Check

9. Where do you define access control for roles in Tomcat?

10. What is a *certificate authority*? What role do they play in security architectures?

11. How does the challenge-response mechanism work in certificate-based security architectures?

12. What is the Secure Hash Algorithm? What is one use for such hash functions in Web architectures?

Module 9

Controller and Flow Control in Web Applications

The Goals of This Module

- Understand the responsibilities of the controller in an MVC architecture
- Understand flow control in a Web application
- Learn techniques for building configurable flow control architectures

JavaServer Pages help simplify dynamic Web application development, but Web applications still become complex very quickly. Whenever you build a complex application, you should first establish a strong architecture using proven techniques for flexibility and extensibility. A strong architecture enables the application to withstand the tests of time.

We saw in Module 6 how you can simplify a JSP page using custom tag libraries that help eliminate mixed Java code with HTML. Tag libraries make JavaServer Pages more readable and adaptable. We discussed various design patterns for Web applications in Module 7 and established the need for the Model-View-Controller (MVC) design pattern in Web architectures. Using custom tag libraries to simplify JavaServer Pages (the view in an MVC architecture), while important, is not a complete MVC architecture. In this module, we concentrate on the MVC controller that coordinates communication between the model and the view.

Controller

The controller object encapsulates a Web application's control logic. Its responsibilities include:

- Receiving user requests and application messages
- Creating and acquiring models that manage data and invoke services on them
- Driving the workflow of the Web application (web-flow)

Since the controller is not responsible for any presentation, a developer writes it rather than a page designer. You should generally write your controller as a Java servlet. Figure 9-1, reproduced from Module 7, shows the controller component in a typical Web application.

Let us address in detail each of the three responsibilities of the controller.

User Input Processing

If you've done Web development, then you have noticed that your most common task is retrieving data posted in an HTML form. Servlet containers capture all this data and present it elegantly to your servlet in

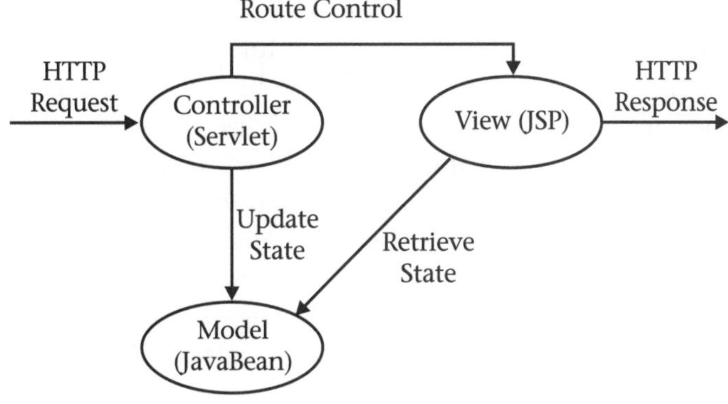

Figure 9-1 Controller in the MVC pattern

a *javax.servlet.http.HttpServletRequest* object. Your controller servlet could directly forward the *HttpServletRequest* object to the model and let it extract the information it needs; but this apparently very practical solution has some drawbacks.

If you let the model extract information from the *HttpServletRequest* object, you tie it inextricably to the view. This is because it must then understand every named HTML input item in the view so that it can retrieve the associated values for these items from the *HttpServletRequest* object. One might argue that this is not so big a deal, since the model's input probably maps directly to the input elements in the view. While this may be true in simple situations, more often than not the model's inputs are either a subset of or a derivation of the inputs from the view. Moreover, making the model aware of view elements clearly violates the separation of model from view dictated by the MVC architecture.

The model provides business logic services that you can use in any application context, not just a Web application context. For instance, your model could provide access to a relational database using JDBC in a two-tier setup or access to an EJB Application Server in a three-tier setup. A native Java client application could access these services as easily as a Web application. When the model must understand HTTP elements, however, the model can only work in a Web context. This also makes it difficult to test the model in isolation, since you must construct HTTP elements, which is difficult outside of a servlet environment.

Further, the HTTP request object normally contains more information than is necessary for the model. This extra information could lead to mistakenly established dependencies that are both unwanted and obscure. These dependencies almost always manifest as bugs.

To avoid these drawbacks, we introduce an intermediary between the controller and the model. This intermediary captures the information from the request that is relevant to the model and invokes the model's services. Model results are encapsulated as data and registered with the *request* object, making it available to the view. You implement this intermediary using a command object following the command pattern discussed in Module 7. The role of this intermediary is shown in Figure 9-2.

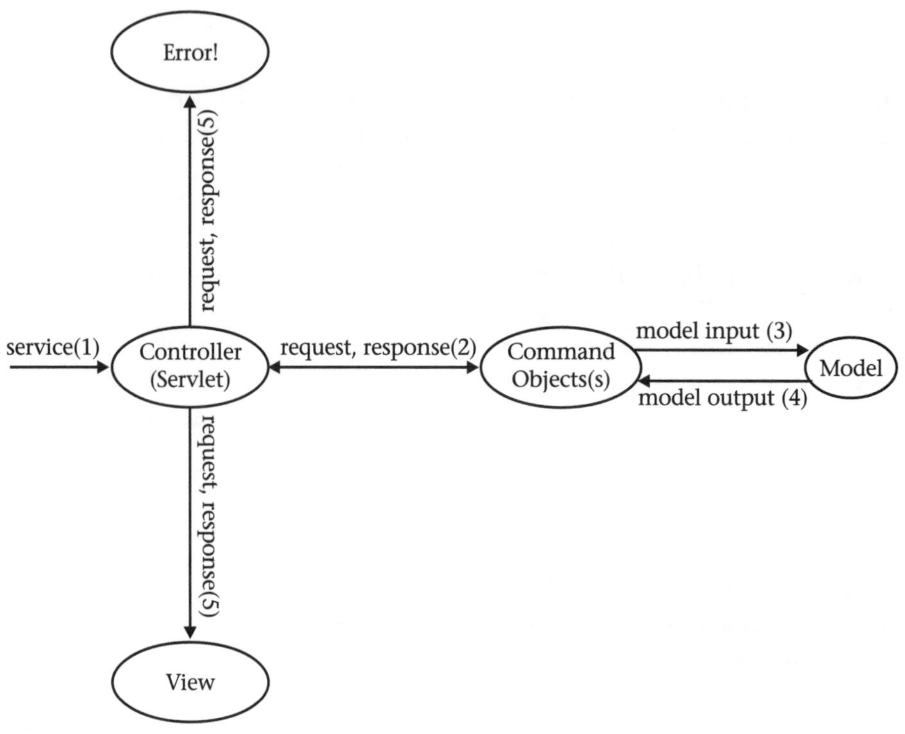

Figure 9-2 Command object interceding between controller and model

Interaction with the Model

You should design model interactions in such a way that you can seamlessly integrate different implementations of the model into your Web application. You can achieve this via the bridge design pattern. The bridge pattern introduces a separation between a model abstraction and its implementation. This allows the abstraction and the implementation to evolve independently. The abstraction serves as the contract to the client, while the implementation serves as the contract to the abstraction. The command objects are the clients that invoke the model's services. These command objects interact with the model abstraction and are completely ignorant of the implementation. Figure 9-3 illustrates this architecture. We go into more detail regarding the design of the model as a bridge in Module 10.

Web Application Workflow and Flow Control

A Web application, like any other application requiring user interaction, has a workflow. For instance, in an e-commerce application, a user typically logs into the application from a login page. Then she browses an inventory of products categorized and presented in multiple pages. While browsing, she selects items and adds them to her shopping cart. When she's ready, either she can move to a checkout page where she is asked to enter credit-card information for billing or she can cancel her order and log out. If the credit is accepted, the transaction is

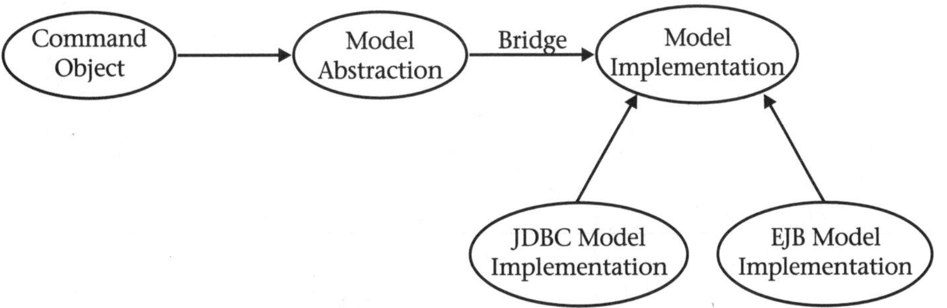

Figure 9-3 Model as a bridge

Ask the Expert

Question: Looking at Figure 9-3, it seems as though the model abstraction is unnecessary. Why can't a command object interact directly with a model implementation and still support seamless integration with different implementations?

Answer: A command object can certainly communicate directly with the implementation. But there are a couple of drawbacks to this setup. If we wanted to extend the services of the model, then we must reproduce this extension for each concrete implementation of the model. Also, not having a model abstraction forces all clients to be aware of granular implementation services rather than a higher level of abstraction.

Having said this, we should note that there are situations where a model abstraction is redundant. Suppose the abstraction interface and the implementation interface are essentially the same and one rarely needs to extend the model services. Rather, one wishes only to provide different implementations of the model. In that case, you can eliminate the model abstraction collapsing it with the client. This is the simplest form of the bridge.

Question: If you can eliminate the model abstraction, how does the result differ from a strategy pattern?

Answer: A strategy pattern provides a common façade for a family of algorithms with different behaviors. The client selects the appropriate algorithm dynamically in accordance with implicit knowledge of the differing behaviors. Clients can interchangeably select the algorithm on each invocation of the service.

A model, on the other hand, has standard behavior. Different implementations of this standard behavior exist, and only one of them is chosen for a particular client. The framework typically preregisters the choice for the client, probably during an initialization phase.

A controller in this architecture creates or retrieves a handle to the model and passes it to the command objects for processing. A controller also reads and manages connectivity parameters for the model from a configuration file such as `web.xml`. This allows for dynamic configuration of the model. In a simple application, a single Java object could completely encapsulate all business logic for the model. In an enterprise setup, however, the services provided by the model might break into several components as in an EJB solution. In this scenario, a command object could specify the model services that it needs and the controller could establish only those model components that provide the selected services and hand it to the command object. These service mappings could be specified in a configuration file as well.

complete and she is directed to a receipt page where she can print out a receipt for her records. This simple workflow is shown in Figure 9-4.

Many things are happening behind the scenes to enable this workflow. But from the user's perspective, she navigates through a series of visual pages.

Consider a *finite state machine*, the most common tool in computer science to model transitions between a finite set of static states. Figure 9-5 shows a typical state diagram for a finite state machine.

Circles in the state diagram are called *states* (the letters in our picture), and the lines connecting two states are called *transitions* (the numbers in our picture). The condition of a finite state machine at a certain time is defined as a state. A mapping of inputs and the current state to the next state is called a transition. The output and the next state in a finite state machine depend on the input and the current state.

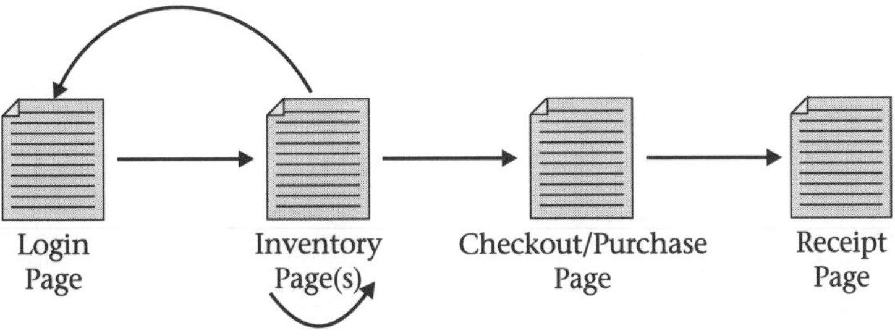

Figure 9-4 Simple e-commerce workflow

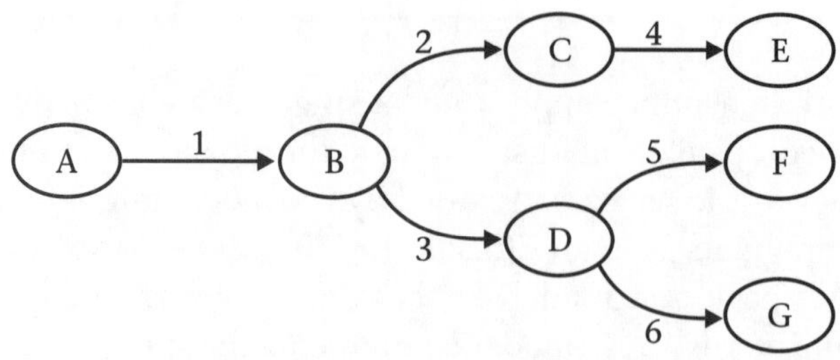

Figure 9-5 State diagram

We can model a user's display of a given page in our Web application workflow (web-flow) as a state. The requests and responses that generate the pages themselves, however, more accurately represent transitions from state to state, rather than states themselves. Recognizing this distinction, we label the state in a state diagram with the page to indicate the fact that the user is viewing that page.

Two facts apply to a user's movement from one page to another:

- The user is displaying a given page
- The user entered some input (or performed an action)

The decision behind this movement can be modeled as a transition. In a state diagram, we can label the transition lines with user inputs or actions to indicate the fact that the user requests a transition. A state diagram for our sample workflow is shown in Figure 9-6.

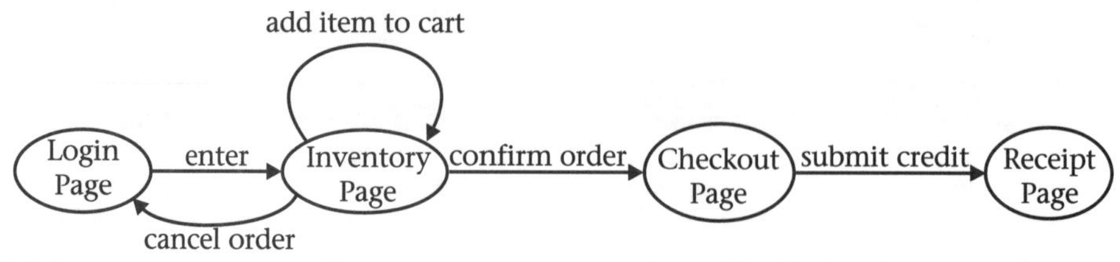

Figure 9-6 State diagram for the e-commerce workflow

Current State	Action	Next State
Login page	enter	Inventory page
Inventory page	add item to cart	Inventory page
Inventory page	confirm order	Checkout page
Inventory page	cancel order	Login page
Checkout page	submit credit	Receipt page

Table 9-1 State transition table for the e-commerce workflow

Another way to view this state diagram is through a state transition table, as shown in Table 9-1.

While restricting states to displayed pages helps us picture web-flow at a high level, this model is insufficient when we dig deeper into the workings of the system. For example, when the user submits her credit card information, the system performs three operations:

- The user requests credit, and if she is authorized, the credit amount is deducted.
- The system updates the inventory to reflect the purchase of items.
- The system generates a receipt and directs control to the receipt page.

9

Only the last operation in this sequence results in a displayed page. The other two operations occur behind the scenes. Yet each operation results in an internal state in the workflow. One could argue that all three operations should be combined into one single operation. Keeping them separate, however, supports reusability in other web-flows. In an MVC architecture, transitions that do not result in a visual page typically create a new state in the model.

Let us expand our workflow to include these internal states. Figure 9-7 shows the refined state diagram starting from the check out page.

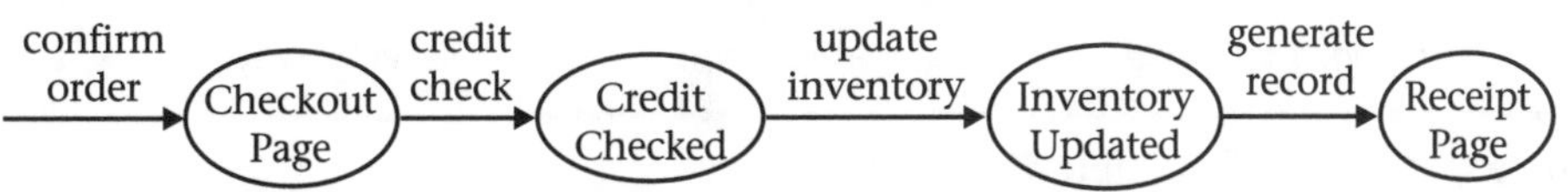

Figure 9-7 State diagram (fragment) with internal states

Current State	**Action**	**Next State**
Checkout page	check credit	Credit checked
Credit checked	update inventory	Inventory updated
Inventory updated	generate receipt	Receipt page

Table 9-2 State transition table with additional states

The state transition table that includes these additional states is shown in Table 9-2.

When you look at Table 9-2, one oddity might catch your eye. The table manifests some of the states as display entities (Web resources) such as "Checkout page" and "Receipt page," but manifests others with descriptive words like "Credit checked" and "Inventory updated." This implies that states need not be displayable. Some states represent changes in the model rather than pages.

State diagrams at this point might seem confusing, since changes to the model are hard to visualize as states. A different approach introduces the term "stages" (also called "destinations") to suggest any physical manifestation that takes an input and optionally produces one or more outputs. A stage in this sense represents any discrete step in a data flow. Table 9-3 shows such a data flow table (not a state transition table).

Notice that the headings now read Current Stage and Next Stage rather than Current State and Next State. The stages now include both the Web resources as well as the Java command objects.

A Web application workflow consists of stages and stage transitions that map the current stage and an action to the next stage. Flow control, a loosely used term in the Web development community, refers to the mechanics of moving from one stage to another in this web-flow.

Current Stage	**Action**	**Next Stage**
Checkout page	check credit	*CreditCheckCommand*
CreditCheckCommand	update inventory	*InventoryUpdateCommand*
InventoryUpdateCommand	generate receipt	Receipt page

Table 9-3 Workflow table

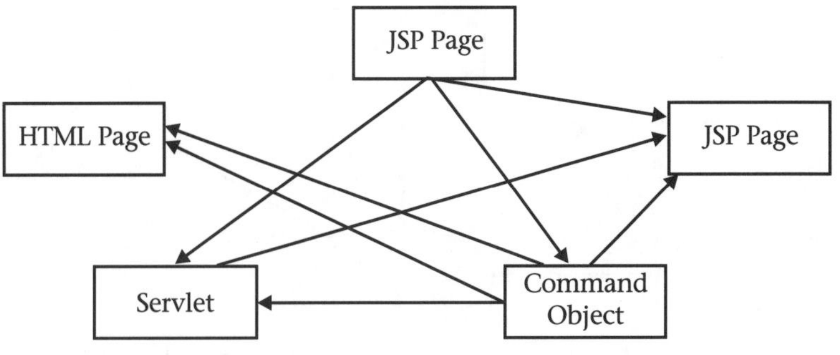

Figure 9-8 No flow control

The most simple form of flow control just hard-codes all destinations that a user might traverse from a given stage. This might suffice for a relatively static Web application involving a handful of JSP pages. But in a complex Web application, the number of Web resources rapidly multiplies. If you haphazardly code transitions into JSP pages, you deliver the messy scenario shown in Figure 9-8.

Such a scenario is hard to modify, and page designers must wade through unnecessary page flow logic in JSP and HTML pages. In Module 7, we discussed the mediator pattern and how it significantly reduces communication paths while eliminating dependencies and promoting reuse. The controller servlet functions as the mediator, routing user requests and application messages between stages in a Web workflow. Figure 9-9 shows this architecture.

In such a setup, only the controller servlet understands the various stages in the Web workflow. You thereby eliminate dependencies between stages. Additionally, you can embed session validation and data validation logic between stage transitions in the controller servlet.

A controller should be able to forward to a visual destination identified by a URL as well as a nonvisual destination such as a command object. Additionally, a controller should allow for modifications to workflow (stage transitions) without affecting code.

This is normally achieved by representing the workflow table in a persistent, structural repository that can be easily modified. The controller then dynamically loads this repository and uses it to drive the web-flow. An XML configuration file quite naturally lends itself to this function.

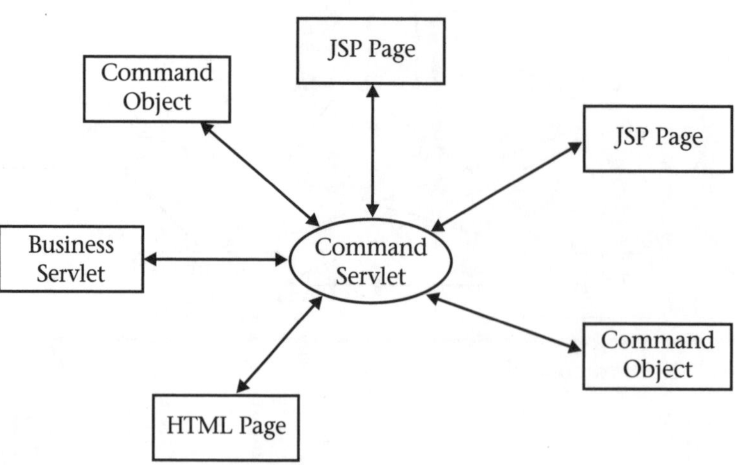

Figure 9-9 Controller as the mediator

Figure 9-10 illustrates a possible flow chart of all responsibilities discussed so far in a controller servlet.

1-Minute Drill

- What are the three major responsibilities of a controller servlet?
- How does the controller dynamically establish a handle to the model?
- Why is it bad for a model to be aware of the HTTP protocol elements?
- What does flow control mean in a Web environment?

In the next section, we present three different implementations of flow control. The first implementation involves a simple servlet that does not use a

---

- A controller servlet is responsible for user-input processing, model interaction, and flow control.
- The controller servlet looks up the model's connectivity parameters from a configuration file such as the `web.xml` file and establishes a handle to it.
- If you make a model aware of HTTP protocol elements, you bind it inextricably to the HTTP environment. Consequently, you cannot use it in any other client-side environments.
- Flow control refers to managing the mechanics of moving from stage to stage in a Web workflow.

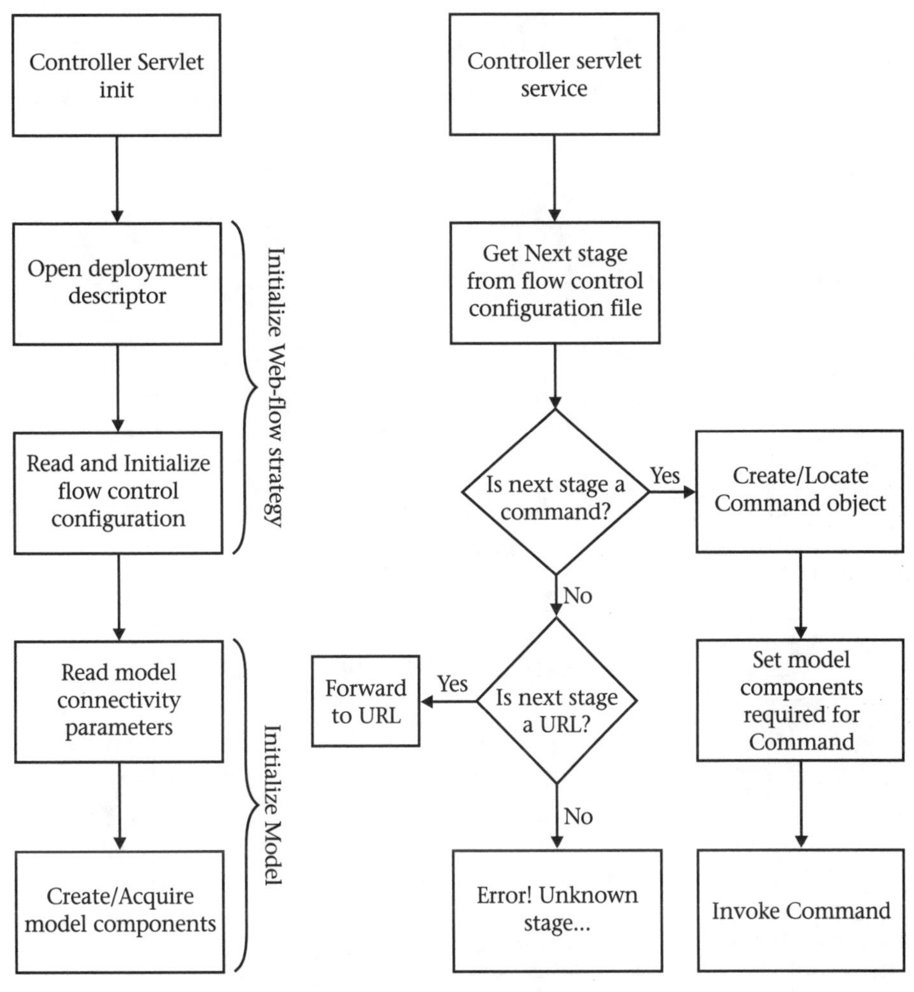

Figure 9-10 Flow chart of the controller's responsibilities

configuration file to define flow control. Each HTML page and JSP page determines the next stage in the web-flow. We present successive implementations, gradually migrating the knowledge of Web workflow out of HTML and JavaServer Pages and into a configuration file.

Simple Flow Control

Let's consider an example that presents a user with a stock transaction page. Here is the HTML page:

```
<HTML>
<HEAD><TITLE>Stock Transaction</TITLE></HEAD>
<BODY>
<H1> Buy/Sell </H1>
<FORM METHOD=POST ACTION="/Book/Broker">
<TABLE>
    <TR>
      <TD> Enter ticker: </TD>
      <TD> <INPUT TYPE=text LENGTH=5 NAME="ticker"> </TD>
    </TR>
    <TR>
       <TD> Number of Shares: </TD>
       <TD> <INPUT TYPE=text LENGTH=3 NAME="numShares"> </TD>
    </TR>
    <TR>
       <TD> Share Price: </TD>
       <TD> <INPUT TYPE=text LENGTH=5 NAME="price"> </TD>
    </TR>
   </TABLE>
<HR>
<TABLE BORDER=1>
<TR>
<TD> <INPUT TYPE=hidden NAME="Buy" VALUE="/jsp/Buy.jsp">
     <INPUT TYPE=submit NAME="action" VALUE="Buy"> </TD>

<TD> <INPUT TYPE=hidden NAME="Sell" VALUE="/jsp/Sell.jsp">
     <INPUT TYPE=submit NAME="action" VALUE="Sell"> </TD>

<TD> <INPUT TYPE=hidden NAME="Cancel" VALUE="/jsp/Cancel.jsp">
     <INPUT TYPE=submit NAME="action" VALUE="Cancel"> </TD>

<TD> <INPUT TYPE=reset VALUE="Reset"> </TD>
</TR>
</TABLE>
</FORM>
</BODY>
</HTML>
```

The page presents a simple form containing input elements for the stock ticker, number of shares, and share price. The user is asked to enter these three elements and make her selection for submission. The user could buy, sell, or cancel the transaction. Figure 9-11 shows the page.

In this example, the HTML page submits three data elements named "Sell", "Buy", and "Cancel". The three data elements represent the three possible actions that this page can produce. Each action is associated with a different destination (or stage). The destinations are specified in an accompanying hidden input element. Notice that all three data elements share the same name: "action".

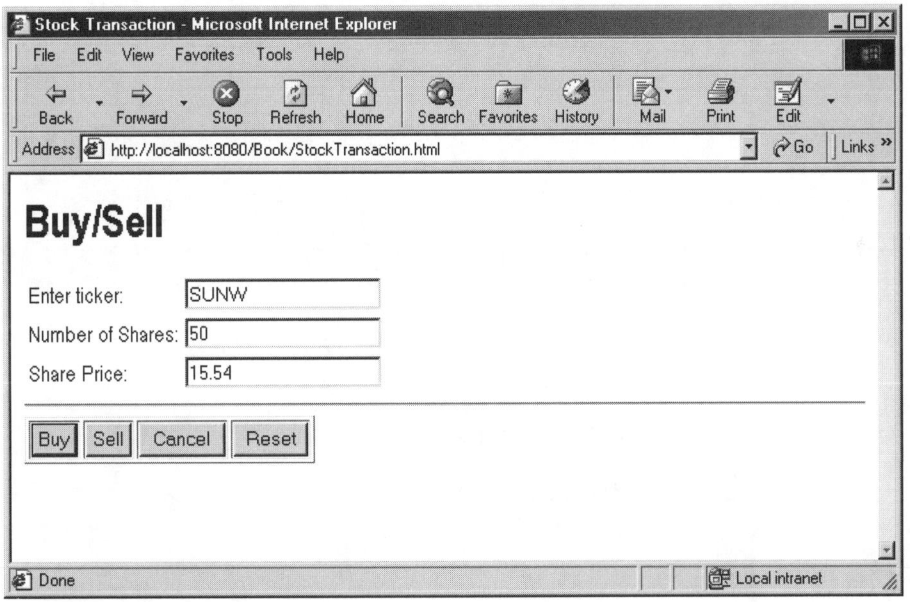

Figure 9-11 Stock transaction page

All submissions on this page are handled by our controller servlet identified by the URL /Book/Broker. Here is the source code for our controller servlet:

```
package simple;

import javax.servlet.*;
import javax.servlet.http.*;
import java.io.IOException;

public class BrokerServlet extends HttpServlet {
    // Forward http get calls to http post handler.
    public void doGet(HttpServletRequest request,
                      HttpServletResponse response)
        throws ServletException, IOException {
        doPost(request, response);
    }
    // Handle requests.
    public void doPost(HttpServletRequest request,
                       HttpServletResponse response)
        throws ServletException, IOException {


        RequestDispatcher rd = null;
        // Get action requested from request.
        String action =
           request.getParameter("action");
        // Get next page associated with action also
        // from request.
        String JSP = request.getParameter(action);
        rd = request.getRequestDispatcher(JSP);

        // Route request to appropriate JSP page.
        if (rd != null) {
            rd.forward(request, response);
        }
    }
}
```

In order to locate the next page in the Web workflow, the servlet retrieves the value of the "action" parameter. This gives it the name of the hidden input element whose value identifies the next page (or stage) in the web-flow.

This implementation is simple and also provides flexibility to change destinations without altering Java code. But this small benefit also introduces unnecessary complexity into the application as the number of page transitions expands. Since each Web resource specifies all possible destination paths from itself, knowledge of the Web workflow disperses into multiple different Web resources. This causes a reverse-engineering nightmare when Web developers seek to alter the web-flow. The controller in this setup merely facilitates the workflow when it should drive it.

We can remove the hidden input elements, which specify the next stage, from our HTML page and put this knowledge into the controller servlet using code similar to this fragment:

```
RequestDispatcher rd = null;
// Get action requested from request.
String action = request.getParameter("action");


if (action.equals("Buy")) {
   rd = request.getRequestDispatcher("/jsp/Buy.jsp");
}
else if (action.equals("Sell")) {
   rd = request.getRequestDispatcher("/jsp/Sell.jsp");
}
else if (action.equals("Cancel")) {
   rd = request.getRequestDispatcher("/jsp/Cancel.jsp");
}
```


While such code centralizes communication channels into our controller servlet, this is clearly not a good solution. It hard-codes the destinations into our servlet, and for each new stage in the Web workflow, it must insert a new `if-else` code block.

A third implementation reads mappings between actions and stages (destinations) from a property file.

```
package simple;
import javax.servlet.*;
import javax.servlet.http.*;
import java.io.IOException;
import java.util.Properties;

public class BrokerServlet extends HttpServlet {
   private static final String MAPPINGS_FILE =
                             "/WEB-INF/config.properties";
```

```
    private Properties properties = new Properties();

    public void init(ServletConfig config)
                               throws ServletException {
        super.init(config);
        try {
            properties.load(
              config.getServletContext().getResourceAsStream(
                                           MAPPINGS_FILE));
        }
        catch(IOException ioexp) {
            System.err.println(
                    "Unable to load property file: " + ioexp);
            throw new ServletException(ioexp);
        }
    }

    // Forward http get calls to http post handler.
    public void doGet(HttpServletRequest request,
                      HttpServletResponse response)
        throws ServletException, IOException {
        doPost(request, response);
    }

    // Handle requests.
    public void doPost(HttpServletRequest request,
                       HttpServletResponse response)
        throws ServletException, IOException {

        RequestDispatcher rd = null;
        // Get action requested from request.
        String action = request.getParameter("action");
        // Get next URL for action from properties file
        String nextURL = properties.getProperty(action);
        // Route request to next destination in workflow.
        if(nextURL != null) {
            rd = request.getRequestDispatcher(nextURL);
            rd.forward(request, response);
        }
    }
}
```

Our controller servlet loads the properties from the properties file in its *init* method. The properties file should be located under /WEB-INF/config.properties in the application context for this example.

Here are the contents of the property file:

```
# Mapping of actions to destinations
Buy=/jsp/Buy.jsp
Sell=/jsp/Sell.jsp
Cancel=/jsp/Cancel.jsp
```

The *doPost* method in our servlet retrieves the value for the parameter "action". It then looks up the destination URL for this action in the property file and forwards to that URL.

Suppose we put a file named Buy.jsp under the /jsp subdirectory in our Book servlet context with the following contents:

```
<HTML>
<BODY>
<%
   String ticker = request.getParameter("ticker");
   int numShares =
      Integer.parseInt(request.getParameter("numShares"));
   float price =
      Float.parseFloat(request.getParameter("price"));
%>
<H3> Bought <%= numShares %> shares of
         <%= ticker %> at $<%= price %> </H3>
</BODY>
</HTML>
```

When we select the Buy button on our StockTransaction.html page, we will get the page shown in Figure 9-12.

Note the URL that is shown in the browser in Figure 9-12. The URL reads http://localhost:8080/Book/Broker. It does not show the final destination, Buy.jsp. This is because, from the browser's perspective, when we submitted the HTML form the destination was /Book/Broker, which we mapped to our controller servlet. We hid the fact that our servlet forwarded control to /jsp/Buy.jsp. By hiding actual page destinations from clients, you help secure them from malicious or mischievous access.

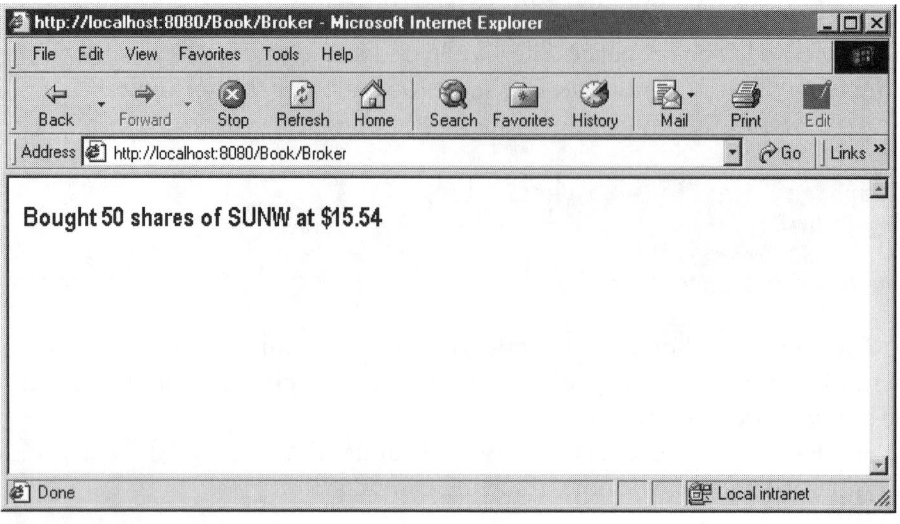

Figure 9-12 Buy.jsp

This implementation is so far the best, since it centralizes all page transitions in a property file managed by our controller servlet. It also provides us a flexible way of altering page transitions without modifying Java code.

The intent here is just to show simple page transition logic. In a "real-world" setup, our controller servlet would also manage user-input processing and model interaction. The following project shows flow control as we implemented it in our Family Center application.

Member.txt
event.txt
household.txt
messageboard.txt
member_role.txt
schmFamily_Center.sql
loadFamily_Center.sql
enter.jar
Family_Center.war

Project 9-1: Address Book Search

As we discussed in Module 7, one of the features of our family center is looking up the contact information for a particular extended family member. We do this by maintaining an address book of all households that are part of the family. We use a MySQL database as our repository for storing household addresses and the family members in each household. Without going into the details of the database schema (which we describe in detail in Module 10), we build the database with all of its schema elements and sample data using predefined scripts delivered with this project. Then we build an address book search page that allows easy lookup of a member's contact information. We provide two basic search mechanisms:

- A textual search of last name or first name
- A letter index search based on the first letter of the first name or the first letter of the last name

We concentrate on the controller servlet, as it handles all three basic responsibilities: user-input processing, model interaction, and management of web-flow.

Step-by-Step: Database Creation

1. Download all the files for this project from the Web site `http://www.osborne.com`.
2. Download and install the MySQL database following instructions in Appendix C.
3. Start the MySQL server as a service following instructions in Appendix C.
4. Create a user account in MySQL following instructions in Appendix C. We will assume the user name and password to be: `bookUser` and `bookPasswd` for our purposes.
5. Log into MySQL using the mysql utility as `bookUser` using the following command syntax.

   ```
   %> mysql -u bookUser -p
   ```

   You will be prompted for the password. Enter it to log in. You should see the prompt change to **mysql>**.
6. Run the script `schmFamily_Center.sql` using the syntax shown here:

   ```
   mysql> source E:/family_center/sql/schmFamily_Center.sql
   ```

   Be sure to modify the location to where you have stored this script. This script creates a database named `family_center` and creates the schema inside this database. The schema is the set of tables and their relationships. Details of the schema will be explained in Module 10 and are not important to this project.
7. Run the script `loadFamily_Center.sql` using the syntax shown next.

```
mysql> source E:/family_center/sql/loadFamily_Center.sql
```

Be sure to modify the location to where you have stored this script. This script populates the database with sample data (family members and their addresses).

8. Quit the mysql utility by typing **quit** as shown here:

```
mysql> quit
Bye
%
```

9. Database creation is complete!

10. In order to access this database from Java, we need a MySQL JDBC driver. Download the MySQL JDBC driver JAR file following instructions in Appendix C.

Now that you have configured the database, let's dive into the Family Center project.

Step-by-Step: Address Book Search

1. Create a directory under `%TOMCAT_HOME%\webapps` named "Family_Center". This will serve as the root context for our family center application.

2. From a command prompt, enter this directory as shown here:

```
%> cd %TOMCAT_HOME%\webapps\Family_Center
```

3. Unjar the WAR file `Family_Center.war` that you downloaded for this project from this directory. It is important that you run the JAR command from within this directory.

```
%> jar xvf Family_Center.war *
```

4. This command will unpack all the files for our family center application creating a directory structure for HTML files, JSP files, images, and others.

5. Create a servlet context element for the Family Center application in the `%TOMCAT_HOME%\bin\server.xml` file as shown here:

```
<Context path="/Family_Center"
   docBase="webapps/Family_Center"
   crossContext="true"
```

```
   debug="0"
   reloadable="true"
   trusted="false" >
</Context>
```

This `Context` element specifies that our family center application will be located under the URL root: `http://localhost:8080/Family_Center`.

Examine the source file `com\jspbg\db\DB.java` located under the `WEB-INF\src` directory in our recently unpacked Web application. This file establishes programmatic connectivity to our MySQL database. It is reproduced here:

```
package com.jspbg.db;

import java.sql.DriverManager;
import java.sql.SQLException;
import java.sql.Connection;

public class DB {
   public static void registerDriver() {
      try {
         Class.forName("org.gjt.mm.mysql.Driver").
                        newInstance();
      }
      catch (Exception exp) {
         exp.printStackTrace();
      }
   }
   public static Connection getConnection() throws SQLException {
      Connection c = null;
      String url = "jdbc:mysql://localhost/Family_Center";
      String args = "?user=bookUser&password=bookPasswd";
      c = DriverManager.getConnection(url + args);
      return c;
   }

   public static void releaseConnection(Connection c) throws
SQLException {
      if(c != null)
         c.close();
   }
}
```

Notice that you must register your JDBC driver in your JVM before you can use the driver for any operation. This is done in the function *registerDriver*. The methods *getConnection* and *releaseConnection* acquire and release JDBC connections that access our database. Pay particular attention to the lines shown in bold in the preceding listing. The function *DriverManager.getConnection* takes a URL and returns a connection to our database. Replace the user name and password in the URL string with your database username and password (e.g., `bookUser` and `bookPasswd`). Recompile this Java file, making sure to have the JDBC driver in your `%CLASSPATH%`, and create a JAR file out of it as shown.

```
%> jar cvf DBAccess.jar com/jspbg/db/DB.class
```

Note

Normally, the database connectivity parameters will be read from a configuration file, so you need not recompile the Java file every time you need to change something. For now, we will go through a manual setup.

6. Copy the following JAR files to `%TOMCAT_HOME%\lib`:

- `Family_Center.jar`
- `DBAccess.jar`
- `mm.mysql-bin.jar` (your MySQL JDBC JAR file)

The startup scripts for Tomcat automatically append all JAR files located under `%TOMCAT_HOME%\lib` to the `%CLASSPATH%`. Unfortunately, this does not work if your Tomcat installation is located under a directory path that has spaces in it, such as `C:\Program Files\Tomcat`. In this case, you would have to manually add these JAR files by updating the startup script `tomcat.bat` located under `%TOMCAT_HOME%\bin`.

Note

Normally, a Web application's class files can either be located under `WEB-INF\classes` or be packaged as a JAR file, which can be placed under the `WEB-INF\lib` subdirectory under the application context. JSP containers automatically load class files from either of these locations. But as you will see in Module 10, we are implementing a security realm that is outside the Web application and should be made available to Tomcat separately and explicitly. A "real word" deployment would isolate the class files relevant to the security realm into a separate JAR and package the rest of the class files into a JAR that is stored under the application context.

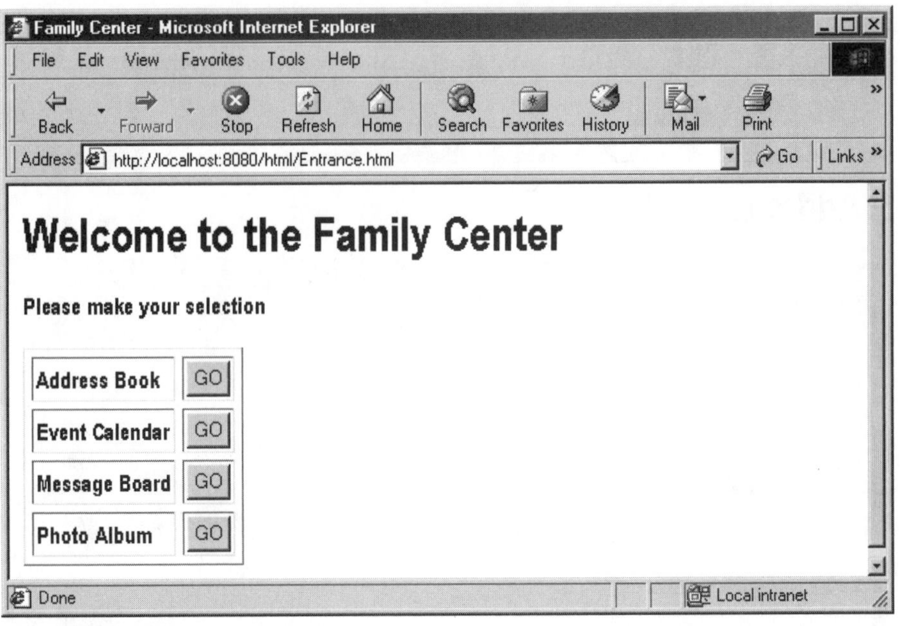

Figure 9-13 Welcome page for Family Center

7. Restart Tomcat and access the URL: `http://localhost:8080/Family_Center`. You should see a page as shown in Figure 9-13.
8. Select the Address Book button and you should see the address book search page as shown in Figure 9-14.
9. The page allows us to search for a member by last name or first name. It also allows us to perform an index search based on the first letter in the last name or first name. The search results page for a sample search is shown in Figure 9-15.
10. If there were no entries that match a search result, you should see a page as shown in Figure 9-16.
11. For the purposes of this project, we will concentrate on the code in the controller servlet. This project, like the Stock transaction example, uses a

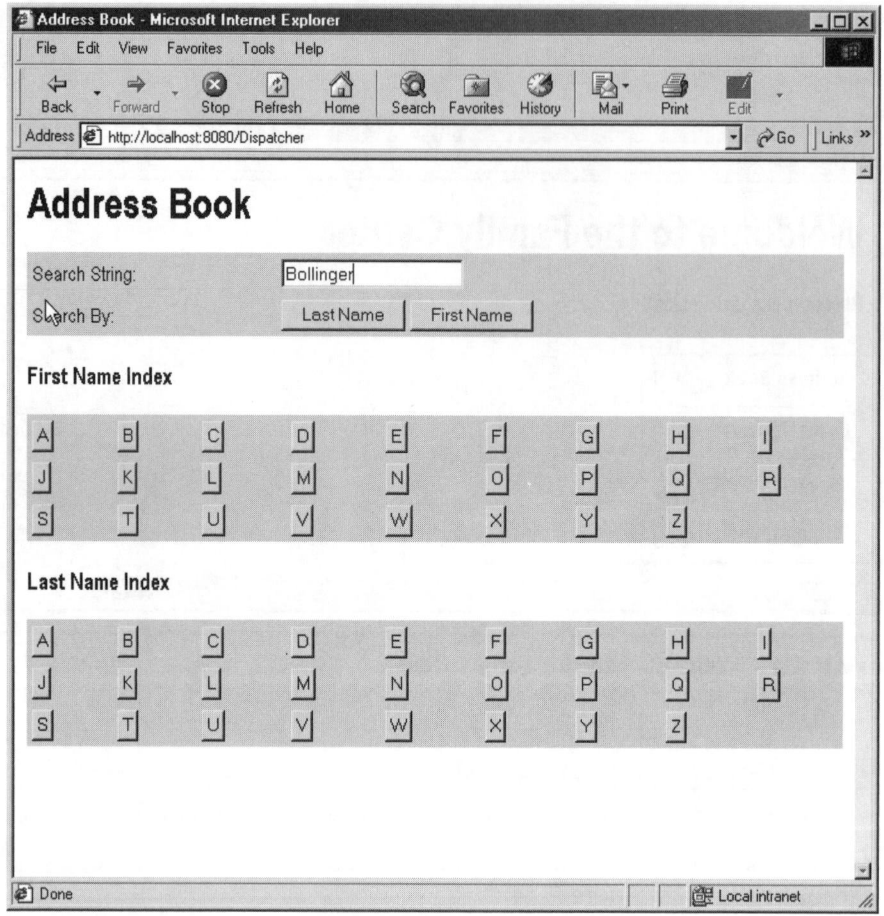

Figure 9-14 Address Book Search page

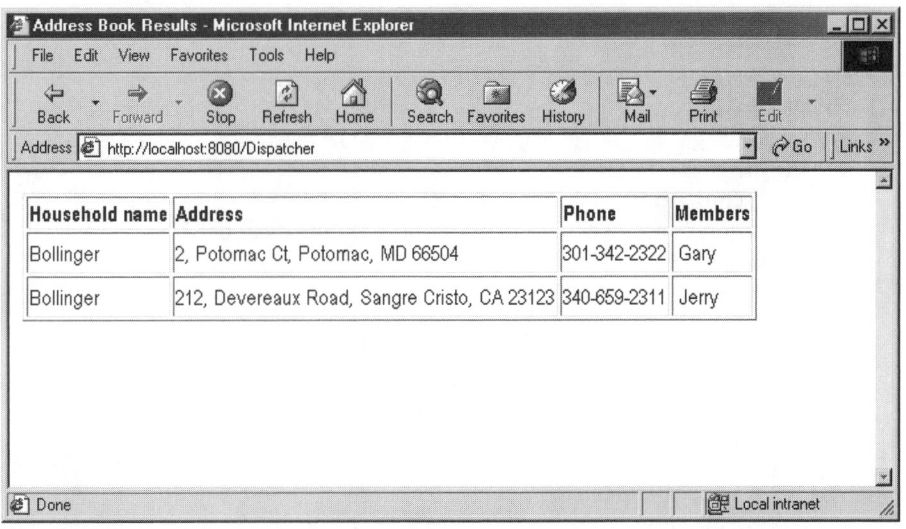

Figure 9-15 Address book search results

configuration file `actions.xml` to establish the relationship between an action and a stage or destination. The file is, however, in XML format. Let's examine its contents:


```
?xml version="1.0" ?>
<!DOCTYPE actions [
<!ELEMENT actions (action*)>
<!ELEMENT action  (command|url)>
<!ATTLIST action
          name    CDATA    #REQUIRED>
<!ELEMENT command (#PCDATA)>
<!ELEMENT url     (#PCDATA)>
<!ATTLIST command
          model   CDATA    #REQUIRED>
]>
<actions>
 <action name="EAB">
    <url>/AddressBook</url>
 </action>

 <action name="SFN">
```

```
    <command model="AddressBookManager">
        com.jspbg.webflow.FirstNameSearchCommand
    </command>
  </action>

  <action name="SLN">
    <command model="AddressBookManager">
       com.jspbg.webflow.LastNameSearchCommand
    </command>
  </action>

  <action name="SFNI">
    <command model="AddressBookManager">
       com.jspbg.webflow.FirstNameIndexCommand
    </command>
  </action>

  <action name="SLNI">
    <command model="AddressBookManager">
        com.jspbg.webflow.LastNameIndexCommand
    </command>
  </action>

  <action name="SABR">
     <url>/AddressBookResults</url>
  </action>

  <action name="SZR">
     <url>/ZeroResults</url>
  </action>

  <action name="SERR">
     <url>/Error</url>
  </action>

</actions>
```

This file contains multiple `action` elements inside a root `actions` element. Each `action` element represents an action in the Web workflow. The action is identified by the `name` attribute. The body of the `action` element contains the next stage for the action. The stage could be either a `url` element indicating a Web resource or a `command` element indicating a command object. Each `command` element could contain an optional `model` attribute that identifies

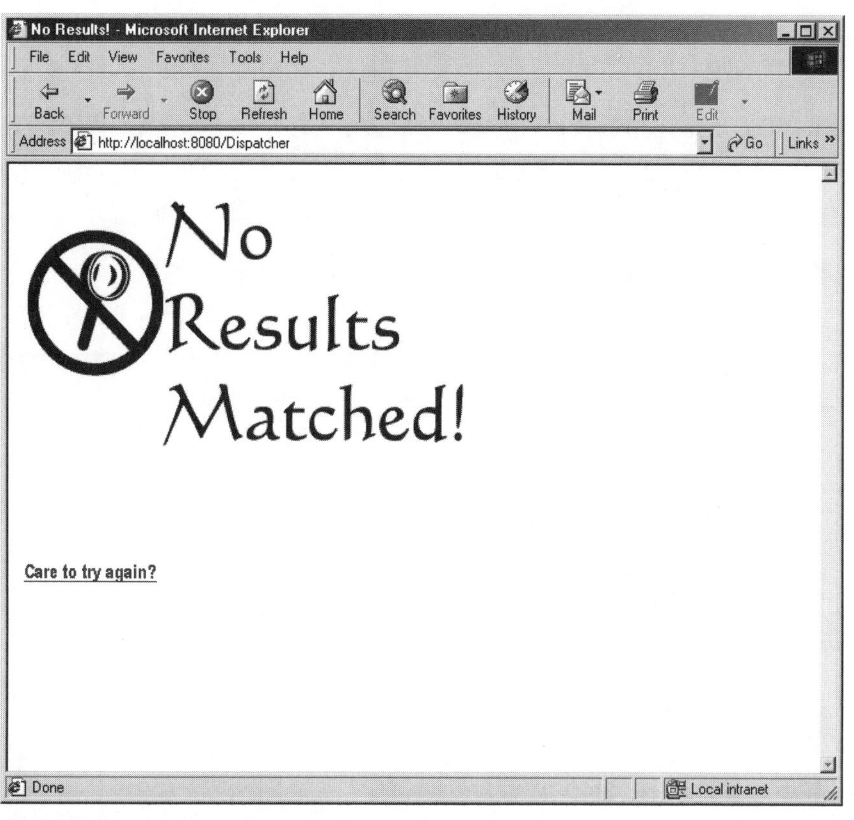

Figure 9-16 No results page

the model that the command intends to use. The controller servlet loads the data in this file and uses it to drive the workflow. For instance, if the action was "EAB" (for Enter Address Book), then the controller servlet looks up the `action` element named "EAB". The destination is a URL, so the controller directly forwards control to the specified relative URL: `/AddressBook`. If the action was "SLN" (for Search Last Name), then the controller looks up the `action` element named "SLN". The destination is a command object. The controller instantiates the command object *com.jspbg.webflow.LastNameSearchCommand*, retrieves the model identified by the name "AddressBookManager", sets it on the command object, and invokes the command.

12. The controller servlet (named *com.jspbg.servlet.DispatcherServlet*) is shown here:

```
public class DispatcherServlet extends HttpServlet {
   private static final String ACTIONS_XML =
         "ACTIONS_XML";

   // Static strings for model-names.
   private static final String ADDRESS_BOOK_MGR  =
         "AddressBookManager";

   /* parser that interprets the actions
      XML that maps actions to commands or URLs.
   */
   private ActionParser actionParser = null;

   // A HashMap of all model components
   private ModelFactory modelFactory = null;

   public void init(ServletConfig config)
         throws ServletException {
      // init parent
      super.init(config);

      // register JDBC driver. Required only once.
      DB.registerDriver();

      // initialize action parser for web-flow logic
      initializeActionParser(config);

      // create model factory.
      initializeModelFactory(config);
   }

   private void initializeActionParser(ServletConfig config)
         throws ServletException {
      ServletContext ctxt = config.getServletContext();

      // Retrieve actions XML file
      String actionsXMLName =
         config.getInitParameter(ACTIONS_XML);
      String actionsXmlFile =
         ctxt.getRealPath(actionsXMLName);
      try {
```

```
        // Construct parser on XML file
        actionParser = new ActionParser(actionsXmlFile);
    }
    catch(ParseException pex) {
        throw new ServletException(pex.getMessage());
    }
}

public void initializeModelFactory(ServletConfig config)
        throws ServletException {
    Map models = new HashMap();
    models.put(ADDRESS_BOOK_MGR,
               config.getInitParameter(ADDRESS_BOOK_MGR));
    modelFactory = new ModelFactory(models);
}

public void doGet(HttpServletRequest req,
                  HttpServletResponse res)
        throws ServletException, IOException {
    doPost(req, res);
}

public void doPost(HttpServletRequest req,
                   HttpServletResponse res)
       throws ServletException, IOException {
    String action = req.getParameter("action");
    try {
        String nextStage = null;
        // While next stage is a Command, retrieve the
        // model component for the command, and invoke
        // the command.
        while((nextStage =
                  actionParser.getCommand(action)) != null) {
            Model model = null;
            String modelName = actionParser.getModel(action);
            // create model if there is one associated
            // with current action
            if(modelName != null) {
                model = modelFactory.makeModel(modelName);
            }

            // forward control to the command
            action = forwardToCommand(nextStage, model, req,
                                      res);
```

9

```
      }

      // If the next stage is a URL, forward control
      // to the URL
      nextStage = actionParser.getURL(action);
      if(nextStage != null) {
         forwardToURL(nextStage, req, res);
      }
      else {
         throw new ServletException(
           "No known destination for action: " + action);
      }
   }
   catch(ParseException pex) {
      throw new ServletException(pex);
   }
   catch(ServiceException sex) {
      throw new ServletException(sex);
   }


}

private void forwardToURL(String url,
                          HttpServletRequest req,
                          HttpServletResponse res)
      throws ServletException, IOException {
   RequestDispatcher rd = req.getRequestDispatcher(url);
   rd.forward(req, res);
}

private String forwardToCommand(String command,
                                Model model,
                                HttpServletRequest req,
                                HttpServletResponse res)
      throws ServletException {
   try {
      // instantiate command object
      Command c =
         (Command)Class.forName(command).newInstance();

      // set model component on command object
      c.setModel(model);
```

```
            // execute command
            return c.execute(req, res);
        }
        catch(ClassNotFoundException cex) {
            throw new ServletException("Class Not Found: " +
                                        cex.getMessage());
        }
        catch(InstantiationException iex) {
            throw new ServletException("Could not Instantiate: "
                                        +iex.getMessage());
        }
        catch(IllegalAccessException illex) {
            throw new ServletException("Illegal Access: " +
                                        illex.getMessage());
        }
    }
}
```

Our controller servlet uses a Java class *com.jspbg.webflow.ActionParser* to parse the `actions.xml` file. It also uses the Java class *com.jspbg.model.ModelFactory* to create or locate model elements. Both of these are initialized in the *init* method of the servlet. The *doGet* method merely delegates to the *doPost* method. This ensures that our servlet will service GET and POST requests uniformly. The *doPost* method retrieves the "action" parameter from the request. It then uses the *ActionParser* to see if the destination mapped to that action is a URL. If it is, the servlet forwards to the designated URL using the method *forwardToURL*. If the destination is a command object, its associated model name is retrieved. The controller then creates the model using the *ModelFactory*. Then control is transferred to the *forwardToCommand* method, where the command is instantiated, the model is set, and then the command is executed.

13. Each command object implements the *com.jspbg.webflow.Command* interface shown here:

```
public interface Command {
    // action: search first name
    public static final String SFN = "SFN";
    // action: search last name
    public static final String SLN = "SLN";
    // action: search first name index
```

```
    public static final String SFNI= "SFNI";
    // action: search last name index
    public static final String SLNI = "SLNI";
    // action: show address book results
    public static final String SABR = "SABR";
    // action: show zero results
    public static final String SZR  = "SZR";
    // action: show error
    public static final String SERR = "SERR";

    public String execute(HttpServletRequest req,
                          HttpServletResponse res)
        throws ServletException;

    public void setModel(Model m);
}
```

The command interface defines two methods. The method *execute* invokes the command. The method *setModel* stores the requested model with the command. Each action in the Web application is defined as a static final *String* in this interface as well.

14. Let's examine the command object for last name search. The class *com.jspbg .webflow.LastNameSearchCommand* extends *com.jspbg .webflow.SearchCommand.* So let's examine that first.

```
public abstract class SearchCommand implements Command {
   protected AddressBookManager addressBookManager = null;

   public void setModel(Model m) {
      addressBookManager = (AddressBookManager)m;
   }

   /**
    * Template execute method that is used by multiple
      sub-classes of this abstract command object.
    */
   public String execute(HttpServletRequest req,
                         HttpServletResponse res)
       throws ServletException {
      String search_str = req.getParameter("SS");

      RequestDispatcher rd = null;
```

```
      try {
         // retrieve the households that match the search
string.
         List households = getHouseholds(search_str);

         // if there are no entries that match, return
         // 'show zero results' action.
         if((households == null) || (households.size() == 0))
         {
            return Command.SZR;
         }

         // set the results on the request and return
         // the action 'show the address book results'
         request.setAttribute("Results", households);
         return Command.SABR;
      }
      catch(ServiceException sexp) {
         // set the service exception with the request
         // and return the action 'show error'
         req.setAttribute("Service Exception", sexp);
         return Command.SERR;
      }
   }

   // abstract method that sub-classes override
   public abstract List getHouseholds(String searchString)
         throws ServiceException;
}
```


This abstract class uses the model *com.jspbg.model.AddressBookManager*. It stores the model using its *setModel* method, which our controller servlet invokes. The *execute* method retrieves the search string from the request named "SS". It then executes the query to retrieve the households that match the search string using the abstract method *getHouseholds*. This is the method that interacts with the model. If there are entries that match, the results are stored in the request and the command object returns the action "SABR" (for Show Address Book Results) indicating that the controller should send control to the stage that matches this action. The controller (our dispatcher servlet) figures out the destination for "SABR" (which, if you examine our `actions.xml` file, is `/AddressBookResults`), to which it forwards the results for layout. If there are no entries, the command object returns the action "SZR" (for Show Zero Results). The controller, upon receiving this action, determines that the destination for this action is `/ZeroResults` and forwards to it. If a *ServiceException* is thrown while executing the model's services, it is captured and stored with the request in the `catch` block and the command object returns the action "SERR" (for Show ERRor). The controller duly looks up the destination for this action (`/Error`) and forwards control to it. This *execute* method is an example of the template method design pattern.

15. The *LastNameSearchCommand* class merely provides the *getHouseholds* method. It does this by requesting the *AddressBookManager* for all households based on last name.

```
public class LastNameSearchCommand
      extends SearchCommand {
   public List getHouseholds(String searchString)
         throws ServiceException {
      return addressBookManager.getHouseholdsByLastName
         (searchString);
   }
}
```

16. The *com.jspbg.model.AddressBookManager* model interface is shown here:

```
public interface AddressBookManager extends Model {
    public List getHouseholdsByLastName(String lastName)
        throws ServiceException;
    public List getHouseholdsByFirstName(String firstName)
        throws ServiceException;
    public List getHouseholdsByIndex(String indexAlphabet,
                                     boolean isFirstName)
        throws ServiceException;
}
```

As you might notice, our model interface is completely unaware of any HTTP elements. This makes it reusable in any client environment.

17. The final element in our Web application consists of the actual Web resources and what each resource must submit in order to participate in this flow control framework. We show a fragment of our `Entrance.html` file here as an example:

```
<script language="javascript">
function submitEntranceForm(val)
{
  document.entrance.action.value = val;
  document.entrance.submit();
}
</script>

<FORM METHOD="POST" NAME="entrance"
ACTION="/Family_Center/Dispatcher">
<INPUT TYPE=hidden NAME="action">
<TABLE CELLPADDING=2 CELLSPACING=5 BORDER=1>
<TR>
  <TD> <B> Address Book </B> </TD>
  <TD>
     <INPUT TYPE=button  VALUE="GO"
      onMouseDown="submitEntranceForm('EAB');">
  </TD>
</TR>
```

The button element for Address Book uses a JavaScript function *submitEntranceForm* passing it an action string "EAB". The function merely sets this as the value for the hidden input element of the form named "action" and submits the form. Our dispatcher servlet handles the form submission.

From this project, you should notice that our controller servlet performs the three major responsibilities of user input processing, model interaction, and flow control. Our controller servlet has introduced a command object intermediary that captures the relevant information from the request and forwards it to the model, keeping the model oblivious of the client-side environment. Our controller servlet also uses the model factory to instantiate the model and set it on the command objects for their use. Finally, our controller servlet uses an `actions.xml` XML configuration file to drive a flexible workflow. The workflow diagram for part of our project is shown in Figure 9-17.

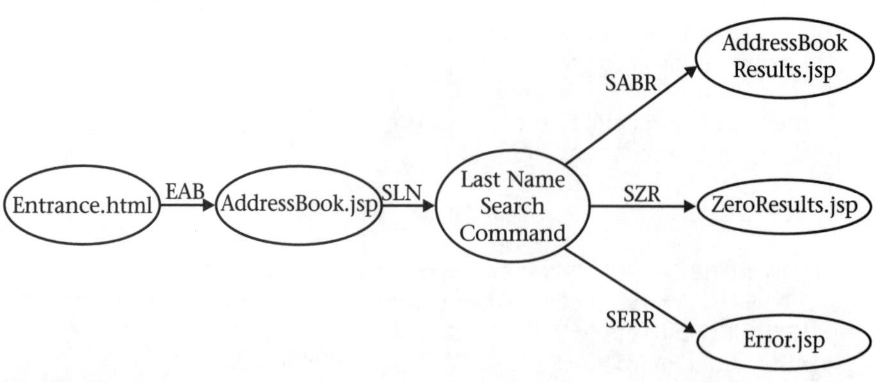

Figure 9-17 Workflow diagram for the project

Advanced Flow Control: The Struts MVC Framework

In January 2001, the Jakarta Project under the Apache Software foundation introduced version 1.0 of an MVC framework for Java called Struts. The Struts framework includes many tools for building model, view, and controller components for a Web application. Some of these tools are:

- Custom tags for building standard forms without using straight HTML or standard JSP utilities
- Custom tags for basic program logic in a JSP page that eliminates the need for Java
- Built in Internationalization support for loading and presenting Java Resource bundles that map message tokens to language-specific strings for a particular *locale*
- Support for setting up Java data sources according to connectivity parameters specified in a configuration file

- A Form Bean mechanism that automatically instantiates and populates a user-provided JavaBean with values from input elements in an HTML form and optionally validates those inputs
- A controller framework that enables powerful and flexible flow control established in a configuration file written in XML

Without going into too much detail, let's examine a sample flow control element in Struts as a contrasting alternative to our solution in the project.

```
<action path="/editSubscription"
   type="org.apache.struts.webapp.example.EditSubscriptionAction"
   name="subscriptionForm"
   scope="request"
   validate="false">
   <forward name="failure" path="/mainMenu.jsp"/>
   <forward name="success" path="/subscription.jsp"/>
</action>
```

This `action` element maps the request URI `/editSubscription` to the action object *EditSubscriptionAction*. An action object in Struts is similar to the command object in our examples. When a JSP page specifies this URI, the controller servlet instantiates the *EditSubscriptionAction* object and invokes the *perform* method on it.

Before it invokes the *perform* method, the controller servlet tries to locate a form JavaBean in request scope under the name "subscriptionForm". If it cannot find one, it instantiates the form bean. The form bean element (also specified in the configuration file) shown next, maps the name to a JavaBean.

```
<form-bean name="subscriptionForm"
   type="org.apache.struts.webapp.example.SubscriptionForm"
/>
```

This form bean is then populated with the parameters in the request according to property method signatures as established by JavaBean introspection. The form bean is then sent to the action object in the *perform* method. This preprocessing step saves the action object from parsing the elements from the request.

The two `forward` elements inside the `action` element indicate the two destinations to which the command object can forward control depending on a "success" or "failure" logical name (action). There can be any number of logical names that an action object could produce with corresponding destinations specified in a `forward` element. These `forward` elements can also appear inside a special `global-forwards` element. This establishes global mappings between logical names and forwarding destinations that any action object can use as default. A sample `global-forwards` element is shown here:

```
<global-forwards>
    <forward   name="logoff" path="/logoff.do"/>
    <forward   name="logon"  path="/logon.jsp"/>
    <forward   name="success" path="/mainMenu.jsp"/>
</global-forwards>
```

All of these elements are specified in a special Struts configuration XML file that is given to the controller servlet as an init-parameter named "config".

We can go into much more detail about Struts, but there is better documentation available on the Struts Web site located at `http://jakarta.apache.org/struts`. You can also download the framework for free from this Web site. The intent of this short description is to stimulate interest so you can learn more about it. The entire Struts framework might prove overwhelming to some. It comes with a lot of well-designed tools, not all of them useful to everybody. Even if you don't plan to use anything in Struts, learning the Struts framework helps you gain good practical insight into Web application design.

Final Thoughts

Fundamentally, all flow control mechanisms involve establishing mappings between actions in a Web application and stages or destinations. These mappings are controlled by a servlet. There can be variants in the destination. We saw a couple in our project: a URL and a command object that implements our *Command* interface. As part of this mapping, one could associate auxiliary information such as the model component in our project or the form bean in the Struts example. There can also be variants in how the next stage in a Web workflow is determined. It can be purely based on the action generated by the current stage, as we've seen in examples in this module. Or, in a slightly more complicated environment, we could envision chains of workflow with reusable stages in each chain. For example, consider Figure 9-18.

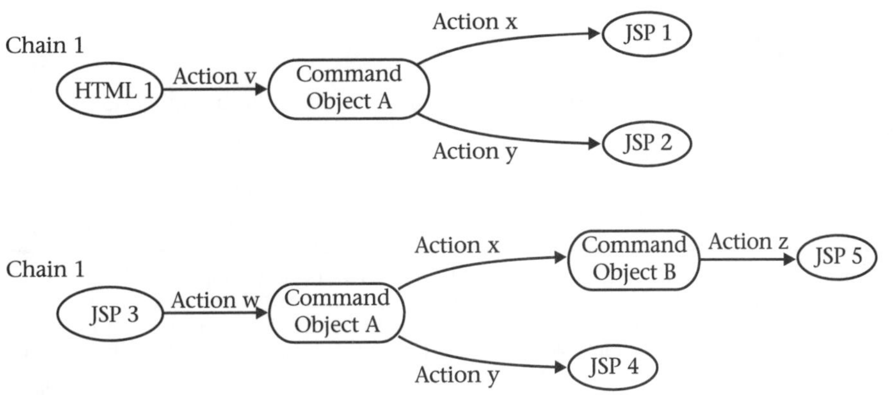

Figure 9-18 Chains of workflow

Two chains of workflow are shown. Command object `A` produces two actions: `x` and `y`. Based on the chain, our example maps the two actions to different destinations. In chain 1, our example maps the actions `x` and `y` to `JSP 1` and `JSP 2` respectively. In chain 2, the same action `x` maps to another command object B and action `y` maps to `JSP 4`. Table 9-4 shows the workflow table that illustrates all the mappings for these two chains.

In essence, the picture illustrates how a controller servlet, by being aware of the current chain in the workflow, could dynamically forward the user to different destinations for the same actions. This makes the stages reusable in multiple web-flows.

Chain	Current Stage	Action	Next Stage
1	HTML 1	v	Command A
1	Command A	x	JSP 1
1	Command A	y	JSP 2
2	JSP 3	w	Command A
2	Command A	x	Command B
2	Command A	y	JSP 4
2	Command B	z	JSP 5

Table 9-4 Chain-Based Workflow Table

1-Minute Drill

- How do you dynamically establish flow control in a Web application?
- What is Struts?
- What do all flow control mechanisms have in common?

- Dynamic flow control can be establish by reading the various stages in a Web application from a configuration file such as a Java properties file or a specially configured XML file.
- Struts is a Model-View-Controller implementation framework developed by the Jakarta project under the Apache Software Foundation. It includes various tools that can be used to easily build model, view, and controller components in your Web application.
- All flow control mechanisms involve establishing mappings from actions in the Web application to stages (or destinations) controlled by a servlet.

Mastery Check

1. Why should you consider it a poor design to make each Web resource aware of the next page(s) or stage(s) in the workflow?

____

2. Consider the following model interface and explain what is wrong:

```
public boolean isCreditApproved(HttpServletRequest request);
public void debitCreditCard(HttpSession session);
```

____

3. What is a common format for storing web-flow information in a Web application and why?

____

4. When designing a flexible Web workflow, is it sufficient just to centralize all stage transition logic in a controller servlet?

____

5. How is a chain-based web-flow different from regular web-flow?

____

Module 10

Integrating a Database

The Goals of This Module

- To explain the role of external content sources in "real-world" applications
- To understand the role of databases in JSP applications
- To present the basics of the JDBC data access API
- To illustrate integration of a relational database into our Family Center application

In Module 8, we presented the different security elements of Web architectures. We also described the login page for our Family Center application. In Module 9 we discussed web-flow and page management in a JSP application. We also described the controller for the Family Center. Now, in this last module we show how to add an *external content source* (e.g., a relational database) to a JSP architecture and describe the Family Center's JDBC (database) implementation of security and data management.

For the purposes of the discussion, we define an external content source to be any *centrally organized and accessible collection of digital content not directly managed by the application*. This definition includes many different kinds of content sources, including but not restricted to standard relational databases. For example, it includes legacy sources of information like SAP R/3 systems or even COBOL finance programs. Relational databases are uniquely important, however, because they are the most universal of external content sources.

Databases and other external content sources are big topics, and we barely touch on them here. Other books, hundreds of them, provide training and expertise on them. In this module, we address the architectural issues surrounding the use and integration of external content sources into a Web application, focusing on relational databases.

The Role of External Content Sources

The most basic question you might ask is: "Why integrate external content sources?" As our discussion of the Model-View-Controller (MVC) pattern in Module 7 explained, you can model the content in a Web application in multiple different ways. The file system, for example, is far simpler to use than a database. Most desktop applications, such as text or graphics editors, use the file system. This means that most computer users are very familiar with hierarchical directory and file systems, including directory search tools.

For some business purposes, the file system is the best choice for content management because it is local. Many other content sources, such as a database, require at least two tiers: client and server. This raises all the issues about network transparency that we described in Module 1. How fast are response times? How common are failures? Will other users share database services, possibly affecting the results of your own database requests? The file system has the same issues, of course, but greatly reduced. Apart from sticking all content in computer memory, you cannot beat a file system for responsiveness. For example, given current technology, you should store high-resolution video content in a local file system rather than a database during sessions with a video-editing tool. But when you need distributed access to content, the file system is not the best solution. It is very limited in preserving data integrity when sharing dynamic content. It also provides only rudimentary security. The point, of course, is that architectures must match business needs to technical capabilities.

So why and when might you integrate an external content source? You integrate external content sources:

- To organize and manage very large amounts of content reliably
- To centralize, secure, and share information
- To provide dynamic content to applications
- To access legacy information systems

Managing Large Amounts of Content

File system storage of content works well when demands are modest. As the amount of content on a local disk expands, however, it grows difficult to find any given piece of content. To organize this content, most computer users create custom directory schemes. For example, many computer users create a special "Pkgs" directory into which they install applications. Windows actually creates such directories by default, including: `My Documents`, `My Download Files`, and `Program Files`.

Such custom schemes quickly fail in a corporate setting. For one thing, it's hard to anticipate how you might want to access the content you produce. Is that PowerPoint presentation you stored in the `/Presentations` directory or the `/DesignMeetings` directory? Do you have two slightly different copies in each directory? Which version is the right version? What filename did you give it?

Another problem is the amount of storage required. There is an adage (maybe a natural law) that says you will fill your disk space no matter how large you make it. Finding content and providing adequate disk space are twin sides of the same problem—scaling information management as the amount of content grows.

External content sources can help alleviate these problems by enabling *index and catalog structures* that label, track, and organize content. The term "catalog structure" originates from library science. The analogy between a book catalog and a content catalog is pretty good. Both types of catalog provide information *about* content—*metadata*. A library catalog provides information, especially including location information, about books and other assets of a library. A content catalog provides information about digital content, including the storage location of that content.

Internet search engines such as Lycos and Web directories such as Yahoo provide familiar examples of content catalogs. A search engine builds an index (a kind of dynamic catalog) of words and phrases that it maps to Web pages that include those words and phrases. A Web directory creates a hierarchical organization of terms or topics into which it maps Web sites. Both supply a way of organizing content that simplifies finding the content.

Centralizing, Securing, and Sharing Content

A natural response to growing amounts of content is to centralize it so that you can protect and share it. That way, you need store only a single permanent copy of any given piece of content. You can also make the most efficient use of the relatively expensive mechanisms required to secure that copy.

Centralizing file storage is familiar to most of us. Almost every organization provides a shared file system managed by a centralized storage device of some kind. Such network attached storage (NAS) is far more cost-effective in general than continuously upgrading disks for every user so that they can store all their content on their own machines.

While a centralized file system can alleviate explosive disk space requirements, however, it does little to enhance management of large amounts of content. Usually such storage is better organized and protected than one's own disk, just because some corporate IT group controls it. But it is a difference of degree, not of kind. You still find directory structures with obscure names, and it is still difficult to find specific files in the corporate haystack.

A first step in managing the haystack is to centralize information about content. The Web catalogs and indexes we mentioned help do this. Such catalogs help you find the content you want but do not themselves manage the content.

The next step centralizes management of both information about content (metadata) and actual content.

When "digital content" meant simply "fielded information" (for example, employee records including such things as name, birth date, and address), centralizing content meant creating a central relational database. Such content still dominates most discussions and is still the most widely recognized information management scenario for most organizations. The importance of such information has been so great that huge corporations (including Oracle, the second largest software company after Microsoft) specialize in the technology of relational databases.

In the last few years, however, the term "digital content" has come to include much richer media than merely fielded content. Digital content now includes such objects as digitized documents, images, and digitized audio and video. New types of repositories have also emerged that can manage such content. Object and object-relational database engines make it possible to model rich media directly in a centralized repository. Modern *digital asset management* (DAM) systems go much further by providing centralized content repositories that integrate metadata, content, indexing and cataloging services, and even delivery of content. The purpose of all these new types of repositories is to centralize, secure, and share digital content.

Note

An interesting but unproven business model based on centralizing, securing, and sharing content hosts both business and consumer content in a central repository. Then it provides management tools to access this content over a variety of devices, including the Web but also including cell phones and personal digital assistants (`http://www.xdrive.com/`).

Providing Dynamic Content

Relational databases are almost uniquely suited to providing dynamic, query-based content to applications. Such dynamic content is important in all kinds of applications. For example, online trading firms rely on it to provide current stock quotes. ATM machines rely on it to allow or disallow withdrawals. Our Family Center relies on it to post and retrieve messages as well as keep security information current. For this reason this module demonstrates integration of a relational database, MySQL, using JDBC, the Java database connectivity toolkit.

The importance of dynamic content derives from the changing character of information. Bank balances ebb and flow (too much ebb, too little flow). The stock market declines and rises. People move, businesses go out of business. Relational databases manage such information best, and applications, including many Web applications, must retrieve and display it.

Accessing Legacy Information Systems

Much of the content that applications must display lies in existing content repositories. For example, large corporations typically store employee information, product information, and financial information in databases. This virtually guarantees that significant corporate Web applications must integrate relational database interfaces to this legacy information. The JDBC data access API provides cross-DBMS connectivity to most SQL databases (including MySQL). We describe this API in the next section.

Recently, Sun Microsystems has released the JDBC 2.0 Standard Extension API. Using this extension you can connect to any tabular data source as if it were a SQL database. For example, you can connect to spreadsheets or delimited files.

Sun Microsystems is also promoting a standard connector architecture for integration of enterprise information systems (EISs). Some examples of EISs are

- PeopleSoft
- SAP R/3
- IBM CICS
- COBOL applications

All these systems store important corporate content that one might need to integrate into an enterprise Web application. Figure 10-1 shows the J2EE Connector Architecture.

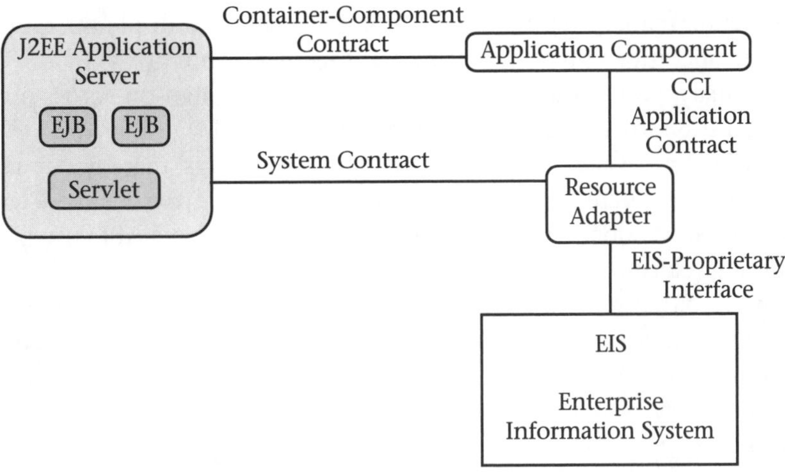

Figure 10-1 J2EE Connector Architecture

The connector architecture has three main components:

- System contracts between the application server and a resource adapter
- A Common Client Interface (CCI)
- A standard packaging and deployment mechanism

System-level contracts define an API for three services:

- Connection management
- Transaction management
- Security management

The primary goal of the connection management service is to provide connection pooling and to provide a Java Naming and Directory Service (JNDI) interface.

Transaction management supports atomicity across multiple operations (i.e., all the operations must be committed together or not at all).

The security management interface supports single sign-on across multiple EISs. It also supports authentication and access control.

The CCI defines a client API for application components, thereby standardizing access to multiple different EIS systems. The intention is to provide a low-level interface for tool vendors, more than it is to provide a complete API for typical application developers.

The hope is that independent vendors or legacy system vendors will write resource adapters for the various legacy information sources. A J2EE-compliant application server should provide simultaneous runtime support for one adapter per legacy system. These adapters run in the memory space of the application server.

Ask the Expert

Question: You mention the Java Naming and Directory Service (JNDI). What is it?

Answer: JNDI is a Java API that presents a common interface to access many different naming and directory services (e.g., LDAP, CORBA Naming Service, DNS, NIS). The purpose of the API is to enable you to simply "plug in" your preferred directory service.

1-Minute Drill

- What are four different reasons to integrate external data sources into your JSP application?
- What is the role of catalog structures?
- What are two Java APIs supporting legacy content integration?
- What is an EIS?

The JDBC Data Access API

The most common form of legacy content integration (and arguably still the most important) is integration of fielded information from relational databases. Relational databases provide the most proven and often the most effective way to model much of the information required by enterprise-scale applications. JDBC provides a vendor-neutral Java API to access relational Database Management Systems (DBMSs).

The JDBC Architecture

Like the J2EE Connector Architecture, the JDBC architecture requires provision of adapters—though restricted to fielded (tabular) information sources. JDBC

- Four reasons to integrate external data sources are: to organize and manage large amounts of data; to centralize, secure, and share information; to provide dynamic content; and to provide access to legacy content sources.
- Catalog structures label, track, and organize content.
- Java supports both the JDBC database APIs and the J2EE Connector Architecture for EIS integration.
- An EIS is an *Enterprise Information System* such as SAP R/3 and PeopleSoft.

drivers adapt applications to vendor DBMSs by implementing a standard Java interface using proprietary protocols and APIs. Figure 10-2 depicts the JDBC architecture.

As Figure 10-2 shows, JDBC supports four types of drivers:

- **Type 1** Accessing an ODBC (Open database connectivity) driver
- **Type 2** Mapping JDBC calls to the native client side API of the database vendor

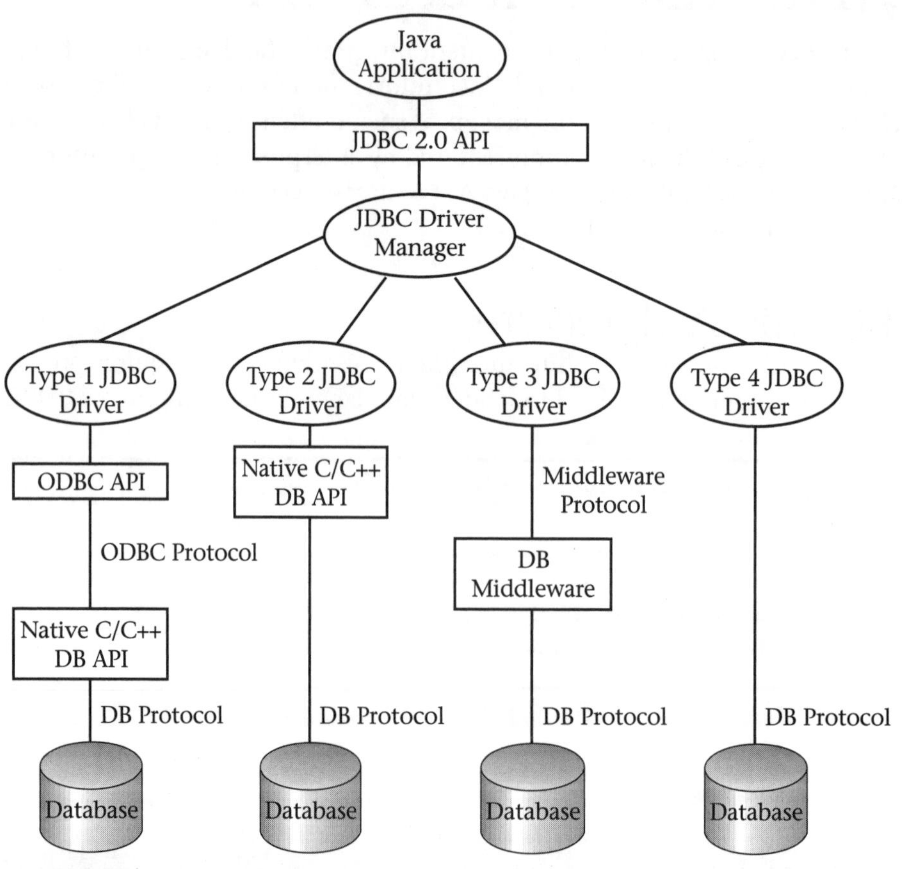

Figure 10-2 JDBC architecture

- **Type 3** Mapping JDBC calls into a middleware vendor's protocol (which is then translated by a middleware server into a DBMS protocol)
- **Type 4** Mapping JDBC calls directly into the database protocol

From the developer's perspective, all the JDBC drivers "look alike," since they share the same interface and developers can only access this interface. In this book, we are using a Type 4 JDBC driver for MySQL.

JDBC Basics

The JDBC API provides three core services:

- Connection services
- SQL services
- Result processing

Connection Services

Connection services include registering a JDBC driver, connecting to the database, and disconnecting from the database. You must first register a JDBC driver with the JDBC runtime framework before you can use it. The JDBC framework supports several ways to do this, but the simplest way to register a driver is to use the Java method *Class.forName*. For example, here is how you could register the MySQL driver (notice that the MySQL driver class is *org.gjt.mm.mysql.Driver*):


```
public static void registerDriver() {
   try {
      Class.forName(
         "org.gjt.mm.mysql.Driver");  ← MySQL JDBC driver class
   }
   catch (Exception excp) {
      excp.printStackTrace();
   }
}
```

This code works because the JDBC specification requires that JDBC drivers register themselves in a static initializer. While simple, this method also has the advantage that you can load the class name from a properties file, which provides an easy way to swap databases—just swap JDBC drivers.

Tip

While *Class.forName* works for MySQL, it may not work for all JDBC drivers (they may not supply a static initializer in accordance with the specification, registering instead in a constructor). This driver bug is common enough that most discussions suggest explicit creation of a driver instance like this: `Class.forName(driver_name).newInstance()`.

Of course, this discussion is greatly simplified. When your application manipulates or creates tables, it requires knowledge of supported DBMS data types and their names. Also, if you use proprietary or advanced features of a DBMS, your code will be difficult to port to a different DBMS.

Once your driver is registered, you must retrieve a connection to the data source. The *DriverManager* acts as a *connection factory*, returning an instance of the first registered JDBC driver it finds that meets the connection protocol. If it doesn't find any, it throws a *SQLException*. The JDBC framework provides a few methods to establish connections, but the simplest just specifies a URL, a username, and a password. The general format of a database URL is:

```
jdbc:subprotocol:subname
```

The only part of the connection protocol that differs between JDBC drivers is the specific format of the connection URL. In the case of MySQL, the specific format is:

```
jdbc:mysql://server-host/database-name
```

Here is the code that establishes a connection to our Family Center application:

```
public static Connection getConnection()
   throws SQLException
{
   String url = "jdbc:mysql://localhost/Family_Center";
   String username = "bookUser";
   String password = "bookPassword";
```

```
   Connection conn =
      DriverManager.getConnection(url,
                                  username,
                                  password);
   return conn;
}
```

Once you are finished with a JDBC connection, you must close it. Here is some code that performs this simple act:

```
public static void releaseConnection(Connection conn)
   throws SQLException
{
   if (conn != null)
      conn.close();
}
```

Ask the Expert

Question: What is a "connection factory"?

Answer: A *factory* is another common software design pattern. A factory provides a method to create an object (a *Connection* object in this case). Typically, in an API framework like JDBC, you use a factory in order to defer responsibility for *what* object to create to the factory, removing this responsibility from the framework. One variation of the factory pattern uses a *parameterized* factory method. The just means that the factory's *create* method takes an argument that specifies the kind of object to create. All the objects created by the factory share a common interface but differ in their implementation.

JDBC uses a parameterized factory method so that it can simultaneously support different JDBC drivers but present the same interface to the application. The JDBC factory method is: *DriverManager.getConnection*. You pass in a URL to this method defining the driver to use to create the connection object. Every JDBC connection object must implement the standard JDBC *Connection* interface.

Question: Is there any way to use JDBC to find out if a given database supports a given feature?

Answer: Yes, JDBC 2.0 supports the *DatabaseMetaData* interface, which provides information about two kinds of database features:

- Information about the database product
- Information about database capabilities to help programmers write DBMS-neutral code

Here is some sample code using some of the methods (there are many others) provided by *DatabaseMetaData* to retrieve some information from the MySQL database:

```
import java.sql.DriverManager;
import java.sql.Connection;
import java.sql.DatabaseMetaData;

public class DBMetaData {

   // register MySQL driver
   static {
      try {
         Class.forName("org.gjt.mm.mysql.Driver").
                        newInstance();
      } catch(Exception exp) {
           System.out.println(exp.getMessage());
      }
   }

   public static void list() {
      Connection conn = null;
      try {
         conn = DriverManager.getConnection(
                  "jdbc:mysql://localhost/Family_Center",
                  "bookUser", "bookPasswd");
         DatabaseMetaData metaData = conn.getMetaData();
```

```
            // database product name
            System.out.println("Product Name: " +
                metaData.getDatabaseProductName());

            // database product version
            System.out.println("Product Version: " +
                metaData.getDatabaseProductVersion());

            // supports batching updates ?
            System.out.println(
                "Supports Batch Updates: " +
                metaData.supportsBatchUpdates());

            // supports multiple result sets?
            System.out.println(
                "Supports multiple result sets: " +
                metaData.supportsMultipleResultSets());
        }
        catch (Exception exp)
        {
            System.out.println(exp.getMessage());
        }
        finally
        {
            try {
                conn.close();
            }
            catch (Exception exp)
            {
                System.out.println(exp.getMessage());
            }
        }
    }

    public static void main(String[] args)
    {
        DBMetaData.list();
    }
}
```

SQL Services

The JDBC 2.0 specification incorporates a model of the latest draft version of the ANSI/ISO SQL standard SQL3 (also known as SQL99).

JDBC supports three basic kinds of calls to the database:

- **Queries** Calls that return tabular data results (SELECT)
- **Data Manipulation Language (DML) updates** Calls that modify data in a database table (INSERT, UPDATE, DELETE)
- **Data Definition Language (DDL) updates** Calls that manipulate a database (CREATE TABLE, ALTER TABLE, DELETE TABLE)

All three kinds of database calls use a *java.sql.Statement* object to specify the SQL that the database executes. This object acts as a container or transport object for JDBC SQL.

The *Statement* object supports four execution methods:

- **executeQuery** Used for queries that return a single result
- **executeUpdate** Used for both DML and DDL statements
- **execute** Used for queries that might return more than one result
- **executeBatch** Used for database calls that must make more than a single update

You should use *executeQuery* for most database calls returning a single result and *executeUpdate* for most database calls that alter the database, database tables, or table data. You should use *execute* when you expect or cannot anticipate the number of result sets that will be returned. If it is available, you should use *executeBatch* to optimize a set of update calls. (JDBC drivers are not required to implement *executeBatch*.)

Note

The JDBC driver we are using, mm.MySQL, does not support *executeBatch*. While it supports *execute*, it does not support multiple result sets—so for MySQL, *execute* and *executeQuery* are equivalent. Compile and execute the code we provided in the previous "Ask the Expert," and you will see that this is so.

This code sample shows how to perform a simple query against a database:

```
Statement stmt = conn.createStatement();   ← Create a Statement
ResultSet rs = stmt.executeQuery("SELECT ID FROM MEMBER");
while (rs.next())   ← Execute the database call
{
   System.out.println("ID: " + rs.getInt(1);   ← Retrieve values from the ResultSet
}
```

As the code sample shows, the basic use of JDBC requires a few very simple steps:

- Create a *Statement*
- Execute the database call
- Retrieve value from the *ResultSet*

Often, you would like to parameterize calls to the database so that you can reuse the same *Statement*. For example, you might want to retrieve each user's valid roles based upon a security id. The query is the same for every user except for the value of the id, which is unique for each user. You would like to reuse the *Statement* but substitute the id value appropriate for each user. JDBC supports parameterized queries with the *java.sql.PreparedStatment* (derived from *java.sql.Statement*). The *PreparedStatement* prepares a SQL string that includes the question mark character (?) to represent parameterized values. Here is some code showing use of a *PreparedStatement*:

```
String sql = "SELECT USERNAME FROM " +
             "MEMBER WHERE ID = ?";
PreparedStatement ps = conn.prepareStatement(sql);   ← Create a PreparedStatement
for (int i = 1; i < 5; i++)
{                                  ← Set the parameterized value
     ps.setInt(1, i);
     rs = ps.executeQuery();   ← Execute the database call
     if (rs.first())
        System.out.println("Username: " +
                              rs.getString(1));   ← Retrieve from the ResultSet
 }
```

Using a *PreparedStatement* is almost as simple as using a *Statement*. It requires just these few simple steps:

- Create a *PreparedStatement*
- Set the parameterized values
- Execute the database call
- Loop through the *ResultSet*

When you use a *PreparedStatement* rather than a *Statement*, you:

- Call the connection's *prepareStatement* method rather than the *createStatement* method
- Call methods on the PreparedStatement object to set parameterized values
- Call execute methods without an argument (e.g., *executeQuery*()) rather than *executeQuery*(*String sql*))

Note

A *PreparedStatment* can also offer optimized querying when the database supports it. It can do this using a database prepared statement to implement the JDBC *PreparedStatement*. MySQL does not support such optimization.

Ask the Expert

Question: **How do some JDBC database implementations optimize *PreparedStatement* queries?**

Answer: When you send SQL to a database, the database engine must parse it before executing it. When it parses the query, the database lays out a *query plan*—a strategy for execution based upon proprietary database structures and optimization rules. SQL supports the `prepare` statement, which precompiles your SQL so that the database engine need not create a new query plan each time you execute the query. Some databases (e.g., Sybase) implement the JDBC *PreparedStatement* using the SQL `prepare` statement. This means that you can use JDBC to gain the performance benefits of a precompiled query. The more times you execute the query, the more benefit you obtain.

Result Processing

JDBC also supports result processing using *java.sql.ResultSet* objects. The essential function of a *ResultSet* object is to traverse query results. This includes scrolling forward and backward through rows of results and retrieving and possibly updating the value of columns in each row.

Scrolling backward and forward is a new feature in JDBC 2.0. In order to scroll, you must send flags to the driver when you create the *PreparedStatement*. Here is an example of such a statement:

```
PreparedStatement ps =
   conn.prepareStatement(sql_query,
                         ResultSet.TYPE_SCROLL_INSENSITIVE,
                         ResultSet.CONCUR_READ_ONLY);
```

JDBC 2.0 also allows you to update the values in a data source (e.g., database table) using the *ResultSet* itself. For example, if MySQL supported it, this code would update the `FIRST_NAME` field in the second row of a *ResultSet* query against the `MEMBER` table in our Family_Center database:

```
// moves the cursor to the second row of rs
rs.absolute(2);
// updates the FIRST_NAME column of row 2
rs.updateString("FIRST_NAME", "Ralph");
// updates the row in the data source
updateRow();
```

Note

MySQL does not support *ResultSet* updates. The JDBC 2.0 specification makes updatable result sets optional. When you try to create an updatable *ResultSet,* MySQL returns a supported *ResultSet* type rather than throwing an exception. Only when you try to use a feature of the updatable *ResultSet* will MySQL throw an exception.

10

You can think of a *ResultSet* as a tabular representation of the data returned by a query. As such, if your SQL requested two fields, `ID` and `USERNAME`, the result set will represent a table with two columns named "ID" and "USERNAME" with zero or more rows of data corresponding to the number of result values returned. A *ResultSet* maintains a cursor (a marker indicating the current row) into the rows in its table. You traverse the table by asking the *ResultSet* object to move its cursor. For example, you retrieve the next result record (the next row) by invoking *next* on the *ResultSet* object. Similarly, you ask for the previous record by invoking *previous*.

You retrieve column values from a *ResultSet* by invoking the appropriate data retrieval method and passing either the column index or the column name as a parameter. We saw this in our earlier code listings. Here is a slightly more complex example:

```
// print the values for the current row.
rs = stmt.executeQuery("SELECT a, b, c FROM Table1");
while (rs.next()) {
    int aVal = rs.getInt("a");
    String bVal = rs.getString(2);
    float cVal = rs.getFloat("c");
    System.out.println("ROW = " + aVal + " " +
                              bVal + " " + cVal);
}
```

Get first column as integer

Get second column as string

Get third column as float

Table 10-1 shows how retrieval methods for column values map to the most common database types.

SQL Type	***ResultSet* Method**
VARCHAR	*getString()*
LONGVARCHAR	*getString()*
CHAR	*getString()*
DECIMAL	*getBigDecimal()*
NUMERIC	*getBigDecimal()*
INTEGER	*getInt()*
BIGINT	*getLong()*
SMALLINT	*getShort()*
TINYINT	*getByte()*
REAL	*getFloat()*
FLOAT	*getDouble()*
DOUBLE	*getDouble()*
BIT	*getBoolean()*

Table 10-1 Mapping Between Common Database Types and *ResultSet* Methods

SQL Type	*ResultSet* Method
DATE	*getDate()*
TIME	*getTime()*
TIMESTAMP	*getTimestamp()*
VARBINARY	*getBytes()*
LONGVARBINARY	*getBytes()*
BINARY	*getBytes()*
BLOB	*getBlob()*
CLOB	*getClob()*

Table 10-1 Mapping Between Common Database Types and *ResultSet* Methods *(continued)*

While it does not support the whole SQL99 draft standard, JDBC 2.0 supports significant functionality beyond JDBC 1.0. Of special interest is its support for two built-in data types not present in JDBC 1.0:

- Binary Large OBject - BLOB
- Character Large OBject - CLOB

Other important features in JDBC 2.0 include:

- Scrollable result sets
- Batch updates
- Connection pooling
- Ability to use the Java Naming and Directory Service (JNDI) for connectivity
- Support for distributed transactions

There are many other features we do not mention here. We recommend that you consult a good JDBC reference for advanced features.

1-Minute Drill

- What is a type 4 JDBC driver?
- What are the three core services provided by the JDBC API?
- How do you obtain a connection to a JDBC driver?
- What four execution methods does *java.sql.Statement* support?
- What is the function of *java.sql.PreparedStatement*?
- What does a *java.sql.ResultSet* object represent?

JavaServer Pages and the JDBC API

You can embed JDBC calls directly into JavaServer Pages. For example, the following JSP fragment accesses our Family_Center database to display all valid users:

```
<% Class.forName(
      "org.gjt.mm.mysql.Driver").newInstance();
   String url =
      "jdbc:mysql://localhost/Family_Center";
   Connection conn = DriverManager.getConnection(url);
   String sql = "SELECT FIRST_NAME, LAST_NAME " +
                "FROM MEMBER";
   Statement stmt = conn.createStatement();
   ResultSet rs = stmt.executeQuery(sql);
   while (rs.next())
   {
      out.println(rs.getString(1) + " " +
                  rs.getString(2));
%>
   <BR>
```

Register MySQL JDBC driver

Establish connection

Create *Statement*

Execute call to database

Loop through *ResultSet*

Retrieve columns and print them

- A type 4 JDBC driver provides a 100 percent pure Java implementation mapping JDBC calls directly into the protocol of the target database.
- The JDBC API provides connection services, SQL services, and result processing.
- You first register the driver, then call *DriverManager.getConnection*, passing in a URL specifying the driver and database.
- The class *java.sql.Statement* supports: *executeQuery*, *executeUpdate*, *execute*, and *executeBatch*.
- The class *java.sql.PreparedStatement* extends *java.sql.Statement* to support parameterized queries.
- A *java.sql.ResultSet* object represents the tabular results returned from a JDBC query.

```
<%
   }
   stmt.close();
   rs.close();
   conn.close(); ←── Close connection
%>
```

Embedding JDBC code in your JavaServer Pages is probably not a good idea. For one thing, JDBC code is more difficult than most Java code to read and maintain. For another, you may wish to use techniques like pooling prepared statements. If you embed your JDBC code in JavaServer Pages, such techniques become impossibly difficult. You can make life much simpler for yourself and other JSP developers who may reuse your pages if you abstract out database access code to a helper JavaBean or a custom action.

The Jakarta Database Access Tag Libraries

A common maxim in software development is *never develop what you can buy or borrow*. Open software makes it especially easy to borrow code, and the Apache project stands out among open software projects. One of those projects is the Taglibs project, which includes the DBTags tag library (`http://jakarta.apache.org/taglibs/doc/dbtags-doc/intro.html`).

The DBTags tag library includes four types of tags:

- Connection tags
- Statement tags
- PreparedStatement tags
- ResultSet tags

These four types of tags correspond to the core JDBC services. Here is a DBTags version of our previous example listing valid users of the Family Center:

```
<%@ taglib uri="dbtags-taglib" prefix="sql" %>
<sql:connection id="conn"> ←── Register driver and establish connection
    <sql:url>jdbc:mysql://localhost/Family_Center
    </sql:url>
    <sql:driver>org.gjt.mm.mysql.Driver</sql:driver>
</sql:connection>
```

```
<sql:statement id="stmt" conn="conn">   <-- Create Statement and execute query
    <sql:query>
        SELECT FIRST_NAME, LAST_NAME from MEMBER
    </sql:query>
                                          Loop through ResultSet
      <sql:resultSet id="rs">
         <sql:getColumn position="1"/>          Retrieve columns
         <sql:getColumn position="2"/><BR>      and print them
    </sql:resultSet>
</sql:statement>                                Close connection
<sql:closeConnection conn="conn"/>
```

When to Avoid Using a Database Tag Library

Even a quick comparison of the JSP scriptlet embedding database code and the JSP page using DBTags provides a compelling argument for database tag libraries over embedded Java database code. Java code is messy and procedural. Tag libraries are clean and declarative. Java code requires Java programmers; the tag libraries do not. That said, there are still circumstances when you should not embed either Java code or database tag libraries in your JavaServer Pages.

The biggest drawback to embedding database tag libraries (or Java database code) in your JavaServer Pages is that it ties you to a particular architecture. Embedded database code is essentially two-tier from the point of view of the JSP container (three-tier from the point of view of the browser). You may want to migrate to an additional tier at some point. Put another way, there may come a time when you will want to migrate responsibility for all database access from the servlet/JSP containers to an Enterprise JavaBean (EJB) container. If you pack your JavaServer Pages with database code, even if this code is the nice, clean, declarative code provided by tag libraries, you will find migration to an additional tier difficult.

Like JDBC itself, DBTags presume the world of a relational database, not an abstract model for data. They display the language of a relational database in their tags, and you could not easily reimplement these tags as an EJB data access tier without distorting them. For this reason, our Family Center establishes its model as a JavaBean interface rather than a tag library.

1-Minute Drill

- Should you embed JDBC code in your JavaServer Pages?
- What is the origin and purpose of the DBTags tag library?
- When should you avoid using a database tag library like DBTags?

Web.xml
MemberEditForm.html
DoMemberEdit.jsp

Project 10-1: Using Jakarta DBTags

In this project, we step through a download of the Apache Taglib project. Then we step through installation of the DBTags. Finally, we use the tags to develop a JSP page to update the `MEMBER` and `ROLES` tables in the Family Center. This project requires you to have installed our Family Center MySQL database following the instructions in Project 9-1. If you have not done this, please ensure that you follow those steps before proceeding with this project.

Step-by-Step

1. Download the files for this project from `http://www.osborne.com`.
2. Create a directory named `database` under `%TOMCAT_HOME%\webapps`.
3. Move the `database.war` file to `%TOMCAT_HOME%\webapps`.
4. Enter the database subdirectory and extract the database application using the `jar.exe` utility as shown here:

```
\> cd %TOMCAT_HOME%\webapps\database
\> jar.exe xvf ..\database.war
```

10

- You should avoid embedding JDBC code in JavaServer Pages. Such code is difficult to read and makes such things as statement pooling impossibly hard.
- The Jakarta group at Apache.org developed and maintains the DBTags tag library. The purpose of the DBTags tag library is to provide a set of tags for embedding database access in a JSP page.
- You should avoid using a database tag library when you may eventually refactor your application to add a database access tier (perhaps using EJB components).

5. You should see a \jsp directory holding DoMemberEdit.jsp, an \html directory holding MemberEditForm.html, and a \WEB-INF directory holding the file web.xml and the directories \lib and \tlds.

6. Now download the Apache DBTags binary distribution from the Apache Web site: http://jakarta.apache.org/builds/jakarta-taglibs/nightly/projects/dbtags/. Pick the most recent distribution for Windows (i.e., the highest numbered release ending in .zip).

7. Use your ZIP utility to extract the DBTags distribution into a temporary directory.

8. Change directories to: *<your-temporary-directory>*\jakarta-taglibs\dbtags.

9. Move DBTags.jar to: %TOMCAT_HOME%\webapps\database\WEB-INF\lib:

```
\temp>move dbtags.jar %TOMCAT_HOME%\webapps\database\
WEB-INF\lib
```

10. Copy dbtags.tld to: %TOMCAT_HOME%\webapps\database\WEB-INF\tlds:

```
\temp>copy dbtags.tld %TOMCAT_HOME%\webapps\database\
WEB-INF\tlds
```

11. Change directory to: %TOMCAT_HOME%\webapps\database\WEB-INF.

12. View the web.xml file and consider the <taglib> block. This block defines the URL that we must embed in our JSP pages to use the DBTags tag library. We want to give apache.org credit for the tag library; hence, we include it in our URI.

```
<taglib>
   <taglib-uri>jakarta.apache.org/taglibs/dbtags
   </taglib-uri>
   <taglib-location>/WEB-INF/tlds/dbtags.tld
   </taglib-location>
</taglib>
```

13. Change directory to: %TOMCAT_HOME%\webapps\database\jsp.

14. View the file: DoMemberEdit.jsp. This is the full code listing for adding records to the MEMBER table in the Family_Center database. Notice that we use a taglib directive (Module 2) to specify our use of the DBTags tag library:

```
<%@ taglib
    uri="jakarta.apache.org/taglibs/dbtags"
    prefix="sql" %>
```

15. The page has three parts: establishing the connection, inserting a table row, and closing the connection. Each part uses its own set of DBTags tags. You can find a tutorial for DBTags in the DBTags distribution. It describes each supported tag and its use.

16. To access the DBTags documentation, change directory to: *<your-temporary-directory>*\jakarta-taglibs\dbtags. Copy the dbtags-doc.war under %TOMCAT_HOME%\webapps. Restart Tomcat and access the URL: http://localhost:8080/dbtags-doc.

17. Finally, change directories to: %TOMCAT_HOME%\webapps\database\html. View the file: EditMemberForm.html. This file presents the form we use to edit the MEMBER table. You should note the correspondence between the form's field names and the request parameters we use in DoMemberEdit.jsp. Also notice that we log into the Family Center database using the bookUser user and bookPasswd password that we added to the database in Project 9-1 (Module 9).

18. Make sure that you add the MySQL JDBC driver JAR file (mm.mysql-bin.jar) to %TOMCAT_HOME%\webapps\database\WEB-INF\lib. (The Tomcat container automatically concatenates any jar found in an application's \WEB-INF\lib directory to the *CLASSPATH* for the application context.)

19. Start Tomcat and enter the following URL in your browser (you should see a Web page that looks like Figure 10-3):

    http://localhost:8080/database/html/EditMemberForm.html.

20. Add some values to the form and push the Add Record button. If the insertion succeeds, you should see a Web page that looks like Figure 10-4.

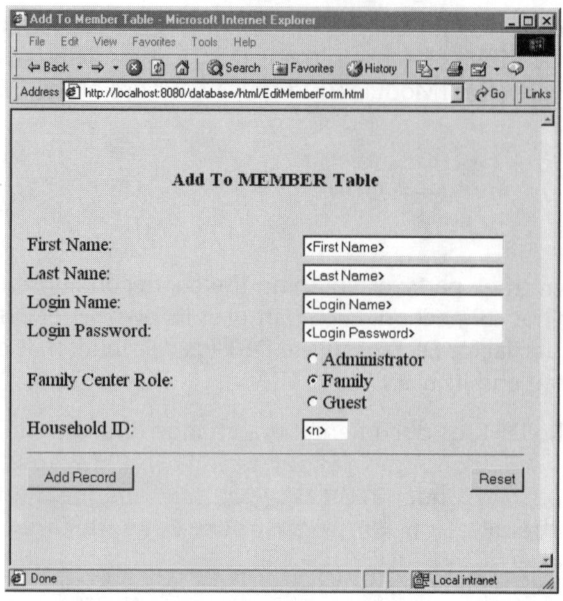

Figure 10-3 Add to MEMBER table form

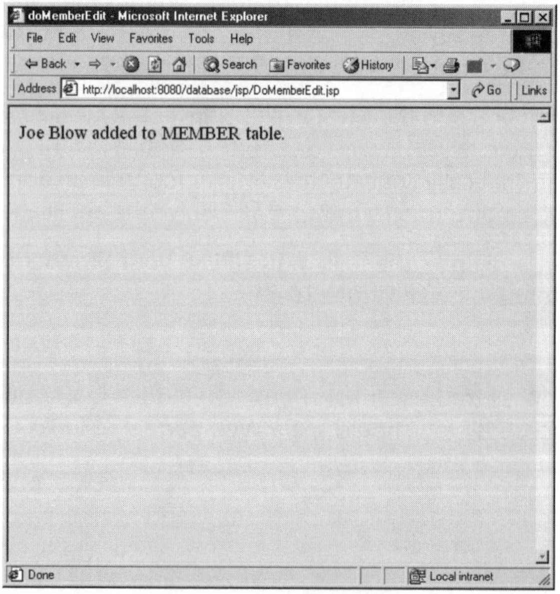

Figure 10-4 Success page

Our goal in this project was to familiarize you with the Jakarta DBTags effort. There are many things we should do to enhance `DoMemberEdit.jsp`. For one thing, we should perform some error checking. For another, we should improve user feedback. We encourage you to explore the DBTags tag library and either enhance this simple example or write your own pages.

The Family Center Data Model

One of the first steps we took when we developed the Family Center application was to model our data. Data modeling is a key part of any "real-world" application, and it can pay dividends to have experts do it. For relatively simple applications like the Family Center, however, we can struggle through without expert help.

At a high level, a data model consists of three types of objects:

- **Entity types** Any type of object of interest within the area being modeled
- **Attributes** An item of information describing an entity occurrence
- **Relationships** A type of association between entity occurrences

Entity Types

Entity types model the things in your application's universe. The tricky job is determining what that universe is—what kind of application are you building? Use cases provide one of the techniques that can help you define the function of your application. Recall that in Module 7 we listed several use cases for the Family Center. Then we mentioned that the pattern of these use cases suggests four features:

1. Address Book
2. Family Calendar
3. Photo Album
4. Bulletin Board

In Module 8 we added a fifth feature:

5. Security

These five features provide the basis for modeling our data because our data must support their function.

We begin by just listing the data elements we think we need for each feature. For pedagogical reasons, we deliberately keep the Family Center simple. To support an address book, we need address information:

- Household name at address
- Family members at address
- Household street, city, state, and country
- Phone

Similarly, to support a calendar, we need information about events:

- Family household holding the event
- Event date
- Description of the event

To support a photo album, we need:

- Family household that is the subject of the images
- Event where the pictures were taken
- Description of the event

To support the bulletin board, we need:

- Family members to whom the message is sent
- The date of the message
- The subject discussed by the message
- The message itself

Finally, to support security, we need:

- Valid family members

- User login names
- User passwords
- Valid roles
- Role descriptions

After listing the anticipated data elements, we notice some patterns. Three entities appear multiple times:

- Household
- Event
- Member

Apart from these three important entities, two others seem necessary and not subsumable by household, event, or family member:

- Message
- Valid roles

We pick these five entity types as the basis of our Family Center data model. We name the five entity types (they will become our tables):

- Household
- Household member
- Household event
- Member messages (message board)
- Member roles

Figure 10-5 shows our data model after defining entity types.

Attributes

Attributes turn abstract entity types into actual entity *occurrences*. By assigning values to attributes, you define an instance of an entity. For example, you define

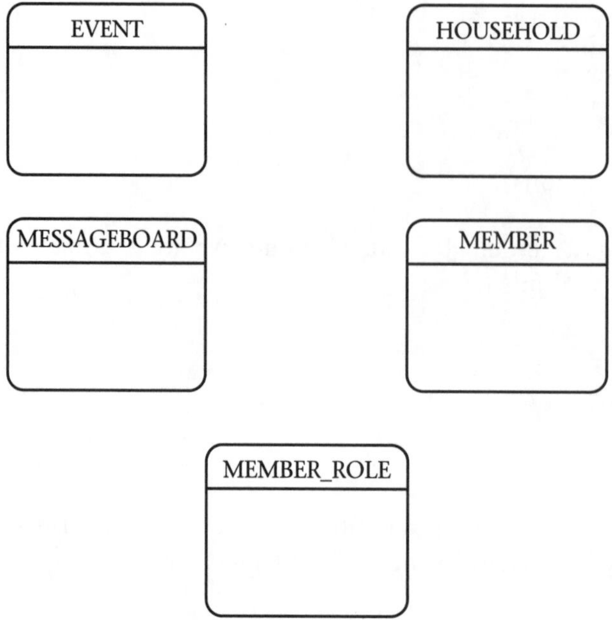

Figure 10-5 Family Center data model after defining entity types

a household instance by assigning actual values to such attributes as household name, household address, and household phone number. You must assign attributes to a single entity type. If more than one entity type seems to require the same attribute (address), then both entity types have a logical relationship to a third entity type to which the attribute properly belongs (addresses). We specify our Family Center attributes by refining the data elements we listed and assigning them to the entity types we defined. Figure 10-6 shows the data model after assigning attributes.

Relationships

Relationships define an association between two entity instances. For example, a member is a *member of* a household. This association does not imply a direction, since another way to describe the `member_of` relationship is to describe it as `has_member`. These are two ways to describe the same relationship, and we

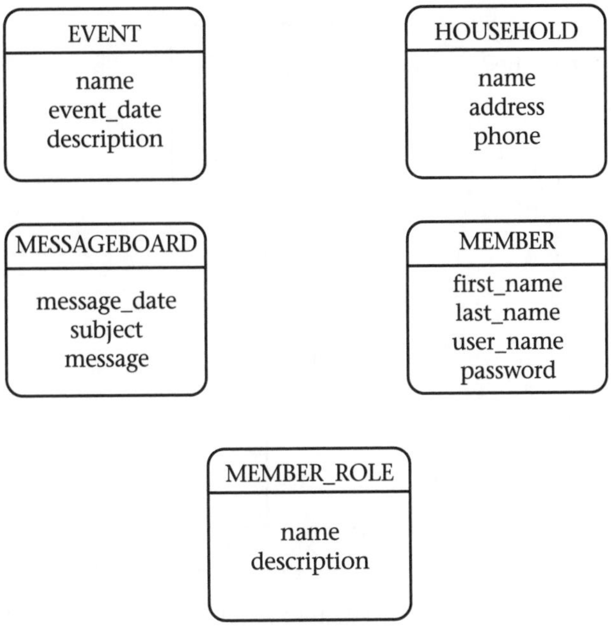

Figure 10-6 Family center data model with attributes assigned

can use them interchangeably. Relationships have *cardinality*. Cardinality refers to the number of entity occurrences possible between entities in a relationship. For example, the `has_member` relationship can relate many occurrences of member entities to a single occurrence of a household entity. This means the relationship has a one-to-many cardinality. There can also be one-to-one and many-to-many cardinalities. Typically, diagrams use a "crows-foot" (three-pronged line) to indicate the "many" side of a relationship.

Relationships require *unique keys* to identify entity occurrences. For convenience and performance, you may often add unique numeric keys to occurrences, just as if they were attributes. A key could also be one or more attributes that together uniquely identify an entity occurrence. In the Family Center data model, we assign a unique numeric identifier to each entity and use the identifier to establish relationships. Figure 10-7 shows the Family Center data model after relationships are defined (we show relationship labels for clarity).

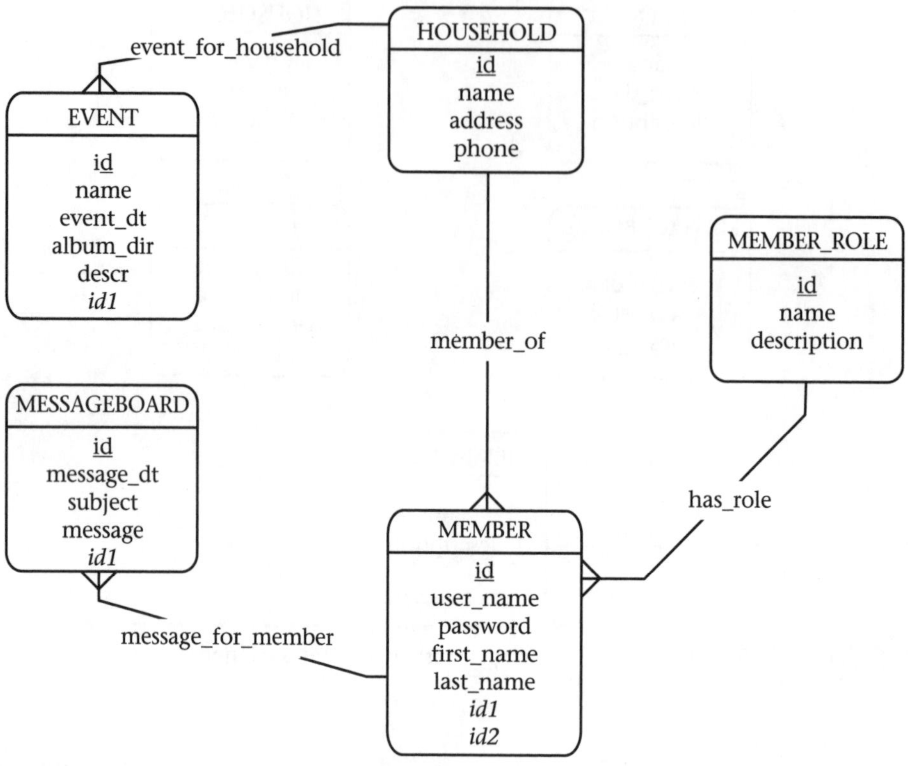

Figure 10-7 Complete Family Center data model with relationship labels

1-Minute Drill

- What three types of objects are included in a high-level data model?
- What is the role of entities in a data model?
- What is the role of attributes in a data model?
- What is the role of relationships in a data model?

- A high-level data model includes: entities, attributes, and relationships.
- Entities model the things in your application's universe.
- Attributes turn abstract entity types into concrete occurrences. They supply the specific characteristics defining an instance of an entity type.
- Relationships define an association between two instances of entity types.

Project 10-2: Adding Security to the Family Center

CustomRealm.java
SQLConstants.java
web.xml
actions.xml
Family.jpg
bluepaper.gif
LoginError.jpg
loginError.jsp
login.jsp

In Project 9-1 (Module 9), we built the database for the Family Center and a simple address book search page that searches for address book entries corresponding to member names. In this project, we continue building the Family Center by adding security to it. Our security implementation enhances the Tomcat request interceptor mechanism we described in Module 8. We built a new custom security realm that authenticates and authorizes users according to information from our Family Center database.

This project requires that you have followed the steps in Project 9-1, created the MySQL database with sample data, and established an application context for our Family Center application. If you skipped Project 9-1, we urge you to complete it before you start this project.

Step-by-Step

1. Download the files for this project from `http://www.osborne.com`.

2. Put the new `family_center.war` into `%TOMCAT_HOME%/webapps/`. This includes all the class files necessary to run the address book search in Module 9 but modifies the `SQLConstants.class` file to include two additional static final *String* variables necessary for security services. All other classes from Project 9-1 remain unchanged. We also add security classes to this core set of Family Center classes.

3. Enter the `Family_Center` subdirectory and extract the revised `Family_Center` application using the **jar.exe** utility:

```
\> cd %TOMCAT_HOME%\webapps\Family_Center
\> jar xvf ..\family_center.war
```

4. Restart Tomcat and access our Family Center application using the URL `http://localhost:8080/Family_Center`.

5. Instead of the `Entrance.html` that you saw in Project 9-1, the Family Center automatically transfers you to the URL: `http://localhost:8080/Family_Center/jsp/secure/login/login.jsp`, as shown in Figure 10-8.

6. Enter a sample login and password. For instance, enter: `jerry` and `jerry`. (You can find sample user names and passwords in the `MEMBER` table in our Family Center MySQL database.) This logs you in and forwards control to the `Entrance.html` page that you should recognize from Project 9-1. The login page authenticates, authorizes, and checks role using values assigned to a given login in the Family Center database.

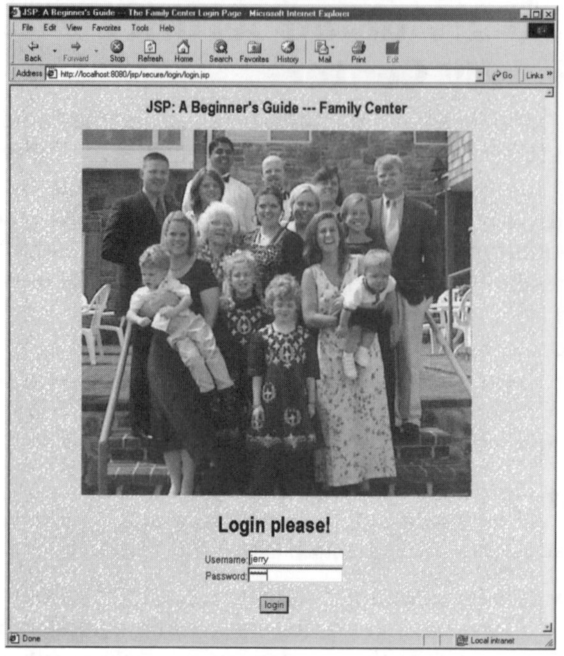

Figure 10-8 Login page for the Family Center application

You have successfully managed to integrate security into our Family Center application. The sections that follow explain the design and the code for the security implementation. You can download the final version of the Family Center application from: `http://www.osborne.com`.

Ask the Expert

Question: I followed the instructions in Project 10-2, but now I can no longer start Tomcat. What has gone wrong?

Answer: The most likely problem is that Tomcat is unable to find *com.jspbg.CustomRealm*. This is the problem if you look in the console window where you tried to run Tomcat and see: **`java.lang.ClassNotFoundException:`**

com.jspbg.interceptor.CustomRealm. Make sure that you have installed this class into `%TOMCAT_HOME%\classes`.

You might also see: **java.lang.ClassNotFoundException: org.gjt.mm.mysql.Driver**. If so, then make sure you have added `mm.mysql-bin.jar` to the Tomcat CLASSPATH (add it to `%TOMCAT_HOME%\bin\tomcat.bat`).

You might also have introduced a typo into `%TOMCAT_HOME%\conf\server.xml`. If you see an error similar to this, you should check the changes you made to `server.xml`:

org.xml.sax.SAXParseException: Attribute names must not start with "<" characters.

An error like this indicates your database is not running: **CustomRealm.authenticate: Unable to retrieve ID. Reason: Cannot connect to MySQL server on localhost:3306**.

The Family Center Data Access Approach

The goal of the data access approach in the Family Center is to create a layer of encapsulation so that we can easily replace any given implementation of the model. It should be possible to "plug in" a new implementation without recoding any part of the model.

The Bridge Pattern

Recall our discussion of the bridge pattern in Modules 7 and 9. As we said there, the bridge pattern decouples an abstract interface from its implementations. Among other advantages, it insulates clients from any platform-specific or proprietary method signatures. Such insulation is exactly what we want for our Family Center. Let's examine how we implement it for security and our address book.

Using the Database to Implement Our CustomRealm

Recall from Module 8 our hard-coded implementation of a custom security realm for Tomcat. We would like to modify the implementation so that it can use a database. But we may someday want to integrate an LDAP directory for access control to the Family Center. To build in such flexibility and extensibility, we must use the bridge pattern to decouple the security interface from any given implementation. We start by defining the interface.

Our interface must support two features:

- Retrieval of a security identity using a login name and password
- Retrieval of all roles assigned to a given user

Here is the Java definition of this interface:

```
package com.jspbg.model;
import java.util.List;
import com.jspbg.data.Member;

public interface SecurityRealm {
   public String getMemberID(String username,
                             String password)
          throws ServiceException;
   public String[] getRoles(String id)
          throws ServiceException;
}
```

Notice that this definition implies nothing about a JDBC implementation. You can use any implementation that supports the method signatures.

Next we must create a JDBC implementation. We first declare the SQL strings as static finals in `SQLConstants.java`:

```
public static final String ID_QUERY =
   new String("SELECT ID FROM MEMBER WHERE " +
              "USERNAME = ? " +
              "AND PASSWORD = ?");
public static final String ROLES_QUERY =
   new String("SELECT t2.NAME FROM MEMBER t1," +
              "MEMBER_ROLE t2 WHERE " +
              "t1.MEMBER_ROLE_ID = t2.ID AND " +
              "t1.ID = ?");
```

Notice the "?" character, indicating that we will be using prepared statements. We declared these as static finals because we reuse them repeatedly but never change them.

Here is the actual JDBC implementation of the interface:

```
package com.jspbg.model;

import java.sql.Connection;
import java.sql.PreparedStatement;
import java.sql.ResultSet;
import java.sql.SQLException;
import com.jspbg.data.Member;
import com.jspbg.db.DB;

public class SecurityRealmImpl
   implements SecurityRealm
{
   static
   {
      DB.registerDriver();     <-- Register JDBC driver
   }
   public String getMemberID(String username,
                             String password)
      throws ServiceException
   {
      String memberID = null;
      PreparedStatement ps = null;
      ResultSet rs = null;
      Connection conn = null;

      try
      {
         conn = DB.getConnection();
         ps = conn.prepareStatement(SQLConstants.ID_QUERY);   <-- Create PreparedStatement
         ps.setString(1, username);   <-- Set username and
         ps.setString(2, password);       password to match

         rs = ps.executeQuery();   <-- Execute query and retrieve security id
         if (rs.first())
         {
            memberID = Integer.toString(rs.getInt(1));
         }
      }
```

```
    catch(SQLException sexp)
    {
       throw new ServiceException(
          "Unable to retrieve ID. Reason: " +
           sexp.getMessage());
    }
    finally
    {
       try
       {
          if(ps != null) ps.close();
          if(rs != null) rs.close();
          DB.releaseConnection(conn);
       }
       catch (SQLException sexp) {}
    }
    return memberID;
}

public String[] getRoles(String id)
    throws ServiceException
{
    String[] roles = null;
    PreparedStatement ps = null;
    ResultSet rs = null;
    Connection conn = null;

    try
    {
       conn = DB.getConnection();
       ps = conn.prepareStatement(
                 SQLConstants.ROLES_QUERY,
                 ResultSet.TYPE_SCROLL_INSENSITIVE,
                 ResultSet.CONCUR_READ_ONLY);
       ps.setInt(1, Integer.valueOf(id).intValue());
       rs = ps.executeQuery();

       if (rs.last())
       {
          int count = rs.getRow();
          roles = new String[count];
          rs.first();
```

If *SQLException* rethrow as *ServiceException*

Close everything

Create *PreparedStatement* returning scrollable *ResultSet*

Set id value to match

Scroll to the last row and get count

```
            for (int i = 0; i < count; i++)
            {
               roles[i] = rs.getString(1);
               rs.next();
            }
         }
      }
      catch(SQLException sexp)
      {
         throw new ServiceException(
            "Unable to retrieve Roles. Reason: " +
             sexp.getMessage());
      }
      finally
      {
         try
         {
            if(ps != null) ps.close();
            if(rs != null) rs.close();
            DB.releaseConnection(conn);
         }
         catch (SQLException sexp) {}
      }
      return roles;
   }
}
```

Collect all roles into a *String* array

We implement both methods required by the *SecurityRealm* interface using JDBC but could as easily implement them using the file system or LDAP. We make sure that if an error occurs, we map the exception to the implementation-neutral *ServiceException* class.

Our next step is to reimplement *CustomRealm* (from Module 8) using our bridge. We first add a new property, *implementation*, representing the security implementation class:

```
public void setImplementation(String implementation)
{
   this.implementation = implementation;
}
```

We will explain shortly how this property gets set.

Then we reimplement the *ContextInit* method:

```
public void contextInit(Context ctx)
   throws TomcatException
{
   if (!inited)
   {
      try
      {
         secMgr = (SecurityRealm)
            Class.forName(implementation).newInstance();
         inited = true; // do it only once
      }
      exception handling code
   }
}
```

In this initialization method, we instantiate the security implementation using the *implementation* property we added.

Next we must reimplement *authenticate* and *authorize*. Here is the new *authenticate* method:

```
public int authenticate(Request req,
                        Response response)
{
   int authValue = NOT_AUTHORIZED; //401

   // Extract login credentials
   HttpSession session = req.getSession(false);
   if (session == null) return authValue;

   String username = (String)
      session.getAttribute("j_username");
   String password = (String)
      session.getAttribute("j_password");

   /*
    * authenticate the username and password
    */
   if (username != null && password != null)
   {
      String id = null;
      try
      {
         id = secMgr.getMemberID(username, password);
         if (id != null)
         {
```

```
            req.setRemoteUser(id);
            req.setUserPrincipal(new SimplePrincipal(id));
            authValue = OK; // 0
         }
      }
      exception handling
   }
   return authValue;
}
```

In this new implementation, if an *id* is returned from *getMemberID*, then the user is authenticated.

Here is the new implementation of *authorize*:

```
public int authorize(Request req,
                     Response response,
                     String roles[])
{
   int authValue = NOT_AUTHORIZED;
   try
   {
      String id = req.getRemoteUser();
      if (id != null)
      {
         String[] allRoles = secMgr.getRoles(id);
         if (allRoles != null)
         {
            int ilen = allRoles.length;
            for (int i = 0; authValue != OK &&
                            i < ilen; i++)
            {
               int jlen = roles.length;
               for (int j = 0; authValue != OK &&
                               j < jlen; j++)
               {
                  if (allRoles[i].equals(roles[j]))
                  {
                     authValue = OK;
                  }
               }
            }
         }
      }
   }
   exception handling
   return authValue;
}
```

The *authorize* method calls the *getRoles* method in our security implementation to retrieve all the roles assigned to a given user. It then compares these roles against the roles authorized for the current resources (passed into the *authorize* method). If there is a match, the user is permitted access to the resource.

Next we must set the *implementation* property in *CustomRealm*. Tomcat uses Java reflection to parse any attribute you provide to your interceptor in `server.xml` and calls the appropriate setter method. Here is our modified `server.xml` configuration for *CustomRealm*:

```
<RequestInterceptor
   className="com.jspbg.interceptor.CustomRealm"
   implementation="com.jspbg.model.SecurityRealmImpl"
   debug="2"
/>
```

Notice that we provide the full class name for our implementation class. We could replace this security handler simply by specifying a different implementation of the *SecurityRealm* interface.

Finally, we must add the necessary security elements in our `web.xml` file for Form-based authentication. The `security-constraint` block is shown here:

```
<!-- Security entries -->
   <security-constraint>
      <web-resource-collection>
        <web-resource-name>Protected Area</web-resource-name>
      <!-- Define the context-relative URL(s) to be protected -->
         <url-pattern>/html/*</url-pattern>
      <!-- If you list http methods, only those methods are protected -->
         <http-method>DELETE</http-method>
         <http-method>GET</http-method>
         <http-method>POST</http-method>
         <http-method>PUT</http-method>
      </web-resource-collection>

      <auth-constraint>
         <!-- Anyone with one of the listed roles may access this area -->
         <role-name>administrator</role-name>
         <role-name>family</role-name>
         <role-name>guest</role-name>
      </auth-constraint>
   </security-constraint>
```

The protected area is identified by the URL pattern "`/html/*`", which is where our welcome page `Entrance.html` is located. The `auth-constraint` block indicates the valid roles for users who access this Web application. This list must match the role names established in our MySQL database in the table MEMBER_ROLES.

The `login-config` block that follows identifies the login form page that should be automatically loaded when a protected area in this Web application is accessed. The error page is loaded when the login authentication or authorization fails.

```
<!-- Form-based login -->
<login-config>
   <auth-method>FORM</auth-method>
   <realm-name>
     Example Form-Based Authentication Area
   </realm-name>
   <form-login-config>
      <form-login-page>
         /jsp/secure/login/login.jsp
      </form-login-page>
      <form-error-page>
        /jsp/secure/login/loginError.jsp
      </form-error-page>
   </form-login-config>
</login-config>
```

The Model for the Address Book

We showed how our Family Center supports flexibility and extensibility by implementing its security model using a simplified bridge pattern. Now let's look at how we do something similar for our Family Center Address Book.

Recall the controller servlet from Module 9 (*com.jspbg.servlet.DispatcherServlet*). This servlet manages web-flow in our Family Center. It also initializes the model for the Family Center. It begins by declaring logical names for the models supporting the Family Center features:

```
// Static strings for model-names.
private static final String ADDRESS_BOOK_MGR  =
   "AddressBookManager";
```

In this discussion, we focus on the ADDRESS_BOOK_MGR. Other managers for event processing and message boards work similarly. You can download the final version from the http://www.osborne.com Web site.

Next, in the *init* method of the *DispatcherServlet* we initialize both the controller strategy (action parser) and the model factory:

```
public void init(ServletConfig config)
        throws ServletException {

   //initialize parent
   super.init(config);

   // register JDBC driver. Required only once.
   DB.registerDriver();

   // initialize action parser for controller logic.
    initializeActionParser(config);

    // create model factory
    initializeModelFactory(config);
    }
```

Here is the initialization method for the model factory:

```
   public void initializeModelFactory(ServletConfig config)
        throws ServletException {
        Map models = new HashMap();
        models.put(ADDRESS_BOOK_MGR,
              config.getInitParameter(ADDRESS_BOOK_MGR));
        modelFactory = new ModelFactory(models);
   }
```

The first point to notice is that we configure the models (assign the specific Java classes that implement the models) using initialization parameters specified in the web.xml for our application context. Here is the fragment of web.xml that does this configuration:

```
<init-param>
   <param-name>AddressBookManager</param-name>
   <param-value>
      com.jspbg.model.AddressBookManagerImpl
   </param-value>
</init-param>
```

After initializing the models, we create a *ModelFactory*, passing in the initialized models. Here is the *ModelFactory* class:

```
public class ModelFactory {
   private Map modelNamesToImplNames = null;
   private Map modelNamesToImplObjects = new HashMap();

   public ModelFactory(Map modelNamesToImplNames)
   {
      this.modelNamesToImplNames = modelNamesToImplNames;
   }

   public synchronized Model makeModel(String modelName)
      throws ServiceException
   {
      /*
         Retrieve implementation class object
         from model-name
      */
      Model m = (Model)
         modelNamesToImplObjects.get(modelName);
      if(m == null) {
         /* Retrieve implementation class name
         String implName = (String)
            modelNamesToImplNames.get(modelName);
         if(implName != null) {
            try {
               // Instantiate implementation class
               m = (Model)Class.forName(implName).
                                          newInstance();

               // Insert it into list for future use.
               modelNamesToImplObjects.put(modelName, m);
            }
             exception handling
         }
      }

      return m;
   }
}
```

The *ModelFactory* creates model instances at first request time. Here is the servlet logic calling the factory reproduced from Module 9:

```
// While next stage is a Command, retrieve the
// model component for the command, and invoke
// the command.
while((nextStage =
       actionParser.getCommand(state)) != null) {
   Model model = null;
   String modelName = actionParser.getModel(state);

   // create model if there is one associated
   // with current action
   if(modelName != null) {
      model = modelFactory.makeModel(modelName);
   }

   // forward control to the command
   state = forwardToCommand(nextStage, model, req, res);
}
```

As you see, the servlet requests a model from the *ModelFactory*, then forwards it to the command object.

The point to note about this architecture for model management is that the model is entirely "pluggable" and replaceable. The specific implementation is determined by the `web.xml` file for a given application context. The specific implementation we use is: *AddressBookManagerImpl*. We define the interface for this implementation using the Java interface: *AddressBookManager*. So long as the models implement the *AddressBookManager* interface, different application contexts can implement different models without any recoding of the *DispatcherServlet* and MVC support classes. Here is the *AddressBookManager* interface:

```
public interface AddressBookManager extends Model {
   public List getHouseholdsByLastName(String lastName)
         throws ServiceException;
   public List getHouseholdsByFirstName(String firstName)
         throws ServiceException;
   public List getHouseholdsByIndex(String indexAlphabet,
                                    boolean isFirstName)
         throws ServiceException;
}
```

Another point to notice is that our Address Book implements a stronger variant of the bridge pattern than our security interceptor. The *DistpatcherServlet* does not hold a direct reference to the *AddressBookManager* interface. Instead it holds a reference to the *Model* interface. Here is that interface:

```
public interface Model {
}
```

This *Model* interface is completely empty, and the *AddressBookManager* interface merely extends it, as do the other interfaces for our models (*EventManager* and *MessageBoardManager*). This enables the servlet to use each of the different models for the Family Center without caring which specific model it is using. Nevertheless, the *Model* interface defines the requirement for our *DispatcherServlet*. The door is open to extend the *Model* interface or implement it as a Java class independently of the specific model interfaces. If we did so, the *AddressBookManager* interface could no longer extend the *Model* interface. Instead, the *Model* class might hold a reference to the *AddressBookManager* and delegate certain calls to it.

Mastery Check

1. What is an external content source?

2. What are two kinds of external content sources?

3. What are four reasons why a JSP application might require integration of external data sources?

4. What two kinds of legacy information sources have Java APIs?

5. Describe the four types of JDBC drivers.

6. What is the purpose of the *java.sql.PreparedStatement* class?

7. What are the primary services provided by JDBC?

8. What is the purpose of the factory pattern?

9. List the steps for using a JDBC *PreparedStatement*.

10. What is the key pattern supporting "pluggable" integration of external content sources?

11. What are the high-level objects in a data model?

Part III

Appendices

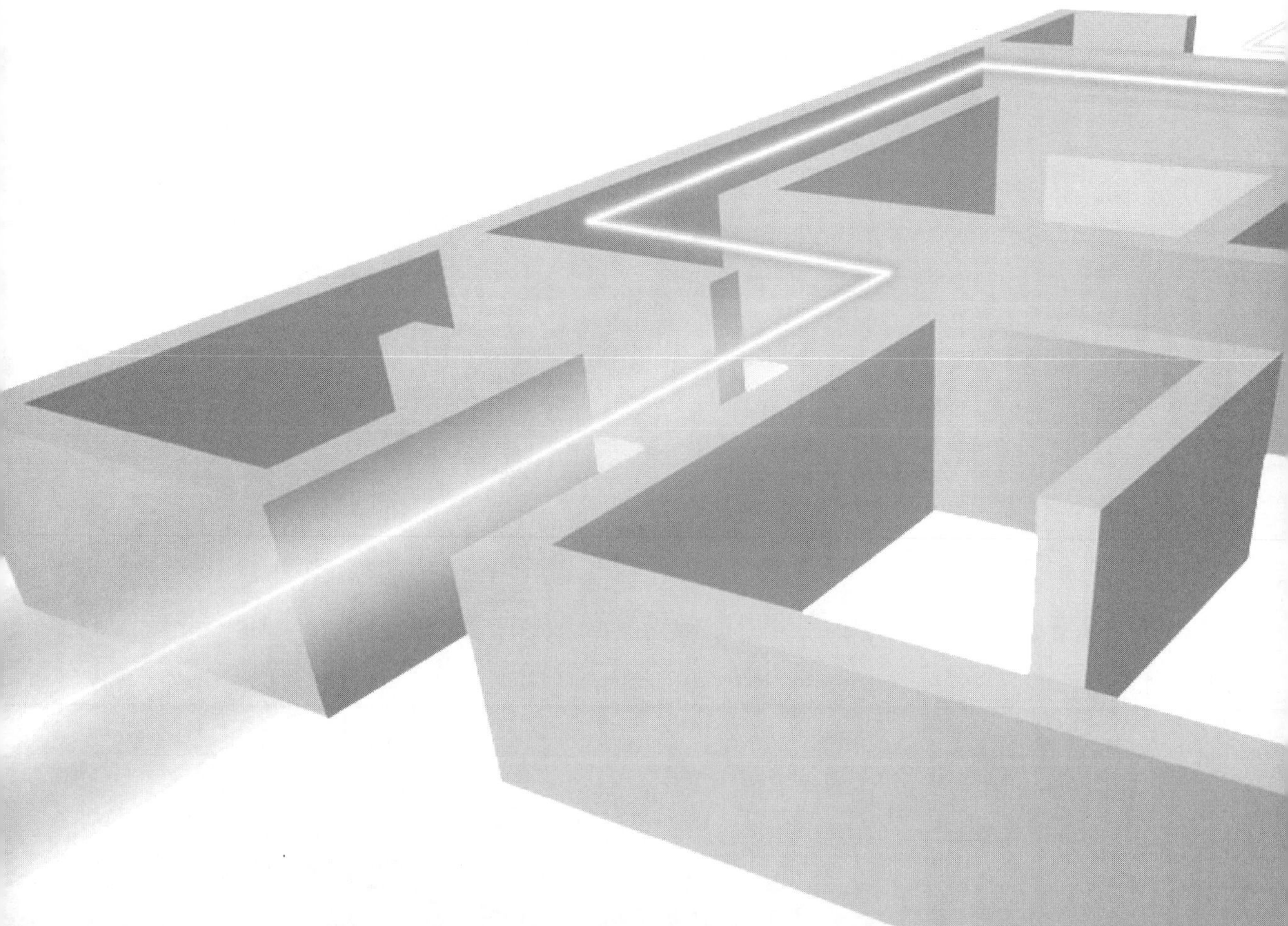

Appendix A

Mastery Check Answers

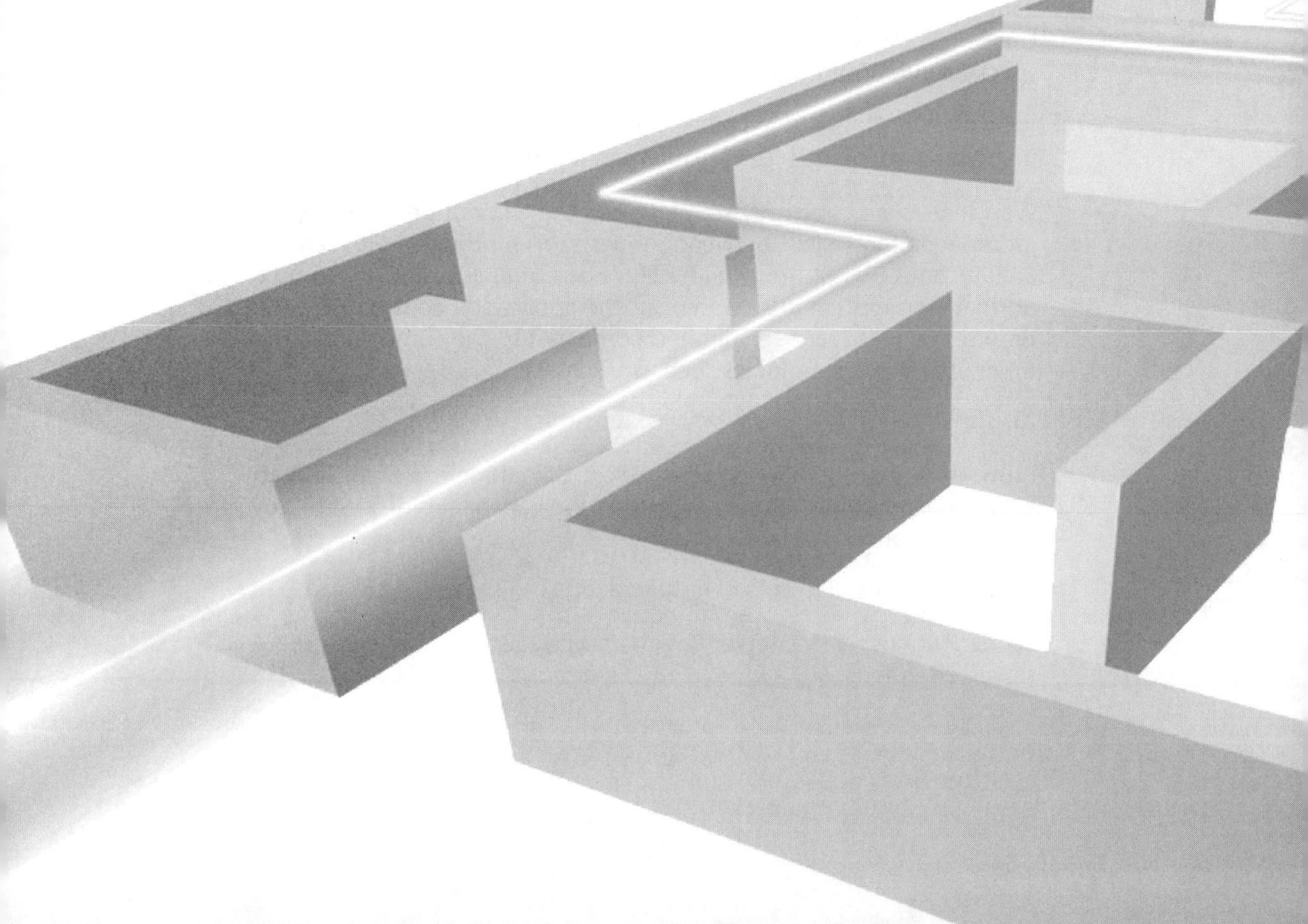

Module 1: Introduction to Internet Technologies

1. HTTP stands for:

   HTTP stands for Hypertext Transfer Protocol.

2. List three computer network traits that make network transparency difficult to achieve.

   - **Latency** The time it takes for requests to travel to servers and responses to travel to clients
   - **Reliability** The likelihood of answers for requests
   - **Concurrency** The execution order of client requests by the server

3. List two types of HTTP requests.

   The two most important types of HTTP requests are GET and POST. GET retrieves a specified Web resource from a remote server. It sends information with the request URI. POST sends and receives data from a remote server. Unlike GET, POST sends the data attached to the end of the request as a special content message.

4. Explain why standard Web browser/Web server architectures fail to provide an adequate basis for many modern Web applications.

   Web servers are essentially stateless; i.e., they do not preserve any "state" information for a client between requests. Web browser/Web server architectures do not provide asynchronous threads of activity common in normal user applications. Moreover, the application controls provided in a browser via HTML are very limited compared to the controls provided by other interface technologies such as Visual Basic.

5. List three types of Web browser extensions:

   Browser plug-ins, JavaScript, and VBScript are three examples of Web browser extensions that help to extend the capabilities of a Web browser as an application interface.

6. List three kinds of Web server extensions:

   Server Plug-ins, Active Server Pages, and JavaServer pages are three Web server extensions.

Module 2: JSP Elements: Comments and Directives

1. What is the problem with this comment declaration?

```
<!-- This variable stores the JSP page context. --!>
```

Output comments start with a `<!--` and end with a `-->` (without a "`!`"). The corrected comment is:

```
<!-- This variable stores the JSP page context. -->
```

2. What is the problem with this comment declaration?

```
<%-- This page was forwarded from <%= sourcePage %>. --%>
```

The JSP container does not send anything between a hidden comment in the response to the client. The JSP expression `<%= sourcePage %>` should not be placed within a hidden comment, since it will never be seen by a client.

3. Your Webmaster has requested that you show a standard logo and a standard title at the top of each JSP page in your Web site. How would you do this without duplicating this information in each JSP page?

You could create a static HTML file that contains the logo and the title and include this HTML file at the top of each JSP page using the include directive.

4. What packages do these page directives import?

```
<%@ page import="java.util.Vector" errorPage="/myError.jsp" %>
<%@ page import="com.mycorp.classes.*, java.util.*, java.text.*" %>
```

These page directives import the following packages:

- *java.util*
- *com.mycorp.classes*
- *java.text*

5. Is there a problem with the JSP page declarations shown here?

```
<%@ page import="java.util.Hashtable" "errorPage=/myError.jsp" %>
<%@ page errorPage="/myError.jsp" %>
```

You can specify the `errorPage` attribute in a page directive only once in a JSP page. The preceding example specifies the attribute in both directives.

6. Can you use a Java class in your JSP page before you specify the page directive that imports it?

Yes, you can. The JSP container translates all packages and/or classes specified in the `import` attribute in page directives into Java `import` statements at the beginning of the translated servlet, regardless of where they appear in the JSP page. We do not recommend such practice, since it is confusing to your JSP page reader.

7. Is this taglib directive valid?

```
<%@ taglib uri="http://www.mywebsite.com/mytags" prefix="" %>
```

The taglib directive is invalid because `prefix` is an empty string. You must provide a prefix string that is not null when you use it in a taglib directive. You must also ensure that the prefix string is unique within that JSP page.

8. Must you specify the taglib directive for your custom tags before you specify them in a JSP page?

Yes, you must specify the taglib directive prior to any occurrence of a custom tag from the tag library declared by that directive.

Module 3: JSP Elements: Scripting Elements

1. Can you find the problem with the following JSP declaration?

```
<%! public String foo() {
        String val = request.getParameter("MyVal");
        return val;
%>
```

JSP declarations can only access variables in object or class scope. They cannot access implicit objects such as the *HttpServletRequest* object *request* that have method scope.

2. What problem does this JSP declaration illustrate?

```
<%! String request = "my request"; %>
```

The declared variable *request* has the same name as the implicit *HttpServletRequest* object *request* that is available in JSP scriptlets and expressions. The declared variable has object scope, whereas the implicit variable has method scope. In Java, a variable that has method scope always takes precedence in a method over a variable with the same name that has object or class scope. Hence the implicit variable *request* completely hides the declared *String* variable *request*. This might not be what the JSP page developer intended.

3. Is there a problem with the following JSP expression?

```
This page was accessed: <%= counter.getNumTimes(); %>.
```

You should not terminate the Java expression inside the JSP expression with a semicolon.

4. What do you see in the following JSP fragment that is cause for worry?

```
<%! Basket basket; %>
<%
   basket = (Basket)session.getAttribute("BASKET");
   if(basket.full()) {
%>
```

A JSP declaration creates the variable *basket*, giving it object scope. A JSP scriptlet assigns this variable a value at request time in the *_jspService* method. Unless you serialize all access to this JSP page (using the isThreadSafe attribute in a page directive), multiple threads could simultaneously modify *basket*, potentially corrupting the variable's value.

5. Is there a better option for the situation in question 4?

There are two ways to avoid the situation in question 4. You can declare *basket* in method scope by including its declaration inside a JSP scriptlet, as shown here:

```
<%
   Basket basket = (Basket)session.getAttribute("BASKET");
   if(basket.full()) {
%>
```

Or you can synchronize *basket*, as shown here:

```
<%! Basket basket; %>
<%
```

```
    synchronized(this) {
        basket = (Basket)session.getAttribute("BASKET");
        if(basket.full()) {
%>
....
<% } %>
```

6. Is there any problem with the following scriptlet?

```
<%
    if(basket.isEmpty()) {
        return basket;
    }
%>
```

A JSP scriptlet cannot return any value, since it translates into a code fragment inside the *_jspService* method of the translated servlet. This *_jspService* method returns `void`.

7. Consider the following scriptlet. Do you see any problems with the way it has been declared?

```
<%
     class LocalClass {
         public String getName() {
               return request.getParameter("Name");
         }
     }
%>
```

The preceding class definition translates into a local inner class inside the *_jspService* method of the translated servlet for this JSP page. A standard restriction imposed on a local inner classes in a Java method is that they can access only local variables that you declare `final`. The method *getName* in our inner class accesses the implicit variable `request`. This variable is not declared `final`, so this script throws a translation-time error.

8. Would the following scriptlet function as you intended?

```
<% if(time.before9AM() || time.after6PM()) %>
        Sorry, our office hours are <%= officeHours %>
```

When you mix Java code with HTML in a conditional, you must enclose the conditional block between braces. This is because what appears as a single statement inside our conditional block actually translates into multiple statements in the translated servlet. So, the correct syntax would be:

```
<% if(time.before9AM() || time.after6PM()) { %>
        Sorry, our office hours are <%= officeHours %>
<% } %>
```

Module 4: Implicit Objects

1. List the implicit objects.

The implicit objects are:

Variable Name	**Description**
request	Provides preparsed HTTP requests
response	Encapsulates HTTP response
pageContext	Encapsulates vendor-specific features. Provides convenience methods to access information from multiple scopes and retrieve other implicit objects. Supplies *forward*, *include*, and *handlePageException* methods
session	Provides mechanism for tracking clients across multiple service requests
application	Provides a set of methods to access Web server information and to write messages to the servlet log file
out	Encapsulates means to write into the HTTP response buffer
config	Supplies initialization parameters
page	A synonym for "this" in the page body
exception	The uncaught *Throwable* passed to an error page

2. In what sense are the implicit objects implicit?

The objects are implicit in the sense that the JSP page developer need not declare them before using them. The variables are automatically available to the developer in JSP scriptlets and JSP expressions in his JSP page.

3. Which implicit object provides access to the application context? Which provides access to the request parameters?

The implicit object *application* provides access to the application context. The implicit object *request* provides access to the request parameters.

4. Why does the JSP container provide a factory method to create the *pageContext* object?

The *PageContext* class is abstract, so JSP container vendors must extend it. You retrieve other implicit objects using methods provided in the *PageContext* subclass. The intention is for container vendors to provide a custom implementation of the *PageContext* object, which returns optimized versions of other implicit objects. A factory method (a creational design pattern) provides the ability for container vendors to return their own custom implementation of the *PageContext* class.

5. Why cannot JavaServer Pages stream binary content?

A JSP container automatically assigns the *JspWriter* (which emulates a *java.io.PrintWriter*), that can send only character data, to the *out* implicit object. This prevents a JSP page from streaming binary content to a client.

6. How does a JSP page developer pass information from one request to another?

A JSP page developer can use the implicit object *session* that refers to the *HttpSession* object to pass information between requests. An *HttpSession* object overcomes the stateless behavior of HTTP by keeping track of a client's information between requests through one of several mechanisms.

7. What are the different ways to pass control from one JSP page to another?

You can *forward, include,* or *redirect* control from one JSP page to another using the *pageContext* implicit object. A *forward* replaces the current page with the destination page. An *include* includes a JSP fragment in the current page. You use a *redirection* in abnormal situations involving exceptions.

8. What are some different ways to track sessions in servlets and JavaServer Pages?

You can track sessions using any of the following mechanisms:

- **URL Rewriting** Session data is added to the end of every URL path for every request participating in a session.
- **Cookies** A special persistent file is installed on the client machine as a cookie.
- **SSL Sessions** The Secure Sockets Layer technology provides a one-time only master key that is used by Servlets and JavaServer Pages to maintain session identity and encrypting and decrypting messages.

9. Why would you want to track sessions in a JSP application?

Your JSP application might need to track sessions if it preserves client information between successive requests from a client machine. For instance, if you are writing an e-commerce application involving a shopping basket into which a client adds items while visiting multiple pages, you might need to track the basket in that client's session.

10. What is the purpose of the *exception* implicit object?

An *exception* implicit object provides access to exceptions inside error JSP pages. This allows for your application to determine the error situation that caused transfer to a given error page.

Module 5: Standard Actions

1. What is the error in this use of `<jsp:useBean>`?

```
<jsp:useBean id="myHelperBean"
             scope="session"
             type="StringProperty" >
<jsp:setProperty name="myHelperBean"
                 property="stringProperty"
                 value="The String Property" />
The String property value is:
   <jsp:getProperty name="myHelperBean"
                    property="stringProperty"/>
```

The `<jsp:useBean>` action either needs to have an empty body or should enclose its body with an end tag `</jsp:useBean>`. In the example, if we consider the `<jsp:setProperty>` standard action to be within the body of the `<jsp:useBean>` action, the proper syntax for it would be:

```
<jsp:useBean id="myHelperBean"
             scope="session"
             type="StringProperty" >
    <jsp:setProperty name="myHelperBean"
                 property="stringProperty"
                 value="The String Property" />
</jsp:useBean>
The String property value is:
   <jsp:getProperty name="myHelperBean"
                    property="stringProperty"/>
```

(Notice the end tag in bold.)

2. How do you set a login name property of type *String* on a helper JavaBean using a request parameter?

   Assuming you name the property "stringProperty" and the request parameter "loginName", you use the `<jsp:setProperty>` standard action like this:

```
<jsp:setProperty name="myHelperBean"
                 property="stringProperty"
                 param="loginName"
/>
```

3. What is the constraint on the Java property types you can initialize using the `<jsp:setProperty>` action?

   If you retrieve the value of a Java property from an HTTP request parameter, then the type of the property has to be a type that you can convert from *String* literals. If you retrieve the value from a JSP expression, then the JSP container enforces no restrictions on the type of the property.

4. What attributes of standard actions can take a JSP expression as their value?

   The following table shows the attributes that can take a JSP expression as their value:

Action Type	Attributes
`<jsp:setProperty>`	value and beanName
`<jsp:include>`	page
`<jsp:forward>`	page
`<jsp:param>`	value

5. Why would you use a JSP expression to set the value of an attribute?

   A JSP expression provides the ability to calculate attribute values dynamically at request time.

6. How do you create a JSP page template using the `<jsp:include>` action?

   You can construct a page layout template from a JSP page (say, `pageTemplate.jsp`) that uses the `<jsp:include>` action for the parameterized sections of the template. You retrieve the pages for these `<jsp:include>` actions from request parameters. Here is an example:

```
<TABLE BORDER="2">
   <TR><TD>
   <jsp:include
```

```
          page='<%= request.getParameter("Cell1") %>'
          flush="true" />
   </TD></TR>
   <TR><TD>
   <jsp:include
          page='<%= request.getParameter("Cell2") %>'
          flush="true" />
   </TD></TR>
</TABLE>
```

There are two parameterized sections, "Cell1" and "Cell2". There can be many instantiations of this template with different values for Cell1 and Cell2. Here is an example:

```
<jsp:include page="pageTemplate.jsp" flush="true" >
     <jsp:param name="Cell1" value="Cell1.jsp" />
     <jsp:param name="Cell2" value="Cell2.jsp" />
</jsp:include>
```

7. What `<jsp:plugin>` attributes map directly into HTML tags?

The attributes code, codebase, align, archive, height, hspace, name, vspace, title, and width in the `<jsp:plugin>` action map directly into HTML tags.

8. What JSP tags can qualify the behavior of the `<jsp:plugin>` tag?

The `<jsp:params>` and `<jsp:fallback>` tags qualify the behavior of the `<jsp:plugin>` tag.

9. Why can't you print output to the JSP response buffer prior to using the `<jsp:forward>` action?

A `<jsp:forward>` provides for the runtime dispatch of the current request to another Web resource terminating the execution of the current page. Any output written in the current page is cleared from the output buffer before the dispatch occurs. If some output has already been sent to the client, a forward is then illegal. Hence, it is not valid to write any output to the response prior to a `<jsp:forward>`.

10. What is the purpose of the `<jsp:param>` action?

A `<jsp:param>` action provides name/value information. You normally use it in conjunction with other standard actions such as `<jsp:include>`, `<jsp:forward>`, and `<jsp:plugin>` to provide auxiliary information for these actions. It has no effect when used independently.

Module 6: Tag Libraries

1. What advantages do custom tags provide JSP developers?

Custom tags provide a specialized sublanguage for JSP developers to insert dynamic functionality in their Web pages. They separate business logic from presentation detail more cleanly than do JSP constructs such as scriptlets, expressions, and declarations. They make a JSP page easier to maintain, since they eliminate Java code in the JSP page. They make a JSP page more readable, since their syntax follows XML syntax rules that are similar to HTML. Packaging them as a tag library provides a single point to extend, test, and correct business services provided by them.

2. What are the main elements of a custom action or tag library?

A tag library contains the following four main elements:

- The definition of the custom actions (i.e., the tags)
- The taglib directive
- The tag library descriptor
- The tag handlers

3. What two types of tag interfaces can a tag developer implement?

A tag developer can implement the following interfaces for a tag handler:

- The *javax.servlet.jsp.tagext.Tag* interface that defines the protocol for a simple tag handler that is not interested in manipulating its body.
- The *javax.servlet.jsp.tagext.BodyTag* interface that defines the protocol for a tag handler that intends to access its tag body.

4. Can a tag handler call the *pageContext.include* method in its *doAfterBody* method?

The *doAfterBody* method is invoked after every body evaluation inside a *BodyTag* handler. Each custom tag with a body is associated with a *BodyContent* object. This *BodyContent* object, a subclass of *JspWriter*, is an "unbounded" buffer that is used to process body evaluations. The *BodyContent* object cannot be flushed, since there is no backing stream that sends its contents to a client. The JSP page pushes a *BodyContent* object for each nested custom tag into a stack maintained by the *pageContext* object. The *JspWriter* that is connected to the client is the item at the bottom of this stack. It is visible only after all the nested tag bodies have been evaluated.

A *pageContext.include* results in an automatic flush of the *JspWriter*. But inside a *doAfterBody* method, the *JspWriter* at the top of the stack is a *BodyContent* object that cannot be flushed. Therefore, it is illegal to invoke the *pageContext.include* method inside a *doAfterBody* method.

5. How does a tag library developer specify that you can provide the value of a tag attribute using a JSP expression?

The `<attribute>` element in the tag library descriptor has an optional subelement `<rtexprvalue>`. A value of `true` inside this element declares that this attribute can take a JSP expression as its value. An example is shown here:

```
<attribute>
   <name>myAttribute</name>
   <required>true</required>
   <rtexprvalue>true</rtexprvalue>
</attribute>
```

6. What is the role of the *BodyContent* object?

The *BodyContent* object is available to *BodyTag* handlers as a property. It is used to process tag bodies in a custom action.

7. What are the roles of the *TagExtraInfo* class?

A custom action uses a subclass of the *TagExtraInfo* abstract class to inform the JSP container about scripting variables that it defines. The class can also optionally provide a translation-time validation method for the attributes specified in the custom action.

8. What are the two recommended ways to share data between custom actions?

The JSP specification recommends two mechanisms for sharing data between custom actions:

- Object ids stored in global data
- Object scoping

9. What is the role of the tag library descriptor?

The tag library descriptor is an XML document that describes the tag library. The JSP container parses the descriptor and gets a comprehensive description of each custom action in that tag library.

10. How do you specify the tag handler class for a custom action?

A tag handler class is specified by the `<tagclass>` subelement within the `<tag>` element that describes the custom action. An example is shown here:

```
<tag>
      <name>readInterestType</name>
      <tagclass>sample.ReadRequestTag</tagclass>
      <teiclass>sample.ReadRequestTEI</teiclass>
      <bodycontent>empty</bodycontent>
      <info> Extracts request parameters </info>
</tag>
```

11. What is the role of the *release* method in the *Tag* interface?

The *release* method in a tag handler is used to release any resources that the tag handler might be holding. The container calls it (via the generated servlet) after all the invocations of the tag handler have completed.

12. When and how many times does the generated servlet call the *doInitBody* method? What is the purpose of the *doInitBody* method?

The *doInitBody* method is called exactly once for each occurrence of a custom action with body in a JSP page. It is called before the *first* time the body is to be evaluated. The *BodyTag* handler can use this method to initialize resources that are necessary while handling the body of the custom action.

13. How does a custom action developer specify that a tag attribute is optional?

The `<attribute>` element in the tag library descriptor has an optional subelement `<required>`. A value of `false` inside this element declares that this attribute is optional. An example is shown here:

```
<attribute>
   <name>myAttribute</name>
   <required>false</required>
   <rtexprvalue>true</rtexprvalue>
</attribute>
```

Module 7: JSP Architectures

1. List three ways in which software patterns help develop quality applications.

Patterns provide a vocabulary for describing development projects, thereby enabling more concise communication between developers. Patterns teach good software design practices that produce elegant, adaptable, and reusable software. Patterns facilitate debate about solutions to problem contexts, thereby helping in problem analysis.

2. How long have software patterns been part of the environment for software development?

The general idea of patterns as applied to software development has been prevalent since the early 1990s.

3. What are some important themes that have emerged from the general discussion about software patterns?

Patterns name and explain solutions to recurring practical problems. They are not academic inventions; rather, they are a kind of received wisdom from a community of problem solvers. This makes them demonstrably useful. Patterns function as "idea factories" crossing multiple problem domains.

4. What are some different types of information systems architectures and what are the respective roles that they play?

The types of information systems architectures are:

- **Physical architecture** Defines the hardware and the network infrastructure on which the application runs.
- **System architecture** Defines the software infrastructure within which the application runs.
- **Database architecture** Defines the data model for an application.
- **Application software architecture** Defines the software elements of an application and the flow of data between them.

5. What are some advantages of three-tier architectures over two-tier architectures and in what contexts are such advantages important?

The three-tier architecture scales better and is more flexible than single-tier or two-tier architectures. But the addition of a network layer slows performance and makes support and troubleshooting more complex. This additional complexity might be overkill for simple desktop and workgroup applications. But Internet applications are usually better off using three tiers rather than two.

6. Why would a Web application architect choose the MVC pattern?

The MVC pattern cleanly partitions a Web application into separate data management (model), presentation (view), and control components. It thereby encourages independent evolution and reuse of the separate components. It also makes better use of other patterns such as the mediator, command, strategy, and bridge.

7. What is the purpose of the mediator pattern in software architecture?

This mediator pattern controls interactions between software subsystems by encapsulating related functionality behind a manager object that separates messages with purely internal relevance from messages that must pass outward to other subsystems. This dramatically reduces hard-coded communication paths between components and converts these dependencies to decision rules.

8. Why would a Web application designer introduce the command pattern?

The *command* pattern wraps an operation (behavior) in an object so that you can register it for execution by a different object. In a Web application, the command pattern helps you separate behavior from control logic, thereby allowing changes to the behavior independent of the changes to the control logic. By providing an encapsulation on the operation that is performed, it makes the operation easily interchangeable. It also enables a separation between the model and the application environment in which the model services are invoked, thereby making the model reusable in other application environments.

9. What is the purpose of the bridge pattern and why might this be important to Web application designers?

The *bridge* pattern decouples an abstract interface from its implementations. By insulating the client from implementation detail, it enables pluggable architectures—an architecture that supports different implementations of the same abstract functionality. In a Web application, the model is a good candidate to follow the bridge pattern so that one can have multiple, pluggable implementations of the model's services.

10. How does the strategy pattern work together with the command pattern to manage web-flow in a JSP architecture?

The *strategy* pattern defines a family of algorithms and encapsulates each algorithm in an object. The controller servlet in a Web application uses a strategy to drive the web-flow that maps application messages to requested operations. You should encapsulate such requests as commands as in a command pattern.

Module 8: JSP Security

1. Which of the security services addresses the problem of spoofing? What is spoofing?

Integrity addresses the problem of spoofing. It refers to the process whereby an application confirms that messages sent from a user were not modified during transit. Spoofing refers to the possibility of modifying a message in transit, thereby fooling a recipient into providing confidential information.

2. What is a security interceptor? How do interceptors work?

A security interceptor is a security handler that intercepts requests for Web resources from a user and forces them to authenticate before forwarding them to the requested resource.

The security interceptor is registered with the JSP container in a configuration file. Then, the Web application, in its deployment descriptor, defines the protected area as a list of URL patterns. Whenever a user attempts to access this protected area, the interceptor intercepts the request and redirects to a login page (that could be custom or built-in) requiring the user to authenticate.

3. Where do you configure the security realm in Tomcat?

You configure the security realm using the `<RequestInterceptor>` element in the `server.xml` file located under `%TOMCAT_HOME%\conf\`. Here is Tomcat's default realm specification:

```
<RequestInterceptor
 className="org.apache.tomcat.request.SimpleRealm"
 debug="0" />
```

4. Where do you configure the security realm in the Apache Web server?

In Apache, you configure a security realm using the `<Directory>` block directive in the `httpd.conf` file. An example is shown here:

```
<Directory "E:/Apache/htdocs/controlled/wsolney">
   AuthType Basic
   AuthName "wsolney"
   AuthGroupFile "E:/Apache/login/wsolney/groups"
   AuthUserFile "E/Apache/login/wsolney/users"
   require valid-user
</Directory>
```

5. Which of the security services do you consider most fundamental? What are your reasons?

Authentication could be considered the most fundamental of the security services. User authentication establishes the identity of the user who wishes access to the application. All other security services presuppose that an identified user is requesting services.

6. What do "rings of trust" represent?

Rings of trust represent a clustering of various security policy domains or realms based upon the degree of security required.

7. What are some reasons not to use the default security mechanism of Tomcat?

The default security mechanism in Tomcat stores passwords in clear text on the file system. A simple text file that stores users and passwords is hard to manage when the number of users grows large. Also, the default security handler caches the authentication database in memory, needlessly consuming a precious resource.

8. What kind of structure does an LDAP service give its repository?

The LDAP service stores information as entries in a tree structure in its repository.

9. Where do you define access control for roles in Tomcat?

The file `tomcat-users.xml` located under `%TOMCAT_HOME%\conf` defines the users and roles. Your Web application in its deployment descriptor, while identifying a protected area, can specify the roles to which users should belong when accessing the protected area. This is done using the `<auth-constraint>` element. A sample is shown here:

```
<security-constraint>
   <web-resource-collection>
      <web-resource-name>Protected Area
      </web-resource-name>
      <!-- Define the context-relative URL(s)
             to be protected
      -->
      <url-pattern>/jsp/security/protected/*
      </url-pattern>
      <!-- If you list http methods, only
           those methods are protected
      -->
```

```
        <http-method>DELETE</http-method>
        <http-method>GET</http-method>
        <http-method>POST</http-method>
        <http-method>PUT</http-method>
    </web-resource-collection>
    <auth-constraint>
        <!-- Anyone with one of the listed
             roles may access this area
        -->
        <role-name>tomcat</role-name>
        <role-name>role1</role-name>
    </auth-constraint>
</security-constraint>
```

10. What is a *certificate authority*? What role does it play in security architectures?

When certificate-based authentication is in effect, the certificates use public-key/private-key encryption to establish identity. A *certificate authority* is a corporation that can vouch for the identity information stored in a security certificate. Certificate authorities have legal liabilities associated with their certificates, making their testimonies trustworthy.

11. How does the challenge-response mechanism work in security architectures?

In a challenge-response negotiation, the client first requests access to a specific resource. If access to the resource is controlled, the security mechanism intercepts this request and returns an authorization error. The client can then respond with authorization credentials. If the client provides sufficient credentials, the security mechanism allows the request. If not, the security mechanism returns another authorization error.

12. What is the Secure Hash Algorithm? What is one use for such hash functions in Web architectures?

The Secure Hash Algorithm generates a binary signature for a binary input. The algorithm ensures that it would be practically impossible to guess at or spoof the input from the generated signature.

In Web architectures, the sender uses the Secure Hash Algorithm to generate an encrypted message digest that he stores in the message. The recipient generates the same digest with her inputs. By comparing the digests, the recipient can tell that the message was not tampered with. This mechanism guarantees message integrity.

Module 9: Controller and Flow Control in Web Applications

1. Why should you consider it a poor design to make each Web resource aware of the next page(s) or stage(s) in the workflow?

Coding page transitions directly into Web resources becomes a maintenance nightmare when the number of pages multiply. Such a scenario is hard to modify, and page designers must wade through unnecessary page flow logic in JSP and HTML pages.

2. Consider the following model interface and explain what is wrong:

```
public boolean isCreditApproved(HttpServletRequest request);
public void debitCreditCard(HttpSession session);
```

The model methods are aware of the *HttpServletRequest* and *HttpSession* objects. This ties them inextricably to the HTTP environment, making it unusable in any other environment.

3. What does a command object encapsulate in a Web application workflow?

A command object encapsulates a distinct operation in a Web application workflow.

4. What is a common format for storing web-flow information in a Web application and why?

A configuration file in the XML format lends itself as a natural fit for storing web-flow information. This is because it is easily modifiable, can easily be persisted as a file, and has a structured format.

5. When designing a flexible Web workflow, is it sufficient just to centralize all stage transition logic in a controller servlet?

Centralizing all stage transitions in a controller servlet does not in itself provide a flexible Web workflow. A configurable resource should be used to specify the workflow, and this resource should be dynamically loaded by the controller servlet.

6. How is a chain-based web-flow different from regular web-flow?

In a regular web-flow, the controller servlet is aware of the action requested and maps this action to a stage in the web-flow. In a chain-based web-flow, the controller servlet is also aware of the current chain of activity and, using this knowledge, it is able to forward control to different destinations for the same actions. This makes the stages reusable in multiple web-flows.

Module 10: Integrating a Database

1. What is an external content source?

An external content source is any *centrally organized and accessible collection of digital content not directly managed by the application.* This includes standard relational databases, SAP R/3 systems, or even COBOL finance programs.

2. What are two kinds of external content sources?

The two kinds of external content sources are standard relational databases and legacy information systems such as SAP R/3.

3. What are four reasons why a JSP application might require integration of external data sources?

A JSP application might integrate an external data source:

- To organize and manage very large amounts of content reliably
- To centralize, secure, and share information
- To provide dynamic content to applications
- To access legacy information systems

4. What two kinds of legacy information sources have Java APIs?

Java APIs exist for accessing SQL databases (e.g., ORACLE) and enterprise information systems (e.g., PeopleSoft).

5. Describe the four types of JDBC drivers.

The four types of JDBC drivers are:

- **Type 1** Accessing an ODBC (Open database connectivity) driver
- **Type 2** Mapping JDBC calls to the native client side API of the database vendor
- **Type 3** Mapping JDBC calls into a middleware vendor's protocol (which is then translated by a middleware server into a DBMS protocol)
- **Type 4** Mapping JDBC calls directly into the database protocol

6. What is the purpose of the *java.sql.PreparedStatement* class?

The *java.sql.PreparedStatment* (derived from *java.sql.Statement*) provides the ability to invoke parameterized queries. The *PreparedStatement* prepares a SQL string that includes the question mark character (?) to represent substitutable values. This allows for the query to be reused on multiple invocations of the same query with different values for the parameters.

7. What are the primary services provided by JDBC?

The primary services provided by JDBC are:

- Connection services
- SQL services
- Result processing

8. What is the purpose of the factory pattern?

A factory provides a method to create an object. In an API framework, a factory is used to defer responsibility for *what* object to create, removing this responsibility from the framework. This allows for simultaneous support of multiple implementations of a function.

9. List the steps for using a JDBC *PreparedStatement*.

The steps for using a *PreparedStatement* are:

- Create a *PreparedStatement*
- Set the parameterized values
- Execute the database call
- Loop through the *ResultSet*

10. What is the key pattern supporting "pluggable" integration of external content sources?

The bridge pattern is the key pattern supporting "pluggable" integration of external content sources.

11. What are the high-level objects in a data model?

The high-level objects in a data model are:

- **Entity types** Any type of object within the area being modeled
- **Attributes** An item of information describing an entity occurrence
- **Relationships** A type of association between entity occurrences

Appendix B

Creating a Development and Deployment Environment

Goals of This Appendix

- Be able to install the Apache Web server and the Tomcat servlet/JSP container
- Know why we picked Tomcat (and optionally Apache) as the environment for this book
- Build a Web Application directory structure and generate a WAR file for deployment in multiple Web environments
- Configure Apache and Tomcat to communicate with each other when handling servlets and JavaServer Pages

In order to develop JavaServer Pages, we must establish a server-side environment that interprets, compiles, and executes the pages that we write. This appendix explains how to install and configure a development environment for JavaServer Pages. It also explains how to package your JavaServer Pages into a deployment package.

Web Servers and Containers

JavaServer Pages provide a server technology to generate dynamic Web pages. Like servlets, they extend the functionality of a Web server. Some popular Web servers are Apache, Microsoft IIS, and Sun Microsystems iPlanet. These industrial-strength servers provide features that support high scalability and improved performance. To support servlets and JavaServer Pages, such Web servers rely on special applications called *servlet and JSP containers.*

Containers are special Java classes to which the Web server directs HTTP requests when the resource requested is a servlet or JSP page. Such containers manage one or more Java virtual machines (JVMs) to execute the servlets and JavaServer Pages. Some containers (e.g., Tomcat) support both stand-alone and hybrid configurations. Support for the stand-alone configuration means the container provides a Web server as well as the servlet and JSP containers. All of our book projects assume Tomcat in this stand-alone configuration.

Web servers handle static resources best, while servlet and JSP containers handle servlets and JavaServer Pages best. This means the hybrid configuration can improve response times and scalability. In the hybrid configuration, the Web server redirects requests for servlets and JavaServer Pages through an adapter to the servlet container. You need not set up this hybrid configuration to do the book projects, but you can. Figure B-1 shows the hybrid configuration.

JavaSoft has a table of currently available servlet containers at the URL: `http://java.sun.com/products/servlet/industry.html`. The table also lists the servlet and JSP specification versions these containers support. Most current containers support the Servlet 2.2 specification and the JSP 1.1 specification.

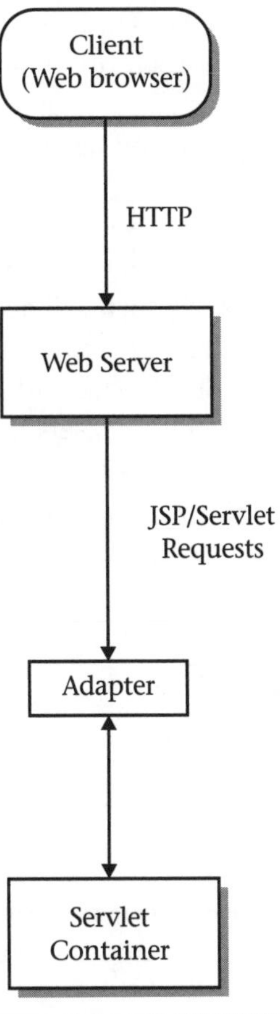

Figure B-1 Web Server and container interaction

Apache and Tomcat

The Apache Software Foundation (`http://www.apache.org`) is an open source, not-for-profit organization with members all around the world. It funds, organizes, and sustains several important software projects.

The Apache HTTP Server is the best-known Apache project. The Apache Web server currently supports more than half the Web server market (`http://www.netcraft.com/survey`). It runs on most desktop and server operating systems including major UNIX variants and Microsoft Windows NT/2000.

The Apache Software Foundation also supports the Jakarta servlet and JavaServer Pages project with the mission "to provide commercial-quality server solutions based on the Java Platform." The Jakarta project provides the Tomcat servlet and JSP container. Tomcat is the official JavaSoft-endorsed reference implementation for the Servlet 2.2 and JSP 1.1 specifications.

While you can run both the Apache Web server and Tomcat on many different platforms, we have chosen Windows NT/2000 as the platform for this book. JavaServer Pages is a Java technology requiring a JVM. Our book assumes that you have installed version 1.3 of the Java Development Kit (JDK).

Installing Tomcat

If you have not yet installed the JDK 1.3, download it from `http://java.sun.com/j2se/1.3`. Install the JDK into a directory on your machine.

You can download both Tomcat source and a Tomcat binary distribution. We will install a binary distribution. Tomcat provides Milestone, Nightly, and Release builds of the software. The Release build is the most robust and most compatible implementation. Download the latest Release build of Tomcat from their Web site: `http://jakarta.apache.org/site/binindex.html`. The download file is a WinZip file with the name *jakarta-tomcat-#.zip*, where the # character is the version number. You can install Tomcat in four simple steps:

1. Unzip the downloaded file under a Tomcat home directory. The contents of this directory should look something like this:

```
E:\Pkgs\tomcat\jakarta-tomcat-3.2.1>dir
 Volume in drive E is CHACHU
 Volume Serial Number is 1321-17F0
 Directory of E:\Pkgs\tomcat\jakarta-tomcat-3.2.1
12/16/2000  07:33p      <DIR>          .
12/16/2000  07:33p      <DIR>          ..
12/12/2000  01:36p               2,811 LICENSE
12/12/2000  01:39p      <DIR>          webapps
12/12/2000  01:36p      <DIR>          conf
```

```
12/12/2000  01:36p      <DIR>          doc
12/12/2000  01:37p      <DIR>          lib
12/12/2000  01:36p      <DIR>          bin
12/12/2000  01:36p      <DIR>          src
12/12/2000  01:36p      <DIR>          logs
12/16/2000  07:45p      <DIR>          work
               1 File(s)          2,811 bytes
              10 Dir(s)   5,683,662,848 bytes free
```

Here are the important subdirectories:

- *bin* Batch scripts for startup and shutdown (`startup.bat`, `shutdown.bat`) of the servlet container
- *logs* Runtime logs for the container
- *conf* Configuration files including the main configuration file: `server.xml`
- *webapps* Web application deployment directory
- *work* Intermediate files (such as compiled servlets from JSP pages)
- *doc* General documentation about Tomcat such as a user's guide

2. Create a new environment variable called *TOMCAT_HOME* and point it to the Tomcat home directory (`E:\pkgs\tomcat\jakarta-tomcat-3.2.1` in the example for this exercise).

3. Set the environment variable *JAVA_HOME* to point to the root directory of the JDK hierarchy.

Note

Tomcat and other Servlet containers require the Java compilation tools normally packaged with the JDK to compile the generated servlets from JSPs.

4. Set the *%PATH%* environment variable to include the Java interpreter (`java.exe`).

Starting and Stopping Tomcat

You start Tomcat using *startup.bat*, located in `%TOMCAT_HOME%\bin`. So go to `%TOMCAT_HOME%\bin` and invoke the batch script like this:

```
E:\>cd pkgs\tomcat\jakarta-tomcat-3.2.1\bin
E:\pkgs\tomcat\jakarta-tomcat-3.2.1> startup
```

You should see a console window pop up with several messages on it as shown in Figure B-2.

To ensure that Tomcat is running properly, start a Web browser and enter the URL: `http://localhost:8080`. You should see a page on your browser as shown in Figure B-3.

By default, Tomcat runs on network port 8080. The default document root for Tomcat is that of the "ROOT" Web application and is physically located at `%TOMCAT_HOME%\webapps\ROOT`. We explain Web applications in the next section.

To shutdown Tomcat, use the script `shutdown.bat` located in `%TOMCAT_HOME%\bin`. This shuts down Tomcat and removes the Tomcat console window.

Web Applications and the WAR Format

A Web application includes many different components:

- Servlets
- JavaServer Pages
- Java utility classes
- HTML files
- Images and sounds
- Applets

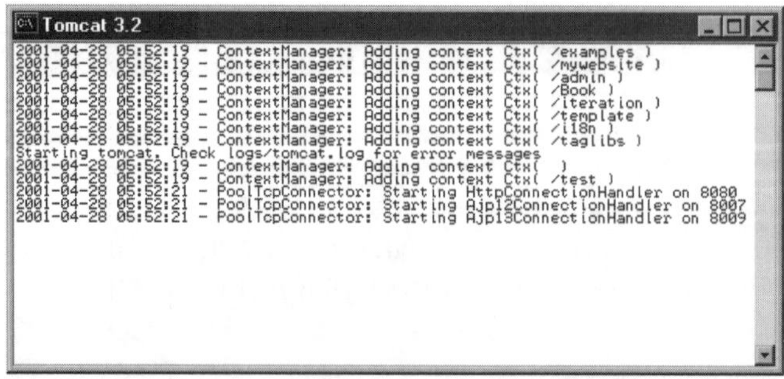

Figure B-2 Startup window for Tomcat

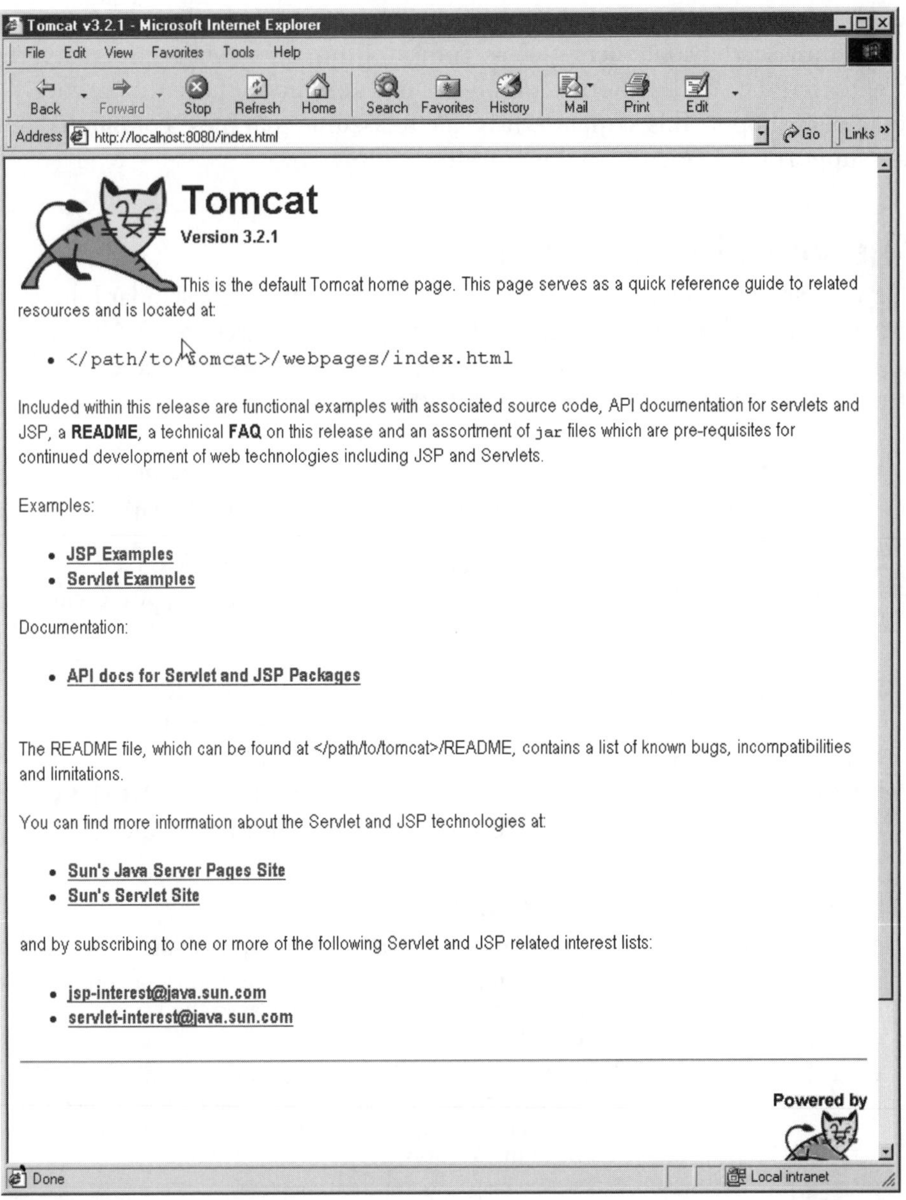

Figure B-3 Initial page for Tomcat

Beginning with the Servlet 2.2 specification, JavaSoft introduced a standard for organizing all of these Web application components. If you follow the standard, you help ensure that you can deploy your Web application in any conforming servlet containers such as Tomcat, JRun, or WebLogic. It is important to note that the specification recommends but does not require that servlet containers support this standard. It is safe to assume that most containers will support this standard, and many already do.

The WAR Directory Structure

The Web application (webapp) deployment conventions use a standard directory structure from which you can create a Web application archive (WAR) file. You do this using the Java utility `jar.exe` to *jar together* the deployed directory structure. Here are the features of this directory structure:

1. You store all files for a Web application under a root directory. This root directory also serves as the document root for this webapp.
2. You store all application files (e.g., JavaServer Pages, HTML pages, and images) directly under the application root. Typically, you create subdirectories for each resource type.
3. There must be a special directory named "WEB-INF" under the root directory that contains information to tie application files together. The specification requires that you cannot serve any of the files in the `WEB-INF` directory as a resource to a client request. Table B-1 shows the contents of the `WEB-INF` directory as listed in the specification:

WEB-INF contents	Description
`/WEB-INF/Web.xml`	The deployment descriptor for the application
`/WEB-INF/classes/*`	A directory for Java utility classes. The container automatically loads these classes. They need not be in the `%CLASSPATH%` of the container
`/WEB-INF/lib/*.jar`	A directory for Java ARchive (JAR) files that contain servlets, JavaBeans, and other utility classes for the Web application. The container automatically loads these classes. They need not be in the `%CLASSPATH%` of the container

Table B-1 Contents of WEB-INF

4. An example might help illustrate the directory structure. Consider a root directory %TOMCAT_HOME%\webapps\eCommerce. The directory structure for this simple application looks like this:
   - /welcome.html
   - /jsp/Inventory.jsp
   - /jsp/Receipt.jsp
   - /images/logo.gif
   - /WEB-INF/classes/CustomerServlet.class
   - /WEB-INF/web.xml

Creating a WAR File

You can package the contents of a Web application directory structure using the standard Java archiving tools into a Web ARchive format (WAR) file. Here are the simple commands that do this with the directory structure we showed in the previous section:

```
%> cd E:\pkgs\tomcat\jakarta-tomcat-3.2.1\webapps\eCommerce
%> jar cvf ../eCommerce.war *
```

The Web Application Deployment Descriptor

Before you can deploy a Web application, you must place a deployment descriptor (Web.xml) into the application's WEB-INF directory. This file ties together all the components of a Web application. The Servlet 2.2 specification provides details for creating the deployment descriptor. Let's look at a simple example:

```
<!DOCTYPE Web-app PUBLIC "-//Sun Microsystems, Inc.//DTD Web
Application 2.2//EN"
http://java.sun.com/j2ee/dtds/Web-app_2_2.dtd>
<web-app>
   <display-name>My E-Commerce Web site</display-name>
   <servlet>
      <servlet-name>Customer</servlet-name>
      <servlet-class>myClasses.CustomerServlet</servlet-class>
```

```
        <init-param>
            <param-name>catalog</param-name>
            <param-value>Spring</param-value>
        </init-param>
    </servlet>
    <servlet-mapping>
        <servlet-name>Customer</servlet-name>
        <url-pattern>/customer/*</url-pattern>
    </servlet-mapping>
    <session-config>
        <session-timeout>30</session-timeout>
    </session-config>
    <welcome-file-list>
        <welcome-file>welcome.html</welcome-file>
    </welcome-file-list>
    <error-page>
        <error-code>404</error-code>
        <location>/404.html</location>
    </error-page>
</web-app>
```

This simple deployment descriptor illustrates these important points:

1. The `<web-app>` element is the root element for the deployment descriptor.
2. The `<display-name>` element specifies that "My E-Commerce Web site" is the displayable name of this Web application in GUI tools.
3. The `<servlet>` element and its subelements provide a name for a servlet used by this Web application. That name is "Customer." Its fully qualified class name is *myClasses.CustomerServlet*, and it gets an initial parameter named "catalog" with the value "Spring." You can retrieve this parameter using the *application* implicit object variable, which we describe in Module 4.
4. The `<servlet-mapping>` element states that the URL pattern `/customer/*` is mapped to the servlet *Customer*.
5. The `<session-config>` element states that the default timeout interval for all sessions created in this Web application is 30 minutes.
6. The `<welcome-file-list>` states that `welcome.html` should be automatically loaded when our Web application is first accessed.

7. The <error-page> element establishes the rule that whenever the HTTP error code 404 is encountered, the URL /404.html should be loaded. Java exception types can also be mapped to error locations.

This is a very simple example. You can specify several additional elements in the deployment descriptor. You can find the Document Type Definition (DTD) for this XML file (web.dtd) in your %TOMCAT_HOME%\conf directory. It provides helpful comments for each element. You can also find information in the Servlet 2.2 specification.

Web Applications in Tomcat

Tomcat associates an application context (*ServletContext* object) with each Web application. An application context maps a relative URL to a physical root directory. You define an application context in Tomcat using a <Context> element in the server.xml file located in %TOMCAT_HOME%\conf. For example, the following <Context> element associates the relative URL "/Book" with the physical location %TOMCAT_HOME%\webapps\Book.

```
<Context path="/Book"
         docBase="webapps/Book">
</Context>
```

You should declare this element within a <ContextManager> element in server.xml. You can also specify absolute paths for the docBase attribute. Here is an example:

```
<Context path="/somewhere"
         docBase="D:\somewhere" >
</Context>
```

Installing Apache

While none of our book projects require a Web server other than Tomcat, you might find it useful to try the hybrid configuration we described. Apache provides a binary distribution of its Web server for Windows platforms, so installing it is easy. You can download the source and build Apache for Windows, but that is beyond the scope of this book. You can find the latest information for the Apache Web server at `http://www.apache.org/httpd`.

You should download the binary build of Apache for Windows named "apache_1_3_#-win32-no_src.msi". The `(#)` character stands for the current point release of Apache. So if the latest current release is "19," the file that you should download is `apache_1_3_19-win32-no_src.msi`. On Windows 2000, you can directly execute the ".msi" file to start the installation process. On Windows NT, you must first download the Microsoft Windows Installer package from an Internet link specified at the Apache download site.

When executing the ".msi" file, the installer wizard will prompt for relevant information such as "Server name," "Domain name," "Administrative email account, "and "Root directory." It will provide an option to start the server as a 'service'. Make sure to choose this option. This automatically starts the Apache Web server when your machine starts.

When finished, the installer will attempt to start the Apache Web server. If you encountered no problems, the installer will present you with a success message. To check if the installation was successful and whether the Web server started successfully, start a Web browser and enter the URL `http://localhost`. You should see a page as shown in Figure B-4.

You can find general documentation supporting the Apache Web server at the URL: `http://httpd.apache.org/docs`. You can find documentation on using Apache with Microsoft Windows at `http://httpd.apache.org/docs/windows.html`.

Once installed, your apache root directory might look like this:

```
E:\Pkgs\apache>dir
 Volume in drive E is CHACHU
 Volume Serial Number is 1321-17F0
 Directory of E:\Pkgs\apache

04/28/2001  03:20p      <DIR>          .
04/28/2001  03:20p      <DIR>          ..
04/28/2001  03:58p      <DIR>          cgi-bin
04/28/2001  03:58p      <DIR>          conf
04/28/2001  03:58p      <DIR>          bin
04/28/2001  03:58p      <DIR>          htdocs
04/28/2001  03:58p      <DIR>          icons
04/28/2001  03:58p      <DIR>          include
04/28/2001  03:58p      <DIR>          lib
04/28/2001  03:58p      <DIR>          libexec
04/28/2001  03:58p      <DIR>          logs
04/28/2001  03:58p      <DIR>          modules
```

```
04/28/2001  03:58p      <DIR>          proxy
02/28/2001  12:33p              20,480 Apache.exe
02/28/2001  12:33p             323,584 ApacheCore.dll
02/16/2001  10:11a              14,567 ABOUT_APACHE
02/26/2001  10:59a               5,651 Announcement
06/05/2000  01:28p              41,421 KEYS
01/15/2001  10:26a               2,885 LICENSE
12/15/2000  09:04a               4,202 README-WIN.TXT
11/06/2000  11:57a               1,342 WARNING-WIN.TXT
02/28/2001  12:32p              20,480 Win9xConHook.dll
02/28/2001  12:33p              40,960 xmlparse.dll
02/28/2001  12:33p              73,728 xmltok.dll
              12 File(s)      2,375,100 bytes
              13 Dir(s)   4,292,317,184 bytes free
```

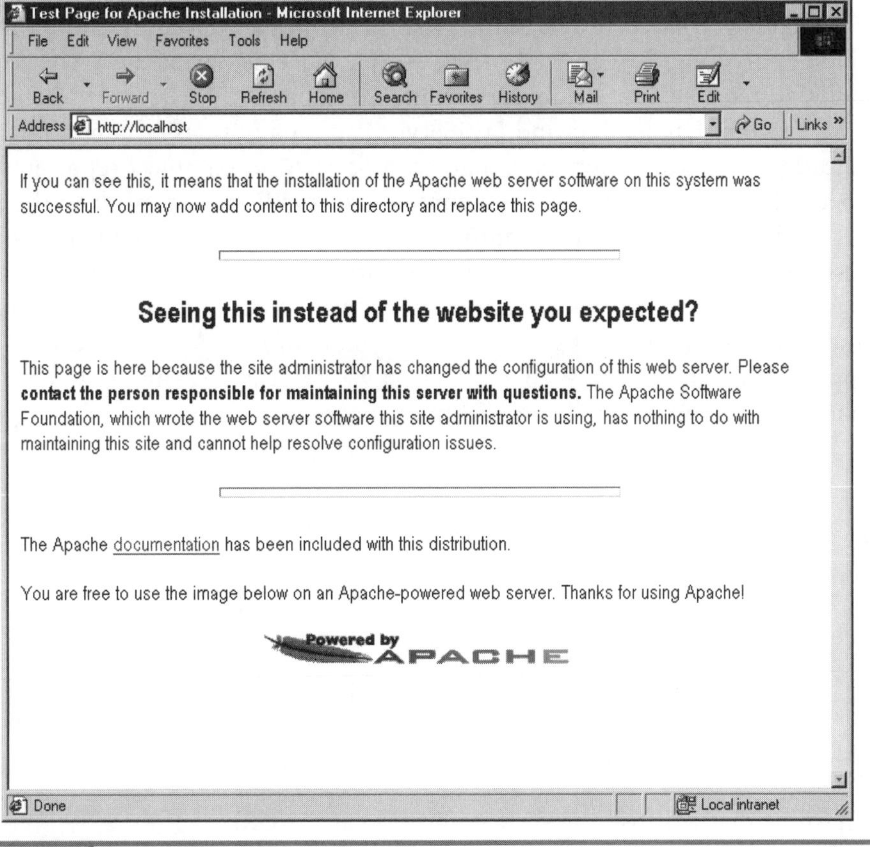

Figure B-4 Initial page after Apache

`Apache.exe` is the executable, and `ApacheCore.dll` is the main library. Here are the important subdirectories:

- *conf* Configuration files
- *logs* Runtime logs
- *modules* Apache plug-in modules
- *htdocs* Documents describing the Apache Web server

Connecting Apache and Tomcat

A corporate Web site probably should use Tomcat as a Servlet/JSP add-on to an industrial-strength Web server such as Apache. This means the Web server handles all requests first before forwarding servlet and JSP requests to Tomcat.

We've seen that servlets and JavaServer Pages have an associated Web application context in a servlet container. A *ServletContext* object represents each application context, and each context has a URL path relative to the root URL for the Web site. So, our configuration should ensure that whenever we access our Web application via its relative URL, the Web server recognizes that this is something the servlet container should handle and forwards the request to the servlet container. Let's examine how you configure Apache to do this mapping. We will use the Web application we described earlier. Our Web application contains the following components:

- `/welcome.html`
- `/jsp/Inventory.jsp`
- `/jsp/Receipt.jsp`
- `/images/logo.gif`
- `/WEB-INF/classes/CustomerServlet.class`
- `/WEB-INF/web.xml`

Assume that we host our Web application at the URL: `http://www.myHost.com/eCommerce`. This means that when a customer using a Web browser goes to this URL address, our Web application should present its welcome page.

The Apache-Tomcat connector's guide (`%TOMCAT_HOME%\doc\tomcat-apache-howto.html`) answers three important questions:

1. How does Apache know which request/type of requests should be forwarded to Tomcat?
2. How does Apache forward these requests to Tomcat?
3. How does Tomcat accept and handle these requests?

Let's address the questions in reverse order.

Configuring Tomcat (Answer to Question 3)

There are three steps to configuring Tomcat for use by Apache:

- Define a context for our application.
- Establish an Ajpv13 protocol (or Ajpv12) connection handler to communicate between Apache and Tomcat.
- Define Tomcat worker(s) that will execute the servlets.

Defining a Context for Our Application

As we saw earlier, in order for Tomcat to handle requests, we need to define a context for our Web application. We do that by defining a `<Context>` element in the file: `%TOMCAT_HOME%\conf\server.xml`. Here is how you do it:

```
<Context path="/eCommerce"
         docBase="webapps/eCommerce">
</Context>
```

This element states that every resource beginning with `/eCommerce` should be mapped to `%TOMCAT_HOME%\webapps\eCommerce`.

We can ensure that this configuration works by starting Tomcat and accessing the URL `http://localhost:8080/eCommerce`. If the domain name for our machine is *www.myHost.com*, then we can also access this Web application from other machines using the URL: `http://www.myHost.com:8080/eCommerce`.

Establishing the AJP Connector

The AJP connector element in `server.xml` is the mechanism Tomcat uses to communicate with Apache. You must add these lines to `%TOMCAT_HOME%\conf\server.xml`:

```
<Connector
      className="org.apache.tomcat.service.PoolTcpConnector">
   <Parameter name="handler"
value="org.apache.tomcat.service.connector.Ajp13ConnectionHandler"
   />
   <Parameter name="port" value="8009" />
</Connector>
```

Ajpv13 is the most recent protocol supported by Tomcat. Apache also supports an older protocol called "Ajpv12," whose handler uses port 8007. Apache recommends Ajpv13 because it is faster and supports Secure HTTP (HTTPS) requests.

Defining Tomcat Workers

Tomcat workers are Tomcat instances that execute servlets and JavaServer Pages on behalf of a Web server. You can define multiple workers for a single Web server. You configure Tomcat workers in the file `%TOMCAT_HOME%\conf\workers.properties`. The default `workers.properties` file defines the correct workers for most applications. But you must define three important values:

- *workers.tomcat_home* This should point to the *TOMCAT_HOME* directory.
- *workers.java_home* This should point to the *JAVA_HOME* directory.
- *ps* This should define the file system separator. ('\' for windows NT/2000)

Here is a sample `workers.properties` fragment:

```
workers.tomcat_home=e:\pkgs\tomcat\jakarta-tomcat-3.2.1
workers.java_home=e:\pkgs\jdk1.3
ps=\
worker.list=ajp12, ajp13
```

```
worker.ajp12.port=8007
worker.ajp12.host=localhost
worker.ajp12.type=ajp12

worker.ajp13.port=8009
worker.ajp13.host=localhost
worker.ajp13.type=ajp13
```

The fragment defines two workers ajp12 and ajp13, and properties for each. The properties state a host and a port for each worker as well as the Apache protocol they use. The ajp12 worker uses the Ajpv12 protocol, and the ajp13 worker uses the Ajpv13 protocol.

Installing the Adapter (Answer to Question 2)

As we illustrated in Figure B-1, the Web server must use an adapter to forward requests for servlets and JavaServer Pages to the Tomcat servlet container. Apache currently provides two adapters:

- mod_jserv
- mod_jk

The mod_jk adapter is more recent and recommended by the Apache Software Foundation. This adapter is available in binary form as a DLL (`mod_jk.dll`). Download the DLL from this URL: `http://jakarta.apache.org/builds/jakarta-tomcat/release/v3.2.1/bin/win32/i386`.

Note

The Tomcat version as of this writing is 3.2.1. The preceding path assumes that version. Alter the path appropriately for the latest version of Tomcat. Basically, the best bet is to locate the adapter in the `win32/i386` subdirectory under the binary location where you downloaded Tomcat.

Copy the downloaded file to the `modules` subdirectory under the Apache home directory.

Configuring Apache (Answer to Question 1)

The final step tells Apache how to load and initialize the adapter, and that certain requests should be forwarded to Tomcat by the adapter. Tomcat already does most of this job for us.

There are two files under `%TOMCAT_HOME%\conf` that help us configure Apache to use Tomcat:

- `tomcat.conf`
- `mod_jk.conf-auto`

We are interested in the second one, since we are using the mod_jk adapter. This file supplements Apache's main configuration file (`httpd.conf`) with directives necessary to make Apache aware of Tomcat. In order to add these directives to Apache's configuration, we must edit `conf/httpd.conf` in the Apache home directory. We add the following line at the end:

```
include E:/pkgs/tomcat/jakarta-tomcat-3.2.1/conf/mod_jk.conf-auto
```

Tip

Use the forward separators (/) regardless of the operating system.

Next, we must stop the Apache Web server (if it is running), remove the file `%TOMCAT_HOME%\conf\mod_jk.conf-auto` (if it exists), and restart Tomcat. Restarting Tomcat re-creates `%TOMCAT_HOME%\conf\mod_jk.conf-auto` with information properly configured by `%TOMCAT_HOME%\conf\server.xml` and `workers.properties`.

Tip

Generally this is all that is necessary. You do not usually need to create a custom `mod_jk.conf`.

Finally, restart Apache to finish the configuration. Now, when you access the URL `http://localhost/eCommerce`, the Apache Web server handles the request initially, then forwards it to a Tomcat worker. The Tomcat instance then handles the request by executing our Web application. If our machine had the domain name `www.myHost.com` that is visible to the Internet, then our Web application could be accessed from any other machine on the Internet using the URL: `http://www.myHost.com/eCommerce`. We are ready for business!

Appendix C

Creating a MySQL Database

The Goals of This Appendix

- Understand the utility of the MySQL database engine
- Learn how to download MySQL from the Internet
- Install and configure a simple MySQL database
- Perform simple administration on the MySQL installation
- Create tables in your MySQL database

Most good developers practice their craft on their own time, learning and trying out new technologies outside the pressures of their jobs and the anxieties of their managers. Database development poses a challenge to such practice, however, because most relational database management systems (RDBMS) are either expensive, difficult to obtain, or both. For example, developers can freely download Oracle 8*i* for Windows NT at this address: `http://technet.oracle.com/software/products/oracle8i/software_index.htm`. This download takes all day, however, unless developers use a high bandwidth Internet connection. For the purposes of this book, we chose a more modest database engine, MySQL.

MySQL and a similar database engine, MiniSQL (mSQL), fit into the category of small to mid-scale application tools. Enterprise level database engines like Oracle, Sybase, or Informix aim at full SQL support, proprietary advanced features (such as support for Java in the database), and scaling to huge sizes with tables storing terabytes of data. Such tools are expensive and require advanced training to configure, tune, and maintain. MySQL and MiniSQL, on the other hand, aim at basic features, fast queries, and little cost. They are also easier to download over narrow-band Internet connections because they weigh in at about 10MB for the Windows version compared to the more than 500MB size of Oracle 8*i* for Windows NT.

We chose to use MySQL for this book rather than MiniSQL because, while both are inexpensive or free, MiniSQL is available only as a source-code release while MySQL also has binary or precompiled versions. Our purpose in this book is to get beginner JSP developers up and running with a usable database engine. For this purpose, a precompiled version for Windows NT is a great advantage. MySQL also seems to have captured mind-share in the small to mid-sized database category, but this is a more subjective judgment. For our purposes, we care more about the JDBC driver available for the database engine than we do about specific features or performance characteristics. You must get a database up and running. You can use MySQL, MiniSQL, Oracle 8*i*, or even Microsoft Access, and the examples in this book will work because a JDBC 2.0 driver exists for all these engines. (There is also a JDBC/ODBC bridge for Microsoft Access.)

Downloading MySQL

The first software you should download is the database engine itself. In the United States, you can go to MySQL's main Internet site, `www.MySQL.com`.

MySQL also has many mirror sites—sites that mirror the links and pages of the main site—worldwide. You access these mirror sites from the main site after clicking the *Downloads* link. In the following procedure, we describe the current link sequence for downloading. Keep in mind, however, that as Internet site managers enhance or recast their sites, such links can change.

1. On the main page for MySQL, click the *Downloads* link.
2. Click the *MySQL* link. This should bring you to a page displaying the currently supported versions.
3. For the purposes of this book, the highest version is probably usable. This book was written using version 3.23. Click a version link at release 3.23 or higher. You will see a page of platform-specific releases for the selected version. Click on the binary version of the database for your platform (we will assume it is Windows).
4. Windows next prompts you with a browser dialog box to save the file to disk. Follow the prompts to save the compressed form (a `.zip` file in Windows) of the release to a temporary location on your hard drive.

Downloading a JDBC Driver for MySQL

After downloading the MySQL database engine, you should download a JDBC driver. JDBC drivers provide a Java programming interface to databases. You need a JDBC driver for MySQL because you will be writing database access routines in Java. Sun Microsystems provides a Web site that helps developers find JDBC drivers appropriate to their needs: `http://industry.java.sun.com/products/jdbc/drivers`.

Several JDBC drivers support MySQL. We will use a free driver authored by Mark Matthews: `mm.mysql.jdbc`. This is a type 4 JDBC driver. Type 4 JDBC drivers provide a 100-percent pure Java programming interface that uses the database's native network protocol. Versions of the MySQL driver support both the JDBC 1.2 and the JDBC 2.0 specification. We are interested in the version that supports JDBC 2.0. To download the JDBC driver, navigate to the Internet address `http://www.worldserver.com/mm.mysql/`. Toward the bottom of the page is a section of links providing stable JDBC 2.0 driver versions. The release we used for this book is 2.0.4 (`mm.mysql-2.0.4-bin.jar`).

1. Click on the release with the highest version number. A browser dialog box will prompt you to save the file to disk.

2. Follow the prompts and save the driver to a directory where you store Java libraries.

Installing MySQL

Once you have downloaded the binary distribution of MySQL, you must unpack it into the temporary download directory. Follow these steps. (These steps assume you will install into the `c:\` directory.)

1. In Windows, unzip the file using WinZip or PKZIP.

2. After unpacking the distribution, use Windows Explorer to find a `SETUP.EXE` file in the installation directory. Double-click it.

3. Follow the instructions of the install program but do not change the deployment directory from `C:\mysql`.

4. After running the setup program, open a command prompt window. Change to the `C:` drive if you aren't there already:

```
E:\>C:
```

5. Change to MySQL's `bin` directory:

```
C:\>cd mysql\bin
```

6. Install the daemon program as a Windows service in the Service Control Manager:

```
C:\mysql\bin\>mysqld -install
```

7. To complete configuration of the MySQL database engine, launch the Service Control Manager. In Windows 2000, you choose `Start Menu` | `Settings` | `Control Panel`. Then double-click on `Administrative Tools`.

8. Next, double-click on `Services`.

9. After launching the Service Control Manager, select the MySql line. In Windows 2000, choose Action | Properties.
10. When the Properties dialog box appears, set the Startup Type to Automatic.
11. Next, click the Start button.
12. Finally, click OK to close the Service Control Manager dialog box.

After installing the database engine you must install the Java JDBC driver. You do this by adding the path to the driver's Java archive file, mm.mysql-2.0.1-bin.jar, to your Java *%CLASSPATH%* variable using the System dialog. Here are the steps:

1. In Windows 2000, you choose Start Menu | Settings | Control Panel. Then double-click on System.
2. Selected the Advanced tab of the System dialog.
3. Click on the Environment Variables... button.
4. Append the path to mm.mysql-2.0.1-bin.jar to the value for your *%CLASSPATH%* variable. (If the variable does not yet exist, create it.)

MySQL Administration

A database administrator must:

- Make sure the database is running
- Create and destroy database instances
- Create users
- Create and drop tables

The first task tests the database to make sure it is available. The second task creates and destroys database instances. Each database instance is a set of tables storing data. Each table is a collection of data. Database administrators must also add user identities and permissions so people can use the database. Finally, since a database instance consists of database tables, administrators must create and drop (destroy) database tables. Here is a cursory explanation of these activities as it relates to MySQL.

The mysqladmin Tool

The mysqladmin tool is the primary administrative tool for MySQL. Among many other functions, it can test the running status of the engine as well as create and destroy database instances.

Pinging the MySQL Engine

MySQL should be up and running, but it's a good idea after installing the database engine to test that it's running properly. To test MySQL, run the following command in a command prompt window:

```
C:\mysql\bin>mysqladmin ping
```

You should see a line like this:

```
mysqld is alive
```

If the service isn't running, you may see a response more like this (along with some other messages):

```
mysqladmin: connect to server at 'localhost' failed
error: 'Can't connect to MySQL server on 'localhost' (10061)'
Check that mysqld is running on localhost and that the port is 3306.
You can check this by doing 'telnet localhost 3306'
```

If you see this, return to the `Service Control Manager`, bring up the `Properties` dialog for `MySql` and click the `Start` button.

Creating and Destroying a Database Instance

MySQL database instances are collections of tables. MySQL comes with a default database instance called `MySQL`. To create other database instances, run the mysqladmin tool:

```
C:\mysql\bin>mysqladmin create DATABASENAME
```

Similarly, to destroy a database instance, use mysqladmin:

```
C:\mysql\bin>mysqladmin drop DATABASENAME
```

Note

For the purposes of the examples in this book, it is probably best to stick with the default database, because all our examples will refer to it.

Help for sqladmin

To get help on the commands for mysqladmin, type:

```
C:\mysql\bin>mysqladmin -?
```


MySQL Structured Query Language

SQL defines queries on tabular data. The following table is an example of such tabular data defining purchase orders:

OWNERID	ITEMDESIRED
1010	Red Parka
2020	Blue Boots
3030	Green Pants

Such tables have a name, some columns, and various rows containing the data for each column. Relational databases organize data in this way. We call such databases *relational* because we can define operations on tables by the mathematics of relations, whereby every retrieval operation generates new tables from existing tables. Despite their basis in mathematics, relational database engines never implement pure mathematical operations. This "real-world" element raises the need for another kind of specification.

Accepted standards bodies define the rules for querying relational databases. Both the American National Standards Institute (ANSI) and the International Standards Organization (ISO) help define and support the SQL standard. Major database engines such as Oracle 8*i* implement some superset of the ANSI SQL 92 version (ANSI X3.135-1992/ISO 9075-1992, or SQL2 for short) of the standard. Unlike enterprise database engines such as Oracle, MySQL implements a subset of the most common features of SQL2. What it loses in functionality it tries to regain by being very fast and small. We describe some of its basic operations in the following sections. Be aware that SQL is a complex subject and we barely touch upon it here. In Module 10, where the focus is on using databases in JSP applications, we provide the SQL you need to understand the discussion and Projects.

Adding Users

After installing and starting the MySQL database, you can add users. Follow these steps:

1. Log in to the database as the `root` user. In Windows NT and Windows 2000, the `root` user has full privileges on all databases. Here's the logon command:

```
C:\mysql\bin>mysql -u root
```

2. Execute a standard SQL2 insert statement to add a record to the `mysql.user` table (do not break any SQL commands into lines like we do here for formatting purposes):

```
mysql>INSERT INTO mysql.user
(Host, User, Select_priv, Insert_priv, Update_priv,
Delete_priv, Create_priv, Drop_priv) VALUES
('localhost', 'SampleUser', 'Y', 'Y', 'Y', 'Y', 'Y', 'Y');
```

This SQL statement adds a new user with the login name `SampleUser`, a blank password, and privileges to execute SQL selects, inserts, updates, and deletes as well as to create and drop tables.

3. Finally, you can add a password to `SampleUser` by executing something like the following SQL:

```
mysql>update mysql.user set Password=PASSWORD('foo')
where user='SampleUser';
```

4. To make this password change take effect, type:

```
mysql>flush privileges;
```

5. To login as the new user from the console, type:

```
%>mysql -u NewUser -p
```

And supply the password when prompted.

Tip

Here we gave `SampleUser` the password "foo". We had to use the built-in `Password` function because MySQL expects passwords to be stored encrypted. On the other hand, by default MySQL requires no password from local users (i.e., users on the database machine).

Creating Tables and Adding Records

MySQL supports standard SQL2 syntax for creating tables. For example, the following command creates a MySQL table named `MYSQL`.ORDERS with two columns—`OWNERID` and `ITEMDESIRED`:

```
mysql>CREATE TABLE MYSQL.ORDERS (OWNERID INTEGER NOT NULL,
ITEMDESIRED CHAR(40) NOT NULL);
```

The legal MySQL column types include several numeric types, date and time types, and numerous string types including Binary Large Object (BLOB) data.

MySQL also supports standard SQL2 insert statements. The following command, for example, inserts a record into the MYSQL.`ORDERS` table:

```
mysql>INSERT INTO MYSQL.ORDERS
(OWNERID, ITEMDESIRED)  VALUES (1010, 'Red Parka');
```

MySQL Documentation

Our intention in this appendix has been to cover just enough MySQL database administration to support the requirements of Module10 where we use a database to implement part of our sample application. Those readers who need or want a deeper introduction can find it in *MySQL & mSQL*, by Yarger, Reese, and King (O'Reilly & Associates, Inc.: Sebatopol, CA. 1999). In addition, the MySQL Web site provides a manual and other literature, including a list of other books. Finally, in your installation directory you can find documentation at `file://c:/mysql/docs/manual_toc.html`.

Appendix D

New Features in JSP 1.2

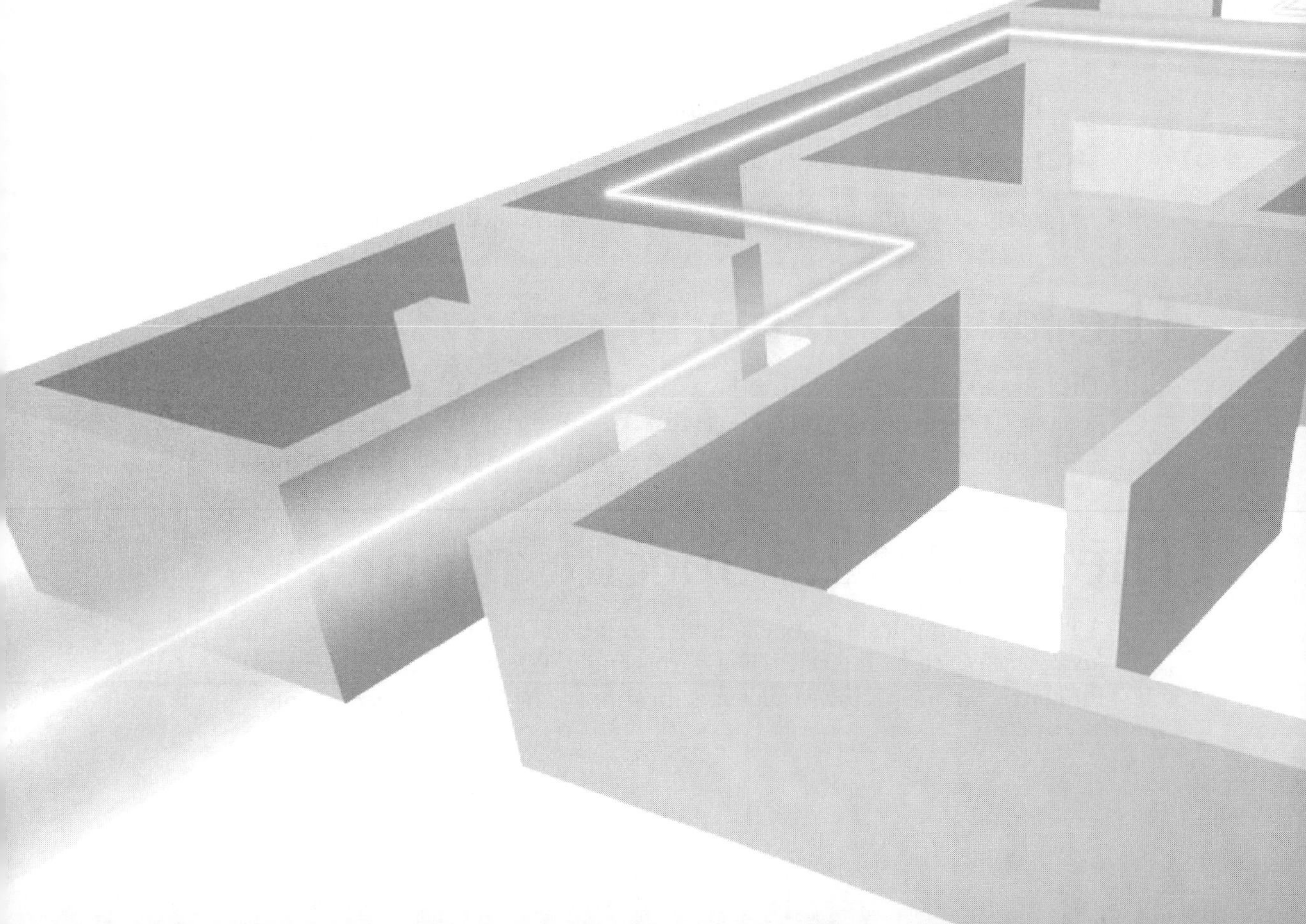

In this appendix, we present and describe anticipated changes between JSP 1.1 and JSP 1.2. Sun has released the "Proposed Final Draft" of the JavaServer Pages 1.2 specification (JSP 1.2). (You can find it at: `http://jcp.org/aboutJava/communityprocess/first/jsr053/index.html`.) This Proposed Final Draft will eventually become the formal Final Release. The Jakarta Tomcat project has already begun implementing it in anticipation of the Final Release in its version 4.0 beta (`http://jakarta.apache.org/builds/jakarta-tomcat-4.0/release`).

The major changes specified in JSP 1.2 are:

- Requiring the Java 2 platform, version 1.2 or greater
- Requiring the Servlet 2.3 specification as its basis
- Fully defining the XML syntax for JavaServer Pages
- Supporting translation-time validation of JavaServer Pages
- Refining runtime support for tag libraries
- Enhancing the tag handler contract
- Providing improved support for page authoring
- Improving character encoding and localization support
- Fixing the infamous "flush before you include" limitation

The Java 2 Platform

The new specification requires Java 2, Standard Edition 1.2 (J2SE 1.2) or greater. Consequently, you can use features from the Java 2 release and have confidence that they will work in all conforming servlet and JSP containers.

The Servlet 2.3 Specification

A JSP page compiles into a Java implementation class that implements the *javax.servlet.Servlet* interface. Not surprisingly, JSP specifications depend intimately upon specific servlet specifications. The JSP 1.1 specification depended upon the Servlet 2.2 specification; now the JSP 1.2 specification depends upon the Servlet 2.3 specification (which, like JSP 1.2, is in "Proposed Final Draft" form).

The biggest changes brought by the Servlet 2.3 specification are support for filters and lifecycle events (`http://www.javaworld.com/javaworld/jw-01-2001/jw-0126-servletapi_p.html`). Filters are "pluggable" pre- and postprocessors that modify a request before it reaches a servlet or modify a response as it leaves a servlet. You could use a filter to perform authentication (perhaps replacing the *CustomRealm* interceptor we introduced in Module 8). You could also perform automatic logging, transformation of XML into HTML using XSL, image transformation, and many other sorts of functions not easily done in Servlet 2.2 containers.

The Servlet 2.3 specification also introduces lifecycle events. Lifecycle events occur when the servlet container initializes or destroys a *ServletContext* object or when you add attributes to the *ServletContext* object or *HttpSession* object. Servlet 2.3 containers will support registration of *listeners* to such events. The container notifies registered listeners whenever such events occur, providing access to the *ServletContext* or *HttpSession*, depending upon the listener type. Such listeners provide a handy centralized way to do such things as synchronization of context or session information with a database or EJB service.

The XML Syntax

The JSP 1.2 specification completes the mapping of JavaServer Pages to XML that the JSP 1.1 specification began. JSP 1.2–compliant tools and containers must support both the standard JSP view of a document and its equivalent XML view. The specification mentions several advantages provided by an XML view of JavaServer Pages:

- Content can be authored in XML editors and passed directly to the JSP container
- JavaServer Pages can be validated against a description of the set of valid pages
- JavaServer Pages can be manipulated by XML-aware tools

- JavaServer pages can be generated from a textual representation using XML transformation technologies like XSLT
- JavaServer Pages may be generated automatically, perhaps by serializing Java objects

Validation of JavaServer Pages

The JSP 1.2 specification lists three reasons to validate JSP documents, as shown in Table D-1.

In JSP 1.1, two mechanisms supported validation of JavaServer Pages:

- Information supplied in the tag library descriptor
- The *TagExtraInfo* class with its *isValid* method (Module 6)

The JSP 1.2 specification has added a *TagLibraryValidator* class and recommends that JSP 2.2 tag library developers use it rather than the *TagExtraInfo* class.

The JSP container gives *TagLibraryValidator* classes access to the XML view of a JSP page (using a *PageData* class). This allows tag developers to perform any validation of the page they may require.

Enhanced Tag Library Support

The JSP 1.2 specification has added some elements to the definition of the tag library descriptor. The `<taglib>` element now includes the additional subelements shown in Table D-2.

Reason	Description
Request-time semantics	A subelement may require data from an enclosing tag
Support for authoring tools	A tool may require an ordering of elements
Methodological constraints	A development group may want to constrain use of some features

Table D-1 Reasons for JSP Document Validation

Subelement	Notes
display-name	Optional for use by tools
small-icon	Optional for use by tools
large-icon	Optional for use by tools
description	Replaces the `info` field from JSP 1.1
validator	Optional specification of *TagLibraryValidator* information
listener	Optional event listener specification

Table D-2 Subelements of the <taglib> Element

The `<tag>` element also adds several subelements, as shown in Table D-3.

A review of the enhancements shows that the general themes behind the tag library enhancements are:

- To increase support for authoring tools
- To improve validation of JavaServer Pages
- To expose Servlet 2.3 features

The JSP 1.2 specification also adds the *IterationTag* interface alongside the *Tag* and *BodyTag* interfaces. In JSP 1.1 containers, any tag library that wanted to iterate had to implement the *BodyTag* interface, even if it never evaluated its body. In JSP 1.2, tag libraries that do not examine or modify their tag body can create iteration tags that implement the *IterationTag* interface rather than the *BodyTag* interface. This creates more efficient and less confusing code.

Sub-element	Notes
display-name	Optional for use by tools
small-icon	Optional for use by tools
large-icon	Optional for use by tools
description	Replaces the `info` field from JSP 1.1
variable	Definitions of zero or more implicit scripting variables
example	Optional illustration of use

Table D-3 Subelements of the <tag> Element

Improved Support for Page Authoring

Support for page authoring is a big theme of the new JSP 1.2 specification. The JSP 1.1 specification emphasized the importance of "hand-authoring friendliness" for the initial adoption of JavaServer Pages. While retaining the original tags, the JSP 1.2 specification emphasizes authoring tools over hand authoring. The increased importance of the XML view of a page reflects this shift, as do special tags supporting tool display, and greater emphasis on validation of JavaServer Pages.

Better Localization Support

Unlike the JSP 1.1 specification, the JSP 1.2 specification includes a chapter on localization issues. In that chapter, it mentions two common approaches to delivering localized pages without giving preference to either:

- Custom tags that retrieve localized strings
- Use-per-locale pages

It suggests that the Java Specification Request for the standard tag library (JSR-052) will eventually address delivery of localized pages (`http://jcp.org/jsr/detail/52.jsp`).

The JSP 1.2 specification also adds the pageEncoding attribute to the JSP 1.1 list of page directive attributes. This new attribute lets you specify the character encoding for your page. The default character encoding is ISO-8859-1 (i.e., Latin-1). You can specify any valid encoding as described by the Internet Assigned Numbers Authority (IANA: `http://www.iana.org/assignments/character-sets`).

Fixing the "Flush Before You Include"

In JSP 1.1, the flush attribute of the `<jsp:include>` tag was mandatory and required being set to `true` (Module 5). JSP 1.2 makes the attribute optional and supports a value of `false`. In JSP 1.2, in fact, the default value is `false`. A goal of the `<jsp:include>` tag is to provide total freedom as to how pages write content to clients. This was not possible in JSP 1.1. By fixing this limitation, JSP 1.2 provides the intended freedom.

Backward Compatibility

Despite the changes, JSP developers should find making the transition to the new specification relatively simple. The JSP 1.2 container is required to support the JSP 1.1 tag library descriptor format alongside the JSP 1.2 format. Further, most of the standard tags and tag attributes remain the same and have the same semantics.

Index

Symbols

A

B

C

E

F

J

N

O

P

Q

R

S

T

U

V

W

X

INTERNATIONAL CONTACT INFORMATION

AUSTRALIA
McGraw-Hill Book Company Australia Pty. Ltd.
TEL +61-2-9417-9899
FAX +61-2-9417-5687
http://www.mcgraw-hill.com.au
books-it_sydney@mcgraw-hill.com

CANADA
McGraw-Hill Ryerson Ltd.
TEL +905-430-5000
FAX +905-430-5020
http://www.mcgrawhill.ca

GREECE, MIDDLE EAST, NORTHERN AFRICA
McGraw-Hill Hellas
TEL +30-1-656-0990-3-4
FAX +30-1-654-5525

MEXICO (Also serving Latin America)
McGraw-Hill Interamericana Editores S.A. de C.V.
TEL +525-117-1583
FAX +525-117-1589
http://www.mcgraw-hill.com.mx
fernando_castellanos@mcgraw-hill.com

SINGAPORE (Serving Asia)
McGraw-Hill Book Company
TEL +65-863-1580
FAX +65-862-3354
http://www.mcgraw-hill.com.sg
mghasia@mcgraw-hill.com

SOUTH AFRICA
McGraw-Hill South Africa
TEL +27-11-622-7512
FAX +27-11-622-9045
robyn_swanepoel@mcgraw-hill.com

UNITED KINGDOM & EUROPE (Excluding Southern Europe)
McGraw-Hill Education Europe
TEL +44-1-628-502500
FAX +44-1-628-770224
http://www.mcgraw-hill.co.uk
computing_neurope@mcgraw-hill.com

ALL OTHER INQUIRIES Contact:
Osborne/McGraw-Hill
TEL +1-510-549-6600
FAX +1-510-883-7600
http://www.osborne.com
omg_international@mcgraw-hill.com

The Apache Software License